Background Screening and Investigations

Background Screening and Investigations

Managing Hiring Risk From the HR and Security Perspectives

W. Barry Nixon, SPHR, and

Kim M. Kerr, CPP

with contributing authors

AMSTERDAM • BOSTON • HEIDELBERG • LONDON
NEW YORK • OXFORD • PARIS • SAN DIEGO
SAN FRANCISCO • SINGAPORE • SYDNEY • TOKYO

ELSEVIER

Butterworth-Heinemann is an imprint of Elsevier

Butterworth-Heinemann is an imprint of Elsevier
30 Corporate Drive, Suite 400, Burlington, MA 01803, USA
Linacre House, Jordan Hill, Oxford OX2 8DP, UK

Library of Congress Cataloging-in-Publication Data
Nixon, W. Barry.
   Background screening and investigations : managing hiring risk from the HR and security perspectives / By W. Barry Nixon and Kim M. Kerr.
      p. cm.
Includes index.
ISBN-13: 978-0-7506-8256-5 (alk. paper)
1. Employee screening. I. Kerr, Kim M. II. Title.
HF5549.5.E429N59 2008
658.3'112–dc22

2007048526

British Library Cataloguing-in-Publication Data
A catalogue record for this book is available from the British Library.

ISBN: 978-0-7506-8256-5

For information on all Butterworth–Heinemann publications
visit our Web site at www.books.elsevier.com

Printed in the United States of America
08 09 10 11 12 13 10 9 8 7 6 5 4 3 2 1

Dedication

This book is dedicated to my father, Max Howard Kerr,
who taught me to "stay in the game."
And to my loving wife, Cheryle: your professional and personal
insights and support have made all the difference.

Kim M. Kerr

I would like to sincerely thank all of the contributing authors who took time out of their
very busy schedules to contribute their expertise to this book.
Your contributions truly make it a who's who work on background screening.
I would also like to dedicate this book to my three moms,
Ella Fields, Eunice Hobbs, and Dorothy Lacy Nixon, whose unconditional love, support,
and belief in me contributed to me achieving a life-long goal: to write this book.

W. Barry Nixon

Contents

About the Authors

Any chapter in this book not identified as contributed material is a collaboration between W. Barry Nixon and Kim M. Kerr.

W. Barry Nixon is the executive director of the National Institute for Prevention of Workplace Violence, Inc., a company focused on assisting organizations to effectively implement programs to prevent workplace violence. Having spent over 20 years in human resources and organization development in Fortune 500 companies, Nixon is well grounded in the real issues that companies face and develops practical solutions based on having been there.

Prior to founding the National Institute for Prevention of Workplace Violence, Nixon studied "general management" in the Executive Management Program, University of Hawaii. He earned a master's degree in human resource development from the New School University and a bachelor of science degree in business administration from Northeastern University. Nixon has also completed the Advanced Human Resource Management program of Babson College, as well as the certification programs in organization development from National Training Laboratories, systems thinking from MIT, and the highly acclaimed "Creating Competitive Advantage Through Human Resources" program from the University of Michigan's School of Industrial Relations. He is a trained mediator, certified anger management facilitator, security specialist, and trauma response specialist, and earned a certificate in background investigations from the Public Safety Institute, Santa Rosa College. In addition, he is an active member of ASIS International's Crime and Loss Prevention Council and served on ASIS International's Workplace Violence Prevention Guidelines Committee. He is also a member of the Security Executive Council of Advising Editors for *Security* Magazine and the past national president of the American Association for Anger Management Providers.

As a specialist in workplace violence prevention, he has gained a reputation for developing comprehensive programs that are practical in nature and that fit the needs of the client. His Workplace Violence Prevention programs cover the full realm of this troubling issue, helping companies to assess their vulnerability, implement readiness programs, establish crisis management teams, train employees and managers, address physical security issues, and revise or add new policies to effectively address this critical issue. In essence, he helps organizations to implement an effective program to minimize the likeliness of a major workplace violence incident occurring and to be ready in the event one should actually occur.

He served as the workplace violence prevention consultant for the State of California for over 9 years, providing consulting and training to managers and employees.

Some of his other clients include Gillette, Canon, Beckman-Coulter, Department of Transportation, Southern California Edison, Orange County Sanitation, National Transit Institute, City of Pasadena, Blue Shield Foundation, Macy's, Peterson Brothers Construction, and District of Columbia Water & Sanitation Authority, among others. He also teaches human resource management courses at several universities.

In addition, Nixon is a frequently requested speaker both in the United States and internationally on the subject of workplace violence and background screening. Most recently he presented at the Singapore World HR Congress held in Singapore and the Background Investigators Conference in India. He has also published numerous articles, including in the highly acclaimed *Complete Workplace Violence Prevention Guide;* has appeared on CBS, CNN, MSNBC, Wall Street Journal Radio, and United Kingdom–National Talk Radio; and hosted the popular radio talk show "Workplace Violence Today" on several North American Broadcasting Corporation affiliates.

Kim M. Kerr is the current vice president and general manager of LexisNexis Risk & Information Analytics Group, Screening Solutions. In his current role, Kerr leads the Screening Solutions division in assisting and collaborating with various corporations and businesses to create screening policies and practices. He manages the overall efforts of the business, including market planning, operations, engineering, product, and customer service, and frequently lends assistance to sales. Kerr and his team of more than 75 LexisNexis employees not only interface with and assist customers to ensure customized, total screening solutions but also analyze current and future market trends in order to produce superior products and services.

Previously, Kim spent 28 years with AT&T serving as an area manager in corporate security. Under AT&T's sponsorship, Kim played a vital role in the successful security operations of the 1996 Summer Olympic Games in Atlanta, Georgia. After completing his career at AT&T, he went on to support the security efforts of both the 2000 Summer Olympic Games in Sydney, Australia, and the 2002 Winter Olympic Games in Salt Lake City, Utah.

Kerr is a leading expert in background screening strategies, corporate security management and investigations, special event security, executive protection, and the creation and implementation of proactive security policy. He frequently lends his expertise in both recognizing and preventing violence in the workplace as he consults with and speaks to businesses around the country. He works directly with human resource and security professionals to create disaster recovery action plans.

Kerr is a Certified Protection Professional (CPP) with the American Society of Industrial Security and recently became a board-certified private investigator in the state of Nevada. Kim graduated from Westminster College with a degree in business administration and economics. He lives in Draper, Utah, with his wife and daughter.

About the Contributors

David Allburn (Chapter 10)

To best understand his chapter David Allburn, Executive Director of Safe Harbor Resources (SHR), suggests readers recall the old fable, "The Emperor's New Clothes" because conventional screening for sexual predators, as well as typical insurance coverage for that peril, is like a mirage: it seems to offer what it doesn't. Based on deflection, not detection, on conflict-of-interest, not crime-and-punishment, on supplemental posthire inquiry, not pre-employment background checking, and on risk-reduction, not "catching perverts," his new screening methods and the new legal framework facilitating them go far toward solving the liability dilemma in worker screening while avoiding naming or shaming individuals.

David Allburn, BSEE/MBA, is a retired software project manager and former military officer trained in countermeasures, the shadowy world of threat assessment, impersonation, infiltration, imposters, concealment, and deception. When he started a tiny after-school project in Appalachian Ohio, that state's worker screening law became effective. In trying to obey it for his staff, Allburn became curious why the law seemed deliberately designed to be ineffective, and to practically attract the very sexual predators it was being advertised to repel. A few months later 9-11 occurred, and America's attitude toward worker screening changed. So did Allburn's.

He founded Safe Harbor Resources (www.SafeHarborResources.org), a research and development nonprofit specializing in thwarting sexual predators that infiltrate youth-serving groups. At this writing he has invested 6 years of full time study, industry participation, and pilot testing to develop The New Precautions™, a modern suite of inquiries and interventions more effective at reducing children's risk-exposure to molestation than is traditional background checking. In the process SHR staff invented a new, economical way to capture FBI standard fingerprints of up to 200 people at a time in under 30 minutes total. They developed daily perpetual monitoring of newspaper arrest-articles, pioneered eliciting nonpublic children service agency and domestic protection order data for screening purposes, and began training phone room operators how to locate and interview baby-sitting clients of workers who were teenagers fifty years ago.

The results led to a popular invited workshop, "Solving the Liability Dilemma in Worker Screening" presented to major national groups such as the American Professional Society on the Abuse of Children, the Social Enterprise Alliance, the Association of Sexual Abuse Prevention, and the National Crime Victims Bar Association. They also led to an appointment for developing the congressional position-paper and internal best practices on child protection screening for the National Association of Professional Background Screeners (NAPBS), www.napbs.com.

And it has attracted a sector of the insurance industry that protects the assets of wealthy persons who often serve on nonprofit boards-of-directors, especially boards of youth-serving groups vulnerable to lawsuits for molestation by staff. Since the molestation constitutes harm-to-a-person, when a jury assigns responsibility to the youth-serving group for negligent selection, it is not just negligence. It is "gross" negligence, a definition that bypasses state immunity guarantees and conventional insurance coverage to directly expose the personal assets of board members. A board member's "gift" to his youth-group of new insurance based on The New Precautions™ is a wise gift indeed. Not only are premiums lower with higher limits, but also important gross negligence risks are covered. Interested board members should do an internet search on the term "New Precautions" to bring up the website and learn more about this evolving coverage improvement.)

Robert S. Blumberg (Chapter 2)

Robert S. Blumberg is the Office Managing Shareholder (partner) of the Los Angeles office of Littler Mendelson. He has 15 years of experience representing public and private sector employers. He regularly counsels and represents clients in state and federal court on a myriad of employment and labor issues, including wrongful discharge, discrimination and harassment, as well as wage and hour claims and class actions. Mr. Blumberg has particular expertise in advising employers on the protection of trade secrets and other proprietary information, covenants not to compete and other restrictive covenants, workplace investigations, and related issues.

Mr. Blumberg can be contacted at (310) 772-7250 or rblumberg@littler.com

Littler Mendelson is *The National Employment & Labor Law Firm.*® With more than 600 attorneys practicing in 43 offices coast-to-coast, Littler Mendelson is the largest law firm in the United States to exclusively represent management in employment law and labor matters. With multiple attorneys in every significant area of labor and employment law, Littler has more experience in more jurisdictions than any other labor and employment law firm in the country.

William J. Bollinger (Chapter 8)

William J. Bollinger, Executive Vice President of National Background Data, LLC (NBD), is responsible for leading business development, the formulation and direction of sales, the company vision, and overall growth strategies. As a co-founder of NBD, Bill has built NBD as the leading provider of criminal history database information to the background screening industry.

NBD is the leading provider of criminal history database information to the background screening industry. With the nation's largest privately held criminal records database, NBD provides efficient and economical access to multi-jurisdictional data. NBD's comprehensive database search services are only available through its network of Solution Providers. NBD helps screening companies reduce operating costs and optimize profits by providing an efficient, quality service unmatched in the industry. NBD's success also lies in its commitment to superior customer service and unparalleled loyalty to its Solution Providers. Whether the goal is to provide an employment screening package or to screen applicants for a dating service, NBD partners with Solution Providers to provide a high quality, low cost, complete solution tailored to meet the needs of the end customer.

Prior to NBD, Bill owned and operated a retail and resident screening company. Bill also spent 17 years with consumer finance credit and third party debt collections. His previous positions in sales, operations, and management give Bill a broad functional experience in a variety of markets and businesses. Visit www.NationalBackground-Data.com to learn more.

Kenneth Coats (Chapter 11)

Founder and chairman, Kenneth Coats, launched ArrestFree.com – a revolutionary concept that is the first technology driven expungement service in the world. The need for this service was driven by recent changes in the law. Since 9/11, policies like the Patriot Act have bought intense scrutiny on a person's background record. Currently people with even minor arrest records can be denied employment, housing and even education opportunities.

ArrestFree.com was built to bring affordable expungement service to citizens with minor offenses in need of a second chance. By offering expungement assistance for those with minor offenses, citizens are given an opportunity on becoming productive contributing citizens in society.

Since its launch the website service has been well received by top legal minds, politicians and media alike. The company has been featured exclusively on Fox News as well as written about in the *Chicago Sun-Times*.

Our mission is to expunge 1 million eligible citizens with minor offense records in accordance with local state laws. Our goal is to do everything we can do to make our mission a reality, to help citizens' live better, and more effective in their pursuit of happiness. If you have any questions, or want to know more, visit ArrestFree.com.

Michael Damm (Chapter 12)

For the past 10 years, Michael Damm has had the pleasure of being President and a Partner in ISB Canada. The head office is located just west of Toronto, Canada, in the beautiful town of Milton. ISB has grown to be the largest document retrieval company in Canada known for its service, speed and price. Throughout the years, ISB has processed hundreds of thousands of documents for the Canadian Insurance Industry, with many exclusive services and products. With that experience came a true understanding of Canadian Privacy laws surrounding the access and handling of confidential and personal documents.

Michael Damm's own background played a role in taking the company where it is today, with over 10 years experience in handling insurance claims and specializing in both litigation and special investigation of fraud related files. One had to work within the strict insurance policy in a very litigious environment while maintaining optimum customer service.

ISB's formal move into the pre-employment screening arena was a natural progression, and it has proved to be both a personal growing experience as well as for the business.

Education is key to anything you do, both in educating yourself or others. Mr. Damm has had the pleasure of giving numerous presentations and educational seminars on information and documents throughout Canada and into the U.S. over the years while meeting some terrific people.

He has enjoyed the opportunity to contribute to this guide in the hope that it will shed some light on the differences in conducting Pre Employment Screening in Canada.

Rick Dyer (Chapter 8)

Rick Dyer is an experienced law enforcement officer who has helped lead Liberty Alliance to its present success. As the vice president of national sales, he oversees the sales team and manages the company's marketing strategy. He also automated the Liberty Alliance system in 2005.

Mr. Dyer previously was a detective with the City of Anaheim Police Department, where he worked for nearly 30 years. He led numerous investigations and provided testimony at court trials. His major achievements include building a field training program and helping develop an automated CAD program for the department.

Prior to working in law enforcement, Mr. Dyer was a purchasing agent for Bender Machine in Vernon, California, for two years. He purchased equipment and material for this repair shop, and created an automated ordering and tracking system. Mr. Dyer also streamlined accounting and helped increase sales by 15%.

Mr. Dyer received a Bachelor's degree in administration of justice from the University of California - Los Angeles. He also holds an Associate of Arts degree from Fullerton College. Mr. Dyer is a current member of the NAPBS, the American Society of Industrial Security, and the Society of Human Resource Managers. He has also completed over 800 hours of additional training through the California Department of Justice, Department of Motor Vehicle, Federal Bureau of Investigation, Western States Vice Investigations, Orange County Burglary and Theft Investigators Association, Western States Burglary and Theft Investigators Association, Orange County Auto Theft Investigators Association, Western States Auto Theft Investigators Association, and the California Highway Patrol.

Liberty Alliance sells employment background check solutions that help large and small organizations nationwide implement detailed screening programs. Many businesses utilize Liberty Alliance because the company delivers effective, customer-focused solutions. Liberty Alliance is known for its efficiency and quick results. The company's success has been brought about by its development of customizable pre-integrated employment screening services using HR-XML interfaces. The goal of the company is to achieve the highest level of customer service, client satisfaction, personal phone interaction, and professional accomplishment by providing the fastest turnaround time available for each client with accuracy and clarity. In May 2007, Liberty Alliance was among a select group of organizations to receive Safe Harbor Certification from the U.S. Department of Commerce. This certification recognizes U.S. companies that have more than adequately satisfied the rigorous personal data and privacy policies of the European Union.

Nick Fishman (Chapter 12)

Nick Fishman is the Chief Marketing Officer and Executive Vice President of **employeescreenIQ**, a global leader in the employment screening industry. Nick earned a Bachelor of Arts degree in Political Science from The Ohio State University and has extensive experience in the development of successful sales and marketing campaigns for both large and small businesses. Nick has also served a term as co-chair of the Public Awareness Committee for the NAPBS. Nick resides in Chicago, Illinois and proudly serves on the Chicago Board of Prevent Child Abuse America.

employeescreenIQ is a global background screening company dedicated to superior client service. Their smarter, comprehensive research techniques produce thorough, accurate screening reports that meet the unique needs of their clients and the standards of federal and international employment guidelines. They keep abreast of evolving compliance laws, use the latest marketplace technologies and conduct intensive court-level record investigations. For more information, please visit www.employeescreen.com

Wanda Hackett, Ph. D. (Chapter 13)

Dr. Wanda Hackett is an organization consultant and trainer who works with Fortune 500 companies, child welfare organizations, public and private schools, non-profit organizations, and individuals across the United States to attain enhanced organization effectiveness. Her areas of expertise include: strategic planning facilitation and organization goal setting, high performance work system design, team development consulting and coaching, valuing and utilizing workplace diversity, process improvement and program evaluation, large system change consulting, and life coaching.

Dr. Hackett has a unique background which includes experience as an administer of early childhood education programs including having designed and implemented the first entirely multicultural early childhood education curriculum in the State of Washington in the 1970s. Additionally, she spent 8 years as a human resource professional in a Fortune 50 corporation and brings her experience working with a variety of organizations and teams to her consulting and training practice.

While working in industry, Wanda received numerous cross-functional excellence awards for her consulting efforts contributing to company productivity and financial success. She is featured as a member of the "expert panel" on the PBS training video "Diversity and High Performance Work Teams." Wanda holds a Ph.D. in Human and Organizational Systems from The Fielding Graduate Institute and double Master of Arts degrees, one in Special Education and Human Development from The George Washington University and the other in Human and Organizational Development from The Fielding Graduate Institute. Recent publications include reports on cultural competence and on racial disproportionality in the child welfare system.

Robert P. Hennessy (Chapter 2)

Robert P. Hennessy is an associate in the Los Angeles office of Littler Mendelson. He represents and counsels employers in a broad range of employment matters, including wrongful termination, discrimination, harassment, and wage and hour claims. Mr. Hennessy handles all types of traditional labor law matters, including collective bargaining negotiations and unfair labor practice investigations. He advises management on various compliance issues, including compliance with the Fair Credit Reporting Act, and its state law equivalents. In addition to his work on background check laws, Mr. Hennessy authored an update to the 50-State survey of wrongful discharge law for Littler Mendelson's 2007-2008 **National Employer**®.

Mr. Hennessy can be contacted at (310) 772-7283 or rhennessy@littler.com

Thomas Lawson, CFE, CII (Chapter 13)

Thomas Lawson's expertise has served a variety of industries including law; medicine; government (Department of Defense, FDIC, RTC); law enforcement on local, state and federal levels; banking; gamings; securities; sports; and professional associations among many others.

Over the years, Lawson has helped formulate many standards for the industry. He developed the "Employment Screening and Asset Search Specifications" for the Resolution Trust Corporation (RTC). These standards, as well as a comprehensive set of factual employment screening guidelines also developed for the RTC were published in the

'94 & '97 editions of *White Paper,* now known as *Fraud Magazine,* for the Journal of the Association of Certified Fraud Examiners. He also authored the "Pre-Employment Screening" series, published in The Complete Workplace Violence Prevention Manual, which is used as the gold standard of Best Hiring Practices.

Lawson authored the interpretation and application of FCRA/CCRRA Compliance Guidelines for the Association of Certified Fraud Examiners (ACFE) and related credit reporting and securities industries.

Currently, Lawson also serves on the Editorial Review Board for *Fraud Magazine.* Other notable published references include *Business Week, Los Angeles Times, Orange County Register, Orange County Business Journal,* as well as CBS syndicated talk radio, and interviews with ABC's American Agenda and NBC's EXTRA! Lawson was also a contributing resource for the startling expose, "Privacy for Sale," authored by Jeffrey Rothfeder and published by Simon & Schuster in 1992.

Lawson has led the industry through involvement with numerous professional organizations, including being a founding member of the NAPBS, a "lifetime member" of ACFE and he is Chairman Emeritus of the award-winning Orange County Chapter of the American Society of Industrial Security (ASIS). He is also affiliated with American Society for Industrial Security (ASIS), Society for Human Resource Management (SHRM), Professionals in Human Resources Association (PIHRA), National Public Record Research Association (NPRRA), Council of International Investigators (CII), World Association of Detectives (WAD), World Investigators Network (WIN), Public Record Research Network (PRRN), and the Forensic Expert Witness Association (FEWA).

Lawson, 51, resides in Coto de Caza, California and continues to serve APSCREEN clients from his headquarters based in Rancho Santa Margarita, California.

Founded in 1980, APSCREEN is the originator of the factual employment-screening concept. APSCREEN provides nationwide coverage for businesses seeking the highest caliber, most comprehensive background checks for pre-employment screening. APSCREEN also offers tenant screening and employee locate services. More information is available by calling toll-free (800) 277-2733 or register online at www. APSCREEN.com.

Thomas Lawson pioneered the background check industry in 1980 when he was among the first to provide corporations with a comprehensive pre-employment screening service. His first clients were from the aerospace industry, who demanded the highest level of background checks.

A Certified Fraud Examiner and Certified International Investigator, Lawson is also recognized as one of the first court-certified "expert" witnesses on cases requiring testimony (in trial and depositions) related to negligent hiring; human resource management and compliance; employment screening; and use, interpretation as well as compliance with FACTA/Fair Credit Reporting Act/CCRRA/Gramm-Leach-Bliley (Financial Privacy) Act in the Human Resources context. He has been listed in O'Brien's Legal Experts since 1993 and also has testified regarding hidden assets research, white collar crime/fraud, embezzlement, factual due diligence, internal theft and investigative standards of care.

Billie Lee (Chapter 8)
Billie Lee is president for First Advantage Corporation's Transportation Services division, which includes First Advantage ADR, a national leader in driver and vehicle information

services. Lee joined the management team of First Advantage Corporation in June 2004 as vice president, strategic planning.

Prior to joining First Advantage, Lee's career was aligned with the growth of the transportation industry screening provider, DAC Services, a division of Total Information Services Inc., which was acquired by US Investigative Services (USIS) in 2002. Lee started her career with DAC in sales and subsequently held management positions of increasing responsibility. Her tenure culminated with her appointment as DAC Services Division president in 1998 and continued as senior vice president of operations for the USIS Commercial Services division following the acquisition. Lee served in that capacity until February 2004 when she decided to pursue new interests to apply her strategic talents.

Lee is involved with numerous human resources and transportation industry-related associations, including the Society for Human Resource Management, Association of Independent Information Professionals, National Private Truck Council, and the American Trucking Associations. Her involvement has included effective lobbying on the grass roots level, as well as in Washington, DC. As a recognized screening expert, she frequently speaks on related topics and participates on panels for industry groups. She can be reached at Billie.Lee@FADV.com.

Jason B. Morris (Chapter 12)

Jason Morris founded employeescreenIQ, formerly Background Information Services, Inc, in 1999 and serves as Chief Operating Officer and President for the company. Morris is a Licensed Private Investigator in the States of Ohio, New Jersey, and Nevada with licenses pending in other states.

Prior to founding employeescreenIQ, Morris served as Vice President of Operations for a Cleveland, OH-based private investigation company. He has also held management and investigative positions with two other security companies also located in the greater Cleveland area.

Morris is a frequent speaker at industry events that focus on background checks, global screening, recruitment, and staffing and often discusses best practice initiatives as they relate to organizational pre-employment screening programs. He was recently included on Cleveland Crain's Business "40 Under 40 List" for innovation in the workplace and serves as a board member of the NAPBS. Morris was the 2005–2006 Co-Chairman for the organization and will serve the next term as past Co-Chairman & Treasurer. employeescreenIQ is a founding member of NAPBS.

As Co-Chairman of NAPBS, Morris made frequent presentations to government agencies including members of the U.S. House of Representatives and the U.S. Senate. The focus on these presentations were amendments to the FCRA, and various provisions to the forthcoming Privacy Bills and Immigration Reforms. Morris has lobbied on behalf of the screening industry and has consulted with officials from the FTC, Department of Homeland Security (DHS), and the U.S. Department of Justice. Morris' comments were published on the U.S. Department of Justice Website regarding pending legislation on the Federal Register.

Cleveland, OH-based employeescreenIQ is a best practices leader in the pre-employment screening industry dedicated to providing its customers with the information they need to make informed hiring decisions. For more information, call 800.235.3954 or visit www.employeescreen.com

Lester S. Rosen (Chapter 12)

Lester S. Rosen, Esq., is an attorney at law and founder of Employment Screening Resources (www.ESRcheck.com), a national background screening company headquartered in Novato, California.

He is a nationally recognized consultant, writer, and speaker on the FCRA, pre-employment screening and safe hiring issues. He is the author of "The Safe Hiring Manual - Complete Guide to Keeping Criminals, Imposters and Terrorists Out of Your Workplace" (Facts on Demand Press), the first comprehensive book on employment screening. He is also the author of the first online professional education course on safe hiring and background checks.

He has qualified and testified in the California and Arkansas Superior Court as an expert witness on issues surrounding safe hiring and due diligence. His speaking appearances have included numerous national and statewide conferences. Mr. Rosen is a former deputy district attorney and criminal defense attorney, and his jury trials have included murder, death penalty, and federal cases.

In 2002, he worked with the California Legislature to amend A.B. 655, a law that affected employers in the area of reference checks and hiring in California, and testified on amendments to the law before the California State Legislature.

Mr. Rosen was the chairperson of the steering committee that founded the NAPBS, a professional trade organization for the screening industry, which has over 500 members. He was also elected to the first board of directors and served as the first co-chairman in 2004. He can be reached at lsr@esrcheck.com.

Kenneth F. Sekella (Chapter 8)

Mr. Sekella is an accomplished business executive with almost two decades of experience as a Senior Vice President of Human Resources/Loss Prevention for Fortune 100 companies. Ken spent the early part of his career in education as an Adjunct Professor, and Head Basketball Coach at Kean University in New Jersey. He began his corporate career with a retail division of Macy Corporation and subsequently moved on to an R&D and Manufacturing Division of Squibb Corporation.

From 1978 to 1998, he held Senior Vice President positions in Human Resources/ Loss Prevention for Gimbels East in New York, The Vons Companies, Inc. and Bugle Boy Industries, Inc. He worked creatively and collaboratively to successfully negotiate precedent setting collective bargaining agreements in New York City and Los Angeles. From 1998-2003, Ken leveraged his former corporate experience as he consulted with Fortune 1000 companies to developed non-qualified executive benefit plans designed to retain key corporate executives.

In 2003, he began a professional relationship with a group of business executives and former INS officials to develop the business model that eventually led to the creation of Form I-9 Compliance, LLC.

Throughout his corporate career, Ken developed leading edge metrics to monitor the effectiveness of the Human Resources and Loss Prevention Programs he administered. He successfully set in place measures to ensure the integrity of corporate databases and systems applications for both of these functions. Further, he ensured that they were sufficiently robust to globally support their respective strategies across each organization.

While at Vons, Ken developed the "Employment Triangle Model" that emphasized the importance of legal, credible, and focused employment practices. In 1986, he established comprehensive procedures for the administration of the newly created, legally mandated Form I-9 process. He further leveraged the employer mandates that emerged from the Immigration Reform and Control Act (IRCA) to implement rigorous background checking and interviewing metrics. These processes markedly contributed to increasing the quality of hires and to a significant reduction in employee turnover.

Ken holds an MBA from New York University in Organizational Behavior and a BA and MA Degree in Social Science from Montclair State University in New Jersey. He is accredited as a Senior Professional in Human Resources (SPHR) by the Society for Human Resource Management and is a past member of the Human Resources Round Table (HAART) at the UCLA School of Industrial Relations. He resides with his wife in Newport Beach, California.

Scott Silverman (Chapter 11)

Scott Silverman is the Executive Director and Founder of Second Chance, a non-profit organization founded in 1993. Second Chance is committed to breaking the cycle of unemployment, poverty, and homelessness that plague San Diego. This is accomplished by offering job readiness training, job placement, and affordable housing to men and women who desire to change their lives.

In 1998, Scott brought STRIVE, the nationally recognized job readiness training program from Harlem, New York to San Diego. STRIVE is now a division of Second Chance, offering a three-week intensive classroom experience, assistance with job placement, and a two-year follow-up program to participants. Additionally, our Prisoner Reentry Employment Program (**PREP**) targets the thousands of prisoners being released in San Diego each year. PREP allows parolees to participate in the STRIVE class and live at one of Second Chance's eight alcohol- and drug-free homes, creating a positive environment. These housing facilities offer over 150 bed spaces to individuals who have made a commitment to sober living.

Second Chance's programs and initiatives are designed to address the workforce development needs of the "hardest to serve" segments of San Diego's population. By assisting individuals who are committed to becoming self-sufficient, positive members of their community, Second Chance helps to prevent chronic social problems, including homelessness, hunger, crime, public health risks, gang activities, substance abuse, and family poverty. The agency has grown and adapted to meet these escalating needs, while retaining very high ratios of success with the clients we serve. You can learn more about their programs at www.secondchanceprogram.org

Foreword

Identity Security and Required Background Screening in the Workplaces of the 21st Century

In less than two decades, the use of background checks in the hiring process has evolved from an expensive optional formality to a serious security and human resource necessity. This transformation has been facilitated and made affordable by changes in technology. The 21st century workplace is premised on the assumption that the employer has selected qualified people and provided them with a secure environment allowing for maximum productivity. At the close of the 20th century, the Internet and the digitizing of vast data banks were starting to make background checks much more available to human resource professionals as a means of verifying the qualifications and training of applicants. Better and more informed hiring decisions promised greater retention and productivity. At the same time the legal system was using the growing availability of searchable conviction records to increasingly hold employers accountable for reasonable hiring decisions. While this trend existed, it was dramatically accelerated by the attack on the World Trade Center. Legislators, judges, and the public all demanded greater care in establishing workplace identities and backgrounds. At the same time it was recognized that identity theft was one of the fastest growing forms of crime, and employee and customer data needed greater safeguards. Suddenly human resource and security professionals were expected to be experts on background checks, including the rapid changes in technology, law, and societal values associated with establishing and protecting identity in the workplace. A massive educational effort has been taking place to meet this expectation. In this effort, Kerr and Nixon and a group of experts have created an essential learning tool and practical resource guide. Beyond the basics, this treatise explores the new focus on protecting personal identification information; the need for continuous background checks; strategies for temporaries, consultants, and vendors in the workplace; and the growing demand for international background checks.

If the above represented the entirety of the efforts of Kerr, Nixon, and their colleagues, it would be essential reading for those responsible for the hiring process. However, the treatise continues providing a fascinating picture of the future of background checks, coming changes in technology, and some of the social concerns that can arise in a transparent world where an ex-convict will have difficulty obtaining employment. Indeed the practice and law of background checks often relate to anticipating the future. Events that occur today are often examined in the legal system years later. While community expectations and the foreseeability of harm from the failure to do adequate background checks should not be judged through hindsight, we have entered a post-9/11 world in which almost anything is possible. Without question, the second, third, or fourth terrorist attack is foreseeable. Identity theft is foreseeable. And the rapid progress of technology is suggesting that solutions may be available that have to be considered now.

Looking at Background Screening and Identity Security From the Future

One of the best ways to understand today's needs and requirements is to travel to the future. When one looks back from this vantage point, the decisions and actions of today take on a new meaning. This is especially true in evaluating the adequacy of today's background screening and identity security standards. Below is a very predictable picture of the future of the hiring process:

> Jessica Hartman is nervous as she arrives at the headquarters of Global Strategic Partners, Inc. for her "dream job" interview. It is her first choice of the five positions she is seeking through her Internet application. She is handed a six-page consent form on an electronic reader. It has the same warnings and permissions as the sample form she had seen on the company Website. She applies her thumbprint, signaling her agreement. This leads to the standard retina verification and scan of her personal identification chip. A green light flashes three times, indicating that her retina identification matches the "V-chip" conveniently embedded in her left arm. Instantly the computer screen is filled with background information. Jessica continues to be amazed at the speed of the process, imagining what it must have been like when this information needed to be entered by hand on an application form.
>
> "Ms. Hartman, Ms. Ashii is ready to see you now," the receptionist announces. "Please follow me and I will take you to her office." The office door opens and a petite woman smiles, inviting her to enter.
>
> "I am Hirokio Ashii, and I am with the Human Resources Department of Global Partners. I have a few preliminary questions and then I would like to introduce you to the department manager." Ms. Ashii glances at her computer screen and turns back to Jessica. "You list your degree from Northwestern University's School of Communication as being issued in June 2015, but our information is showing January 2016."
>
> Jessica nods her head in agreement. "Yes, I graduated with the class of 2015, but there was one course still needed. I completed it online and the actual degree was issued in January 2016."
>
> Ms. Ashii returns to the screen and continues, "Yes, I now see the notation on your transcript."
>
> Defensively, Jessica states, "Sometimes there is confusion over my last address in Spain. It is correct, but the residence is in the name of my domestic partner."

> *Ms. Ashii again smiles, "Thank you for that information, but please don't be concerned. We only have access to certain prehire information from our background checking service. If a job offer is made, then we receive and examine much more detailed information, including a lot of personal data that are not needed or relevant in making the hiring decision. You would be able to clarify anything needed at that time. It is amazing that in the third decade of the 21st century when almost everyone has their digital family history on YouTubeII, we are still very much limited in what can be considered during the hiring process."*

The above exchange is fictional, but the technology already exists. Ms. Hartman's interview envisions a future in which something close to the perfect identifier has been fully developed and deployed. When did this happen? When are certain technologies commercially available and in wide enough use to influence community standards about a reasonable background search? These are hard questions to answer even though the authors do a good job of describing what is now possible. The critical message is that technology is rapidly changing, such that at the time a negligent hiring case reaches a jury, much of the technology will likely already be in common use. This is similarly seen through TV programs such as "CSI" and the advanced advertising of technological marvels, where the public often believes that computerized solutions are in place and common well before they have hit the market, been fully proved, and made cost-effective. The bottom line is the need to stay current with the fast-changing technology of background checks and to be prepared to explain why the organization's solution is consistent with the technology actually in use.

A second lesson from Ms. Hartman's interview is the need to understand the law of background checks and newly developed identity information protections. This law will not and cannot stop the forward push of technology in its quest to find the perfect identifier. The "V-chip" already exists and is called the "Veri-Chip." It can be painlessly inserted in an arm and provide enormous benefits for patients with severe memory loss (such as Alzheimer's disease). The chip can be made to give off a faint electronic signal that would help locate a lost patient. Legislating against the development of this type of technology would not only be counterproductive, it would completely fail given its multiple applications and the fact that research and development can be done globally. The role of law is not to stop the technology but to define when and how it can be used. This is particularly relevant when considering information used in hiring decisions, not the least of which requires absolute verification of the applicant's identity. With a proper understanding of the legal rules, the interviewer is supplied only with the verified information needed.

The Convergence of Three Great Forces: Technology, Privacy, and Security

By looking into the future and then turning back to today, it is apparent that at least three great forces are converging in the area of background screening and protection of personal identification information—technology; the deeply cherished value of privacy; and the need for national, workplace, and personal security.

Obviously technology is greatly expanding what is possible. Biometrics, retina scans, and DNA testing are only some of the examples of how we can now establish identity. Soon the time necessary for and the cost of DNA testing will greatly decline, promising to make it a commercially available tool. Indeed, technology in its many forms has the potential to all but eliminate personal privacy. When we make our first cellular telephone call, buy a latté with a credit card, board an aircraft, or drive in a car with a GPS mapping system, we create a digital record. Nonetheless, privacy is one of our most deeply held values and many legislative and judicial restrictions have been applied to limit access to this digital record of our lives. Most states have already passed legislation prohibiting the use of DNA testing in the making of employment decisions (fearing that those with expected high future medical needs would be discriminated against). Indeed, new privacy legislation was pending in Congress and expected to pass, when a third force appeared and instantly silenced those calling for privacy protections. This was the need for national, workplace, and personal security, as demonstrated by the events of 9/11. Suddenly the importance of the government having access to bank records, cell phone transmissions, and e-mail exchanges was deemed greater than our need for personal privacy. On a lesser scale, a similar balancing process takes place in the workplace between the employer's need to provide a safe workplace and personal privacy. Moreover, because the applicant or employee is voluntarily entering the workplace, it is possible for the employer to decrease the expectation of privacy through proper notice.

The above forces can be seen at play in the workplace of Jessica Hartman. Technology has made verification of identity and background information a ubiquitous option for employers. In the time it takes an applicant to walk to the interview room, his or her life's history can be displayed on a computer screen. The importance of knowing who is being hired in the future is speculation, but in a world that promises to be at war with terrorists for decades, it is inevitable that countries will be forced to identify everyone within its borders. This is the underlying issue in the current debate over immigration reform. When car bombings come to America, the concept of a national identification system will be publicly mandated. This might come in the form of more sophisticated driver's licenses, but it is not too extreme to imagine that one option would be to have implants containing vital information injected into our arms much like flu shots. While this seems to be the material of science fiction or a recreation of Orwell's *1984*, the need for being able to establish one's identity and prevent anyone else from taking it is a force at least as strong as our fear of government control. The key to making any of these visions of the future workable is the role of law in regulating how information is used. Indeed, this is what Jessica encountered when she volunteered information about her personal life that was beyond what could be legally requested by her prospective employer. If or when she had a domestic partner should not play any role in the hiring process. There clearly was no need or effort by the employer to learn more about her prior address in Spain at that stage of her hiring. Once given a job offer, it may be appropriate to verify that Ms. Hartman resided in Spain. At that point, the employment decision has been made. Of course, if there is no employment-related purpose for verifying the residence in Spain, then it is likely that even after employment such personal information would be unnecessary and potentially legally protected.

While the trend toward mandatory background screening for all employees intensifies, Kerr and Nixon have included a chapter written by Ken Coates entitled, "The Other Side of Background Screening." This chapter provides a strong case for the value of privacy that is threatened with universal background screening. For example, if we use the available technology to provide complete records to all employers of each applicant's background, then those with criminal convictions will have an extremely difficult time reentering society. While this can be justified for certain sensitive positions, there are many others that would not be threatened by someone with a past criminal conviction. This is increasingly true the older the conviction becomes. Nonetheless, knowing about the conviction will undoubtedly constitute a concern for many employers. Does this justify a more limited application of background checks?

The answer to the above question is a resounding "no." Identity of even the most unskilled of workers may be essential for national security and employment that is premised on the assumption of a correct identity. For example, an undocumented worker who contributes to Social Security through a "borrowed" number will not have the benefit of those contributions if he or she cannot establish identity at the time the benefit is to be claimed. Clearly identity is important, if not essential, to our ability to function in a global society dependant on the open use of technology. Abuses created by dramatically increased access to information will be best controlled by the application of law coupled with compliance technology. For example, criminal records can be "expunged" through a proper legal process. Indeed this may need to be expanded, but it is a channel for greatly restricting the information from being made available to private employers or (if known), used by private employers. Currently, the records are not electronically altered when they are "expunged." Often what occurs is a note is added to the file showing the order of "expungement" without removing the original conviction. Clearly technology could be refined to eliminate the underlying criminal record in a standard background screening, all the while keeping the record available to law enforcement or the courts for proper purposes that are unrelated to employment. Society can determine the rules of employment that apply to those with a criminal history, and compliance technology can restrict access to the out of date records.

Regarding the role of law in establishing enforceable boundaries for information, strong legal tools are available. For several years it was assumed that small violations of wage and hour laws were often beyond the enforceable reach of the law. This has dramatically changed with the growth of class action litigation. While such tools can be the source of great abuse and questionable social value, in the context of background checks they certainly have the potential to almost guarantee enforcement. While individual abuses of information gained through a background check will occur and must be addressed by each employer, policywide abuse is an invitation for class action litigation. One example is legislation that mandates that full account numbers cannot be on receipts because these can easily fall into the hands of the wrong people. Only the last four digits of the account number are to show on the receipt. When the law became effective, several employers were in noncompliance. In some cases, software changes had not been made restricting the information, while in other cases proper preparation had not occurred. Within a few weeks of the law's effective date, dozens of class action lawsuits were being filed. Predictably, enforcement was almost immediate. While background screening has many differences, the principle is the same. If policies are not being enforced that apply equally to large numbers of applicants or employees of a single employer, enforcement tools are available to ensure that the law is followed. We now have a well-established and well-funded plaintiff's bar more than able to provide the necessary assistance. Moreover, the Internet has made the existence of these plaintiff attorneys and their efforts well known and easily researched.

The Employer's Challenge

The world of background screening and the protection of personal information is expanding, driven by the need for security, the demand for greater workforce productivity, and the increasing online availability of information. This creates a serious challenge for employers to properly use the available technology while protecting the rights of applicants and employees. Kerr and Nixon's book is a critical resource for human resource and security professionals who need practical compliance information and guidance. It is the proper use of available information that will keep government from becoming "Big Brother." Employers must now navigate in a new world that calls it "negligent" to hire someone without proper background screening, and yet is unforgiving if the collected personal information is stolen or misused. Clearly, Kerr and Nixon have made an excellent first effort in providing a blueprint for navigating between the colliding forces of technology, privacy, and security that define the 21st century workplace.

Gary Mathiason
Senior Partner and Vice-chair of Littler Mendelson

Acknowledgments

The authors would like to acknowledge Kristen J. Overton for her hard work, editing skills, attention to detail, and overall coordination of this work. We sincerely appreciate her dedicated efforts.

Introduction

As part of the planning for the 2002 Winter Olympic Games, one of the co-authors was asked to help set up a background checking policy and process for the Salt Lake Organizing Committee for 120,000 individuals who would have varying levels of access to the 2002 Winter Olympic Games, held in Salt Lake City, Utah. This group of constituents was a combination of athletes, employees, volunteers, contractors, consultants, vendors, law enforcement, National Guard, and U.S. military.

Initially, it was believed that this process would be quite routine, and ultimately, "no big deal." In order to complete the task at hand, the Salt Lake Organizing Committee, also known as "SLOC," would simply need to run the applicant names through some sort of database in order to gather the information necessary to either accept or decline each application.

As weeks turned into months, it became increasingly evident that this "simple screening assignment" was much more complicated than was initially believed. A number of organizations were involved in the volunteer selection process. Consequently, a plethora of opinions and ideas from varying and conflicting schools of thought had to be reconciled, latticed together, and then tailored to each situation in an attempt to meet the underlying screening objective in the most ethical, efficient, and systematic way possible.

Heavily involved in the volunteer selection process, The SLOC Human Resources Department was primarily concerned with the skill set of each applicant. They wanted clear acceptance/rejection criteria and the information necessary to create a "yes," "no," or "please review" format when reviewing the applicants. However, they also wanted the power to veto a rejection due to an impressive letter of recommendation from a member of the Olympic board, Olympic sponsor, venue manager, etc.

Salt Lake City law enforcement also had an opinion on how the applicant revision process should be handled. Their procedural views were pretty much black and white. All Olympic participant hopefuls who had been convicted of certain crimes, particularly violent felonies, should be immediately terminated from the pool of applicants, no questions asked.

The CIA, FBI, and federal law enforcement agencies involved lobbied for a more extensive, far-reaching screening approach. In addition to criminality, they were also concerned with examining watch lists and anti-American associations. Keep in mind, the 2002 Winter Olympic participant background screening process took place prior to 9/11. However, the actual games took place only a few short months after the tragedy occurred. Historically, the Olympic Games have been a violent political arena, as exhibited in Munich 1972 and in Atlanta in 1996, and therefore, all precautions had to be taken in order to ensure the safety of the athletes, administration, volunteers, and spectators. Simply put, the CIA and FBI had their own way of conducting background checks and operating event security. They often denied entry badges and/or accreditation with little or no explanation.

The U.S. State Department also contributed to the screening effort as they prohibited the access of "marked" individuals that could potentially cause a disturbance due to past radical behavior. They combed lists of anti-American groups and parties and then ensured that these individuals were banned from any and all Olympic participation. This was a great help to SLOC and the FBI as it freed these organizations to focus specifically on problematic Olympic attendees during the 2 weeks the games actually took place.

The U.S. Secret Service acted as the lead federal agency in the planning phase of the games. They advocated uncomplicated and straightforward screening methodology. Employing the Reagan view to trust but verify, they allowed other agencies, like SLOC and the FBI, to conduct background checks; however, the Secret Service still required that everybody coming into the games be searched. They devoted a great deal of time, money and manpower to ensure that everyone that was granted access to an Olympic venue was not carrying or concealing anything dangerous. Their approach was truly reminiscent of the early days of the Transportation Security Administration (TSA). They snatched away Grandma's sheers, tweezers, and the ever-favorite fingernail clippers. This practice was well overdone, causing a multitude of access problems in the early days as it did initially at the Olympic Games; however, as operational efficiency improved, so did the entrance into the Olympic venues.

The Salt Lake Winter Olympic volunteers turned out to be a fascinating constituency. For those who are not already aware, the games would never work without the volunteers - they are truly the backbone of the games. People come from all over the world, on their own dime, to share in the magic, spirit, talent, and camaraderie of the Olympic Games. Most of the volunteers, however, come right from the local population. They act as greeters, drivers, event services staff, athlete services staff, security, guides, etc. Through their dedicated and generous efforts, they constitute the largest group to participate in the games. Consequently, they require the greatest amount of time and energy to screen.

Contractors, vendors, sponsors, volunteers, and the SLOC employees themselves were screened at least once, sometimes twice. Initially, background checks were conducted at the point of hire or when an individual was given access to the planning committee. A second background check was conducted at the point an individual was actually accredited to participate in the games.

The 2002 Salt Lake Winter Olympic Games were a great success! Due to the very thorough, systematic, and security-conscience procedures carried out prior to and during the games, no major incidences occurred. And due to the careful and methodical background screening process that took place, for the most part, all involved, particularly the volunteers selected, were capable, sharp, trustworthy, and very deserving of their participation in the games. Although they did not take home any gold, silver, or bronze medals, these volunteers are all true winners!

This example demonstrates two important issues. First, many security professionals may have misconceptions about the screening process, needs, and complexities, as SLOC did in its early days of security planning. Second, it is our contention that part of the success of the games was due in some part to the screening effort and making sure the volunteers, staff, and contractors were not bringing preventable activities into the games. Just as it was necessary to properly screen all those participating in the Olympic Games, it is equally as important for all organizations, large and small, to screen the people who will be the facilitator for whatever activity your organization is undertaking. When proper screening is not conducted, businesses take on major risk and liability that can easily be addressed early and economically in the initial hiring process.

Companies, corporations, churches, day care centers, health care facilities, philanthropic organizations, the government, and even individuals who make up the general public typically conduct some form of due diligence when deciding whether or not to develop a relationship with an "outsider." Big businesses and individuals alike seek healthy, mutually beneficial relationships. As individuals, we want physicians who are not only highly educated but honest about their credentials and expertise, we want competent and morally sound caregivers tending our children, and we want friends who do not speak ill of us behind our backs. The same goes in business. Corporations, large or small, need to know that the employees, vendors, contractors, suppliers, resellers, brokers, and whatever partners they choose to work with are who they say they are, have the credentials they claim to have, and operate with overall honestly and integrity.

Choosing to open up your business to an outsider is monumental as no corporation would ever knowingly hire the employee who would commit a dishonest or violent act. Negligent on-boarding impact becomes very real when an organization is made aware of and truly considers the gravity of all of the potential costs associated with hiring or contracting with the wrong person or organization.

The decision to work with, trust, and grant access to sensitive company data is, no doubt, a monumental one. Would a company ever knowingly employ a CEO or CFO who would "cook the books" and lie under oath, ultimately damaging and even destroying the company reputation? Of course not! Would a business ever willfully hire an employee destined to commit a dishonest or violent act? Of course not! When thoughtfully considered, the impact of these hiring decisions comes with extremely high costs to the overall success and life of the business. And believe it or not, these hiring decisions are made by companies literally on a daily basis without the proper information necessary to make a good decision.

How can a company safeguard itself when hiring? Is it really necessary or even feasible to verify all applicant information prior to the hire? Does the applicant in question really have a Ph.D. in Egyptology or management experience with a Fortune 500 company? Does the applicant really have the ability and skill set, as depicted in the resume, to do the job well? When questions such as these are not answered with the best data available, via a background check, corporations take on major liability including potential lawsuits, public relations debacles, revenue loss, damaged reputations, etc.

For instance, one such company, which will remain anonymous, failed to perform a proper background check on a newly hired CFO. Screening for criminal behavior was conducted, however, the individual's education, experience, and credentials were left unchecked. After being relocated at the company's expense, this individual stepped into his role as the CFO of a large manufacturing firm. Unfortunately for the company, it was not long before he was let go due to incompetence. However, the story does not end there. The newly fired CFO sued the company for stock options. It was only in the midst of this corporate fiasco that the company, as a means of protecting itself, conducted a thorough background check costing several thousand dollars as the services of a law and private investigation firm were employed. From the background check, it was discovered that nearly all of the experience and credentials listed on the CFO's resume were either false or grossly inflated. The education level achieved was a bachelor's rather than a master's degree as stated, and the university he allegedly attended was phony. His work experience, job titles, and responsibilities were clearly overstated.

Because of this blunder, a new CFO had to be recruited, hired, and relocated. Reasonable spin-up time was needed in order to move toward operational efficiency and effectiveness, so expensive delays and loss of focus for the CEO and other senior managers occurred. Not only did this misstep result in doubling the expense, but the company lost a vast amount of time and the production and credibility of the senior team suffered.

Maybe some of the readers have experienced a similar blunder in their organization or even made a similar mistake themselves. This screening blind spot is not a unique situation and has been seen in many organizations throughout the country. Good screening strategies go far beyond a look at prior criminality. It really means asking whether this candidate fits the job from several angles, including work experience, education, and professional certifications. Even if a candidate has a sterling recommendation from a trusted source or fellow member of your team, take the time and expense to verify key aspects of the resume.

This phenomenon extends past the private world. Consider the case of George O'Leary, former Congressman Wes Cooley, TV evangelist Pat Robertson, and RadioShack Chief Executive Dave Edmondson. They all had discrepancies in their resumes that raised some sort of public review. The impact as such was a public relations nightmare for the organization or individual or both.

The gamut runs from football to politics and a sprinkle of spiritual leadership to corporate leadership. Ellis's and Cooley's military service was called into review, and O'Leary was not the football player he claimed to be. Also, his degrees were overstated for over 10 years on resumes that were not checked by various hiring schools. Do you wonder how much money, time, and effort was spent to make a decision on a coach for such a prestigious university. So, the win/loss record was the real deciding factor, and the rest overshadowed his accomplishments. He resigned after 5 weeks.

In the case of Dave Edmondson, it was religion and psychology that were found to be the culprits. Edmondson, the CEO of RadioShack, inflated or misstated certain credentials he had listed on his corporate biography.

There are several myths relating to background screening. Some of these myths relate to the laws surrounding the legal process for the use of background information in the screening process. Other myths relate to the industry or data sources that can be used to do the actual screening. We will attempt to address some of the more common myths to make the rest of the discussions around the screening process more meaningful.

Myth No. 1

Background screening purely relates to criminality!

If a company or organization really wants to unleash the full capability of screening an individual or business, that company would have to alter their understanding or knowledge of the power and usefulness behind a properly conducted background check. Thorough screening substantially reduces the risks associated with hiring new employees as well as vendors and contractors who might not share in and/or uphold the company values and standards. Additionally, does screening guarantee that a candidate or business entity will undoubtedly add value to your organization? For example, does the applicant or entity in question have the education, work experience, and/or skills to do the job for which they are applying? Even if the person has a clear record, does their past employer confirm the job responsibilities and skill level the applicant is claiming?

Pay careful attention to the chapters on use of employment verifications, education verifications, and job skill testing. You may be limiting your ability to make a good job hire who will not jump at the first rough patch or move for an additional dollar an hour.

Myth No. 2

Getting a driver's license or the equivalent is enough for identification verification.

There are a number of reasons to check identity from a third-party provider. If for no other reason, to make sure the information provided is indeed accurate. There are a number of false IDs that look authentic. Unless you have all the up-to-date security devices in the ID you're looking at, you may just get fooled. Many of the IDs produced today use highly effective antiforgery techniques, but you still need to use the newest security devices to detect forged documents.

More detailed personal identification documents and records may have items that can be used to find old address information from which to verify the application information in order to know where to do your criminal searches. Most screening services have very good ID tools. This is usually the cheapest search to do, is non-FCRA, and can be run at any time during the hiring process once you have identifiers.

Emerging technology allows potential employers to easily access "out of wallet" information to ask in the early stages of the hiring process. For example:

Did the applicant ever live in the following counties?

1. Arapahoe County, Colorado
2. DeKalb County, Georgia
3. Los Angeles County, California
4. Maricopa County, Arizona

OR:

Have you ever had the following vehicles registered in your name?

1. 1989 Buick Regal
2. 2001 Chevrolet Tahoe
3. 2005 Chrysler 300
4. 2006 BMW 330I

These questions could be increased to give the hiring entity an adequate level of reassurance in the hiring decision. Why waste time with someone who is not going to be able to pass a more-specific and more-costly screen down the road?

Maybe a more logical approach is to layer the in wallet and out of wallet via a data collection site, before a candidate shows up to an interview.

Identity verification is not a background check, nor is it part of an FCRA background check. It should be done before the background check is even conducted. We discuss strategies of ID verification in the chapter on identity verification and fraud later on in the book.

Myth No. 3

Consents and waivers are not needed for some types of background checks.

Be careful here! Again, it is highly advised that waivers and consents be reviewed and signed early in your relationship with an applicant, a volunteer, or a contractor. Why? The applicant is much more willing to sign a consent form during the on-boarding or initial stages of the relationship as a newly hired employee, contractor, volunteer, etc. Once the individual is part of the organization, the cooperative relationship might change as the crucial "impression period" is over. This is especially true if an investigation of wrongdoing occurs.

Therefore, whenever possible, and in those states that allow such agreements, be sure to obtain a signed consent authorizing the right to conduct a background check any-time during the individual's tenure. This is especially helpful if you intend to do routine moving violation record checks or employment credit reports or if the employee is in a position where theft is possible. Do not get into a consent debate – just get the agreement and make it "evergreen" if possible.

Investigations can be compromised if consent is requested in the midst of contro-versy as it will likely become a warning signal or red flag to the wrongdoer. This may result in loss of evidence, the coordination of stories and perspectives by guilty parties, and overall stonewalling by suspects. Investigative background checks will be covered in a later chapter in greater detail, but suffice it to say at this point, be proactive in the obtaining of waivers and consents immediately upon the formation of any business relationship.

Myth No. 4

The FCRA does not apply in certain hiring circumstances.

Again, a word of caution: all applicants are also consumers, and the FCRA was written to protect consumers. So if you intend to use any consumer reports for your back-ground check (i.e., a credit report), be sure to obtain a waiver and consent. If you make any portion of your decision based on an FCRA compliant report, make sure you are in compliance.

An FCRA complaint could and likely will result in costly fines, potentially bad public relations and/or press, disruption within the business operations, and added stress.

Myth No. 5

Background checking companies do not have to be licensed.

Beyond the normal business licensing requirements, some states require companies to have private investigative licenses. Most national companies are licensed to operate in all 50 states, and all companies will provide proof of licensing when asked.

Myth No. 6

A multistate or nationwide database is comprehensive and is an efficient and economical background screening resource.

Law enforcement and government agencies have access to the National Crime Information Center (NCIC), a contributory database. Law enforcement "runs" a name and gets what appears to be a comprehensive criminal record about an individual in seconds. Rather than discuss the completeness of the NCIC database, suffice it to say, this is unavailable to the public sector and is not FCRA compliant. Use of this database for hiring purposes is a violation of federal and state law. It is for law enforcement purposes only. But when companies use the phrase "national database" or "national criminal file," it gives the impression it is equally as comprehensive and even possibly a subset of this file. However, this could not be farther from the truth. The multistate files are aggregations of public databases obtained, sometimes for a fee, from state and local government agencies, compiled and stored in a database.

The use of these data in the hiring or background checking motion in the private sector is a fairly new phenomenon. It has really only been around for approximately 6 or 7 years. Many of the large background companies use a multi-state or national type search. Many tout a "proprietary" database, or "secret sauce," that makes theirs better than the competition's.

Some public criminal databases exist and can be aggregated to create a large footprint for a database. Some of the sources are very good and up-to-date. If the aggregator is diligent in the updates, the database can provide some good information and can add a dimension to the check. For example, if you determine your applicant has lived in Atlanta all their life and you do a metro type search, it is highly likely you will get some valuable information. But what about those gaps in employment? Was your applicant doing time in Texas for a crime committed while on the road or during a spring break adventure? It might not be significant, but this type of check does cast a wider net and catches more pieces of information. Also, if you live in New York, for an example, the New York Statewide is a very good check, although very expensive. It covers all 62 counties. But it is stand-alone and not sold as part of any multistate file.

Many states are represented in these databases in a Department of Corrections (DOC) database. So only those who were incarcerated in state prison are covered.

But the real question is should you use the national criminal file as the sole source on which to base your decisions? Probably not! It is not comprehensive in all jurisdictions. Also, the logic in most databases is fuzzy at best and most, if not all, do bring back false positives. So be careful here.

We will cover the proper use of the multi-state database in more detail later on. But just be aware, these sources are incomplete and, therefore, need to work in conjunction with other types of checks in order to make them useful and lawful.

Myth No. 7

You cannot ask for a date of birth without offering the candidate a job.

Brutus' wife is credited with the adage of it not only has to be above reproach but it has to have the appearance of being above reproach. The application here is the idea that if you do not ask for the birthdate, you could not be violating any age discrimination laws because you did not ask the candidate for a date of birth.

Asking for a date of birth to do a background check prior to offering a candidate a job is permissible. In fact, to do a criminal background check, you need a birthdate because most jurisdictions require this in order to provide the information obtained from a criminal background check. This is very important with common names. The birthday is used to find John Jones in Covington, GA, who has applied for a job in your organization.

So, well-documented processes will suffice here. However, if you are really concerned, there are many suppliers that have self-service tools so the applicant can provide the data identifiers directly to their systems. This also saves on administrative costs by off-loading data entry to the applicant.

Myth No. 8

Hiring someone with a criminal past is just bad business.

Hiring employees who have a criminal past is increasingly becoming a controversial topic. This is especially true as the labor market contracts. According to the U.S. Department of Labor, the U.S. labor market is at 4.5% unemployment. In some areas of the country, we are at full employment at the time of this writing. Salt Lake City, Utah, is hovering around 2.5%. A partial solution might be to relax the standards of who you hire.

Hiring ex-criminals is hotly debated because of the moral and social implications involved. It is a double-edged sword. On one hand, you want to help the down trodden get back on their feet; on the other hand, you do not want to put your business and employees at risk.

For example, there may be several skilled job categories that could be filled by a certain qualified applicant, but the work or personal history of the individual is questionable or risky. For example, a felon who has served his or her time has limited legal options in the workforce. So the issue is not whether a background check is run and criminality is validated; the question is whether you should hire the individual who has a past.

Programs are being developed to attack this issue. Training individuals with a troubled past for the workforce is a progressive view. It allows employers to find a way to get qualified workers who could be high producers and good additions to their workforce if the risks are known and evaluated. The real question is, was the information disclosed by the applicant allowing the employer to evaluate the risk? In other words, the information was asked for during your application process and disclosed freely by the applicant. It is the view of the authors that three issues have to be kept mutually exclusive:

1. Did the applicant disclose a past and provide you with accurate information that can be validated?
2. Once the information is validated via a background check, what was the charge, conviction, and adjudication information? If these are answered to your satisfaction, you can now move onto No. 3.
3. How long ago was this instance and what has gone on since the occurrence?

Let's talk about the third question: how much time has elapsed since the event? If a college student is arrested and charged with disorderly conduct or worse, what is the risk to your business if that same individual is now 22 years of age and entering the workforce? Does your hiring practice allow flexibility to make a good hiring decision? What if the incident occurred 5 years ago and there has been no incident since? The applicant could have stayed out of trouble, but what if the individual has been in prison for the last 5 years?

A much more challenging aspect is the felon example. If that applicant is a nonviolent burglar, what is the risk to hiring them as a software engineer? This takes the concept of "break in" to a much higher level! The question is what are you going to do if your senior vice president of operations is willing to sponsor this person into your business?

It is our contention that policies and processes can be developed that address this very thing. You can have guidelines and processes that show due diligence, identify associated risks that allow you to make good hiring decisions that make sense in light of a diminishing hiring labor pool in some areas. We would hope that this is a possible alternative to exporting your jobs or making hiring decisions without a full understanding of the risks.

Therefore, hiring workers with imperfect backgrounds should be considered in many occupations, even those that are highly skilled and demanding positions. Security managers are probably frowning right about now, but please read the chapter on hiring alternatives before you give the whole idea the thumbs down.

Myth No. 9

Resumes are normally fairly accurate and should be good enough to make the initial hiring decision.

Let's assume that a hiring organization is having a job fair and has done their due diligence to make sure the person who is being interviewed is, in fact, who they say they are. The company runs a check on this particular "John Smith" and it is the one who came in for an interview. The resume looks phenomenal. It's professionally printed on card stock and contains all the resume "buzz" words that appeal to an employer. And WOW! Look at those degrees and former work experience. Impressive! He signs a consent (which is a must!) and he isn't a sex offender or a convicted criminal in any of the states I checked. So is he good to go? What about the list of prior experience and educational accomplishments? Surely they are accurate and the candidate did pass the criminal background check.

Think again! Various studies report that anywhere from a third to half of all resumes contain overstated, misleading and/or false information, blatant errors, and intentional omissions. So, you may be making a real hiring mistake here even if the candidate passed the criminal portion of the background check. Also, consider that getting a current reference that is objective and reliable has challenges that you may not be able to overcome. You need to use objective sources like education and prior job histories as a benchmark. So, if you are looking for someone with 5 years of experience, we recommend you confirm that fact along with the title and responsibility of that title, if possible. Or, did you ask the question to weed out a few hundred applicants who are just entering the market who might not have any real job experience? Make sure your screening process matches your decision process in that you want to build in verification strategies of information that is critical to a good job fit.

The documents that should be used for hiring decisions are the application in addition to the resume. Both include important information. However, the application is the legal document that allows you to initiate the hiring decision. It will also be signed with some attestations of accuracy. It can also refer to the applicant's permission to allow you and potentially a third-party provider to complete a background check. However, we recommend a separate consent and waiver be signed that asks for specific information you will want to verify, like dates of employment, location of employment, supervisors' names, colleges and universities, degrees earned, birthdate, and previous names an/or addresses.

Screening of applicants involves having baseline information that can be verified. It is not your job to find out the information that is left out. It is the applicant's responsibility to provide you with information you can verify. That job is hard enough. Your human resource department is not a detective agency, and holes should be filled by the applicant, not by you. Your process is to verify the accuracy of the information provided and make sure your applicant is not trying to hide negative information.

If an applicant lies on the application, which is an important document, what else will they lie about once they are on your team? This is a hiring decision that will also test the character of the individual. If the applicant discloses seemingly negative information, will it eventually demonstrate the behavior of the applicant has changed from the date of the original issue? Some say honesty is the first step in any healthy relationship. Starting out on broken promises may be a risk you cannot afford.

There are probably many more myths out there, but suffice it to say, a well-rounded, robust process has many touch points with both good business and legal standards. We try to discuss most aspects of screening and hopefully assist you in developing an effective screening process as part of your on-boarding process and retention strategy.

In this book, we will bring two views of the screening process from complementary disciplines of human resources and security to helping the security and human resource professional establish a worthwhile, effective screening program. The authors will use a process of point-counterpoint discussions to outline the subtle and other opposing views of these two organizations on this subject. Also, at the end of each of these chapters, a summary of key points is listed.

1

Managing Risk in the Hiring Process
What Are We Risking by Not Having an Appropriate Screening Process?

Some definitions of the word *risk* are "the chance of something going wrong; the danger that injury, damage, or loss will occur; somebody or something likely to cause injury, damage or loss. To put something in danger; to place something valued in a position or situation where it could be damaged or lost, or exposed to damage or loss." In other words, to take a risk is "to do something despite the danger; to place something valued in a position or situation where it could be damaged or lost; exposed to damage or loss; or to incur the chance of harm or loss by taking or not taking an action" (dictionary. reference.com/browse/risk).

Risk can occur whether you act or fail to take action. The authors of this book are practitioners who work with clients and customers to create strategies and solutions in order to prevent risky hiring decisions, poor employee retention, and workplace violence. So our definitions of risk have a common sense dimension. But we would like to start with a discussion of risk as the basis for conducting screening of all persons associated with your organization including employees, volunteers, contractors, consultants, and vendors.

Staffing is the most fundamental and critical driver of organizational performance. In the simplest sense, staffing is putting people to work. It begins with workforce design and includes recruiting, assessment, development, workforce planning, and retention. Today, staffing may involve any combination of employees, contingent workers, contractors, consultants, and outsourced operations working around the world. And although it may involve thousands of employees, staffing recognizes the importance of every single person: the individual worker is the ultimate performer (www.staffing.org/staffinga-z/).

The American Society of Industrial Security (ASIS) has produced a Protection of Assets (POA) manual that is considered the foremost expert guide on how to create, maintain, and adjust corporate security strategy, processes, and policies. The POA suggests that "an effective security plan or program must be based on a clear understanding of the actual risks it faces." We agree that a frank discussion of an organization's risk should occur before a proper screening strategy plan or process can be launched. Taking time for such a discussion is vital if an organization is truly serious about identifying, addressing, and ultimately mitigating the risks it faces. This is true for every business concern from the smallest of businesses to the largest of corporations.

The following is a discussion on how to address risk in the *real world*.

The Avoidance of Risk—is This Possible?

Frustration can arise, especially with the small business owner who rolls his eyes when told of the importance of doing a background check, knowing that his primary focus is on running the day-to-day business. Small business owners are not always aware of simple risk-mitigation strategies that could reduce or eliminate sometimes show-stopping issues like violence in the workplace.

You can try to do all the work yourself. Maybe your business is small enough and business model simple enough that no additional staff is required. But what if your business utilizes vendors, temporary workers, or consultants? And what if you get sick and can't work: What do you do then? Do you have time to make the necessary telephone calls to verify a potential employee's education, work history, etc.? Perhaps it is more relevant to ask: *Will* you take the time necessary to conduct a thorough background check on your own?

On the surface, employee screening appears to be a fairly simple, straightforward process. However, when proper screening measures are taken, a degree of complexity is involved, as is clearly demonstrated in the 2002 Winter Olympic Games example discussed in the introduction. These strategies should also include policies on the hiring and retention of personnel, procurement of professional services, and utilization of vendors and volunteer organizations. It is our contention that there is a superior, more cost-efficient strategy that will give any organization a greater return on investment and the ability to make better hiring decisions, which will significantly stabilize their workforce and avoid, or at least mitigate, organizational disruption.

Starting a business or participating in any sort of business relationship has inherent risk factors. There are countless books that talk about risk as a part of life, and there are many experts in the risk management and risk information business that dedicate hours of discussion to the impact of various risks. But for our discussion, let's keep it simple and basic.

Let's start with a discussion of strategies to address risk (specifically risk mitigation).

Mitigating Risk Through Insurance and Indemnities

You could attempt to transfer risk to another entity like an insurance company. Most of us are familiar with this strategy. We buy policies that cover our homes, businesses, vehicles, and medical needs. If an insured event occurs, we call our insurance provider and file a claim. If the incident or event is covered, we are compensated, reimbursed, or made whole. If the event involves more serious issues like loss of life or livelihood, the coverage will have limits. In everyday life, we make risk/reward decisions all the time. The cost of risk can be quite high in many industries and is a true *risk management* decision. This is extremely important in businesses that require working with the elderly and children, driving of vehicles, shipping of cargo, and the operation of publicly accessed businesses like retail stores, amusement parks, and shopping malls.

There is no question that insurance is very important; however, is it the *total* solution to providing the greatest security and protection possible within an organization? Violence, theft, and loss of proprietary information or trade secrets cannot always be entirely restored with insurance alone. Employee goodwill and morale can be greatly impacted in ways not easily measured. Further study should be conducted in an attempt to weigh out or assess the risks or costs involved in forming all business relationships. It must be determined if the employee, contractor, vendor, etc. with whom the relationship is being formed is well aware of, and in compliance with, the overall organizational function and mission.

Mitigating Risk Through Contracting and Outsourcing

You can transfer risk by contracting the activity or work to some other party. Transferring risk to a third party can sometimes be accomplished by outsourcing the activity or task to an outside provider of goods or services. Vendors, temporary agencies, consultants, and contractors are examples. Many companies use this model in various industries like construction, call centers, and other labor-intensive areas that require a particular expertise. Gaming, for example, has many outside suppliers that are necessary to run a casino or a related facility, like a hotel or restaurant that might be associated with the gaming business. However, the net effect of outsourcing is often more costly and less effective in the employee-screening area because most outsourcing companies will charge for functions that can be done cheaper and more effectively through internal control of the hiring process. This is especially true in the highly skilled areas where you want to truly own the work product.

This transferring of risk is especially prevalent in the background check industry by transferring the liability for mistakes to the outside vendor used in the information retrieval process. In other words, if the screening company makes a deliberate mistake or is negligent in their screening process, the consumer can attempt to hold the hiring company and the screening company liable. However, assigning liability to an outsourced company can be tricky because both the hiring company and the screening company should, ideally, do their utmost to ensure the accuracy of the background check. Both have a vested interest in returning up-to-date information that is attributable to the applicant. However, there are numerous risks involved in background screening that must be addressed. For example, it is extremely difficult to retrieve the correct background information on people with common names. How many people named John Smith or Jose Lopez live in Northern California? For this reason, good background screening companies utilize sophisticated computer applications and employ a great deal of time and manpower sifting through reams of information. In fact, a good background-screening company actually spends more time in the beginning of the process by verifying personal information as opposed to investigating the applicant. A strong process of collecting and matching identifiers (i.e., DOB, addresses, full names and alias, etc.) is critical. If the screening company has strong initial data, they can accurately retrieve information from courts, former employees, and educational institutions.

Risk Acceptance

At some point, every organization must accept some degree of risk. The risk-mitigation strategies discussed here can significantly lower the likelihood of a negative outcome and are therefore extremely important; however, no one strategy or strategies collectively offer a 100% accurate outcome. In fact, the cost to be, let's say, 99.9% sure of the accuracy of every detail could be enormous and/or would slow down a hiring model to such a degree that an organization's ability to efficiently conduct business would be negatively impacted. And so risk acceptance, to some degree, is inherent in all business relationships and decisions.

On the other hand, if you are constantly having to hire new employees because your current hires are ill equipped to perform the job or if their background includes a history of behavior counter to your work culture (such as instances of threats or acts of intimidation), your business could have significant problems, such as understaffing and low morale. In some organizations, the only recruiting requirement is verifying the legitimacy of the applicant's work background. Yet even this basic requirement, in some hiring models, is ignored. For example, many employers, particularly in industries such as construction, farming, and food services, dismiss the importance of proper documentation as it applies to an individual's ability to work within the United States. Legal penalties more and more companies are beginning to receive for knowingly hiring illegal immigrants is a perfect example of this kind of neglect in verifying an applicant's background.

Many companies have been unsuccessful in streamlining hiring processes and procedures largely due to politics, bureaucracy, and the "we've always done it this way" excuse. While all hiring models must include some form of applicant screening, background screening is a necessity in this day and age that no employer can afford to forgo. As discussed, the risks involved in bringing in an "outsider" are too great for any organization to accept without proper security measures.

And so the acceptance of risk is something all employers must accept when forming business relationships; however, the degree of risk, whether it be high, low, or somewhere in the middle, is determined by the efficiency and effectiveness of the hiring model. Again, a high degree of risk acceptance is very common in the unskilled and temporary workforce industries. In many cases, hiring entities believe the screening process is too slow and costly to implement. Therefore, these organizations rely on interviews and gut instinct, and in doing so, accept an unnecessary amount of risk that can prove to be a costly mistake. In August 1990, Christina Appleton was stabbed to death by Arvie Carroll, a co-worker who had been convicted of murder. Carroll was placed with Iron Horse Vineyards by a staffing agency that failed to conduct a background check. After a lengthy trial, Christina Appleton's family was awarded $5.5 million from the hiring company due to their neglect.

Mitigating Risk Through Proper Security Planning and Activity

Another risk-mitigation strategy for an organization involves utilizing some form of reasonable activity that can reduce risk through knowledge of key information. The level and thoroughness of this activity must make both financial and time investment sense. For example, if you have a well-thought-out process for screening applicants where the third party provider understands your business, you can reduce your hiring and retention risk significantly by making employee screening as seamless as possible. Don't fall into the "cookie cutter/one-size-fits-all" trap when approaching screening. Job responsibilities should drive the type of screens, not vice versa.

The trick here is to stick to the basics of consistency/risk. In this book, we examine the various aspects of managing risk with a consistent, thorough process that minimizes the risk in hiring by using a screening strategy that layers a series of filters to identify inconsistencies or holes in the information provided by the applicant. The concept of background screening will be expanded to make the screening portion of your hiring or decision process part of a totally integrated hiring and security plan. Screening should be viewed as standard business practice because it is an effort to make not only a decision that includes as little risk as possible but also a business decision that is in compliance with the objectives and future of the organization. Without utilizing these criteria when making a hiring decision, you end up having to make expensive reactive changes, which ultimately slows your ability to create and execute a viable, sustainable business model.

In the chapter addressing the legal issues surrounding background screening, we focus on negligent hiring and negligent retention. Basically, this refers to making an uninformed decision in an environment where you should have been aware of who and what type of person is in your workplace. Remember, the workplace can also extend into the residences or business locations of your customers. In other words, it involves everyone in your organization who is interacting with customers and customer information, shareholders, other employees, technology, and trade secrets.

In the discussion involving proactive screening activity, it is beneficial to look at what risks are common in the hiring cycle (or on-boarding) and retention process that should be addressed using a life cycle approach. For example, there are different types of screening risks at different points in the hiring cycle.

The following table (Table 1-1) demonstrates a layered approach in the hiring process and incorporates a series of filters to address risk.

In-house vs. Outsourcing

Making the decision either to retain all work within the business or to outsource must be weighed carefully because a number of factors should be considered. In fact, this decision

Table 1-1 Background Risks in the Hiring/On-boarding Cycle

Recruiting	Interviewing	Offer	Training	Ongoing
Identity verification.	Obtain an application and consent to do a background check. This is a good time to conduct a national criminal search on all serious candidates. Low cost. Rough filter.	Most businesses do their complete background check here. Criminal; Employment verifications; Education verifications; Drug testing; and Reference checks.	Depending on the industry, fingerprinting may be required. If submitted during the offer period, there will likely be a delay. Results from fingerprinting.	Life changes, such as moving violation records, credit history, criminality, etc.

is a hotly debated issue in many industries. Traditionally, tasks involving facility security, temporary workers, cleaning and cafeteria services, IT support, delivery services, etc. were services that were typically outsourced.

□ □ □ ██

Important tip: Businesses that choose to outsource open themselves up to a certain degree of liability as valuable business assets and sensitive information are now accessible to "outsiders." This aspect of outsourcing is often overlooked in the screening process.

██ □ □ □

Keeping It In-house

If a business chooses to incorporate a particular task in-house rather than outsourcing, the job description, requirements, and expectations must be carefully thought out and clearly stated. Does the job description accurately reflect the skill set, knowledge, and level of responsibility the candidate will need to possess in order to successfully carry out all duties pertaining to the position? The job function is actually important in determining what types of screens to do and when. For example, in addition to the standard preemployment screening (i.e., sex offenses, criminal behavior, etc.), an employer would most likely want to consider conducting different types of screening when hiring an accountant versus a software engineer. In other words, thorough screening should be tailored to the job rather than generically conducted across all departments and positions.

If your hiring model and approach to the hiring market are consistent, you still may be failing to leverage the screening process. For example, your job descriptions and hiring pools are often completely dissimilar between the factory and the front office. You may want to do an ID verification on the applicants, not just final candidates. Often, ID fraud will cause rework in high-turnover positions (i.e., factory), whereas in other jobs that tend to be more stable, this could delay the entire screening motion until the job offer is made.

How many types of jobs have similar risk patterns? Work on grouping the job descriptions and then determine what types of screens to use for these groups. Do most entry-level jobs have similar access to property, people, and information? If this is the case, these prospective employees might represent a large percentage of your hiring, which will allow for a uniform screen. What if employees move to a different position? Will you refresh your screen? Most security professionals recommend the hiring screen be refreshed if the risk to your company changes with the job. We suggest you link the type of background check to the job description.

Outsourcing

Where are you going to source the candidate? Web searches, temporary agencies, and employment agencies often offer different types of candidates. There are strategies to employ when using each type of staffing source in an effort to prescreen candidates before you ever interview them. For example, some Web search firms allow the potential candidate to do a voluntary background search on themselves, provide the information of the search to a potential employer, and (here's the best part!) pay for the search themselves. This process, if used in addition to your own screen, could prevent many false starts in the hiring process by weeding out undesirable candidates at the beginning.

Temporary agencies also prescreen candidates. But be cautious here: Make sure you are comfortable with the quality of screen being utilized. Also, make sure you are allowed to view the screen results as well as the criteria involved in determining a "passed" or "failed" outcome. Employment agencies should do a good job verifying the information included on an applicant's resume. Their reputation as a quality source of staffing will depend on this. Partner with credible agencies in developing the first layer of screening.

Are you sure of the identity of your candidate? An entire chapter has been devoted to identity verification. Therefore, we just briefly touch on this subject now and go into greater detail later in the book. Included in the identity verification screen is the candidate's legitimacy to work within the United States. It is important to answer this question early in the screening process before a great deal of consideration, money, and interview time with a candidate is spent. Document experts can usually spot a phony piece of ID, but can you? There are some pretty good forgeries out there. Make sure you know who you are hiring.

Biometrics or fingerprints are sometimes helpful in these circumstances but not always. A match is helpful in identifying a person if you have a document you can compare to the fingerprint. There are a lot of rules and regulations around this process, and it can be costly and time-consuming, so think carefully before adding this feature to your hiring procedure.

Establishment of a Sound and Effective Background Screening Policy

How crucial is an established background screening policy to the security and overall function of a business? For starters, all businesses first need to ask themselves, "Do we even have a corporate policy for conducting background checks, let alone one that is effective and efficient?" If the answer is no, we highly recommend you consider the amount of risk a business accepts when background screening is ignored. Take some time to contemplate the many consequences an employer could likely face after making a poor hiring decision—everything from theft, to workplace violence, to costly lawsuits. And then decide if it's worth it to you to take that kind of gamble.

After realizing the importance of establishing a sound background screening policy, it's time to think about what a comprehensive policy should entail. Later in the book, we discuss and dissect the various aspects of a superior background screening policy. But for now, we focus on the risks associated with bad hires, slow hires, bad matches in skills and employment background, and hiring of undocumented workers or job jumpers. What costs are inherent within the on-boarding process, and how can these costs be avoided, or at least curtailed, as much as possible?

The online resource Staffing.org (www.chrysaliscorporation.com/tv_hiring_costs.htm) estimates "the cost of hiring one employee at $4,263 in 2003 ... too many organizations don't know how much recruitment, staffing and turnover cost their companies. If the cost of hiring an employee is $4,263, then the company loses an equal amount on the balance sheet if that employee doesn't work out and the hiring cycle starts all over. One hiring mistake now costs $8,526 to replace a single employee. When all is said and done, the cost to hire one employee in a competitive industry can cost nearly 30 percent of the employee's annual salary. This expense doesn't even take into consideration the cost of training, lost opportunities, impact on morale of co-workers, and strain on productivity." In fact, studies show that replacing an employee can go as high as costing the organization more than three times the employee's annual salary.

One survey shows that "the direct cost to fill a $60,000 position ranges from $9,777 to $49,000; however, indirect costs can be even higher" (www.jdapsi.com/Client/Articles/Default.php?Article=coh&Mode=Print).

Workplace Violence

The following figure (Figure 1-1) is a mass murder survey. How concerned should businesses be about violence in the workplace? According to the Society of Human Resource Management (SHRM), over 5,500 acts of violence or violent threats occur in the workplace each day. That equates to over 2 million instances of violence in the workplace every year! The cost of workplace violence is undoubtedly in the billions when you

Mass murder survey

Situational factors related to public incidents of mass homicide

AGE OF OFFENDER		WEAPON	
YEAR	AVERAGE AGE		NUMBER OF VICTIMS
1997	36.2	Firearms	4.86
1998	18.5	Arson	8.5
1999	17.5	Explosives	86.5

LOCATION	PERCENTAGE OF INCIDENTS
Restaurant	16.1%
Retail store	14.5%
Government office/facility	12.9%
School/university	9.7%
Factory	8.1%
Street/sidewalk/parking lot	7.3%
Nightclub/bar	6.5%
Bank/financial institution	4.0%
Business office	4.0%
Church/temple	3.2%
Other location	13.7%

Commercial location	**40%**
Workplace	**31%**

DAY OF THE WEEK	INCIDENTS	TIME OF DAY
Monday	21.8%	*Mass murders occurring between 9 a.m. and 5 p.m.*
Tuesday	14.5%	
Wednesday	13.7%	
Thursday	14.5%	
Friday	13.7%	**48.9%**
Saturday	8.1%	
Sunday	12.1%	

Source: Homicide Research Working Group

FIGURE 1-1 Mass murder survey published in the press. (Source: www.deseretnews.com. Used with permission.)

consider loss of production, potential loss of employment and subsequent rehiring costs, lawsuits, and numerous other costs, including damaged goodwill with customers and employees. The good news is there are various background checks that retrieve an abundance of historic behavioral information that employers can use to make the best hiring decisions possible. These types of background screens can prove to be invaluable because a good predictor of an employee's future behavior is his or her past behavior.

Here are some things you can check for:

- *Criminal activity by type and level of crime* (i.e., felony theft vs. shop lifting).

- *Length of time* that has passed since the incident occurred. Is there some consideration that can be given for how long it has been since the offense? A misdemeanor conviction for possession of marijuana or underage drinking charges at the age of 18 might be excusable if the person is now 22 and holding down steady employment or working toward a degree. Should you consider a time factor?

- *Sex offences.* This could be a check that is critical and even mandatory in certain industries or states. Make sure you know the laws in your state and your industry guidelines.

- *Education history and licensing status.* If you are making a hiring decision based on skill, this is critical for the younger employee who may not have as impressive work history as other potential candidates. In the technical fields, these might be certifications or professional licenses.

- *Work history.* This is critical for the more seasoned employee. Their education may even be irrelevant, but their work history is paramount, especially for the more key positions.

- *Driving history.* If the employee is driving a company vehicle, this may be an insurance requirement or a legal requirement for certain types of vehicles. Also, consider people who drive their personal vehicle on company business. Often, an employee will drive a rental car on company business.

- *Credit history.* This is a controversial area. Many feel there are clear risks associated with hiring people who have poor credit and/or lack the ability to handle their own finances. The employer should be able to clearly articulate how credit checks and the results thereof directly relate to the job responsibilities. For example, it would be very logical to run a credit check on a bank teller who will be given access to customer accounts/funds; however, it may not be necessary to pull credit on an applicant applying for a teaching position.

- *Professional sanction sites* (i.e., the Office of Inspector General for persons who are restricted from practicing medicine).

- *An Office of Foreign Asset Control or OFAC.* This is a standard check since its inception in 2002, but what is its real value because it is a name-only search? Other related sites are routinely checked today, including the FBI Most Wanted and Interpol sites. If you are in the United States, many IRA members are listed with common names, so false positives are common. The real value here is using this check in concert with all other types of checks. In and of itself, the value may mean little and, yes, Osama Bin Laden is listed! This check is increasingly being used for employment and vendor checks.

- *Vendor or contractors checks.* A lot of companies grant the same or similar access to sensitive information to vendors or contractors as they do to internal employees. Should a check be done on the contractor or vendor? If so, by whom? Should this check include temporary and casual day labor as well? Where do you draw the line, or do you draw a line at all?

- *Visitors to sensitive facilities or with access to privileged information.* Is a signed nondisclosure agreement sufficient? Or, in certain instances, would a company be wise to keep sensitive information completely sensitive? How dangerous is leakage of company trade secrets? For example, many franchised restaurants now use premixed spice packets that include all of the ingredients required in a recipe combined into a single packet in order to prevent cooks from knowing exactly what spices a dish includes and in what portions. This protects the restaurant from losing one of its most valuable assets—the recipe! The most valuable asset being the customer, of course.

There are key activities in the hiring cycle that can reduce the risk of making a bad hiring decision in all industries and organizations. To the experienced security or human resource (HR) professional, these steps might seem obvious, but it is our experience that some of these steps are overlooked in order to expedite the on-boarding process. This, of course, is a major mistake. So we recommend doing all of the following, no matter what types of checks you perform or who does your screening.

1. Require an application from every serious candidate. Make sure you ask the question: Have you ever been punished for a crime? Also notify the applicant of the requirement to successfully pass a background check early in the hiring process.

2. Get a waiver and consent to do a background screen. Make this a separate document in the application packet so it can be sent to former employers or educational institutions that require it before they release information. It will prevent rework later and avoid slowing down the hiring process.

3. Make sure you have a written background checking policy (see Chapter 5). This is a general statement that all employees and potential employees are given.

4. Have an internal document that outlines your background checking procedure and require that it be followed by all your hiring/recruiting personnel. This activity will ensure consistency.

5. If you're going to have an appeal process incorporated into your hiring model (for either alleged mistakes in the information or if someone in the hiring process wants to make an exception), make sure you have a petition process that reviews exceptions or appeals at a level where the risk is fully vetted and understood. This appeal should be done at a very high level in your organization and should include legal counsel, a senior executive for the hiring department, HR vice president or the equivalent, and corporate security officer (CSO). In other words, decide who in the organization has the authority to make an exception.

You'll notice the above suggestion of having a documented appeal process in your procedure. Does that mean that there are factors in the hiring motion that would drive exception-based thinking? You may want to ask yourself the following set of questions before determining that your company will never deviate from a set policy of hiring a known felon.

1. What is the availability of workers in your market? If you have a very strenuous criterion, will you be able to find enough workers?

2. If in fact the labor market is tight, what can you do to mitigate the increased risk involved in relaxing hiring standards? Could you institute an additional layer of security because you cannot fill your openings and need help immediately? If so, who in your organization should determine how you should manage the increased hiring risk?

3. Did the applicant disclose the information, or did you find the negative information as the result of doing a background check? If it was not disclosed by the applicant, then this is falsification of the application and may indicate a deeper issue of integrity that cannot be ignored.

4. The critical element in risk mitigation is in understanding the problems you are likely to encounter. Without knowing the background of the candidate, making an informed decision is impossible.

The complexity of the hiring process can increase when you break down the areas of risk you may want to address.

And what if your real business risk is that you are unable to find enough qualified applicants to fill your open positions? For example, your business may be located in an area of high employment or the demand for skilled employees in the discipline you are seeking might be so competitive that you are unable to find a sufficient number of qualified applicants.

To combat a deficiency in the number of qualified applicants, HR departments often hold job fairs, list jobs on the Internet, and even offer substantial signing bonuses. Many companies go to great lengths and expend substantial funds in the hiring process with no guarantee that the "right person" will emerge. Even as salaries blossom, many businesses are finding that the well of qualified employees is getting dry and prospects of it getting dryer are increasing in the future.

According to the National Association of Manufacturers, 83% of U.S. manufacturers cannot find enough skilled workers. This, in turn, puts pressure on their ability to stay competitive. An even grimmer statistic is that 80% of companies are reporting more than a moderate shortage in unskilled labor and severe shortages in skilled workers like technicians, operators, and machinists. These shortages of available workers can increase the risk of overlooking dishonesty and potential liability for negligent retention or hiring.

There appears to be an ongoing debate between statisticians and economists. On one side of the coin, it is argued that the exportation of jobs has fueled and will continue to fuel the unemployment predicament in the United States. In fact, the U.S. Labor Department paints a grim employment picture in a number of job specialties and industries. The phenomenal growth in India's economy due to recent U.S. outsourcing is becoming increasingly alarming.

However, on the flip side, industries are complaining there are just not enough qualified people to fill the jobs at the salaries their business model can support. For example, there is a shortage of medical professionals in the southwestern United States. In response to the shortages, Las Vegas is offering signing bonuses to registered nurses to the tune of $2,000.

This leads us back to the overarching topic at hand—background screening. What kind of background checks are being conducted in the job specialties and industries that are struggling to find qualified applicants? How effective is the screening process in weeding out risky candidates if there aren't enough candidates to weed? Is having a current valid driver's license sifficient? The details are vague and varied. In areas and industries where quality applicants are few and far between, an attitude of "take whatever you can get" often prevails in the hiring process regardless of the thoroughness of the background check and what it uncovers.

As just discussed, many companies are choosing to outsource jobs overseas in order to cut costs. However, companies that choose to take business outside the United States must consider the following: How prevalent and reliable are background checks conducted in foreign countries? Are the costs of doing these checks so expensive that they offset some of the financial benefits gained through outsourcing overseas? Should you insist on a contractual relationship with the provider to ensure against part of the risk? And even if you do ensure your organization against negative occurrences, what about the real risk? For example, what happens when a child care facility inadvertently hires a sex offender? Would the insurance policy keep such a facility in business or prevent the loss of benefactors to a volunteer organization? Loss of donations and loss of future volunteers often result in a cut in funding and therefore a reduction in programs.

These are questions that need to be asked by every HR and/or security professional who wrestles with these issues every day. These professionals have jobs to fill and face the new realities of risk in the hiring process.

Background Checks: Quality Results vs. Speedy Turnaround Times

Background result turnaround times and costs—what is the tradeoff? Do you lose something by using only instant products? Is there loss of training and orientation time when conducting a time-consuming check, or do you compensate with better process models? "We have a candidate and a job opening; what is holding it up?" exclaims the frustrated operations manager. "We're waiting for the background check to come back," replies the HR recruiter. "That's not my problem, we are missing our production schedules," responds the frustrated production boss.

Therefore, the organization decides to invoke the inevitable "work around." Do something that is cheap and quick. This leads, in part, to the rise of "national criminal files" as an alternative solution to county court searches that, for many years, have been considered the gold standard in criminal background checking. No more waiting for court researchers to go to a court house in Sanpete County, Utah, that only pulls records on Tuesday. Could this be the panacea? Some third party providers will tell you "yes." But the reality is there are some significant risks involved with this process. Most states have limited databases that vary from nonexistent to quite inclusive. We take some time to give valuable suggestions on the use of national criminal files for hiring purposes.

What about the associated costs of doing a background check? What should you pay for a background check, and who should do it? This presents an "in-house" versus "outsource" dilemma. The real issue here is to understand what types of risks you are trying to mitigate, and what risks you are willing to accept. For example, if you are a retailer who is concerned about theft and have a high rate of turnover among employees, you may want to invest primarily in criminal background checks and spend the rest of your funds on skills testing. As a result, you will prevent known thieves from entering the business and ensure that your new hires can do the job you are asking them to perform. The screening process is attempting to filter out a problem and identify a qualified candidate among those who can pass the criminal background check.

As to the actual cost of performing the background check, the average across all industries currently is about $30 per search according to LexisNexis Screening Solutions, a nationwide screening provider. The types of searches vary by industry and company, but the cost is relatively low when considering the risks of hiring a criminal or an unqualified applicant.

The tricky part is managing the data appropriately through the hiring process and understanding the legal and practical implications of taking corrective action based on the background check results. The question arises, could you be missing out on a good hire with incomplete or old data?

There continues to be a widespread concern with the availability of qualified candidates. The angles of debate range from the baby boomers who are leaving the job market to the current immigration policy. The surface facts seem to raise many questions.

For example, in 2002, 12.4% of the U.S. population was past the age of 65. In the next 30 years, this percentage will almost double to 20% (Bureau of Labor Statistics). There are 39.4 million workers in the 26- to 35-year-old age bracket versus the 44 million in the 36- to 45-year-old age group (Employment Policy Foundation).

This issue is not limited to the United States; the aging population is a worldwide trend. Other countries with similar predicaments include the United Kingdom, Japan, France, Germany, and Spain (Employment Policy Foundation).

In the United States, the baby boomers are congregating into certain states. Over 50% of the boomers reside in nine states based on the year 2000 numbers. These states are California, Texas, New York, Florida, Pennsylvania, Illinois, Ohio, Michigan, and New Jersey (MetLife Mature Market Institute).

As workers migrate and retire, it may mean that qualified candidates will be harder to find. And by utilizing background checks, the pool of candidates will be further reduced. It is important to note that currently 9% of all candidates have a criminal record of some sort. This does not mean that the offense would necessarily eliminate them from being hired. There is nothing illegal, in most instances, in hiring someone with a record. But it means that if your criteria for hiring are too generalized, you may pass on a candidate who could be a valuable asset to your company because of, for example, a misdemeanor marijuana conviction in the 1960s, although the woman is now in her 50s with no subsequent convictions. So your hiring criterion has to make sense based on the risk, type of crime, and length of time since occurrence. People do change behavior over time and consideration should be given to someone who has made significant and positive lifestyle changes over time.

One example hits close to home: a high-ranking police commander and personal friend encountered a potential reputation-damaging situation. In his 20s, he was arrested for driving under the influence of alcohol (DUI). A news reporter for the local newspaper was doing a story on police officers who had been convicted of DUIs and who were still actively engaged in law enforcement. The reporter found the old charge against the commander and contacted him for a statement. The officer had been in recovery from alcoholism for more than 30 years when he was contacted by the reporter. The reporter chose to respect the nature of the situation as he took into account the many years that had passed since the occurrence. As a result, he chose not to include the man by name in his newspaper article. A full understanding of the facts took the DUI issue to another level in that the commander had changed his lifestyle and become a model citizen. A well-decorated officer with a tremendous career could have been passed over for hire had the police department not taken all the factors into account.

The arrest of Governor Mitt Romney (R-Mass) is another classic example. An over-zealous Department of Wildlife officer took Mr. Romney into custody for launching his boat with an expired license. This arrest made the newspaper a couple of weeks prior to Mr. Romney's unsuccessful bid for the Senate to unseat Edward Kennedy. Interesting timing! When all the facts were known, it became obvious that this incident was little more than an officer who lost his temper and used bad judgment. The charges were almost immediately dropped and an apology to Mr. Romney issued.

Therefore, the important issue to consider is the risks associated with doing background checks versus not doing background checks. If any organization chooses to hire someone for a job, the business must be cognizant of the fact that they have given that individual the keys to the business' reputation, information, assets, involvement with other employees, etc. This includes not only new hires but also all current employees, volunteers, vendors, consultants, temporary hires, and contractors. All of these players, to varying degrees, have a role in the overall success or demise of the business.

Throughout this book, we dissect pertinent background screening concerns and shed new light on the realities of the hiring process in today's business environment in order to assist your organization in finding strategies and solutions that work! It is our intent to demystify the issues concerning employee screening and help create practical approaches, policies, and programs that make sense in your particular circumstance.

Table 1-2 provides a "point-counterpoint" discussion.

Table 1-2 Point-Counterpoint

Risk is often in the eye of the beholder. Security and HR professionals often view the risk from differing perspectives. Let's see how our authors view the area of risk in the hiring process and the differing points of view on this subject.

Security	Human Resources
A clear process of criteria should be decided on before the first job notice is posted. This policy and process should be strictly enforced with few exceptions.	A policy is only a guideline. There needs to be some flexibility in dealing with individual cases. Therefore, each applicant should be reviewed based on his or her own merit.

(Continued)

Table 1-2 Point-Counterpoint—Cont'd

Security	Human Resources
A good identity verification process is vital. Make sure you know whom you are dealing with from the beginning.	Excellent point! Make sure you know whom you are dealing with. You'll lose valuable time and effort if you don't do a thorough job here.
Have a robust criminal check strategy. This is by far the most important portion of the background check process.	The criminal background check is important but the bigger issues concern job task competencies and the nature of the crime as it matches to the responsibility of the job.
Failure to pass the check based on preset criteria should be reason enough to disqualify the applicant. Don't take risks on known previous offenders.	Business is about taking risk. If we dig deep enough, all of us have something in our backgrounds that would potentially disqualify us. So we need to be flexible in deciding our absolute disqualifiers.
Security should be the lead on adjudication. Ultimately, if the employee is hired with a less-than-stellar history, it will be corporate security's responsibility to clean up the mess.	Hiring people is the domain of HR. Security should have input into the process, but ultimately it is decision of HR and management who gets the job.

In Summary

1. Know your risks and discuss them at length in those with your organization's departments who are responsible for corporate security, HR, functional management, and legal issues.
2. Review those risks against your screening plan to ensure that you are addressing those issues as you understand them.
3. Use the set of standard risk mitigation activities discussed in this chapter to minimize your risk.
4. Team with security, legal, and HR personnel to ensure your policies and procedures will address the known or suspected risk.
5. The changing employment landscape may affect your risk discussions.
6. If there is potentially problematic information in a background result, perform the proper due diligence and gather the facts before disregarding a qualified applicant. An arrest or even a conviction might include mitigating factors that should be considered, so give the applicant the opportunity to address your concerns. It is the right thing to do.

2

Legal Issues in Background Checks

Robert S. Blumberg and Robert P. Hennessy

This chapter is to provide an overview of some of the main legal issues concerning the use of background checks, primarily focused on the use by employers and prospective employers. First, this chapter describes some of the basic legal requirements involved in properly conducting backgrounds checks. Second, the chapter discusses some of the considerations that face companies when contemplating whether to conduct background screening. Third, this chapter addresses the legal implications for properly conducting background checks, including the consequences for violating background check laws. Finally, it addresses some of the reasons why conducting background checks is essential from a legal standpoint, despite the potential liability associated with it.

There are myriad laws impacting background checks. Before moving forward, employers and security professionals should be aware that the relevant legal considerations often vary depending upon the particular situation and from state to state. As such, the discussion in this chapter should not supplant the advice of experienced employment law counsel.

What Laws Govern Background Checks?

Determining which laws govern and regulate the use of background checks for employees or employee applicants can be a perplexing enterprise. While certain federal statutes affect the use of background checks nationwide, many states also have their own legal requirements. To further complicate matters, several statutes that do not directly regulate background checks have relevant provisions that still bear upon the use of the information thereby obtained.

Since the Fair Credit Reporting Act (FCRA) was first enacted nearly 40 years ago, Congress has recognized the central role background screening plays in modern society. In doing so, Congress noted that consumer reporting agencies must exercise their "grave responsibilities" with fairness and impartiality to ensure "respect for the consumer's right to privacy."[1] While protecting an individual's right to privacy is vitally important,

---

[1] 15 U.S.C. § 1681.

Congress itself acknowledges that the entire banking system is dependent upon a legal scheme enabling fair and accurate credit reporting. Legal restrictions on the use of background checks, and on the information they contain, seek to strike a balance between these sometimes conflicting interests. Just as the means of commerce have changed dramatically in the past 40 years, the FCRA and its uses have also changed significantly. What was once a law that primarily concerned the procurement of credit reports by the major credit reporting agencies, now governs a growing industry of background checking professionals from coast to coast.

Likewise, many state legislatures have asserted their own ability to govern background checks. These efforts have increased in recent years, with the advent of the Internet and increasingly more sophisticated identity theft schemes. For example, in enacting its own Investigative Consumer Reporting Agencies Act, California's legislature noted that "The crime of identity theft in this new computer era has exploded to become the fastest growing white collar crime in America."[2] For this reason, California, like many other states, has explicitly imposed requirements beyond those required under federal law.

Federal Law—The Fair Credit Reporting Act

Scope of the FCRA

The primary federal law governing the use and acquisition of background information on consumers is the FCRA, 15 U.S.C. § 1681, *et seq.* The title of the FCRA is a bit misleading in that it appears to refer simply to "credit reporting," implying that its requirements apply only to credit reports. In fact, the FCRA has a much broader scope. In addition to consumer credit reports, such as those prepared by one of the three major credit reporting agencies, the FCRA applies to any report regarding a consumer's character, general reputation, personal characteristics, or mode of living.

Nearly everyone deals with these reports at some point in the course of seeking employment, purchasing a home, or financing a vehicle. The term "consumer reports" refers to virtually any report of information prepared by a consumer reporting agency. Consumer reports bear upon the credit worthiness of an applicant or employee, as well as his or her character, general reputation, and personal characteristics. A consumer report can include literally anything from factual information such as where the person went to school, whether they pay their bills on time or how many speeding tickets they have, to opinions of friends and neighbors regarding whether they drink too much at cocktail parties.

The term "consumer report" does not, however, refer to reports regarding a specific transaction between a consumer and the person making the report. For example, a report by a bank regarding a mortgage holder is not a consumer report, even if the report is given to an affiliated entity such as the bank's credit card division. Likewise, surveillance by a private investigator or a drug test analysis report by a laboratory may not be considered a consumer report under the FCRA because it is limited to a single specific transaction or incident and concerns information developed by the reporting entity.[3]

---

[2]   Cal. Civ. Code § 1786(c).

[3]   *Salazar v. Golden State Warriors*, 124 F. Supp. 2d 1155 (N.D. Cal. 2000); *Hodge v. Texaco, Inc.*, 957 F.2d 1093 (5th Cir. 1992).

"Investigative consumer reports" are a subset of consumer reports involving similar information, but where that information is obtained through personal interviews with the friends, neighbors, or business associates of an employee or applicant.[4] This may include such routine items as an employment reference check, where the former employer is interviewed regarding the quality of an applicant's prior work.[5] Persons seeking investigative consumer reports have additional disclosure requirements under federal law.

In enacting the FCRA, Congress specifically delineated the permissible purposes for conducting background checks. Specifically, background checks are only to be provided by a consumer reporting agency if requested by the consumer or if the consumer reporting agency believes that it is being obtained for one the following purposes: (1) for a credit transaction between the party requesting the report and the consumer; (2) for employment purposes; (3) for underwriting of insurance for the consumer; (4) for determining the consumer's eligibility for a license or other benefit granted by a governmental agency; (5) for evaluating credit risk in association with an existing credit obligation; or (6) as related to a legitimate business transaction or ongoing business relationship.[6]

Congress also limits some of the information that can be provided in consumer reports. For example, under the FCRA, consumer reporting agencies are not permitted to report bankruptcy filings that are more than 10 years old. Likewise, paid tax liens, civil suits, and civil judgments that occurred more than 7 years before the report is prepared cannot be included.[7] Arrests that occurred more than 7 years before the report cannot be disclosed. Interestingly, Congress amended the FCRA in 2003 to eliminate the bar on reporting records of indictment and conviction that are more than 7 years old. This restriction does, however, still exist in some state laws, which also prohibit the reporting of arrests that did not result in conviction.[8]

In the employment context, background checks do not solely concern prehire determinations of an applicant's qualifications and experience. Rather, permissible background checks can include checks concerning existing employees. In fact, the FCRA defines "employment purposes" as including decisions regarding hiring, as well as promotions, reassignments, or even retention of an employee.[9] Employment history, education verifications, criminal background checks, credit history checks, and motor vehicle records checks are among the most common types of consumer reports regularly obtained by employers. The FCRA has, however, been clarified to indicate that the notice and authorization requirements do not apply to investigations concerning suspected workplace misconduct, such as theft or sexual harassment.[10,11]

---

[4] But be wary. Certain states, such as California, do not differentiate between them, and consider any consumer report to be an investigative consumer report. Cal. Civ. Code § 1786.2(c).

[5] Simply verifying the prior employment dates and position is generally not considered an investigative consumer report.

[6] 15 U.S.C. § 1681b.

[7] 15 U.S.C. § 1681c.

[8] See, e.g., Cal. Lab. Code § 432.7.

[9] 15 U.S.C. § 1681a(h).

[10] 15 U.S.C. § 1681a(x).

[11] Although the FCRA does require that if adverse action is taken following such an investigation by a consumer reporting agency, the employer must provide a summary of the report upon which the action is taken.

Legal Procedures for Entities Obtaining Consumer Reports

Under the FCRA, users of consumer reports and investigative consumer reports, such as insurers and prospective employers, may only obtain and use background information if they strictly adhere to several important procedures. Although not intended as a comprehensive discourse on the detailed requirements of the FCRA, the basic procedures for obtaining a consumer report for employment purposes can be summarized in four steps: (1) disclosure and authorization, (2) certification, (3) pre-adverse action notice, and (4) post adverse action notice.[12] This is in addition to the many requirements placed upon the consumer reporting agencies regarding what information may be obtained and procedures that are required to increase the accuracy of the report.

- **Disclosure and authorization:** The FCRA recognizes the vital importance of consumer right to privacy. Accordingly, before obtaining a consumer report, the party seeking the report, such as a current or prospective employer, must give the individual being investigated a special written notice stating that the employer intends to request a consumer report. The employer *must* also obtain the individual's signed consent. This notice and authorization must be a separate document, and cannot be buried in the boilerplate language of a lengthy contract, or placed in the back of an employment application or handbook. One of the more interesting issues to arise in recent years is how to comply with this requirement in the preparation of online application processes.

- The FCRA does, however, permit an employer to obtain a "blanket" authorization from an employee, which will apply throughout employment. At least one court has held that it is permissible to require current employees to provide authorization, and to terminate an employee who refuses to provide such authorization.[13]

- When medical information is sought, specific notice and consent to the release of medical information must be obtained.[14] Additional procedures are also required in order to obtain an investigative consumer report, i.e., a report involving personal interviews. In order to conduct an investigative consumer report, specific notice should be given, as a blanket authorization may not be sufficient.[15] Rather, the party seeking to obtain an investigative consumer report should provide additional notice that such a report is being obtained, along with the scope of the investigation. With this special notice, the party obtaining the report must also provide a summary of the individual's rights under federal law.

- **Certification:** In order to obtain a consumer report regarding a prospective or current employee, the employer obtaining the report must certify to the company performing the background check that they will comply with the FCRA's procedures. Specifically, the party obtaining the report must certify that they are seeking the information contained in a consumer report only for one of the specifically delineated permissible purposes set forth in the FCRA, such as for employment purposes.[16]

---

12   Similar requirements exist for obtaining reports for insurance or other business transactions.

13   *Kelchner v. Sycamore Manor Health Center*, 305 F. Supp. 2d. 429, 435-436 (M.D. Pa. 2004).

14   15 U.S.C. § 1681b(g).

15   See *Kelchner v. Sycamore Manor Health Center*, 305 F. Supp. at 431.

16   15 U.S.C. § 1681b.

- **Notice *Before* Taking Any Adverse Action:** Among the stated purposes of the FCRA is to provide consumers with notice concerning their personal information. With the rise of identity theft and the many mistakes that may occur in background checks, it is essential that the consumer be given notice when the contents of the background check may have an adverse impact on him or her, whether it is the denial of insurance or the loss of a job opportunity. Where a consumer report influences any decision—such as the decision not to hire an applicant—the party obtaining the report must first provide the individual with notice of the anticipated adverse action, a copy of the consumer report upon which the decision will be based, and *A Summary of Rights Prescribed by the Federal Trade Commission.* The party seeking to make the decision based upon the consumer report must then give the consumer an opportunity to correct information within the report.

- **Notice *After* Taking an Adverse Action:** After the party obtaining the report has provided the documents above, it must wait a reasonable time period prior to taking the adverse action. A reasonable time period may be as short as 5 business days. Once this reasonable period has elapsed, the party relying upon the consumer report must provide a formal notice that an adverse action is being taken based, at least in part, upon the contents of the consumer report. The FCRA's requirements for this notice are detailed. The adverse action notice must, at a minimum, contain the following information:[17]

  ○ *Consumer reporting agency contact information,* including the name (Lexis/Nexis, etc.), address, and telephone number of the agency that provided the report.

  ○ *Statement that agency is not the decision-maker.* This statement must explain that the consumer reporting agency is unable to inform the consumer of the specific reasons for the adverse action.

  ○ *Statement of right to obtain a free copy of the consumer report* upon which the entity bases any adverse decision. Although the consumer will have already received a copy of the report *before* any action is taken, the individual must be notified of his or her right to obtain an *additional* copy.

  ○ *Statement of right to dispute report.* The consumer must be notified of his or her right to dispute the accuracy or completeness of any information in the report.

Failure to comply with these federal requirements can result in legal actions, as discussed later in this chapter.

State Laws—Background Checks

In addition to the FCRA's numerous requirements, employers must also be aware that many states have their own laws directly regulating background check reports, including Arizona, California, Colorado, Georgia, Kansas, Louisiana, Maine, Maryland, Massachusetts, Minnesota, Montana, New Hampshire, New Jersey, New Mexico, New York, Oklahoma, Rhode Island, Tennessee, Texas, Virginia, and Washington. Although the number and

---

[17] 15 U.S.C. § 1681m.

variety of state laws preclude even a summary discussion of each, a few representative examples are in order.

Many states with laws pertaining to background checks in the employment context contain only minor differences or exceptions to the requirements of the FCRA. Arizona law, for example, does not generally impose any more extensive requirements than does the FCRA.[18] Likewise, Kansas law provides that if the information contained in a consumer report results in a denial of employment, employers "shall so advise the consumer against whom such adverse action has been taken."[19] This is essentially akin to the adverse action notice required under the FCRA.

Other states such as Maine, New York, and Washington actively impose greater requirements than those under the FCRA. Maine law provides that employers must retain all records of disclosures made to an applicant or employee in the course of obtaining a consumer report for 2 years.[20] New York requires that employers give notice to an applicant or employee *before* the employer requests an investigative consumer report, whereas the FCRA allows the notice to be given shortly after the request is made.[21] Unlike the FCRA, which permits a single blanket authorization, Washington state law imposes an additional requirement that Washington employers give successful applicants a second written notice that it may use a consumer report for other employment purposes *after* they become employees.[22]

California has such an extensive set of state laws governing background checks, it could fill the entire chapter of this book by itself! California has separate statutes governing credit checks, as well as other types of background checks: the California Consumer Credit Reporting Agencies Act (CCRA) and the California Investigative Consumer Reporting Agencies Act (ICRA). These laws impose several additional requirements beyond those of the FCRA.

While the CCRA applies to all individuals investigated for employment purposes who have a mailing address in California, the coverage of the ICRA is unspecified and could be assumed to apply to anyone who lives in California, as well as anyone who applies for work or insurance in California.[23] Thus, the ICRA may apply when any part of the background check process is connected to California. If the investigated employee *intends* to work in California, for example, the ICRA may apply to any investigation conducted on him. It may apply where the records being searched are located in California, or even if the background check agency itself is located in California. Such ambiguities counsel employers and security professionals to think expansively about the possibility their actions will fall under the requirements of the ICRA.[24]

California has certain requirements that go beyond the FCRA in terms of the notice and authorization itself. For example, in California, the party seeking the report must notify the consumer of the name, address, and telephone number of the consumer

---

[18]   Ariz. Rev. Stat. Ann. §§ 44-1691–44-1696.

[19]   Kan. Stat. Ann. §§ 50-701–50-722.

[20]   Me. Rev. Stat. Ann. tit. 10 § 1320.3.

[21]   N.Y. Gen. Bus. Law § 380-c.

[22]   Wash. Rev. Code § 19.182.020.

[23]   Cal. Civ. Proc. Code § 1786.

[24]   In a similar situation, a court in Kansas asserted personal jurisdiction over a resident of Wisconsin when that person intentionally conducted an improper background check concerning a Kansas resident. *Cole v. American Family Mutual ins. Co.*, 333 F. Supp. 2d 1038 (D. Kan. 2004).

reporting agency. This may create an administrative burden if an employer does not have a consumer reporting agency that they use regularly. California, like several other states, including Oklahoma and Minnesota, specifically requires that the consumer be given the opportunity to obtain a free copy of the consumer report any time one is requested. This must be done by providing a check box in the authorization form itself. There is also some question as to whether a blanket authorization can be utilized in California for all reports sought during the course of employment based upon the requirement that the employer provide notice of the "nature and scope of the investigation *requested*."[25]

As state laws are constantly being added or amended, entities utilizing background checks must be vigilant to make sure that they are complying with the current laws in their jurisdiction.

State and Federal Laws—Other Statutes

As if the interplay between the FCRA and its state law equivalents did not create sufficient intricacy, there are an assortment of additional state and federal laws impacting the use of some types of information contained in a background check report. This added layer of complexity again emphasizes the potential need for an experienced background check company and legal counsel well versed in working with the various applicable statutes.

Criminal background checks, for example, represent one area in which sometimes conflicting laws bear upon the use of certain information contained in the report. Employers regularly inquire as to the criminal history of a prospective employee—they are often required to do so by law. Under the FCRA, consumer reports may permissibly contain records of *arrests* occurring any time within 7 years prior to the report.[26] As noted above, the FCRA has eliminated the restriction on the reporting of convictions. However, many state laws specifically prohibit employers from considering information about arrests that did not lead to conviction when making employment decisions. California generally prohibits both public and private employers from utilizing this information as a factor in "determining any condition of employment."[27,28] California has a registry regarding sex offenders but specifically states that the registry shall not be used for employment purposes.[29] Hawaii merely prohibits *public* employers from considering such information.[30] Rhode Island law prohibits all employers except law enforcement from making any inquiry regarding arrests not leading to conviction, calling such inquiries "unlawful employment practices."[31] In New York, inquiring into an arrest that did not result in conviction may be considered illegal discrimination.[32] To make this provision a little more convoluted, the New York legislature made the

---

[25] Cal. Civ. Proc. Code §1786.16.

[26] 15 U.S.C. §1681c.

[27] Cal. Lab. Code § 432.7(a).

[28] However, California does make certain exceptions for law enforcement and health care organizations.

[29] Megan's Law: Penal Code § 290.46(j)(2).

[30] Haw. Rev. Stat. § 378-2.5.

[31] R.I. Gen. Laws § 28-5-7(7).

[32] N.Y. Exec. Law § 296(16).

law applicable only to the arrest records of employee applicants, not to employees. This does not even begin to consider the intricacies involved in determining whether a particular court action is a "conviction" or when the "conviction" occurred for the purposes of these laws.

The proliferation of state laws affecting background checks extends beyond laws restricting the use of arrest records. In fact, while the above-mentioned laws concern restrictions *on the use* of information obtained though background checks, other state and federal laws place affirmative duties to obtain and/or disclose certain information in the background check context. Laws dictate that when requested, certain employers *must* provide information regarding their employees' drug test results. For example, employers in the trucking industry are subject to the federal regulations of the Department of Transportation (DOT). The Federal Motor Carrier Safety Administration Regulations mandate that current or former employers must accurately respond to a prospective employer's inquiry regarding whether a truck driver tested positive for a drug test, and whether the driver actually agreed to take the test, or has ever refused.[33]

Other federal laws forbid employers from even requesting certain types of information. Under the Americans with Disabilities Act (ADA), for example, employers may be prohibited from using information about a prospective employee's disability when making the decision to hire.[34] Moreover, the ADA authorizes employers to seek medical exams or inquire about medical information only after all non-medical components of the background check are complete and the applicant has been given a "real" offer of employment. Where an employer is unable to demonstrate that the single remaining aspect of its background check is the requested medical examination, courts are unlikely to find the requisite job offer on the table. Without a qualifying job offer, the employer's request violates the ADA.[35] As an example, courts have found that where a medical exam is conducted prior to receiving a conditional offer of employment, the employer failed to comply with the ADA.[36]

The Driver's Privacy Protection Act of 1994 (DPPA) restricts disclosure of personal information maintained at the state level by departments of motor vehicles. Such personal information includes anything that could identify an individual, including the individual's photograph, Social Security number, and address.[37] The purpose of the DPPA is to add another layer of protection for individual privacy, ensuring that citizens have fully consented to any release of private, personal information. To that end, Congress amended the statute in 1999 to prohibit the practice of "implying" consent when an individual was merely given the option to block the release of information. Now, states are required to affirmatively obtain consent prior to any such release.

This discussion of the varying statutes bearing upon the release or use of information typically at play in background checks could continue at length. Other issues, including those related to the use of drug screening, or polygraph testing, remain to be

---

[33]   49 C.F.R. § 40.25.

[34]   42 U.S.C. § 12101 *et seq.*

[35]   *Leonel v. American Airlines, Inc.*, 400 F.3d 702, 709-711 (9th Cir. 2005).

[36]   *Buchanan v. City of San Antonio*, 85 F.3d 196, 199 (5th Cir. 1996) (offer conditioned on completion of medical examination, as well as polygraph test, assessment board, and extensive background investigation was not conditional offer of employment under ADA).

[37]   18 U.S.C.A. § 2725(3).

considered. Laws such as the Health Insurance Portability and Accountability Act (HIPAA), and even the Federal Rules of Evidence, bear upon the ways in which this information may be properly and legally utilized. The real impetus for directly engaging the array of laws discussed, however, comes into stark relief when considered in light of the equally extensive consequences for failing to do so.

The Legal Implications of Conducting Background Checks
Liability for Violation of the FCRA

Given the litigiousness of current American society, the legal implications for not properly conducting background checks can be serious and costly. As the sophistication and detail of background screening have increased, so too has the number of potential forms liability can take when there is a failure to adhere to the numerous requirements of the laws governing them. As one might expect, individuals denied employment, or who suffer any adverse employment action based on information contained in a background check report, will frequently seek whatever recourse is available to them. This can lead to a positive outcome, such as when identity theft is uncovered and inaccurate information corrected. All too frequently, though, the result is legal action.

The FCRA contains specific provisions for violations of its provisions whether by the consumer reporting agency or by the person seeking the report.[38] Although no liability can be imposed if a user of consumer reports maintains reasonable procedures to comply with the law, where noncompliance with the requirements of the FCRA is the result of negligence, the agency or employer that fails to comply may be held liable for any actual damages suffered by the subject of the report. This may potentially include, for example, lost wages or emotional distress for a person wrongfully terminated based upon an improperly received or prepared background check report.[39] Moreover, when an FCRA-based suit is successful, the losing defendant must pay the plaintiff's attorney's fees and costs.[40] It is important to note that the law in this area is still nascent and evolving. Although the FCRA does not define what constitutes reasonable procedures, it does have many detailed requirements. Anyone utilizing information contained in a consumer report would be well advised to, at a minimum, maintain policies and procedures strictly adhering to the express requirements of the statute. Furthermore, companies should have strict requirements regarding who within an organization is authorized to request and obtain the results of a background check. Companies have clear responsibilities under the FCRA and should expect to be held liable for any violations of those requirements.

The FCRA's more draconian civil liability provisions may be imposed for instances of willful noncompliance. Where the violation is willful, the party in violation will still be liable for any *actual* damages suffered by the employee or consumer who is the subject of the report. Just as with negligent noncompliance, a prevailing party is entitled to attorney's fees where willful noncompliance is found. The violator may also be liable for "such amount of punitive damages as the court may allow."[41] In order to award punitive

---

38 15 U.S.C. § 1681n-s.
39 *Veno v. AT&T Corp.*, 297 F. Supp. 379 (D. Mass. 2003).
40 15 U.S.C. § 1681o.
41 15 U.S.C. § 1681n.

damages, the court would need to find that the violation was the result of conscious disregard for the consumer's rights, or that the violation was deliberate and purposeful.[42]

Potentially more important, willful noncompliance can also result in civil fines of "not less than $100 and not more than $1,000" for each consumer affected by a noncompliant action. Thus, for example, a seemingly innocent failure to comply with the technical requirements of the FCRA, such as including the FCRA authorization in a job application rather than as a separate document, could result in significant liability. In a single instance, this type of liability is not particularly burdensome. However, plaintiff's attorneys have become adroit at sniffing out technical violations of laws, such as the FCRA, which are systematically repeated. A mid-size company with a few hundred employees, or a background screening agency conducting several thousand screenings per month, could potentially have a lawsuit filed seeking aggregate damages in the millions of dollars. The cumulative, fixed penalties assessed for certain FCRA violations are particularly amenable to class action status. In fact, recent years have seen an explosion in the number of class actions filed against employers in other contexts.[43] Furthermore, if the intentional violation is deemed malicious, the party may be subject to common law tort claims of defamation and invasion of privacy as well.[44]

Given the potentially heavy liability for "willful" noncompliance with the FCRA, one may reasonably ask, "What exactly does 'willful' mean under the FCRA?" This is where the still evolving legal climate for claims asserted under the FCRA comes into play. For although the definition of such a central term in the statute would seem straightforward, there is a sharp disagreement even among different courts. According to some courts, the definition of willful noncompliance includes any action that is in "reckless disregard" for the law.[45] This interpretation means that ignoring the law's requirements could constitute an intentional action. Willful noncompliance may be found even where users of background checks rely on the opinions of lawyers interpreting the FCRA. In fact, one court explicitly noted that it had little patience for "creative lawyering."[46]

Other courts have embraced a less expansive interpretation of "willful" under the FCRA. According to that view, "willfulness" requires *actual knowledge* that the defendant's conduct violates the FCRA, such as the "knowing and intentional commission of an act the defendant knows to violate the law."[47]

To resolve this ambiguity, the U.S. Supreme Court joined the fray in October 2006, and concluded that willfulness covers "not only knowing violations of a standard, but reckless ones as well."[48]

Moreover, an employer's liability may exist even for conduct of its employees that is outside of the course and scope of employment. At least one court has found that

---

[42]   *Spector v. Trans Union, LLC*, 301 F. Supp. 2d 231 (D. Conn. 2004).

[43]   See, *e.g.*, The Class Action Fairness Act of 2005, 28 U.S.C. §§ 1332(d), 1453, 1711-1715, recently passed by Congress to control, in part, the "explosion" of state class action litigation.

[44]   15 U.S.C. § 1681h.

[45]   *Reynolds v. Hartford Fin. Servs. Group, Inc.*, 435 F.3d 1081, 1099 (9th Cir. 2006); *Philbin v. Trans Union Corp.*, 101 F.3d 957, 970 (3d Cir. 1996).

[46]   *Reynolds*, 435 F.3d at 1099.

[47]   *Phillips v. Grendahl*, 312 F.3d 357, 368-369 (8th Cir. 2002).

[48]   *Safeco Ins. Co. of Am. v. Burr*, 127 s.ct. 2201, 2208 (2007).

an employer could potentially be liable when its employees improperly conducted a background check on the ex-wife of one of the employees.[49]

Liability for Common Law Torts

The FCRA generally preempts most common law tort claims based upon the failure to comply with its provisions. This preemption prohibits claims for defamation, invasion of privacy or other related torts. This preemption is lost, however, where the consumer asserts that the violation was willful and malicious.[50]

Companies should take note, however, that potential liability for actions in the course of conducting background checks does not lie solely with the company seeking the information or consumer reporting agency actively conducting the background check. Former employers are also at risk. A basic step in nearly every background check involves contacting former employers to confirm employment dates and, in many cases, to inquire as to the former employee's performance. Jilted applicants—denied employment based in part on a former employer's negative reference—have brought actions for defamation or even retaliation. Where a former employer makes a statement to a third party that appears to be based on fact not just opinion, and which could damage the reputation of the employee, that statement must be reasonably believed to be true. Of course, the line between what constitutes a statement of opinion and what constitutes one of fact is difficult to discern and may only be determined following costly litigation. For example, calling a former employee's work record "unsatisfactory" was considered a statement of opinion and, hence, not actionable as defamation.[51] However, a statement that a former employee was terminated for "unsatisfactory performance" *was* considered actionable.[52] Although at least thirty-four states have laws granting limited immunity to former employers when giving references,[53] the scope of this privilege is often only discerned following litigation, and will not prevent an employer from being sued.

Employers should not, however, provide misleading or falsely positive recommendations for former employees for fear of being sued. This is especially true if the employee is known to be violent or dangerous. In one instance, a school district was held liable for falsely providing a recommendation for an employee suspected of child molestation, when another school district hired the individual based upon the recommendation.[54] Former employers' references may also expose them to liability under several other legal theories. For example, where the agent of an employer unreasonably provides false or inaccurate information regarding the subject of a background investigation, the employer may be liable for the tort of negligent misrepresentation.[55]

---

[49] *Cole v. American Family Mut. Ins.*, *supra*, 333 F. Supp. 2d, at 1046.

[50] 15 U.S.C. § 1681h(e).

[51] *Kakuris v. Klein*, 410 N.E.2d 984 (Ill. App. 1980).

[52] *Adler v. American Standard Corp.*, 538 F. Supp. 572 (D. Md. 1982).

[53] Matthew W. Finkin, *Privacy in Employment Law* (2nd ed., pp. 763-789), BNA Books, 2003.

[54] *Randi W. v. Muroc Joint Unified School Dist.*, 14 Cal. 4th 1066 (1997).

[55] To be actionable, the recipient of the false information must rely on it in making an adverse employment decision, and the plaintiff must suffer damages as a direct result of the misrepresentation. See, *e.g.*, *Singer v. Beach Trading Co.*, 876 A.2d 885 (N.J. App. 2005) (plaintiff fired after former employer falsely stated that she had been a customer service representative, when she had actually been a vice president).

The Legal Implications of *Not* Conducting Background Checks

Given the many technicalities and the potential consequences for failing to properly conduct background checks, one may justifiably wonder whether an employer should give up on the process entirely and hope that employees and employee-applicants are all entirely qualified, upstanding citizens. Not surprisingly, the legal ramifications for failing to conduct background checks in certain circumstances are often as severe as those for improperly conducting them.

Employers in many fields are required by law to conduct background checks on prospective employees. This includes employees who might come into contact with children, who operate large machinery, who operate the instrumentalities of interstate commerce, who deal with sensitive financial information, who work for government agencies, as well as physicians, lawyers, and teachers.

As readers of this chapter are undoubtedly aware, an employer can sometimes be held vicariously liable for the actions of its employees. This liability is based on the idea that if an employee of XYZ Company negligently performs his job in a way that injures a third party, XYZ may itself be liable for the employee's negligence. The legal term for this is *respondeat superior*—"let the master answer." Where a delivery truck driver hits a parked car, his employer will have to answer for the damage. Employers may be held vicariously liable for the consequences of an employee's drug use or intoxication, for example.[56] Employers may also be liable for the discrimination or harassment of its supervisors, even if the company was not aware of, and did not approve of, the conduct.

Fortunately, vicarious liability usually attaches only when an employee is acting within the scope of his or her duties. Thus, on Monday morning, when one of XYZ's software engineers strikes a passerby, XYZ will have a strong argument that it should not be vicariously liable for that injury. Employers are not normally liable for the actions of an employee who is on a "frolic and detour." This distinction between activities within the scope of employment, and those resulting from a so-called frolic, has enabled employers to avoid untold fortunes in liability over the years.

Employers may lose the benefit of this distinction, however, when they fail to conduct a background check. That is to say, while an employer may potentially avoid vicarious liability for employees' actions "outside the scope" of employment, the employer may still be *directly* liable under a theory of negligent hiring or negligent retention. Liability for negligently hiring an employee is based on the idea that if a reasonably prudent employer would have uncovered the danger posed by an employee at the application stage, the employer should bear liability for losses resulting from the employee's wrongdoing. Analogously, employers may be directly liable for the actions of their employees under a theory of negligent supervision or retention. The only real difference between these two tort theories is the timing of the employer's alleged negligence—prior to hiring an employee, or during the course of employment.

Both negligent hiring and negligent supervision may lie where an employer *should* have foreseen that an employee or applicant *might* pose a threat to the people the employee would reasonably be expected to contact. The result may be different, if, unlike

---

[56] See *Mulroy v. Olberding*, 29 Kan. App. 2d 757 (Kan. 2001) (employer can be held liable for injuries caused by employee driving while intoxicated).

the example of a software engineer randomly striking a passerby it turns out that the employer is a restaurant, and the employee is a waiter with a history of violent crimes. Thus, it has been held that an action can be stated when an employer hires an employee whom the employer knew or should have known has a propensity for violence.[57] Of course, the actions giving rise to liability must have *some* connection to the employee's job. On the other hand, employers are often insulated from charges of negligently hiring an employee when the employer has conducted a proper background check, even if it failed to uncover the employee's potential for wrongdoing.

Apart from the threat of lawsuits, there are countless practical reasons background checks are absolutely imperative from a legal standpoint. Improperly screened applicants may engage in theft of employer property. The costs and loss of revenue caused by utilizing company resources to take legal action against such employees provide their own impetus for properly conducting preemployment investigations. There is also the potential for drug use among employees and the loss of productivity or quality of work when a company gets stuck with an unqualified worker. On the most basic level, hiring a qualified applicant the first time around reduces the possibility a company will have to expend resources searching for, interviewing, and training the unqualified employee's replacement. The need for background checks may not end upon hiring. Employers may have incentive to regularly conduct background checks regarding existing employees to determine whether they have engaged in criminal conduct, have a poor driving record, or are having significant financial problems that may impact their work.

The now infamous story of George O'Leary and the Notre Dame football program illustrates the practical problems associated with failing to conduct a proper background check. Coach of the Notre Dame football team would be the dream job of many Americans. In 2001, O'Leary realized that dream—for 5 days.[58] O'Leary's resume was strong. He had been a highly successful coach with three decades of experience. It was his experience Notre Dame took interest in, not that he claimed to have played 3 years of varsity college football in the 1960s, or even that he had received a master's degree in the early 1970s. Yet when it was discovered that O'Leary lied about his qualifications, O'Leary was forced to resign. Notre Dame was held up to national scrutiny and ridicule, and critics openly questioned the competency of a program that failed to catch such blatant inaccuracies.

Had Notre Dame conducted a fairly routine background check before offering him the job, the entire mess could have been avoided.[59] Although the university has since recovered from the episode, other employers are not as fortunate. Smaller companies are not so well positioned to withstand the negative publicity, or the financial burden, that can result when the failure to conduct a background check leads to hiring an unfit employee.

---

[57] *Underwriters Insurance Co. v. Purdue*, 145 Cal. App. 3d 57, 69 (1983); *Monty v. Orlandi*, 169 Cal. App. 2d 620, 625 (1959); See also, *Bradley v. Stevens,* 329 Mich. 556 (1951).

[58] See John W. Fountain with Edward Wong, Notre Dame Coach Resigns After 5 Days and a Few Lies, *New York Times,* Dec. 15, 2001.

[59] The story has a happy ending. O'Leary was given another chance to coach and, in 2005, led one of the greatest turnarounds in college football history at the University of Central Florida.

Conclusion—Moving Forward

With the ascendancy of electronic communication, concern over identity theft and personal privacy has resulted in a proliferation of laws further restricting both access to and the use of personal information. At the same time, concern for safety and security in the post-9/11 era has brought about an expansion of laws mandating more comprehensive background screening. As the law evolves, so too must the policies and procedures of anyone engaged in such endeavors. The combined efforts of employers, security professionals, background screening agencies, and experienced employment law counsel will be necessary to successfully adapt to these changes.

3

The Role of Security in the Hiring Process

One of the primary roles of any security professional is to protect the assets of the business. Management and courts alike have maintained the position that companies have a duty to establish a work environment that is safe and secure so the organization is free to conduct legal business that is beneficial to the owners or stockholders. Security then should touch all areas of the business that affect this mission even if the administration of this mission is outside of the traditional security organization. Screenings of individuals who will have access to, control, sell, or dispense these assets are of major importance to the security professional. This activity can proactively and dramatically reduce the overall losses or damage of business assets. Even better, if the company starts out on the right foot and has a policy of preemployment background checking from inception, the mission of reactive security investigation can be greatly minimized.

A logical extension of this mission touches all individuals who have access to the same space, information, systems, customers, or assets as does the employee. These individuals carry a variety of titles such as temporary worker or "temp," consultant, contractor, vendor, and even visitor. All, under the right circumstances, have access to many of the same assets as employees.

Human resources (HR) is not always the lead in bringing these individuals into your organization. The lead group could be procurement or even the functional organization itself. The contract janitorial staff sometimes has access to some of the most secure areas of the business and some of the most confidential information. The movie "Wall Street," in which the main character, played by Charlie Sheen, gets a job as a janitor in a law office that handles mergers and acquisitions, comes to mind. As he fulfills his janitorial responsibilities, Sheen is able to collect sensitive information off the desks and out of the trashcans of the senior partners.

Security departments often write, or at least assist in writing, policies that involve these individuals who are granted access to the "inside." However, from a more practical standpoint, other departments might be better positioned to administer some sort of an ongoing program that ensures due diligence is used in screening these parties into the organization. As it pertains to employees, for instance, the HR department usually has the most interfaces with the new hires in both the recruiting and on-boarding process. Therefore, they are often the department that administers the screening program for new hires.

As a matter of course, HR is usually the lead group and the first line of defense against a bad hire. One of HR's primary purposes is to manage the hiring effort based on current processes. For example, at LexisNexis Screening Solutions, the efforts around screening are lead by the HR department in well over half of the companies in their clientele. But in other cases (approximately 15% of the time), corporate or organizational security is the lead group. The emerging model is actually a hybrid of both security and HR working jointly, complementing the strengths both departments bring to this activity.

The on-boarding process has certainly changed over the years and especially since 9/11. A real interest in the background screening process brought security more and more into play. At a minimum, policies and procedures are being reviewed and even signed off by the chief security officers (CSOs) along with the various legal, HR, and senior management policy makers.

The quality of background checks themselves can be a problem for many companies that choose to disengage security from the hiring process. For example, in cities like Atlanta, where there are many counties that make up the larger metropolis, conducting a check in only the county of residence might leave out valuable information. It is vitally important that the screening strategy employed is based on both crime patterns and searching surrounding counties in addition to the counties where the individual lived, worked, or studied.

Healthy organizations create an environment in which departments are able to align themselves together with a common purpose and unified initiatives. Unfortunately, this alignment is not always the case between the security and HR departments. Failure to execute a thorough and systematic background check process could eventually end up creating problems down the road. On the other hand, HR needs flexibility and often wants some ability to make common sense decisions that may mean appealing rigid hiring constraints that the security department may want. Qualified candidates are often difficult to find and severe hiring rules can make finding qualified pools of candidates even harder.

From a practical point of view, security is certainly affected by the policies and procedures of any background screening process and should be considered a key stakeholder in any screening process. Security should be involved early in the planning, enhancing, and/or expansion of the hiring process no matter who actually administers the day-to-day activities. If you look into your own security or HR case files, you can often identify patterns and/or evidence of prior behavior that was linked to an incident investigation. And we all know that the best predictor of future behavior is past behavior.

There is no greater area of concern for security and HR alike than incidents of violence in the workplace. This is increasingly, and unfortunately, becoming an almost daily occurrence. These violent individuals, who lash out on people, property, or both, are not exclusively employees or former employees. They can be vendors, temporary workers, consultants, contractors, etc.

The basic statistics are pretty frightening. Let's look at some of the statistics and trends:

- According to the National Institute for Occupational Safety and Health (NIOSH), *workplace violence* is any physical assault, threatening behavior, or verbal abuse occurring in the work setting. It includes, but is not limited to, beatings, stabbing, suicides, shootings, rapes, near suicides, psychological traumas such as threats, obscene telephone calls, an intimidating presence, and harassment of any nature, such as being followed, sworn at, or shouted at.

- NIOSH found that an average of 20 workers are murdered each week in the United States. In addition, an estimated 1 million workers—18,000 per week—are victims of nonfatal workplace assaults each year.

- Workplace violence is the second leading cause of work-site death in the United States for men and the number one leading cause of work-site death for women, according to the U.S. Department of Labor. However, according to the NIOSH, men are at three times higher risk of becoming victims of workplace homicides than are women.

- Homicide is also the leading cause of death for workers under 18 years of age.

- The majority of workplace homicides are robbery-related crimes (71%), with only 9% committed by coworkers or former coworkers. Additionally, 76% of all workplace homicides are committed with a firearm.

- Murder is the leading cause of work-site death in the service, retail, and finance industries.

- According to the Bureau of Labor Statistics Census of Fatal Occupational Injuries (CFOI), there were 551 workplace homicides in 2004 in the United States, of a total of 5,703 fatal work injuries.

- Most nonfatal workplace assaults occur in service settings such as hospitals, nursing homes, and social service agencies. Forty-eight percent of nonfatal assaults in the workplace are committed by a health care patient. Nonfatal workplace assaults result in more than 876,000 lost workdays and $16 million in lost wages. Nonfatal assaults occur among men and women at an almost equal rate.

- The U.S. Department of Justice (DOJ) National Crime Victimization Survey statistics, published in July 1994, found that almost 1 million workers were victims of violence while working. The survey excludes homicides because it was based on interviews with victims. According to the survey, one in six violent crimes in the United States—an estimated 8% of rapes, 7% of robberies, and 16% of assaults—occurs at work. An indicator of the seriousness of the workplace violence problem was the finding in the study that 30% of the victims were confronted with armed offenders, one-third of whom carried handguns. The study noted that 16% of violent workplace incidents resulted in physical injuries and 10% required medical care.

- In addition to the human cost, businesses suffer economic losses when workplace violence occurs. According to the DOJ survey, assaults at work cost 500,000 employees a total of 1,751,100 lost days of work each year, which averages out to 3.5 days per crime. In terms of just lost wages, the estimated annual total was more than $55 million. When lost productivity, legal expenses, property damage, diminished public image, increased security, and other factors are included, total losses from workplace violence probably can be measured in the *billions of dollars.*

These statistics are representative of only those instances that are reported. It is unknown exactly how many threats or simple batteries occur and go unreported. So, needless to say, the problem is real and should be a considerable factor in deciding who should be given access to your employees, customers, property, and good name on a daily basis.

Let's list some specific examples of actual incidents that could have been avoided by the use of a simple criminal background check.

Twenty-eight-year-old Christina Appleton was stabbed to death by co-worker, Arvie Carroll, a convicted murderer placed with Iron Horse Vineyards by a temporary agency that did not conduct a background check. The case went to trial and the jury awarded the family $5.5 million.

According to industry experts, California employers lose negligent hiring suits 60% of the time, and the average verdict award in such cases is $870,000.

The Kirby Company, an in-home, door-to-door vacuum cleaner manufacturer, along with University Vacs, Inc., owned by William L. Urie, hired Michael Molachek as a door-to-door dealer in December 1983. The employer failed to conduct a background check before hiring Molachek. During the year prior to Molachek's employment with Kirby, he was convicted of two assault charges and two weapons charges in Minnesota. Additionally, a Minnesota charge of criminal sexual conduct in the third degree was still pending when he was extended the job with Kirby. On December 8, 1983, Linda McLean allowed Molachek to enter her apartment to demonstrate a vacuum cleaner. Molachek also brought with him a set of knives, provided by the distributor. Molachek used the knives in assaulting and raping McLean. McLean sued Kirby, Urie, and Molachek and was awarded $150,000 in damages.

Other types of behavior can also be cause for concern. As with violence, a history of theft or dishonesty can also be a strong predictor of future propensities for similar behavior. It is realistic to suspect that an individual who has been convicted of felony theft and is on probation for such might be a risk to work in a bank. According to SHRM, approximately 56% of all "shrinkage" comes from internal theft. Shoplifters have a tendency to take smaller items with lower price points. But the real issue is at what point is an incident not an indicator of the honesty of an individual? It is important to consider the amount of time that has passed since the incident in question. Was the crime committed last week or last decade? If the applicant can stay out of the system and clean up his or her record, maybe that person could be a real value to your business. In other words, the incident at 19 years of age should be weighed carefully for the now 35-year-old candidate. More often than not, however, the issues are not quite so black and white but rather a dull shade of gray.

Roles and Responsibilities of Security and Human Resources in the Screening Process

It is apparent that each approach has validity contingent upon the company policy, industry standards, and organizational philosophy coinciding with the screening process in place. In some cases, the screening process is a joint responsibility, and in other cases, one department will take the lead and the other a more supporting role. For example, skill-based testing and employment and education verifications could be an HR mission, leaving the criminal background checks to be overseen by security.

One common model is to have HR managers work with line and operations departments to understand the hiring requirements and jobs needed. Their recruiting function, whether conducted by an HR manager or a recruiting specialist, then swings into action to match candidates with openings based upon resumes and applications. Once the candidates are sourced, a series of interviews are initiated. Sometimes companies use panel interviews for *key* hires that might include corporate security directors or CSOs. It is recommended that identity verifications be completed before the first interview. This practice is highly cost effective as it can prevent the wasting of both your employee's and the applicant's time and effort.

Some organizations and industries require skill testing to ensure the applicant has the baseline skills needed to complete the job before the interview process spins up. These tests are almost always conducted in the retail and semiskilled arena. Again, why spend valuable time interviewing candidates who cannot perform the basic job responsibilities?

Once you know the applicant is who he says he is and the testing and interviewing phases are complete, an offer is made subject to the successful completion of a preemployment background check. A background consent signed by the applicant also allows for routine screening during the course of the applicant's employment (see Appendix A for sample forms).

Now the results come back. Oops, what if the applicant has a conviction for vehicular homicide or maybe disturbing the peace or aggravated assault? If the application does not send any red flags, what do you do? Should you withdraw the offer? What does the charge mean? And what is a delayed adjudication? What does that mean? If it happened 6 years ago, should the conviction be a deciding factor? Maybe your security professional can assist here. Perhaps they need to "sign off" on any hiring involving a conviction. Often, the policy of the business requires security to review all screening results that have a criminal hit.

It is our experience that security is very good at demystifying the criminal codes and significance of the charges. Most comprehensive screens require a review by a security professional with conviction interpretation. This is one of the many valuable services the security professional can provide to the HR manager or recruiter. Some HR departments rely on help from the third party screening provider to assist here. It is highly recommended that the security department be consulted on security risk decisions when hiring an employee who has a criminal past.

A very important question regarding the integrity of the applicant is, was the negative information disclosed voluntarily by the applicant prior to the background check? If nothing was disclosed, this may be considered a falsification of a company record and the need to interpret the charge is moot. There is no need to proceed with the hiring motion if the applicant is hiding a conviction.

It is possible there has been a mistake in the information provided. Maybe the court runner made a mistake or it's a "false positive." These are good questions to ask. If you have such questions, your third party provider can assist in providing answers. Your policy should allow the applicant to explain the inconsistency in the application and screening results. You don't want to pass on a qualified applicant if a mistake has been made. A good third party provider will validate the information at no additional charge.

If you have an in-house process, the process should be done by the security department. They know how to work with courts and should be your lead in any in-house program.

Sending the screening results directly to the security department, in the case of any hits, is also a good alternative for final review. They can review and resolve many of the questions the HR manager would likely have if the results were initially sent to HR.

There are no real rules or legal requirements of who should be the lead here; however, a comprehensive review of how hiring is conducted within your organization is critical. Operations and line departments' participation in the planning process will reduce the frustrations of turnaround time complaints as these are issues that need to be communicated to the ultimate "customer"—HR and security.

This information flow is now being managed with automated tools such as Applicant Tracking Systems (ATS) and Human Resource Information Systems (HRIS), which can allow review of candidates via a privileged password-protected system if multiple departments need to sign off on less-than-stellar backgrounds.

The most critical path in the equation is timely and accurate communication of all results to the party/parties doing the actual hiring as they are accepting the risk(s) associated with hiring a particular candidate. This is especially true if a candidate has the necessary skills but has failed to comply with the hiring policies and/or hiring expectations established by the organization. It is recommended that a clearly articulated appeal process be put into place in order to account for such discrepancies. Senior managers who are ultimately responsible for the organization should be well briefed and sign off on any policy waivers. If you have a waiver process, make sure it is well documented and reviewed by your legal department or outside counsel.

Now that we've set the table for some good discussion on the topic of organizational security and hiring processes, let's delve into the meat of the issue.

1. Let's begin with policy. In order to create a process you must first decide what your policy will be in relation to screening. In this document, you should state your purpose for screening applicants, current employees, and even temporaries, volunteers, contractors, consultants, and vendors. Normally, this statement is general in nature and does not outline the actual nuts and bolts of the screening process. It is rather a framework to support your screening procedures, even if they vary across departments or job descriptions. In most organizations, this policy is part of the employee handbook, Code of Conduct, or similar document and may be reprinted on the application and circulated for employees to review. The security department should help write this document or, at a minimum, review the document as a key stakeholder. All policies should be reviewed by the in-house legal department or a labor law firm. Senior management needs to sign off here because this will be one of the building blocks of the hiring model and may impact the type of employees who will be part of the organization.

2. Procedural documentation is normally not for general publication. This is an internal document that actually details the process. This may include the types of checks that will be done and when. Because most companies perform a check that is structured to catch most criminal activity or uncover education inflations and artful employment creation, it is important to keep this information confidential. Security should take an active role here in order to ensure the approach is sound based upon their knowledge of court coverage, strengths and weaknesses of database searches, and possible schemes to hide information. Your legal advisor needs to verify that the procedure is in accordance with current Federal Credit Reporting Act (FCRA) interpretations and state and local laws governing hiring in the states where applicable. There are other legal implications involving the American with Disabilities Act (ADA), Equal Opportunity laws, and other statutes that should be considered. A full review by your legal team will ensure compliance.

3. Your commitment to screen each applicant should be clearly stated at the earliest possible point of contact with the applicant. In fact, it is best practice to inform all potential candidates of the background screening that will take place prior to the submission of an application. This allows the potential candidate the opportunity to select out of the application process if he or she so chooses. This practice will avoid unnecessary costs and loss of time and effort on candidates who know they will fail the process. Your HR team should explain the process and strongly encourage disclosure. Disclosure should not mean immediate disqualification, however. Security professionals can be used as subject matter experts as they understand best the gravity of the convictions. They should also be helpful in assisting the policy and procedure makers in factoring the length of time from the conviction. For example, if there was a conviction for shoplifting 5 years earlier with no recurrence, there might be some thought of how this might not indicate a theft pattern that might negatively impact the hiring decision. This is especially true if there was complete disclosure by the candidate. Security can also be helpful in helping the HR manager or the hiring manager to understand the impact of plea bargaining and how courts often reduce the conviction degree from the original charge. If you use an outside agency or third party provider, they can also help the organization establish a screen based on the risk and consistent with budget constraints. In certain cases, it might be beneficial to contact a consultant familiar with the various types of searches available.

4. Make sure the policy adheres to the adverse action procedures as outlined by the FCRA. This is a protection for the consumer (in this case, an applicant) as it gives them the opportunity to correct any errors that are associated with their name. Although rare, mistakes do occur in the courts. Sometimes, the most up-to-date court filings may not be in the record, which could substantially change your decision to pass on an applicant. Also, if court runners are used to gather information, mistakes can be made by the runner or the court clerk or both. Again, candidates should be given an opportunity to correct errors in your report. Therefore, when you get the adverse information, you should give the applicant the opportunity to dispute the results. If you use a third party service, they should rerun the report for no additional charge. The appeal process can be lengthy; and therefore, it is necessary to keep the opportunity open for a reasonable period of time. Although it is not clearly outlined in the FCRA, most legal experts agree that 5 days is ample time to rerun a check. There may be exceptions, but 5 days is considered standard.

5. Outline the process of obtaining waivers and consents to do the background check. This is a requirement in all cases where the information gathered is used under the FCRA and most state laws. In most cases, an "evergreen" or perpetual consent can be obtained. This alleviates the need to go back to the employee for a second consent. However, many organizations by policy obtain a second consent if an additional screen is required later. In the state of California, you must get consent if you conduct an additional screen. Later in this chapter, we discuss when this is advisable.

6. On a rare occasion, an organization may want to make an exception to policy. Because the policy procedure may insist a check be conducted, the actual

enforcement of the policy should be clearly detailed as well. What this means is the applicant is sponsored by the hiring department that would like an exception to the procedure. This can happen from time to time and should be allowed for in the procedure. Security has a critical voice in the process, as they will give input into these sorts of appeals. Being responsible for the protection of the organization and its assets, security will offer valuable perspective to these types of situations.

    a. These appeals should be in writing, outlining why the exception should be made.

    b. The appeal should be cleared through the highest level of the department that is endorsing the applicant.

    c. Legal, the director of security or the CSO, and HR vice president should be included in the decision-making panel, along with the leader of the sponsored department. The decision to grant the exception should be unanimous.

7. A good mission for the security organization is to review all adverse information that is uncovered in the screening process. If the screen is clear, there is no reason to slow the process down by requiring further review. According to LexisNexis Screening Solutions, approximately 9% to 12% will have a hit in a criminal background check. These hits may not eliminate the candidate, but security has the trained eye to review the risk involved. Security can compare the results to the policy and adjudicate the process. This will create checks and balances within your hiring model.

Another area that is increasingly becoming standard procedure in the screening process involves the screening of current employees. Many organizations will run annual or semi-annual screens on current employees under certain circumstances. This should be outlined in your screening policy. As previously discussed, the waiver and consent documents will give the employee the opportunity to disclose possible infractions at the point of hire. However, this type of check is similar to a balance sheet. It is only current at the point the screen is run. This is a good reason to get additional consent before an annual check is run, to give the employee the opportunity to disclose any incident that might have gone unnoticed or unreported since the preemployment check was run. If information is uncovered during the subsequent screen and the employee failed to disclose it, then the nondisclosure or falsification of company record issue should be reviewed before taking any adverse action based on the issue that was uncovered in the screen.

As discussed earlier, HR is often the hiring lead, but security should be the adjudicator of the adverse information that is uncovered for the same reasons described above. Security will often conduct background checks for investigative reasons. This is a separate activity.

Some reasons that an additional screen might be done on the employee include:

1. The employee is moved to a job that has different or expanded responsibilities involving driving, cash handling, or cash disbursements.

2. The employee is moving to a position where they will have access to proprietary information or trade secrets.

3. The employee will be required by a government agency to pass a clearance background check.

4. A certification is now required or a certification needs to be verified for licensing or insurance purposes. This is often outlined by statute. Many practitioners must by recertified on an annual or semiannual basis.

5. Customers may require your employees to be screened in order to do business with your company. This is part of a vendor-certification process. Furthermore, government outsourcing requirements may be imposed if you work for the government. If you do not currently have a background checking process in your company, you would be required to background screen your current workforce.

Security will often be tasked with the responsibility of establishing or helping to establish the mix of background checks that will be performed either in-house or through an outsource provider. There are advantages and limitations to every type of check and each one has a price tag attached to it. So, the use of certain types of checks needs to be discussed to enable the security professional to recommend a product or screening suite to best meet the guidelines of the hiring policy.

The use and value of personal references should be discussed at length between HR and security. This check is often extremely subjective. In this process, the applicant is asked to provide names that the hiring organization can contact to ask about the individual's particular behavior in prior assignments. The names usually include co-workers (current or former), relatives, or professional associates whom the applicant believes will provide positive personal information. If your organization chooses to use this type of check, you may want to "consider the source," and then look for secondary sources that can be contacted to obtain a more objective evaluation.

Identity verification is critical. This is sometimes overlooked or assumed to be accurate based upon information provided on the application or resume. Make sure the suite of verifications include a check of names, any other names used by the applicant at any time, current address, former addresses, date of birth, and Social Security number. This check is meant to determine the validity of these data points and how they belong to each other. Most outsourcing companies offer products that provide the matching logic and database to not only validate the data but also provide all the known addresses associated with the names.

Be careful here—you should still validate the information provided with government issued identifications. This could include the birth certificate, driver license, passport, work visa, school identification card, state identification card, etc., but even these can be suspect. Think about using a product that offers "out of wallet" questions (i.e., old addresses, vehicle types registered in the candidate's name, etc.) that could eliminate identity fraud in your organization. You should also use the Social Security Administration service to validate the Social Security number provided.

Multistate or countrywide databases are also helpful to screen candidates. These are compilations of criminal databases from various state and local agencies. Some of the data is very comprehensive and up-to-date. North Carolina is a good example of a state where data are often included in these databases that are fresh and comprehensive. Other data might be provided by the state Department of Corrections, including the names and information of individuals who have spent time in the prison system of a particular state. However, this will not include jail information. Not all criminal activity rises to the level of requiring the perpetrator to spend time behind bars. For example, some felonies have a sentencing process that is satisfied with a combination of jail time and probation. So, it is recommended you understand the breadth and scope of the coverage of this type of database. There is a term floating around—"National Database"—that makes it sound like there is some mainframe database containing records of all criminal activity in the United States. This gives the casual reader the misconception that this is national coverage including a compilation of data that are common between all states. This is not true. Have your source give you a copy of the coverage map and check out the data sources. Be sure to ask what types of crimes or sentences are included in the data.

Another common issue is the logic behind the search/screen results. Often the matching logic can be too broad or inherently fuzzy. This creates false positives. False positives will slow down your process and often create confusion for the reviewer. Common names often lead to false positives. For example, common names frequently match your applicant. You must then carefully evaluate the data to make sure it belongs to your candidate.

Another obstacle to consider is out-of-date data. Using information that may or may not be current is never a good idea. Make sure your process includes a disposition update to ensure that you are not making decisions on information that has been changed in additional court action. This makes the database information old and therefore not FCRA compliant. Most companies that sell this type of search should counsel buyers on its limitations. Be leery of any provider that contends this type of search is in any way completely comprehensive.

Many of the multistate files do, however, include a comprehensive sex offender database among the data sources. This file, in and of itself, is a good addition to the screening and is often justification enough to use this search. The sex offender data are compiled, by law in most states, and available for public review. However, checking all 50 states individually can be a tedious process. Therefore, checking the information in this type of consolidated database makes a lot of sense.

The gold standard of background checking remains the county court search. This is the most up-to-date record of any incidences of state offenses. Consequently, this search should be included in all criminal screening strategies in some form. This check is the most commonly used vehicle in verifying information provided in the countrywide searches.

However, because there are approximately 3200 counties in the United States, it is necessary to use the first two strategies to narrow the searches. ID verifications or tools will usually provide a list of counties that are associated with the name and other data points to help your organization to direct your county criminal searches. According to LexisNexis Screening Solutions, the average number of counties a person will bring back in its ID tool is 1.96 counties per name submitted. Therefore, checking at least two counties is often a good metric to follow. A more aggressive or comprehensive suggestion is to search all the counties brought back by your source. Many providers can bundle this type of request to fit your budget.

This search can often take a substantial amount of time in a screening process. Many counties do have highly automated ways to recover this data that can be returned in a matter of hours or, at maximum, 2 days. But there are also counties that still use paper files or logs, which slows down the entire process and inevitably results in lengthier turnaround times. Most providers should give you a time estimate that you can use to gauge when you can "green light" the various candidates.

Some companies or organizations also map federal searches to overlay the addresses of the counties provided. There are 97 federal districts within the federal court system, which includes U.S. possessions (i.e., U.S. Virgin Islands, Puerto Rico, etc.). Checking the provided addresses against these districts can also be done. Make sure you have a good risk discussion, as outlined in Chapter 2, to decide what your risk analysis is. The crimes that come out of this search range from wire fraud to drug trafficking. Criminal activity that would normally be charged at the state level can often appear here if the offense was on federal property (i.e., a national park). The information here is found within the PACER court system and is sometimes troublesome because the data are name only and often produce false positives. Regardless, this is an excellent data process to get clearances on most applicants.

Another type of search that may have application is the statewide search. This is becoming increasingly popular for a couple of reasons: (1) the coverage is greater, and (2) the cost is cheaper than doing the search county by county. Statewide searches have two flavors to consider: (1) the search comes through the law enforcement community, normally the state police, and (2) the search is from the state office of the courts. The court case systems are only available in 15 states, and the turn-around time is also a factor. Also worth noting, the law enforcement reports can take up to 2 weeks to get back. And you must be sure that the information you are using for your decision is compliant with FCRA and the states involved. This report is comprehensive and can contain arrest information that should not be used in the decision process. Receiving current information can also be an issue depending on the counties' diligence in updating the files.

In addition to the delays in getting the data, there might be incomplete data sets, and even missing dispositions. Further, the fees associated with these types of searches, especially the offline police reports, can be high. It is highly recommended that you consider your risk model and even consult with your legal counsel to make absolutely sure you are clear on and in compliance with your use of the statewide searches. What seems to be a relatively adequate and cheaper solution might just backfire. So, unfortunately, the county criminal search is still the best option if you want to be in full compliance.

The next type of search that you may want to consider is the civil court. This search often coincides with the search patterns of the state or county searches. In this area, you will find judgments, liens, bankruptcies, and cases involving torts or contract disputes. This search is meant to determine the judgment of your candidate, more specifically if his or her focus is impaired. This is a common search for executives, financial managers, and auditors. Even HR and security personnel are considered prime candidates for this search.

Often an organization wants to understand the specific civil court issues, if any, involving an applicant. Civil cases include noncriminal activity where two parties are involved in a claim for monetary damages ascertaining that one of the parties, through actions or nonactions, is liable and owes a settlement or monetary judgment to the other party. Civil cases involve *torts,* which by definition is "a wrongful act, not including a breach of contract or trust, that results in injury to another's person, property, reputation, or the like, and for which the injured party is entitled to compensation" (www.Dictionary.com).

In a tort case, the sued party either acted or failed to act in a manner that caused loss or injury. The most common of the tort cases is a car accident where neither party has a contract but, due to the negligence of one of the parties, an incident occurred that caused a loss to the other party. In a contract situation, there are provisions of the contract that are in dispute, and one of the parties is claiming a violation of the contract and want some form of remuneration. Either way, the case(s) may demonstrate or predict a certain behavioral pattern that could raise a red flag to the organization considering hiring the applicant involved in such a case. Most states separate the civil courts between a lower court (less than $10,000) and upper (greater than $10,000). This information might prove interesting when considering a position of trust within your organization.

There are also federal civil court cases that are very large in scope and/or involve cases between governmental agencies or even class action suits.

Searching all of the various courts can be tricky. When searching multiple courts, the costs and turnaround times may increase.

Another challenge is simply guaranteeing that you have the right person. Often the case lacks identifying information that would help you determine if the "John Smith" you are screening is the same as the one in federal civil court.

Verification services are provided by most third party providers. This is often done in addition to or in place of the references. What this search does is allow the organization to determine the accuracy of the resume or application information and find any variances that may indicate resume inflation or application fraud. If you are hiring an employee whose experience or education is a key indicator, these types of services are invaluable. Often companies or organizations make final decisions based on these verifications.

For example, if you are hiring a Harvard graduate who went through the honors program and you find out that the university and degree are accurate but the honors issue is inaccurate, you may consider asking the applicant some clarifying questions. Or, if the candidate was a district sales manager of a software company and the software company is reporting that the applicant was a software telemarketer or software support technician, you will definitely have some issues to clear up. The inconsistency may be legitimate, but leave it to your adjudication process to reconcile these types of inconsistencies. Furthermore, wide variations in the dates of graduation or employment may indicate the applicant is choosing not to report time out of school or a bad job that they would rather forget.

The key here is to avoid nondisclosure and inaccuracy. You want to start your relationship with this individual without lapses of information, which may indicate lapses in judgment. Remember, bad hires are extremely costly to a business. Some sources list the hit as much as $4,000 to $10,000 for an entry-level position and as high as $300,000 for an executive. In addition to monetary outlay, bad hires can potentially weaken the organizational morale and reputation.

If professional licensing is important, do the verification now. Do not assume a lawyer is licensed and in good standing. If your position requires the applicant, consultant, or vendor to be licensed, verify this at the beginning of the relationship. If the applicant is touting the license as part of why you should hire him or her and the certification is needed to perform the duties, make sure your HR partner includes this check.

There are several sites that are publicly available that can help in the on-boarding decision process. They are as follows:

Table 3-1 discusses sources of background information and offers a Website to each source.

BRB Publications publishes *The Source Book to Public Record Information*. This publication provides a comprehensive guide to county, state and federal public record sources (www.BRB.pub.com).

Table 3-1 Background Screening Source Descriptions and Locations

Social Security Number Check and Validation: This is the unique number that is issued by the U.S. government and is a good way to validate the identity of an individual and the information provided. The Social Security number can be compared against the application information or the information provided on the background check waiver and consent form. Information related to the use of Social Security numbers and how they can be validated and used in accordance with current regulations can be found on the on the Social Security Website.

Website: www.ssa.gov
www.socialsecurity.gov/foia/highgroup.htm.
To obtain information about the Social Security Death Master list, go to www.ntis.gov/products/ssa-dmf.asp?loc=4-0-0

Federal Court District Nationwide: Within the 97 U.S. federal district court systems, there are many offenses that might be important in determining the risk and background of your applicant. This search would be for a record of a federal offense. Crimes committed on federal property (i.e., government offices, national parks, and reservations) and violations of the U.S. federal criminal statutes are contained within this database.

The Public Access to Court Electronic Records (PACER) system is the repository of this information. PACER is maintained by the Administrative Office of the United States Courts. The U.S. Party/Case Index contains pertinent information from the court files, such as names and case numbers. The challenge here is that the data are given in name only and creates search issues with common names; however, it is still a very comprehensive database.

Website: www.pacer.psc.uscourts.gov
There are 89 district courts in the 50 states. District courts also exist in the District of Columbia, Guam, the Northern Mariana Islands, Puerto Rico, and the Virgin Islands. The total is 97 districts.

Fingerprinting: The use and submission of fingerprints to an agency for comparison against federal, state, and/or local criminal fingerprint records are often considered an excellent way to validate identity and find offenses that could be helpful in the on-boarding decision-making process. However, fingerprint records are not available for all employers. Additionally, the fingerprint repositories are not always available in all states for the various industries.

However, due to a growing demand by the state licensing agencies, this is a fluid area of background checking. It is important to stay abreast of what is going on in your particular industry and the regulations that various states are now imposing. Child care, elderly care, and health care regulatory organizations are increasingly requiring fingerprinting of license holders and employees. A Bureau of Criminal Identification (BCI) or the equivalent is the state agency that is usually charged with this task. Check your state Websites for

Information regarding the comparison of fingerprints to the various fingerprint record databases can be found on the Federal Bureau of Investigation Website at www.fbi.gov/hq/ciisd/fprequest.htm
Websites:
www.aba.com
www.nasd.com
www.theclearinghouse.org

(Continued)

Table 3-1 Background Screening Source Descriptions and Locations—Cont'd

your particular state requirements. Nationally, there are some specific regulations. See the sites in the table for more information.

Sexual Offender Databases: Many states have a registry for sex offenders. However, it is not available in all states. Notable exceptions are Vermont and Washington. But for those that have these registries, the indexes are a list of individuals who have been convicted of a sex crime at either the felony or misdemeanor level. Many of the states have public Websites that can be accessed by anyone. The match logic does vary, so use caution in making sure you have the right person. In some states, the data also include a picture of the individual, which is a clean match.

www.sexoffender.com has all of the states listed and a process to get the information for the state-specific records.

At the national level, visit this public site (shown to the right). This particular site is a cooperative effort between the various states and the Department of Justice. There is also linking to state sites to verify and drill down on specifics. However, there is no clear consistency in application of the levels of severity between the states. Your interpretation of this information might be needed. Security professionals are a good source to sort out the charge levels and severity if questions arise due to discrepancies between states.
In the case of unresolved confusion, the county court search is the best option in obtaining additional details on the offense.

Website: www.nsopr.gov

Incarceration Indexes and Records: The various states have their own Department of Corrections Website. This information can be used to verify the sentences from the county court or federal court searches. These are particularly helpful in resolving disputes. There are various levels of information that can be obtained including release dates and current inmates. These databases also contain information on individuals who may be or have been on supervised probations. This information's value is often geared toward the severity of the offense; felons are the ones who normally do prison time. However, serious or violent misdemeanors are also included.

Federal Bureau of Prisons
Website: www.bop.gov
To obtain state Website information, go to a search engine, type in the state you are interested in, leave a space and then type "department of corrections"; another space and the type in the words "inmate search".

Driving Records: The importance of moving violation records (MVRs) relates to the risk in your employment model. Anyone who is driving on your behalf should have a valid driver's license and be in good driving standing. In other words, suspensions and revocations are factors to consider in some jobs. Often times, employers would, at this point, prefer a national search. But this is not currently possible, and the information is part of the state Motor Vehicle Department charters. Employers search these

As an example of a state Website:
www.dps.state.al.us

(Continued)

Table 3-1 Background Screening Source Descriptions and Locations—Cont'd

records hoping to find driving under the influence of drugs or alcohol charges. However, most of the time, those records are included in the criminal records. Conducting MVR searches in addition to criminal records searches at the county level is highly recommended.

Employment Credit Reports: There is a very specific credit report that should be used in the hiring process. The FCRA specifically prohibits the use of credit sources (Fair Isaac, as an example) or names who are associated with a candidate; a spouse for instance, and is normally bannered "For employment purposes only." This type of credit report will show financial history such as payment history and debt history and will also link the information by Social Security number. Large balances that are inconsistent with the earning and salary history of your applicant might be a concern. If your job requires a fiduciary responsibility, this report may be valuable.

Websites:
www.equifax.com
www.transunion.com
www.experian.com

Office of Foreign Assets Control (OFAC): The U.S. Department of Treasury has, for some time, maintained a database of individuals and countries that are engaged in terrorism, drug trafficking, and criminal conduct that is contrary to the interests of our country and its citizens. The office of Foreign Assets Control (OFAC) maintains a list of these individuals and countries. Checking this list is simple and highly recommended.

Website: www.treasury.gov/offices/enforcement/ofac/

International Criminal Police Organization (Interpol): Interpol is often touted as the "international police" but their real function is to cooperate and coordinate between the various countries' law enforcement entities. The site shown here has the most wanted, which can be accessed by the public. To make this list, the individual will be involved in one or more of the following: human slave trade, drugs, weapons of mass destruction, money laundering, or child pornography.

Website: www.interpol.int

Excluded Parties List: The U.S. General Service Administration (GSA) maintains a "List of Parties Excluded From Federal Procurement," which also extends to nonprocurement programs. The major purpose for this list is to notify all who will be excluded from participation in government let contracts. If you are hiring and the applicant will be dealing with or working on a U.S. government contract, you should make sure this site is used as part of your hiring process.

Website: www.epls.gov/

Office of Inspector General (OIG): Also known as the Health and Human Services Office of Inspector General, this organization provides access to a sanctions list for individuals who are prohibited in participation with Medicare or Medicaid programs.

Website: www.oig.hhs.gov/fraud/exclusions.html

(Continued)

Table 3-1 Background Screening Source Descriptions and Locations—Cont'd

National Practitioner Data Bank (NPDB): This search relates to the medical profession regarding licensing issues, sanctions, and adverse action that might affect a medical professional's ability to perform the tasks you are hiring him or her to perform.	Website: www.npdb-hipdb.hrsa.gov
Federal Drug Administration (FDA) Sanctions List: If you are hiring someone in the area of drug research or pharmaceutical research, this search is vital. This list shows those who might have been disqualified by the FDA from submitting trial information.	Websites: www.fda.gov/ora/compliance ref/bimo/dis res assur.htm www.fda.gov/ora/compliance ref/debar/default.htm

There are other tools that third party providers may be able to assist you with that could be of interest.

- **International Criminal History Searches** can also be helpful in making hiring decisions. The reliability is often difficult, so ask your provider plenty of questions. The use of this in the United States falls under the FCRA and can be used accordingly. However, international background checks for persons living and working in that country can be tricky. Make sure you have a firm understanding of the privacy and hiring laws in that country.
- **Propriety databases** include databases that are offered and maintained by specific consumer reporting agencies or third party providers. These databases are negative histories of individuals who have allowed their information to be placed in the database by an employer. This information is not in the criminal or police records since no formal charges were ever filed. The real value of this information may be questionable since it is usually limited to the contributing entities.

Drug Screening

Security, when coupled with safety concerns, sees a need for drug screening in the on-boarding, and often the ongoing, relationship with the employee. Many companies consider a strong drug testing policy and procedure as part of their overall screening strategy. If your business operations are highly susceptible to dangerous situations and/or physical harm to employees or others (i.e., driving and manufacturing), a strong review of the use of drug testing as part of your overall strategy should be considered.

With the availability of online background screening and the complexities and expense of drug screening, the industry has seen a decline since its inception. But with the proper understanding of the laws and complexities, you can use this process to keep problems in check. Drug use and certainly alcohol abuse can cause a breakdown in your normal work environment and drive good employees elsewhere. Additionally, a strong drug testing policy can prevent someone with a clean background but a drug or alcohol problem from entering your organization.

The screens test for types of drug or panels. The normal number of panels is broken into 5 or 10+ panels. The 5-panel test is focused on the top illegal drug families like marijuana, methamphetamines, and opiate-based drugs such as heroin. The 10-panel test widens the search to include prescription drugs like pain medication that can be abused. A medical review process or medical review officer is often required to review the drug results and interview the applicant to determine if the legitimate use of prescription drugs is causing the applicant to show positive when they are not drug abusers.

The cost of this screening can be quite high. The drug screening is approximately the same cost as the baseline background screen. Therefore, the timing of the check is important. Sometimes, random drug screening can be used to control costs. Also, drug screening should be used in connection with your accident policy.

The U.S. Department of Labor provides a Website source of information as well as the laws in the various states (http://said.dol.gov/StateLawList.asp). Make sure you consider the impact under the ADA and state laws that regulate drug testing.

The Appeal Process

An appeal regarding background check results primarily falls into two major categories. First of all, the accuracy of the check itself may be questioned. This is one of the reasons the FCRA includes a section on hiring (see Chapter 2). The applicant should have the opportunity to dispute any derogatory information that is reported to the organization from a credit reporting agency. This includes the criminal background check results that may indicate a conviction or other major discrepancy from the application. This is one of the reasons it is so important to get an application from every candidate. The FCRA requires that the organization advise the candidate, in writing, that adverse information has been linked to the applicant and the organization may be making a decision based on this information.

If a third party provider is involved, they should help with this process and confirm or correct the original report for no additional charge. You should also factor in a reasonable period of time, normally 5 business days, to allow the information to be reviewed. If the information is not disputed or appealed, you have the right to make the decision based on the information at hand. A final notice should be sent to the applicant of the planned adverse action.

The second appeal is slightly different in that the facts are not in dispute. The applicant has disclosed the issue in the application and the background check has verified the information as accurate. In this case the applicant, the company's management, or hiring department still wants to make the hire despite the associated risk. This sometimes occurs when a candidate is highly sought after because of a unique skill or if sufficient time has passed even if the offense is still current enough to raise concern. A well-documented approach in addressing these situations is highly recommended.

It is important that you establish a section in the procedure of your process that specifically addresses this issue. All appeals should be in writing. A review committee should be established with representatives of security, HR, management, and legal to review the appeal request. These representatives should be the highest ranking individuals in the respective departments due to the sizeable liability that must be taken into account.

Table 3-2 provides a "point-counterpoint" discussion.

Table 3-2 Point-Counterpoint

Security should have a place at the table when determining the course, use, and types of background screening to be conducted. The specific operational role is often times an area of dispute. Security and HR professionals often view the role of security in the screening process from differing perspectives

Security	Human Resources
Security often ends up dealing with the mess a bad hire creates. Therefore, their input is tremendously helpful in evaluating the types of checks to conduct and the criteria used to make the final decision.	I agree that security should be part of the hiring process because they have a keen sense of how applicants should be evaluated from another vantage point.
Security should review all of the hits in the criminal background check area. They are better suited to evaluate the risk associated with certain types of charges.	While security should have input to the process, many of them still have the "lock 'em up or lock 'em out" law enforcement mindset. We must follow the EEOC guidelines and be willing to give people a second chance.
Selection of a third party provider or contractor who will oversee this process should include the security professional. They can ask questions that will help determine the source of information as being in line with the organization's concerns.	Security should participate in the selection process, but HR should have the final say since ultimately they will be held accountable for the effectiveness of their hiring process.
HR's role is to understand the skill and/or qualifications of the applicant. Security will be more focused on gaps and inaccuracies. For example, if the applicant falsifies dates of employment, what else could he or she be hiding?	HR professionals are very capable of assessing gaps and inaccuracies. Inserting security into the hiring process will only slow down the hiring process.
Security should have the right to veto hires. They are a full partner in this process. This is certainly true in the appeals process as well.	Let us not forget that line management is the one ultimately responsible for hiring. Security and HR should have courage and commitment to assert recommendations. A best practice in this area is to have a Background Screening Review Committee. Their role will be to review and audit checks being dependent on the date of submission.

Summary

1. Because the primary role of security is the protection of employees and company assets, they need to be included in the screening process design and implementation.

2. While the extent of security's involvement in the background checking process is negotiable, at a very minimum, they should help in deciding the types of searches to conduct and participate in any necessary adjudication and appeal.

3. Violence in the workplace continues to be the number one reason to have a thorough screening process in place. Security can help by reviewing applicant convictions once they are uncovered or returned from the provider.

4. Document the policy and process and be consistent based on your risk model using job description as a guidepost.

5. Consider conducting ongoing screening for existing employees.

6. Know the types of searches and research various search sources in order to understand the strengths and weaknesses of the searches you perform.

7. Define your appeal process.

4

Insights From Background Screening Surveys[1]

In June 2005, PreemploymentDirectory.com conducted the 2005 Employers' Practices in Background Screening Survey to identify the current practices that businesses were using to conduct background screenings. The survey was initiated because of the changing face of background screening and we believed that businesses needed to have more information about this emerging business practice.

I doubt that we could find a manager involved in the hiring process today who would not agree that this is a turbulent time for employers who are competing for talent. Hiring quality people has become one of the business issues of the 21st century, and the competitiveness in the recruitment arena is escalating at a torrid pace. Further complicating the hiring process, firms are finding themselves being challenged by issues such as identify theft, fraud, workplace violence, theft, sabotage, terrorism, negligent hiring, and retention, to name a few.

Due to these concerns, background checking has skyrocketed to record levels and is continuing to grow annually. The number of firms that provide outsourced background screening services has leaped to well over 2,000 and is growing daily.

In parallel with the unprecedented growth of the background screening industry, we have seen more concerns about privacy and security of the data obtained. ChoicePoint recently settled an issue surrounding a breach of their data for $10 million. This case, plus numerous other high-profile cases with major organizations such as Time Warner, Eastman Kodak, Motorola, MCI, ADP, Equifax, Fidelity, and the Veterans Administration, have thrust this issue onto the national political agenda, and inevitably this will lead to new data protection laws. This subject of data protection is covered fully in Chapter 7.

Many are predicting the days of using birthdate and Social Security numbers as identifiers are numbered and will give way to biometric solutions, some of which border on science fiction. Consequently, the landscape of background screening is continuing to evolve and employers will need to be diligent in keeping their employment and hiring professions up to speed.

A very promising trend that has emerged in background screening is that we are increasingly seeing stand-alone screening feeds being integrated into firm's human resource information systems (HRIS).

A pressing issue that is confronting background screeners is the proliferation of the fake diploma and degree mills. Simply verifying educational background is no longer

---

[1] This chapter is primarily based on the published results of the 2005 Background Screening Survey conducted by PreemploymentDirectory.com and The National Institute for Prevention of Workplace Violence, Inc.

sufficient. Screeners must now verify that the source of the education is legitimate and, for foreign degrees, their equivalency.

There are also clear signs that background screening is increasingly going global as the economies in India, China, Europe, and so on continue to prosper and recruiters span national borders to find people. The international marketplace is likely to be the brave new world that background screening must master.

Despite the challenges that will be faced, there is no question that background screening has become an integral part of the hiring process. The need to know whom they are hiring and to discover the best information possible to make quality hiring decisions will continue to make a background screening valuable for years to come.

With all of the above in mind, the survey set out to explore, in depth, the full realm of checking applicants backgrounds ranging from the types of checks conducted, to the content contained in background screening policies to key selection factors in choosing an outsourced background screening firm, if one was used. (See the complete survey in Appendix B.)

Who Conducted the Survey?

PreemploymentDirectory.com is the largest and most comprehensive Web-based directory of background screening firms designed to make it easy for employers to quickly and easily find a company to meet their screening needs. The directory has over 1,000 companies listed and is continuously growing. The directory consists of four sections to guide employers quickly to the company that will serve them best:

1. U.S. Domestic Section (firms are listed by their location, state by state)
2. International Section (firms that conduct background screening internationally)
3. Vendor Showcase (firms that provide services to the background screening industry)
4. Alphabetical listing

Participants

The survey questions were developed by an advisory committee specifically formed for the purpose of creating the survey. The advisory committee was composed of a variety of human resource (HR), employment, background screening, security, and management professionals.

An invitation to participate in the online survey was emailed to approximately 7,000 security and HR managers. Recipients of the invitation were sent an email invitation containing a link that directed the participant to the online survey. Three email reminders were sent out to sample members in an effort to increase the response rate.

In addition, an invitation to participate in the survey was posted on the home page of The National Institute for the Prevention of Workplace Violence, Inc. Website (www. Workplaceviolence911.com).

Responses

There were 273 responses to the 2005 Background Screening Practices of Employer Survey. Demographically, respondents came from firms of varying sizes. Figure 4-1 shows the size of the firms surveyed.

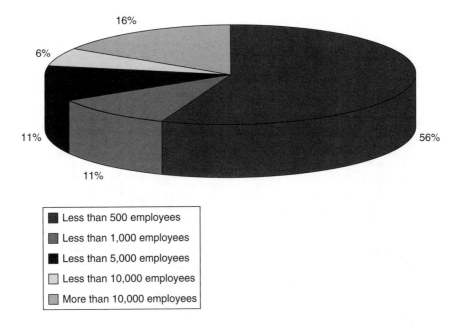

16%

6%

11%

11%

56%

- ■ Less than 500 employees
- ■ Less than 1,000 employees
- ■ Less than 5,000 employees
- □ Less than 10,000 employees
- ▨ More than 10,000 employees

FIGURE 4-1 Size of the firms surveyed.

In addition, 69% of responding firms were in the private sector, and 31% were public or government entities; the distribution of industries represented is itemized below in Figure 4-2. Figure 4-3 shows the revenue distribution of participants. Figure 4-4 shows the top seven focus areas for background checks.

It should be noted that based on conventional statistical methods, the 273 responses do not meet our defined criteria to be statistically significant. While we believe the data are informative and present a representative picture of employer practices, readers are advised to be cautious in drawing definitive conclusions based on these data alone. Later in the chapter, we make a comparison to an earlier study conducted by the Society of Human Resource Management's (SHRM) 2004 Reference and Background Checking Practices to see where there are similarities and differences.

Please note that the SHRM study reflects the combined results of reference and background checking practices, while PreemploymentDirectory.com's focus was solely on background checking practices. Accordingly, while the comparisons are potentially useful to get a sense of how businesses are dealing with these aspects of the hiring process, it is important to keep the different focuses of the respective surveys in mind.

Also, to add clarity regarding the differences in reference checking and background checking, we are sharing the following definitions from Paul W. Barada's book *Reference Checking for Everyone*: Mcgraw-Hill, January 21, 2004.

> **Reference Checks**—an objective evaluation of a candidate's past job performance, based on conversations with people who have actually worked with the candidate on a daily basis within the last 5 to 7 years.

> **Background Checks**—checking the accuracy of basic information provided by a candidate for employment on a job application or resume. It includes preemployment screening, candidate evaluation, employment verification, and candidate screening.

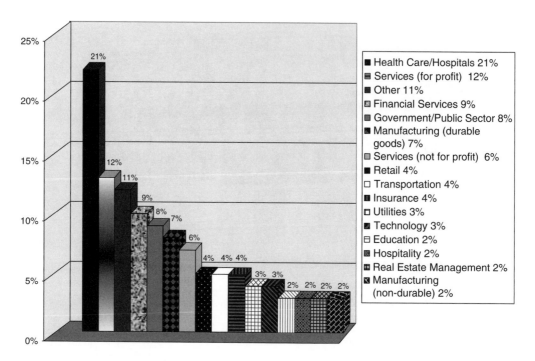

FIGURE 4-2 Distribution of industries.

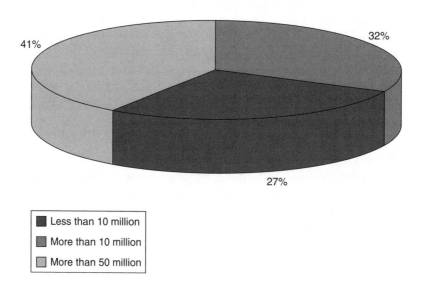

FIGURE 4-3 Revenue distribution of survey participants.

Who do Businesses Conduct Background Checks on?

Approximately 80% of firms are conducting background checks on employees in the United States, which means we can definitively conclude that preemployment screening has become an integral part of the employment and hiring process in this country.

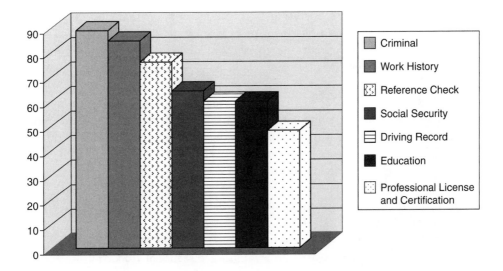

FIGURE 4-4 Top 7 focus areas for background checks.

The SHRM study indicated that 96% of respondents conduct some form of reference checking or background screening. Please note that the SHRM study is focused on practices within the United States.

With this level of background screening occurring across the country and in businesses of all kinds, it is no wonder that the background screening industry has skyrocketed into a billion-dollar industry. This growth is not likely to slow down in the near term because of the nature of the issues that businesses are continuing to face:

- Employee theft is at an all time high; the Annual Retail Industry report noted that employees are stealing from their employers at an all-time high rate.
- Identity theft continues to be a troubling issue.
- From 40% to 60% of applicants lie or misrepresent their backgrounds on resumes or CVs.
- Fake degrees are prevalent and still easy to acquire.
- One of 10 applicants has a criminal background.
- The threat of home-grown terrorists is highlighted as an equally threatening situation to those from outside of the country.
- Employers continue to lose 73% of negligent hiring cases that go to jury trials at a cost averaging over $3 million.

With the prevalence of these issues, I think we can safely say that background screening is going to be with us for some time to come.

In contrast to the number of firms that conduct background checks on applicants, only 58% similarly screen their current employees. We believe this response is indicative of businesses being more aware of the complexities involved with screening current employees, which raises the spectrum of fair employment practices, policy, and employee relations issues. In addition, it may also reflect the reality that employers are more selective in screening current employees and only screening those who are in or apply for jobs that have been identified as sensitive ones. We sincerely hope that the response rate does not reflect that businesses are operating from the assumption that once a person has passed the scrutiny of the preemployment process it means that the individual will for evermore be an honest and upright employee. With the escalating levels of employee, confidential data, and identity theft, this would be a potentially perilous viewpoint to have.

With less than half (47%) of firms conducting background checks on applicants from countries outside of the United States, we are forced to ponder whether businesses have taken the threat of terrorism as seriously as the Homeland Security Department has envisioned. We are also sure that it reflects the complexity that is involved with conducting background checks on individuals from other countries, many of which operate on a different set of data protection laws and have different court and legal systems, varying definitions of criminal activity, and challenging data access issues, not to mention the different cultural norms and view of background screening.

It will be interesting to see where the response rate falls for this question the next time the survey is conducted so we can establish a directional trend. Future responses to this question will likely be impacted by the reality that *background vetting and verifications,* as they are called in many other countries, are picking up steam in many areas of the world. The processes for conducting them and the views about conducting them are changing. An interesting dichotomy that may also occur is that the more time that elapses since the tragic terrorist attacks on the World Trade Center on September 11, 2001, the less concerned U.S. businesses may be focused on this as an issue for which they should be conducting screening. We are already seeing signs of security budgets and funding being reduced from their earlier post-9/11 levels.

With 70% of responses answering that their firms do not conduct background checks on employees who work in countries outside of the United States, we see an apparent pattern that is consistent with the views expressed in the earlier question regarding conducting screenings on applicants from other countries. Businesses are either less concerned about terrorism impacting them outside of the United States or are, again, confronted with the complexity of the task of conducting background checks. It will be interesting to see how this issue is impacted over time.

From the data provided, we conclude that the target of background checks are predominantly U.S.-based applicants for positions and, to a lesser extent, current employees in the United States. Foreign applicants and applicants who apply for positions abroad are much less likely to be the target of a background investigation. The basis for this difference may likely be culturally based, although we have to wonder if the dearth of background screening of foreign applicants and applicants in other countries is wise in the times we live in. All the problematic issues that have been identified that U.S. businesses are facing are also present in the business communities throughout the world, so it is our view that over time background screenings will increase outside of the United States, albeit at a slower pace than security professionals would like to see.

The response clearly illustrate that businesses are most focused on trying to avoid a bad hire who has a dubious history of criminal activity (89%), poor work history, and/or bad references (75%). Despite 64% of firms reporting that they conduct a Social Security trace, it was surprising that more firms are not doing this because it is a way of verifying a person's identity.

Likewise, with all of the high-profile cases of educational background fraud, it was surprising that only 60% of firms check this information.

The SHRM study reported the 66% check degrees conferred and 65% verify that attendance at a college or university.

In an era where a college degree can be bought online and approximately 50% of job applicants misrepresent their backgrounds, this is something that firms may need to revisit. Businesses may inadvertently be contributing to the flourishing of the fake diploma mill industry and people continuing to lie on their resumes, because an applicant has 4 out of 10 chance that their education will not be verified and about a 5 of 10 chance that their professional license or certification will actually not be checked.

At What Point in the Hiring Process are Background Checks Conducted

Consistent with best practices in background screening most businesses, 56%, responded that they conduct background checks only on final candidates because this is the most economical and efficient way to handle screening. Very much in line with this practical approach were the respondents (26%) who indicated that they check backgrounds after an offer, which would represent an even smaller group of individuals. While we did not cross-reference the data, we suspect that the 14% of respondents who check all applicants may be in industries that hire large numbers of people at one time with a minimal hiring process; thus, the screening occurs up front to identify any potential problems.

Sensitive Jobs

Slightly over half (53%) of respondents indicated that they have identified "sensitive or high-risk positions." This is certainly an area that firms may want to look at closer because the courts have been clear in stating that "sensitive jobs" require more aggressive background screening due to the higher potential risk created by an incumbent in one of these jobs. (See Figure 4-5 for information on industry best practices in identifying such

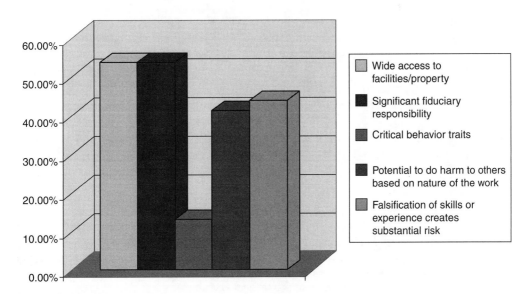

FIGURE 4-5 Five factors consistent with industry best practices for identifying sensitive jobs.

positions.) In addition, as the issue continues to heat up about not discriminating against previously incarcerated persons and not violating the EEOC guidelines on hiring, a solid defense is that you have previously classified a job as sensitive and identified the criminal offenses that would preclude a person from consideration for the position. HR professionals particularly need to pay attention to this point, which is very similar to firms building an affirmative defense against discrimination claims by disabled applicants by having built clear physical and mental requirements into their job descriptions.

For firms that identify sensitive jobs, Figure 4-6 depicts the top factors that are generally used to qualify a job to be classified as sensitive.

The responses to this question were very revealing regarding the specific information included in the release form and the specific information requested. Given that the release form is a legal document, it was quite surprising that only 40% of firms stated that their form was either created by or had been approved by a labor attorney. This is particularly

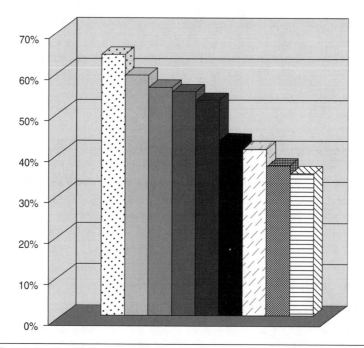

☐ States that applicant releases your firm from legal liability for providing information regarding their employment history

▨ Makes generic statement that comprehensive background checks will be conducted

▩ Provides a check box indicating that an applicant has the right to obtain a copy of the report that is provided

▨ Specifically identifies the types of background checks that may be conducted such as criminal records or educational records

■ Requests date of birth

■ Form was created by or has been approved by labor attorney

☐ Has provision that grants permission to perform future background checks if the person becomes an employee

▨ If date of birth requested also includes statements regarding purpose for request and that providing information will not be affect hiring decision

▥ States time period that the Release is valid for/date of expiration

FIGURE 4-6 Top factors that identify a job as sensitive.
Since multiple factors are possible, each bar represents the percentage of companies giving this response.

alarming given some of the information that is actually included, such as "request for date of birth" and "a statement that releases the firm from liability."

Having the applicant provide their date of birth information directly to your business can raise the spectrum of age discrimination. Also, it is a violation of the Fair Credit Reporting Act (FCRA) to include a waiver of liability within the disclosure form granting you permission to conduct a background check. These two reasons alone are sufficient to make sure your labor attorney reviews your release form.

Use of External Background Screening Firms

Sixty-eight percent of respondents reported that they use an external firm to conduct their background checks.

The SHRM study reported that 52% of firms outsource reference and background checking to an external service provider.

This partially explains why the background screening industry continues to grow at a steady pace, and we expect that this pattern will continue for some time to come as outsourcing continues to grow. In addition, the complexities of background screening and increasing legal requirements may make the specialized services of background screening firms even more attractive.

For firms that use external background screening services, 44% of respondents reported that they find their providers through referrals from other companies and 41% indicated they find a provider by using internal research processes.

The top factors that businesses use to determine which provider to select are listed in Figure 4-7.

The most significant selection factors that respondents reported were, unsurprisingly, types of checks performed, the scope of those checks, and the turnaround time for conducing them. The next tier of reported factors provides an interesting insight into how businesses view cost of services that one would have assumed would have made the top tier given all the talk about background checks being a commodity. When we view the selection factors that were marked "very important," cost of services actually ranked fifth on the list.

We believe it is also noteworthy that these responses indicate that businesses are very concerned that a provider is legally compliant, provide appropriate training to keep their staff's knowledge and skills current, and want a high-quality level of customer service. Interestingly, based on what we are hearing in the marketplace, many of the businesses that are changing providers are doing so because they want better customer service. While this premise is not research based, it does suggest that perhaps businesses need to be more diligent on the front end in evaluating the type and level of customer service provided by external background screening firms during the selection process.

While "Firm performs hands on checks" was ranked eighth with regard to level of importance, we believe this is one of the cornerstone factors that is necessary to ensure accuracy of background checks, and it should be considered more important. We also recognize that businesses may have ranked this lower because there is an awareness of the vast network of court researchers that now exist across the country to which, in general, all firms have access, too, so it may be less of an issue for a specific firm to have this

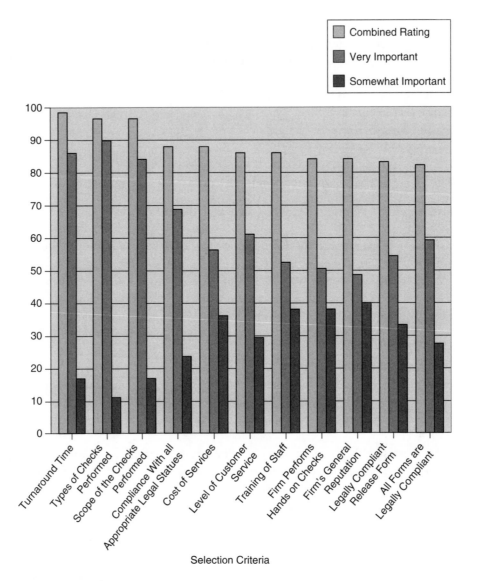

FIGURE 4-7 Top factors in selecting a provider.

capability. The real good news is that businesses ranked this factor more important than "Firm uses a national database," which suggests that efforts to communicate the risk and challenges of relying on a national database are being effective.

Two areas that were not ranked in the top tier that likely will move up in future surveys are the firm's technology capability and system security. With 2005 having been named "the year of the data breach" and the subsequent level of data breaches that are reported regularly, this subject has come to the forefront. Likewise, we believe that technology is rapidly becoming a driving force in the background screening industry and that its role will continue to escalate in years to come.

The top factor that drove client satisfaction dealt with the number one area that businesses focus background screening on, the *identification of a criminal history*. Not surprisingly, this was closely followed by the background screening firms' capability to handle sensitive data and to conduct Social Security verifications.

The following top 10 list of factors that drive customer satisfaction identify the areas that background screening firms need to pay attention to as they work to drive their clients, satisfaction upward.

Figure 4-8 shows customer satisfaction with the background screening providers.

There were no surprises in the response to the question, "How important do you consider the services provided to be to your firm?" Respondents overwhelming indicated that their businesses considered criminal background checks to be the most important

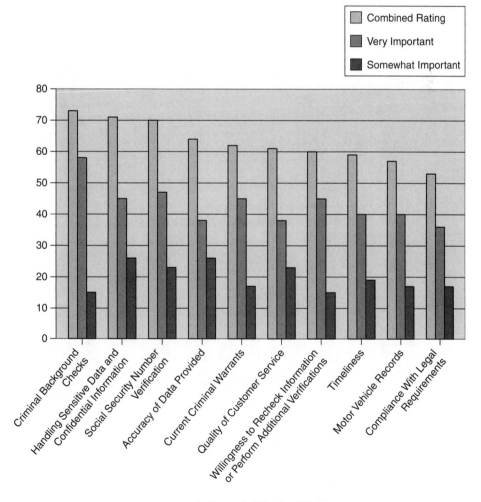

Customer Satisfaction Drivers

FIGURE 4-8 Customer satisfaction with background screening provider.

(96%), which is at the heart of why most businesses conduct background checks. This was followed by timeliness in providing the data, as well as the firm's capabilities in handling sensitive data, and being in legal compliance. Probably the most noteworthy insight gained from this question was that only 53% of respondents thought that professional licensing/certifications were important to their firms, and a lowly 30% thought that terrorist searches were important.

Figure 4-9 shows customer satisfaction drivers.

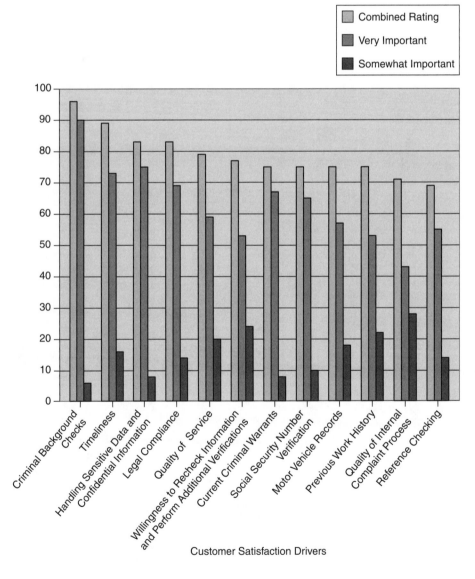

FIGURE 4-9 Importance of specific aspects of service provider.

Which Function is Responsible for Background Screening?

Overwhelming, respondents reported that the HR function has responsibility for oversight of the background screening activity: 83% indicated that HR had this responsibility, while 12% reported that security had the responsibility.

The SHRM study reported that 61% of firms reported that HR staff are responsible for conducting reference checks.

Training for In-house Background Screening Staff

Overwhelmingly, the training that is provided for internal background screening personnel is internally driven by "on-the-job training," which 59% of firms provide, and internal experts from HR or security typically deliver 38% of the training.

The SHRM study reported that over half of HR professionals (52%) indicated that their organization provides training for those conducting references to learn to look for "red flags" in the process. In organizations where a security clearance is required for some positions, 67% offer such training. Forty-four percent of all SHRM responders said that they train reference checkers to be more productive.

It was surprising that only 28% of respondents indicated that training was received on a firm's background screening policy. This would appear to be an essential ingredient that should be central in any training delivered. The amount of training that is received from outside is low.

This may be because there has been a lack of externally provided training that has been focused on the background screening industry. We see this starting to change, with more marketplace initiatives becoming available for background screening professionals to receive training. An example is the Background Screening Certification Program offered by the National Institute for the Prevention of Workplace Violence, Inc. and HR Tutor, a professional online training firm. (See Appendix C for an outline of the certification program.)

Figure 4-10 shows a breakdown in the types of in-house background screening training.

Background Screening Policy

Respondents reported that 63% of their firms have background screening policies in place.

The SHRM study reported that 38% of firms have a reference checking policy in place for their employees to follow.

It is interesting to note that our study indicated that 81% of the background screening policies the firms have created have been in place for more than 2 years, while 21% were created in the last 12 months. The predominant reasons cited for creating the policy were that it is normal process to create a policy when a new process is introduced and to reduce the likelihood of inconsistent treatment of applicants and employees.

In contrast to the above, the SHRM Reference and Background Checking Survey found that "Just over one-fifth of HR professionals indicated that their organization has implemented new or different reference or background checking policies or procedures as a direct result of the September 11, 2001, terrorist attacks. Organizations where

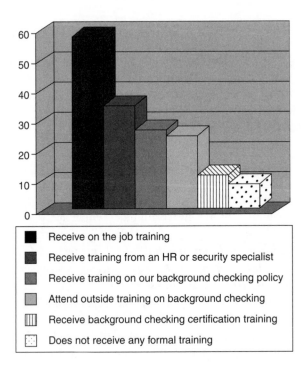

FIGURE 4-10 In-house training in background checking.
Since multiple factors are possible, each bar represents the percentage of companies giving this response.

some positions may require security clearance are more than twice as likely as other orga-nizations to have implemented new measures."

A closer examination of the reported data reveals some very interesting insights about the content of these policies. With regard to the policies paralleling the legal responsibilities identified in the FCRA, the percentages of firms addressing key legal requirements are lower than they should be. In addition, with only 64% of firms indicating that their policy "Specifies criteria to be used in checking background such as nature of criminal record, date of offense or relevance to work, number of years past history that is checked or where checked," it would appear that 36% of businesses are walking the tightrope regarding the risk of discrimination issues. Inconsistent treatment of employees is the root of many discrimination issues, and failure to have guidelines to guide manager's behaviors could have dire consequences. In essence, firms that are not addressing this are rolling the dice.

A clear example of the risk of discrimination that firms can face is found in the reported responses. For example, 59% of businesses reported that they have a "Provision that addresses when and how a new hire may start to work before their background check results are completed," which means that 41% of businesses are faced with managers who decided this on their own. Faced with the challenges of trying to fill a critical position and the shortage of talent, it is easy to see how different managers may make different decisions without any common guidance or framework by which to determine their decisions. This is an invitation for a problem. The lack of policy guidelines to provide a framework for consistent decision-making and desired behavior is in direct conflict with firms' stated goal to create a consistent application of background screening practices.

In addition to these issues, less than 62% of respondents to this question reported that their policies do not deal with any of the following issues:

- Requires contractors and temporary agencies to prescreen referrals/Have process to verify agencies are conducting prescreenings
- Separate guidelines for applicants and current employees
- Have process to identify sensitive or high-risk jobs

These are gaping holes in their policies because by not requiring contractors, temporary agencies, professional employment organizations (PEOs), or employment agencies to conduct background screenings, you create a potential loophole in your system that may allow employees with backgrounds of which you do not approve to be in your workforce.

There is an increasing need to have separate guidelines in place regarding how pre-employment practices will be applied to job applicants versus how post employment practices will be applied to current employees. This will increasingly become important as more businesses start to implement continuous screening programs to extend their due diligence beyond the hiring process to the on-going employment relationship. While there certainly will be many common practices between the sets of guidelines, it is also likely that firms will have a different set of rules in place to apply to their employees.

Finally, by not addressing the process of identifying sensitive jobs, firms may find themselves in a position of not being able to defend hiring decisions that are challenged or, even worse, they may make a hiring decision that places a problematic person in a job who subsequently creates liability for the business. This is an open invitation for a negligent hiring or retention lawsuit.

Figure 4-11 shows the types of checks included in a company's background screening policy.

Employment Application Questions

While the employment application is not directly part of the background screening process, it is a very important tool in identifying critical information to be verified via background checking; also, there are important questions that can help with the overall preemployment process.

Ninety percent of firms reported that they notify applicants that making false statements or material omissions may be grounds for termination.

The SHRM study reported that 92% of firms include this statement in their employment application.

Despite the high percentage of businesses that provide a "false statements" provision in their employment application, it is interesting to note that 32% of firms stated that they do not have a process in place to verify that the applicant signed the application. This potentially negates the value of having the original "false statements" in the application because, without the person's signature, it opens up many issues that could otherwise be easily avoided.

Eighty-eight percent of respondents ask applicants in their application about conviction records, while only 36% ask about misdemeanors. While asking about misdemeanors is governed by state laws, many managers would be surprised to find out about the severity of crimes that can be classified as misdemeanors. This is an important area for managers to consider revising their employment application forms to address so that

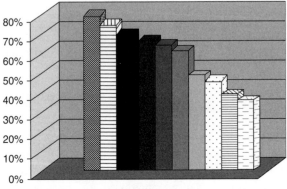

Procedure for notifying applicants that are rejected

Protection of consumer confidential information

Specify criteria to be used in checking background such as nature of criminal record, date of offense, relevance to work, number of years past history that are checked, and where checked

Compliance with FCRA, EEO, and other relevant laws

Management responsibility to use the information and consequences for not using

Provision addressing new hire starting to work before background check results are completed

Process for dealing with alleged inaccurate information

Procedure for dealing with missing information

Separate guidelines for applicants and current employees

Require contractors and temporary agencies to pre-screen referrals

FIGURE 4-11 Checks included in background screening policies.
Since multiple factors are possible, each bar represents the percentage of companies giving this response.

you do not unwittingly hire people with backgrounds you do not want, because you never asked about it.

While it is good that 73% of firms' applications state that marking "yes" to having a conviction will not automatically disqualify an applicant from consideration for employment, this also means that 27% of firms are potentially leaving themselves wide open for discrimination issues by failing to address this. By not addressing this issue affirmatively, you open the door to an applicant who has been previously incarcerated that is fully qualified for the position to claim discrimination because you violated the EEOC guidelines on this matter. Under *EEOC rules*, an employer may not deny employment to an ex-offender unless it is a business necessity, determined by reviewing the following three factors:

- Nature and gravity of the offense
- Amount of time that has passed since the conviction or completion of sentence
- Nature of the job being held or sought

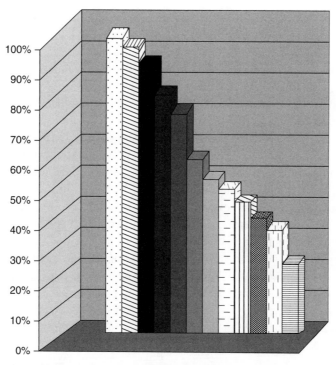

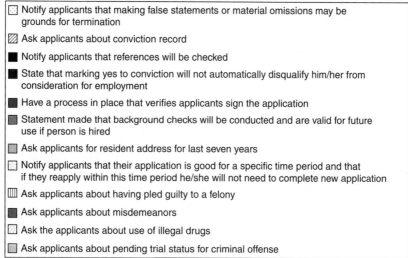

- ▦ Notify applicants that making false statements or material omissions may be grounds for termination
- ▨ Ask applicants about conviction record
- ■ Notify applicants that references will be checked
- ■ State that marking yes to conviction will not automatically disqualify him/her from consideration for employment
- ▦ Have a process in place that verifies applicants sign the application
- ▦ Statement made that background checks will be conducted and are valid for future use if person is hired
- ▦ Ask applicants for resident address for last seven years
- ▦ Notify applicants that their application is good for a specific time period and that if they reapply within this time period he/she will not need to complete new application
- ▥ Ask applicants about having pled guilty to a felony
- ▦ Ask applicants about misdemeanors
- ▧ Ask the applicants about use of illegal drugs
- ▤ Ask applicants about pending trial status for criminal offense

FIGURE 4-12 Items included in employment applications.
Since multiple factors are possible, each bar represents the percentage of companies giving this response.

Figure 4-12 shows the items included in firms' employment applications.

Fifty-four percent of respondents indicated that they include a statement that background checks will be conducted and are valid for future use if the person is hired, while 46% do not include this statement. Although there is certainly no legal requirement that businesses make this statement, it does potentially provide an affirmative defense that the person was notified should the occasion arise. It is one of those business practices that may not hurt you, but it certainly can help you if you are sued.

The number of years in "address history" that you ask about in an employment application should match the time period that you use in your background screening process. While we recommend 7 years, which has become the industry standard, if your firm routinely checks 3 years of history, then you need to match the address history you ask for on the application.

Forty-five percent of respondents reported that they notify applicants that their application is good for a specific time period and that if they reapply within this time period he or she will not need to complete a new application. While we certainly understand the administrative convenience of this practice, it is one that can contribute to a firm making a bad hiring decision because it omits important information that may have transpired in the time that has elapsed since the previous application. For example, a delivery person might have applied for a position 3 months earlier and at the time of completing the application had a clean driving record. However, in the past 90 days, he has had a DUI conviction and was involved in an accident that caused fatalities. If you do not have the applicant complete a new application, you may not be informed about the current situation. This is not a risk that a prudent business should be willing to take.

On a very positive note, only 9% of firms did *not* consider their background screening program to be successful, which is a testimony to how far this process has progressed as it has become an integral part of businesses hiring program—11% of firms considered their program to be extremely successful, 56% considered their program to be very successful, and 24% considered their programs to be moderately successful, which means that 91% consider their program successful.

Summary

It is undeniable that we have reached the point where background screening has become an integral part of the hiring practices of the vast majority of firms in the United States. While about one third of firms conduct their own background screening, over two thirds of businesses now outsource this activity. As a consequence, background screening has become "big business," with well over 2,000 firms involved in this activity, and it has become a billion-dollar industry. The competitiveness in the industry has led to significant innovations that have not only driven the price for background screening down but made the process significantly easier for businesses and more integrated with their other employment related processes.

As the background screening industry continues to evolve, we will continue to see more innovation driven by technological advances in areas such as integration with HRIS, more sophisticated databases that cross-reference a wider array of data, and integration with systems outside of HR such as access control and other security-based systems. The ability of applicants or employees to hide information will become increasingly difficult.

While for many businesses this is great news, it also raises considerable issues with regard to data protection and privacy. The sheer quantity and visibility of significant data breaches, as well as the continued threat of identify theft, are fueling the political winds, which means increases in legislation governing access to and distribution of personal information are likely. One likely target of legislation will be the primary identifiers used to verify the identity of individuals, Social Security numbers and date of birth. With the expected demise of the current identifiers, we will see the rise of new ones likely to come out of the emerging science of biometrics. Beyond fingerprinting, facial recognition, iris scans, etc., there are technologies being researched and developed that come straight out of science fiction and are mind boggling. With these new emerging technologies significantly reducing "false negatives," we will be moving closer to the day when individuals will be able to be positively identified with a virtually insignificant error rate.

On a more mundane level, there remains a number of business practices that need to be addressed for the business community to truly benefit from the capabilities for accessing personal information that exist. One area for businesses to consider goes to the very heart of why they conduct background checks. Today the answer to that question is evidenced by more than 90% of firms conducting criminal background checks, which means firms are trying to secure their organizations and protect their employees and resources from harm or theft. While this is unquestionably a worthwhile focus, we believe that to truly increase the "return on investment" of background screening, businesses must start to focus on how background checks can contribute to hiring a higher quality of employee who adds to the organization's talent pool. This is where competitive advantage is gained. To do this, more emphasis needs to be switched to checking educational backgrounds, professional certifications, and other indicators of achievement. In other words, the focus must change from "How do we screen out the bad guys" to "How do we screen in the good guys." It is a paradigm switch that can fundamentally change the emerging field of background screening.

Background Checking Policy[1]

The intent of this chapter is to discuss the importance of having a well-crafted and comprehensive background screening policy; however, before we dive into this subject, I believe it is very important to define the overall purpose for having a policy, in general.

As I am sure you know, organizations have many types of policies—human resources (HR) or personnel policies, operational policies, and functional policies such as security, safety, marketing, to name a few. A common thread that cuts across all of these different type policies is that they are all established with the intent to provide a framework for people's behavior in the organization. This is a diplomatic way of saying that policies are created to control people's behavior. Before anyone gets upset, this notion of controlling behavior is not a new one for organizations after all; I am sure your parents (the management of your household) had some rules (policies) that you learned about early in life, such as "no playing ball in the house," "wash your hands after using the bathroom," "eat all your vegetables," "be home before dark," etc. These were the forerunners to the policies we implement in organizations where we work. And it does not stop there: upscale restaurants tell us "you must wear a jacket" or others say "no smoking" or "shoes must be worn" or in the parking lot "handicapped parking only." Your behavior is being guided and controlled all over the place.

The purpose for wanting to control the behavior of the people that work in an organization includes ensuring that people are treated in a manner consistent with our societal view of fairness, preventing people from creating legal problems for the organization, reinforcing the maintenance of a desired corporate culture, preserving and protecting the organization's resources, having predictability in dealing with situations, and creating order which includes obeying the law. In addition, policies are a means of communicating what is important to the organization and in many ways form the basis of a *quid pro quo* contract with people who work for the organization. You perform the agreed upon work for us while following this set of rules and we will pay you as agreed for the time you work on our behalf. It is one of the most fundamental forms of a contract that has existed throughout the ages.

Polices are also the infrastructure for decision making in organizations. They provide the framework and criteria by which decisions should be made. With the creation and implementation of good policies, we get predictable decision making and behavior; with poor policies or the lack of them, we get chaos.

To segue back to our intent for having a background screening policy, let's discuss why it is important to have a policy that delineates how we want our managers, supervisors, and employees to behave:

---

[1] This chapter is based upon the Ultimate Background Screening Policy Maker Software.

- **Controlling Behavior**—Very simply put, a background screening policy is intended to provide the guidance for how background checks should be performed, set the parameters under which they should be performed, and identify clear boundaries to be followed.
- **Fair Treatment**—At its most rudimentary level, fairness permeates out of our concept of justice and our beliefs about how people should be treated. A background screening policy should embody the principles of fairness as reflected in actions of upfront notification, providing the right to correct or appeal incorrect information, and notification of intended actions.
- **Avoiding Legal Problems**—A background screening policy must set the tone for an organization to follow the spirit of legal requirements, but also set the processes and procedures to ensure compliance with laws.

The following are some of the legal issues that impact background screening (see Chapter 2 for details).

Laws Impacting Background Screening

- The Driver's Protection Privacy Act (DPPA)
- Fair Credit Reporting Act (FCRA)/Fair and Accurate Credit Transactions Act (FACTA)
- Discrimination laws: Civil Rights Act 1964, Title VII, Civil Rights Act 1996
- Americans with Disabilities Act (ADA) (hiring or terminating dangerous individuals)
- Federal Bankruptcy Act
- Employee Polygraph Protection Act (EPPA)
- Equal Employment Opportunity Commission (EEOC)
  - Uniform Guidelines on Selection (Title VII/Executive Order 11246)
  - Guidelines for hiring previously incarcerated individuals
- Child care worker employee background checks
- The Family Educational Rights and Privacy Act (FERPA)
- Privacy laws
- Records retention and destruction laws

Other Legal Concerns

- Defamation
- Failure to warn
- Negligent hiring, retention, and misrepresentation

    Avoiding Financial Problems—A background screening policy must establish efficient and effective ways of doing things to minimize the impact on cost of operations and incorporate "checks and balances" or audit processes to ensure that legal liabilities are not incurred.

Reinforcing the Corporate Culture—A background screening policy must be congruent with, and an integral part of, an organization's approach to creating a security conscious culture.

Protecting the Organization's Resources—One of the basic tenets of a background screening policy is to reduce the risk to the organization's human, financial, informational, technological and physical resources.

Predictability in Decision Making—A background screening policy must provide clear guidance to managers, supervisors, and employees regarding the behaviors that are acceptable and those that are not acceptable. The true acid test of a truly effective policy is that it provides clear guidelines, but also allows sufficient leeway for making decisions based on the unique circumstances of situations that occur.

Communications—To be effective a background screening policy must be easy to read, easy to understand, and be presented to people in the organization. If a firm does continuous screenings, they need to communicate their policy annually or circulate it to make sure employees understand how they may be affected.

***Quid Pro Quo* contract**—The background screening policy is just one of many policies that employees agree to follow as part of their continuing relationship with the employer.

Having discussed the reason for having a background screening policy, let's talk about the benefits that are derived from having a policy in this area.

The Benefits of Having a Background Screening Policy

1. **Proactive Management of Risk:** As was discussed in the first chapter, risk management is fundamentally about choosing to accept a risk, mitigating the risk, or reducing the risk, and a background screening policy is a clear step to reduce the organization's risk.

2. **Due Diligence and Legal Compliance:** A well-crafted background screening policy will position an organization to exercise due diligence, which ultimately will help them avoid the negative consequences of being out of compliance or breaking the law. This helps the organization avoid unnecessary cost and the distraction of resources to address legal issues.

3. **Improve Hiring Processes:** Background screening provides for the collection of relevant information and verification of the accuracy of the information, which helps an organization to be equipped to make better hiring decisions. Hiring the right person the first time can have the following positive impacts:

   a. Reduce overall cost of hiring

   b. Improve retention rates, thus reducing cost of recruiting, training, replacement cost, etc.

   c. Reduce the cost of dealing with negative employee situations, including lawsuits

   d. Contribute to the acquisition of an effective talent pool

4. **Protection of Information:** One of the side benefits of implementing an effective background screening policy is that it forces an organization to pay close attention to how it protects individuals' personal information, which ultimately reduces the likelihood of the organization having a breach in its data and all of the commensurate problems associated with it.

□ □ □ ▬▬▬▬▬▬▬▬▬▬▬▬▬▬▬▬▬▬▬▬▬▬▬▬▬▬▬▬▬▬▬▬▬

An industry best practice is to have security or HR staff involved in the hiring process to review the background screening policy with a hiring manager when they have an open requisition approved. This will ensure that the policy is understood and fresh in their mind. Some organizations have the hiring manager review a short online course on the background screening policy.

▬▬▬▬▬▬▬▬▬▬▬▬▬▬▬▬▬▬▬▬▬▬▬▬▬▬▬▬▬▬▬▬▬ □ □ □

Reduce Cost and Improve Profitability

An organization that proactively manages its risk, avoids costly employee problems and lawsuits, has an efficient hiring process, and protects individual personal data will reduce its cost of operations, thus improving the flow of dollars to the bottom line.

Creating Your Background Screening Policy

Purpose of the Policy

Sample Policy Language

The purpose of this policy is to support the organization's efforts to hire qualified people, to promote a safe and secure work environment for employees, customers, contractors, and visitors, as well as to protect the organization's property, financial, technological, and informational resources.

Intent.   The intent of the above purpose statement is to make the policy all encompassing with regard to people who will be on your premises, e.g., employee, customers, contractors, and visitors, as well as to define the resources that the policy is focused on protecting.

Considerations.   Choose language that is consistent with your organization's norms and policies. For example, some firms use the term *clients* instead of *customers* or *associates, team members* instead of *employees*.

Scope of the Policy

Sample Policy Language

This policy is intended to cover all work locations in the United States and applies to individuals who apply for employment with the company, as well as to current employees. The policy covers preemployment background checks, reference checks, and post employment background checks.

Intent.   To define the scope and boundaries of the policy with regard to locations that are covered.

Considerations.   You must carefully determine the locations to be included; for example, some firms might want to add in to the above statement "and U.S. properties" to include locations in Puerto Rico, St. Thomas, etc. The language needs to be exact and precise to define the locations that are covered and to exclude those that are not.

Responsible Organization

Sample Policy Language

The human resources (HR) department is responsible for administering this policy and ensuring that all company personnel are in compliance with its provisions. The HR department is charged to work with the security department to ensure that all hiring practices are congruent with, and supportive of, the organization's overall efforts to create a safe and secure work environment.

Intent.   To clearly state which department is responsible for implementing and managing the policy's provisions and to define their responsibility for working with the security department.

Considerations.   Some organizations designate a position that is responsible for implementing and administering their policies, such as the director of security. If this is the case, then your policy should reflect how your organization designates the responsibility.

Sensitive Positions

First, let me define what is meant by "sensitive positions." Sensitive positions are typically the jobs that have the greatest potential to create risk and commensurately liability for the organization because of the nature of the work being performed. This may include jobs:

- That deal directly with the public
- That require employees to go into people homes
- Where employees have contact with children, elderly, or indigent populations
- Where employees have access to sensitive information
- Where employees have broad access to premises
- Where employees handle cash, valuable merchandise, or financial matters
- That are in a position that yields considerable influence on the affairs of the organization
- That have a significant responsibility for internal/external safety and/or security, such as security personnel, nurses, physicians, etc.

Each organization will likely have a unique set of definitions regarding what is considered to be a sensitive job. See the guide and worksheet in Appendix D regarding sensitive positions.

Sensitive Positions Policy Statement

Sample Policy Language

It is the policy of our organization to identify sensitive jobs to ensure that extra attention is paid to conducting appropriate preemployment background checks, references, and/or post-hire background checks on individuals who are being considered for positions designated as sensitive or who occupy such a position.

In addition, we have established a Sensitive Jobs Committee composed of representatives from security, human resources, legal, and operations who are charged with the responsibility to evaluate positions to determine if they should be designated as sensitive.

Definition.   Sensitive Jobs Committee is a committee made up of an HR compensation specialist, or other HR professional knowledgeable about job descriptions, and security, legal, and line management representatives. The work of the committee is to define the criteria to be used for determining which of the organization's jobs will be identified as "sensitive," to define the process to be used to make these decisions, and to ultimately identify the jobs that will be classified as "sensitive." The HR department typically will have responsibility for developing a communication plan to disseminate information regarding the jobs that have been identified as "sensitive" and the criteria and process for determining this to the organization so that managers fully understand the process when they have a position that needs to be filled. It is also important that employees are knowledgeable about sensitive jobs so that, should they apply for a "sensitive" job, they will understand the implications on the selection process and that a background check may be done.

Intent.   The intent in identifying sensitive jobs is to define the jobs that, based on a chosen set of criteria, have high-risk potential for causing injury to individuals, putting organization resources or other resources at risk. In addition, the intent is to define the information-gathering steps associated with background screening that the organizations deems appropriate to take to reduce the potential risk. It also provides clear documentation of the process of identifying sensitive jobs, the criteria on which it is based, and justification for taking specific steps to gather additional information.

Considerations.   The identification of sensitive jobs helps to identify positions for which higher levels of scrutiny may be deemed necessary for applicants. Some firms only conduct background checks on positions that are designated as sensitive, while others choose to conduct background checks on all of their positions. This is a choice that an organization must make. Many organizations that conduct background checks on all of their positions also conduct a higher level of checks on those positions designated as sensitive. This latter approach is the most prevalent in industry at this time.

Targeted Positions

Sample Policy Language

It is the policy of our organization to conduct preemployment background checks and reference checks for all open positions in locations within the scope of this policy. We conduct preemployment background checks and reference checks on all individuals who are offered a position of employment. In addition, we conduct preemployment background checks, reference checks, and post-hire background checks on all individuals who are offered a position that has been designated as sensitive.

Intent.   The intent is to designate the positions for which preemployment background checks, reference checks, and/or post-hire background checks will be conducted.

Considerations.   The important decision that you must make is to determine the target population that most appropriately fits your organization's risk profile.

For example, if your organization is a delivery service and 90% of your employees are truck drivers, you may choose to state that all applicants for truck driving positions will be subject to a preemployment background check and reference checks. You may go even further and designate that any truck driver who goes out on a leave of absence may be subject to a background check upon their return to work.

In another example, if your organization is a manufacturing operation, you may choose to state that only positions that fit the following criteria will subject applicants to a preemployment reference check and post-hire background check—any position that involves any of the following activities:

- Deals directly with the public
- Requires employees to go into people's homes
- Where employees have contact with children, elderly, or indigent populations
- Where employees have access to sensitive information
- Where employees have broad access to premises
- Where employees handle cash, valuable merchandise, or financial matters
- Are in a position that yields considerable influence on the affairs of the organization
- Have a significant responsibility for internal/external safety and/or security such as security personnel, nurses, physicians, etc.

In essence, this would mean that applicants for production jobs in your plant would not be subject to a background check unless at some point in the future an individual applies for another position that involves one of the stated criteria.

There are numerous options regarding designating the target population to be screened. Based on our research, the most prevalent practice is for organizations to conduct screenings on either finalists or individuals who have been offered a position. This is efficient because it is generally a much smaller pool than the original applicant pool, thus making it less expensive and more focused on individuals in whom the organization has serious interest.

Other possible options include the points listed in Table 5-1.

Process for Conducting Background Checks

Sample Policy Language

Intent. The intent is to make decisions amongst the numerous types of background checks that can be performed and how they will be applied to open positions at your organization.

Table 5-1 Target Population to be Screened

- Every job applicant (internal/external), regardless of the position for which they are applying
- Candidates who are considered a finalist for a position
- Candidate who is offered a position
- Applicants for specific jobs that have been preidentified as sensitive jobs
- Candidates who are considered finalists for specific jobs that have been preidentified as sensitive jobs

Considerations. There are numerous *types of preemployment background checking searches* that can be conducted including criminal records, motor vehicles records, educational records, previous employment history, Social Security number, previous addresses, and other records, as deemed appropriate.

Most firms tie the decision regarding "how extensively to search" to the level of responsibility, nature and scope of work, and risk level of the open position. Firms vary widely on their searches, although we recommend checking records in the counties in which the applicant has previously lived and worked. For sensitive jobs, we also recommend a nationwide database search, which may identify other information that may not show up in county searches. Please note that a nationwide database search is not a search of all states, counties, and courthouses across the United States but more of a search of multijurisdictional databases of information from multiple sources (see Glossary for further definition). Other options include searching the current county where the person lives and works, current state where the person lives and works (all counties within the state), the last three counties where the applicant has lived or worked, etc. The predominant point to consider is that we live in a mobile society; consequently, it is imperative to conduct background checks in a wide enough net to have a reasonable chance of discovering undisclosed information or to determine the validity of information provided.

Personnel Actions That May Trigger the Need for a Post Employment Background Check

Sample Policy Language

Definition. Personnel actions are the employment related actions that may trigger the need for a post employment background check. They include when the following actions may move an individual into a job classified as sensitive:

- A promotion
- A transfer
- A job reclassification
- A demotion
- Significant additional job responsibilities and/or duties added to the current position

A post-hire background check may also be triggered by designated individual actions that the organization has defined such as:

- Accident reportable to OSHA
- "At-risk" behavior that would raise reasonable suspicions, e.g., a number of "early warning signs" of workplace violence, etc.

Intent. The intent is to define the types of employment-related actions that may trigger the need for a post employment background check to ensure that employees fully understand when they may be subjected to such screenings and to ensure the organization consistently applies this practice.

Consideration. The primary consideration is to make sure that the organization has a solid business rationale for using the designated "personnel actions" as ones that will trigger a post-hire background check. Predominantly, the reason will be based on the nature of the work and the level of risk that the position presents; however, there may be situations where the organization also chooses to employ background checks when an individual's behavior creates possible heightened risk. The entire rationale should be documented to ensure consistent application and to avoid possible discrimination issues.

Provisional Hires

Sample Policy Language

It is the policy of our organization to avoid making provisional hires. However, in recognition of extraordinary business circumstances, should a manager deem it necessary to make such a hire, the decision must be approved by the following individuals:

- Chief security officer
- Vice president, human resources
- Legal counsel
- Senior operations manager in the chain of command where the position is open

Intent.   The intent of this section is make it clear that provisional hiring is not encouraged and is an exception process that must obtain the approval of senior management who have responsibility for deterring the level of risk the organization is willing to take.

Considerations.   We strongly recommend against the practice of "provisional hiring" because of the substantial liability that can result from this practice should the person perpetuate an incident of violence, theft of proprietary information or property, or other damage to the firm's resources in the interim period, thus exposing the firm to significant legal and financial liability. In addition, should the background check show a previous conviction that would have disqualified the person from consideration, you are now faced with a termination situation that can become complicated. The prospect of making a provisional hire should be required to be approved by the chief security officer, vice president of HR, legal counsel, and the senior operations manager in the chain of command where the position is open. Senior managers who are in the position to appropriately weigh the potential benefit against the potential risk and potential negative exposure should make this determination.

In the end, recognizing that there are occasions where business necessity means we need to take extraordinary actions, should you need to provisionally make a hiring decision of this nature, we recommend that you make the offer contingent on receiving an acceptable preemployment background check and that a derogatory report will subject the person to immediate termination of employment. We suggest that a separate document regarding the contingent nature of the offer be created that requires the applicant's signature so you have this document on file to eliminate any possibility of a misunderstanding regarding the person being hired provisionally.

Hiring Manager's Responsibility

Sample Policy Language

Our organization takes background screening very seriously and considers it to be a very important part of the hiring process. To this end, all hiring managers are expected to not only review background information provided to them, but to give it serious consideration as part of the decision to offer a position to a job candidate.

Intent. The intent is to clearly communicate to managers in the hiring process that it is their responsibility to actively consider the background screening information provided to them and to consider it as a part of their hiring decision.

Consideration. In order for this provision to be effective, you must have the "buy-in" of senior management who ultimately will need to be the ones that drive and reinforce this behavior within their respective departments. Please note that careful consideration should be given to including this provision because if it is not actually adhered to, meaning a monitored process actually exists to ensure that managers are using the background screening information, the policy statement can come back and haunt you in a lawsuit. It is better to not have it than to have it and not follow it.

Training and Communications

Sample Policy Language

It is the policy of our organization to provide hiring managers with the necessary support needed to make effective hiring decisions. To this end, when a manager has an open position he or she will be provided with a short online training program that describes how to appropriately use the background screening information he or she will be provided on candidates, if any.

- Note that the online training program has a certificate at the end into which the manager must input his or her name, employee number, and date of completion, and it will automatically be sent to the human resources department to verify that it has been viewed.

Intent. The intent of this provision is to ensure that hiring managers know how to use the background screening information that is provided to them. Also, if you include the online training provision that tracks when it was used and by whom, it provides irrefutable evidence that a process is in place to ensure that managers are aware of the policy.

Consideration. There are many methods for ensuring that the appropriate information about how to use the background screening information provided to them, and you must determine an effective approach for your organization that is consistent with your normal ways of communicating with managers. Some organizations may choose to deliver this message via a low-tech solution because this is most effective for them, while others may choose a high-tech solution that is consistent with their organization's way of doing things. Some of the options we have seen used are given in Table 5-2.

Adverse Action/Appeal Process

Sample Policy Language

It is the policy of our organization to notify applicants for positions of our intent to not offer them a position when part of the decision to not consider them was based on

Table 5-2 Training Managers on your Company Policy

- Annual classroom training provided on how to handle background checks
- Included as part of management orientation for new hires and promoted employees
- Included as part of supervisor/management training or other designated programs
- Online or CD-ROM training provided to manager when a position is open
- Printed materials provided to manager when a position is open
- HR or training representative meets with a manager when a position is open to explain how background checks are handled

negative or derogatory information identified in a background screening report. All applicants have the right to challenge the negative or derogatory information and to provide additional information that counters the previously reported information within a reasonable time period (note that each firm should specify the reasonable time period that it will apply because the law is silent on this factor).

Intent.   The intent of this section is to give appropriate notification to an applicant that there was derogatory information that resulted from a background check that was used in making the decision to not offer them a position. This notification also gives the applicant the opportunity to challenge the negative or derogatory information and to have an opportunity to provide additional information that counters the previously reported information.

Consideration.   Many firms sidestep providing this information by simply notifying applicants that they had a substantial pool of qualified applicants and that another person was selected that was considered to be a better fit for the position. While we understand the efficiency of this approach, we caution organizations to be aware of the risk, if an applicant suspects that in reality it was a derogatory background check that booted them out of the selection process and challenges the decision. The organization is now faced with a potentially messy situation to clean up and a potential violation of the FCRA (see explanation below). It is easier to do it right on the front end and not have to worry about possibly having to scramble to clean up a situation on the back end.

According to the FCRA, an applicant must be advised of your intent to take adverse action if you use a consumer reporting agency (a background screening firm) or consumer report in any part of the selection process (e.g., deny employment based on derogatory information found as a result of conducting a preemployment background check).

If you conduct background checks with your internal staff, you are not required by the FCRA to provide an appeal process, although some states do require this. Consequently, it is *strongly recommended* that you give applicants an opportunity to *contest derogatory information* collected during a preemployment or post employment background check that is claimed to be incorrect. The FCRA states that you must give the person a reasonable time period to contest the information.

Note that the FCRA is silent on defining the specific time period that is considered reasonable. While ultimately this is an individual business decision, our research indicates the following time periods that are defined as reasonable by many organizations:

- 3 Business days
- 5 Business days
- 10 Business days

Nondiscrimination Clause

Sample Policy Language

It is the policy of our organization to hire applicants on the basis of their qualifications to perform the work available in an open position and we do not discriminate on the basis of any protected class categories as defined in federal discrimination legislation or the states in which we operate (see our Equal Employment Opportunity and Nondiscrimination Policy).

Intent.   Because background screening is part of the hiring process, it is the intent in this section to clearly communicate that no discrimination will occur against applicants on the basis of any of the identified protected class categories in federal and state discrimination laws or Equal Employment Opportunity Commission (EEOC) guidelines.

Consideration.   Beyond the normal nondiscrimination posture that virtually all organizations routinely state in today's work environment, a primary concern is that your organization complies with the EEOC rules concerning the use of criminal records for previously incarcerated persons.

Under EEOC rules, an employer may not deny employment to an ex-offender unless it is a business necessity, determined by reviewing the following three factors:

- Nature and gravity of the offense
- Amount of time that has passed since the conviction or completion of sentence
- Nature of the job being held or sought

Record Keeping, Data Protection, and Destruction

Sample Policy Language

It is the policy of this organization to maintain all information attained from pre-employment or post employment background and reference checks in a strictly confidential manner. All information gathered from background checking and/or reference checking will be kept in a secure file that is separate from the regular human resource file.

In addition, only individuals who have a legitimate business need to know will be allowed to view information obtained in a background or reference check. Hiring managers will only be provided with a notification of potential negative or derogatory information and not the actual background screening report.

Records are retained according to timeframes prescribed by law and based on business necessity.

Intent. The intent of this section is to severely restrict the access to confidential personal information on individuals and to only provide the absolute necessary information to designated individuals who have an established need to know. The select group will generally include the security and HR representatives assigned to a case, and legal counsel should questions or issues arise. A key intent is to avoid the unnecessary exposure of an individual's personal information and any violations of privacy laws. In addition, the intent is to ensure that effective data protection procedures are put in place to ensure that data breaches of personal information do not occur and that all appropriate data protection laws are complied with.

Considerations. In the above sample policy language, we included information about hiring managers having access to information obtained in a background or reference check. The following are additional options that you could consider:

- The employee on whom the background check was conducted will have access to a summary of the criminal background check if conducted in-house, and access to a full copy of the reports provided by a third party preemployment background checking firm.
- The hiring manager for the open position will only receive a summary report that will indicate no derogatory information was found or that derogatory information was found and that additional inquiry may be necessary.
- Designated HR department personnel who have a need to know.
- Designated security department personnel who have a need to know.
- Designated legal counsel who have a need to know.
- Criminal background check review committee, if any—see information given in Table 5-3.
- Other designated personnel who have a legitimate business need to know based on the specifics of the situation.

Data

Here are some additional considerations for defining the data protection and destruction portion of the policy. When considering the life cycle of employee background check records, businesses should focus, in broad terms, on data input, access, storage, and destruction. It should be noted that if your organization has a policy that governs the management of sensitive information, then you should either refer to this policy or replicate its guidelines in this section of this policy.

Table 5-3 Criminal Background Check Review Committees

A Criminal Background Check Committee is a committee that is chartered to review situations when a derogatory criminal record is identified to evaluate the applicant's employability. In general, the committee is used to review criminal convictions that fall into a gray area with regard to the applicant's employability, where a determination needs to be made regarding appropriately applying the EEOC rules for handling individuals with criminal records, or the hiring manager wants to recommend hiring an applicant despite being notified of negative or derogatory information in the background screening report. This type of committee is typically made up of representatives from security, HR, and legal departments.

Data Protection

The department or function that has the responsibility for background screening should also have the responsibility for managing the protection of the data gathered. Based on the survey results of PreemploymentDirectory.com, as indicated in Chapter 4, 83% of the time the HR function has this responsibility and security has it about 12% of the time. Whichever function has the lead, it would a prudent business practice to partner with the security, HR, legal, and information technology functions to develop a complete solution.

A critical starting step is to create a process map of all of the internal and external processes and data flows that involve personal employee information collected via background and reference checks from the initial collection through data destruction. To develop an effective data protection program, you must identify every step "from the womb to the tomb" in the process and totally understand the life cycle of the data.

Your focus is to protect the data at every point along the life cycle. Remember that wherever you have an unprotected or marginally protected point, this will most likely be a weak link that creates vulnerability to a breach.

Data Input

An obvious, but often violated, principle that can help reduce the data protection load is to avoid asking for and collecting sensitive information that is not needed or that is not needed at an early stage in the hiring process. The more data you collect, the more data you have to protect and the larger the volume of data to protect, the more complex it gets.

To illustrate the point about only collecting data when you need it, "don't ask job applicants for their date of birth or Social Security numbers until it has been determined that they are a finalist for a position or have been offered the position (match this to the point identified in your background screening policy)." The convenience of collecting the data all at once upfront may very well be outweighed by the risk this creates for safeguarding the information.

Another important step to take is to not only track the sensitive information that you collect but to also track who has accessed the information. This way you will have a built-in audit trail along the entire life cycle of the data.

Access Issues

In order to limit access to data collected from background screening, you must decide what information will be made available to whom. For example, data should not be made available on a general nature to the security department; it should be accessible to the security professional who is assigned to work on a specific background screening case.

Restricting who has access to data is a vital part of protecting sensitive data. To this point, as a precautionary measure, security and HR personnel who will be involved with handling individual's personal information should themselves be appropriately screened at the time of entry into the position that will involve dealing with sensitive information. In addition, a schedule should be established for conducting post-hire background checks on these individuals to ensure that they continue to meet your qualifications for dealing with sensitive information. It is essential that temporary workers who are bought into the security or HR department also have background checks conducted on them to ensure that they meet your qualifications to deal with sensitive information. Do not assume that the agency that provided them has conducted a sufficient background screening. In general, we suggest that you avoid having temporary workers have access to sensitive data unless it is under very close supervision. This is often a weak link in data protection in many firms.

You should also have a clear policy on who can access applicant- or employee-sensitive data based on a clearly defined business necessity. For example, a hiring manager needs to know if a job candidate has negative or derogatory information in their background report; however, they do not need to know all the details associated with that report. The more you restrict access to information, the better.

Work with your information technology department to have them restrict electronic access to sensitive data using the available technologies. Make sure that they share your concern for system security and also give a high priority to protecting personal sensitive information. In addition, do not overlook appropriate low-tech security measures, such as ensuring that secure file cabinets are used to store information and that they are secured behind locked doors. We suggest you use key cards or access control devices that allow you to track who accessed the room and/or files.

Storing Data

An important tool that can be employed to help protect data is to encrypt as much of these data as possible. Encryption translates the data into a secret code that can be unlocked only by using a key or password.

In-transit Data

In-transit data includes data that pass through a Web portal or company network. A different type of protection is necessary to keep such data secure. Businesses must require individuals approved for access to sign onto company networks through a Secure Sockets Layer (SSL) connection. SSL uses a cryptographic system that uses two keys to encrypt data—a public key known to everyone and a private or secret key known only to the recipient of the message.

A new technology tool that has emerged that can also assist with protecting in-transit data is Outbound Content Control (OCC), which focuses on preventing confidential information from being transmitted electronically. OCC solutions screen outgoing electronic messages for certain sensitive data patterns. For example, if a message has a nine number set in a 3-2-4 sequence, such as a Social Security number, an OCC tool can block that traffic without actually reading the message.

Data Destruction

When electronic and paper files are waiting to be destroyed, they should be kept in a secure area. The information technology department should be able to identify ways to best handle destroying electronic data and the security department should identify ways to destroy paper files. The data destruction requirement of the FACTA amendment to the FCRA should be followed.

Retention of Records

Currently there are no legal requirements stating how long background check results must be kept on file, so we recommend that you plan to keep them indefinitely up to the time period when an employee leaves the organization. Upon termination, the person's record should be destroyed.

Legal Compliance

Sample Policy Language

It is the policy of our organization to ensure that all preemployment, reference, and post employment background checks are conducted in compliance with all federal and state statutes, such as the Fair Credit Reporting Act, as applicable.

Intent.   The intent of this provision is to affirmatively state that the organization is in compliance with the FCRA and all other applicable federal and state statutes.

Considerations.   The FCRA requires employers that use a third party firm to conduct background checks and/or references to obtain a written release from the person applying for a position authorizing the firm to conduct a background and reference check. While employers that conduct their own background checks and references may not be required to obtain an authorization, it is strongly recommended that you do so to minimize liability and exposure due to privacy rights. Also note that separate and distinct authorization releases must be given for permission to conduct a preemployment background check and a reference check.

You also should determine how your organization will respond and whether you want to incorporate language into your policy that states that if a nonemployee applicant for employment refuses to complete the consent and authorization to conduct a preemployment background and reference check, the individual will be advised that it is a prerequisite to be considered for employment.

In addition, a similar determination needs to be made for an employee applying for a position that refuses to complete a consent and authorization to conduct post-hire background and reference check the individual will be advised that it is a prerequisite to be considered for the position being applied for. Please note that this does not mean that the person should be terminated, but more so that he or she will not be considered for the position that is open.

See the overview of FCRA in Chapter 2.

Third Party Suppliers of Employees: Contractors, Temporary Agency, Employment Leasing, or Professional Employment Organization

Sample Policy Language

All labor contracts with contractors, subcontractors, temporary agencies, and employment leasing or professional employment organizations include the requirement for them to conduct background checks for all of their employees assigned to work at any of our locations and regular reports will be provided to verify the agreed upon checks are being conducted or permission to periodically audit their records will be granted.

Intent. The intent of this provision is to ensure that third party suppliers of labor are conducting background checks on their employees. Your intent should be to ensure that these firms are abiding by the same level of checks that you apply to your own applicants and employees.

Considerations. Historically, one of the gaping loopholes in businesses, security processes has been not ensuring that contractors and their employees are held to the same standards that your applicants and employees are held to. Consider the situation where a temporary administrative assistant is hired into the sales department and has access to your customer database as part of his or her duties. When your organization hires a regular employee to fill this position, you conduct a background check because you recognize the person will have access to sensitive company data. You should apply the same standard to the temporary employee that is filling the position.

Policy Auditing Process

Sample Policy Language

It is the policy of our organization to audit the policy, procedures, and practices that we have put in place to ensure:

- That hiring managers being trained appropriately about the background checking policy and process when they have an opening
- That sensitive jobs are reviewed annually to ensure continued accuracy
- That those contractors providing people to work at our sites are appropriately conducting background checks on their employees

Intent. The intent of this section is best characterized by the saying, "You get what you inspect, not what you expect." To ensure that the practices you have put in place are actually happening and are functioning according to plan, you must have a means of evaluating their success and auditing what is occurring.

Considerations. While follow-up, evaluation, and analysis of plans versus actual implementation are necessary ingredients of any successful program and definitely should be applied to this policy, you must also give consideration to whether you want to actually commit this to writing. Inserting the language stated above into your policy creates a commitment that must be adhered to year after year, and in many cases organization inertia sets in after the hot issue that stimulated the policy has cooled down. Despite that reality and the best intentions, the requirement is still sitting in your policy. Should an issue subsequently arise, once having put this commitment in your policy can work against you since your firm may not have kept up with the ongoing evaluations, analysis, and audits. Now the business is faced with a situation where it is potentially in violation of its own policy. This does not work in your favor in a lawsuit.

In our experience, it is better to establish this as a practice by putting the audit or review on your annual calendar and conducting it rather than committing it to being part of the policy.

Continuous Post-Hire Background Checks

Post employment background checks include searching criminal records, motor vehicle records, educational records, previous employment history, Social Security records, immigration records, previous address, and other records, as deemed appropriate, on a current employee.

When screening current employees, legal and practical factors must be considered. There is absolutely nothing illegal about screening current employees as long as all of their rights are respected. Keep in mind that a current employee is entitled to the same legal rights as a new applicant (and if there is a union involved, perhaps even more rights). If the background check is performed by a third party service provider such as a background screening firm, then current employees are entitled to the same rights under the FCRA that would be applied to new applicants This includes a disclosure of rights and a written consent and authorization. Some states have additional rules. We recommend that you have a separate form that employees sign granting permission to conduct background screening that is completed at the time of hire or when you introduce your background screening policy. It is also acceptable to include the consent and authorization as part of your employment application completed at the time of hire.

The other consideration which often arises is whether the employer believes that asking existing employees to consent to a background check will somehow negatively impact the relationship between employees and the company. Will it send the message that you do not trust employees? Will it send the message that management is constantly spying on them? These are practical considerations that must be dealt with by closely examining the organization's corporate culture and understanding the effect of implementing ongoing background screenings.

If management decides it is in the firm's best interest to screen current employees, management should treat the introduction of the process as "change" that needs to be consciously and carefully orchestrated. One of the key ingredients in successfully implementing any change is to clearly explain the problem the organization faces and the rationale that has led to the decision to implement the change. Explaining that post-hire continuous screening is a business necessity that is focused on enhancing the safety and security of employees as well as the organization is an important point to emphasize. It should be made clear that the screenings will impact all employees and is not directed at any specific employee or groups of employees. It is also important that employees understand that all of their rights are going to be respected and nothing will occur as a result of a background check until the employee has an opportunity to discuss any negative findings with the employer. You do not want employees to feel powerless or to be worried that they will face an adverse action without an opportunity to be heard.

With careful change management and implementation planning, you will be able to get the "buy-in" of most employees and decrease resistance.

Table 5-4 provides a "point-counterpoint" discussion.

We have raised some good points that warrant thoughtful consideration. In the end, we agree that it would be foolish to ignore the potential increased risk that hiring a person that has a known criminal background rises in a business environment. It is very

Table 5-4 Point-Counterpoint

Even though we fully understand the EEOC guidelines regarding not discriminating against previously incarcerated persons, we should do everything legally that we can to avoid hiring people with criminal backgrounds because it is just too much of a risk.

Security	Human Resources
In reviewing the background results of a potential candidate or volunteer to join your organization, make sure you understand the conviction and the length of time that has passed since the incident. Some charges, like sexual predator or extreme violence, do not have flexible timelines.	Previously incarcerated persons (PIPs) have paid their debt to society and should be granted a second chance to become contributing members of society. They have done their time; we do not need to continue to punish them for their past indiscretions.
Market drivers should be considered in setting the criteria for hiring. However, if you lower your hiring standards, you might be inviting risk through the door. If you loosen the hiring standards, consider tightening other security layers.	It is getting harder and harder to fill these type positions; we need to take every able body.
Past behavior is normally a predictor for future conduct. We all hope that the criminal justice system is effective in rehabilitating criminals. But be careful here. A long period of gradual improvement or increasing levels of responsibility might be a strategy to ensure the actual changes are fully embraced by the new addition to your organization.	It is in the community's best interest that PIPs have a job and a means of earning a living or else they will have no choice but to turn back to illegal means to support themselves. We should be selective and appropriately match them to the right jobs, but not make a concerted effort to keep them out. That would be a disservice to the greater community.
We are not advocating not hiring individuals with a past. But make sure the applicant discloses all issues and you verify the accuracy of the disclosure and then make your decision based on facts.	Everybody has some skeletons in their closet that if they were known might make hiring them questionable, so let's give these folks a break and not continue to hold their past against them.
Doing background checks on current staff is a tricky situation. I recommend good generalship here. Base final decisions on all factors including current work record. Also, make sure you look at whether the issue was disclosed on the consent to do the background check. Always consider disclosure as a positive sign the employee has indeed changed their behavior.	It is highly likely that we already have employees that have a criminal history since we just started doing background checks in the last three years. Also it is possible for many people to get the criminal past expunged from the records, so this makes it even more likely that PIPs work among us. Let's not let paranoia drive our hiring practices and approach this in a logical rational manner.

important that the organization provides a safe work environment for its employees and minimizes the risk to its other resources. Consequently, we believe the prudent approach to addressing this dilemma involves taking several steps:

- Carefully screen all applicants so that you can make informed hiring decisions based on having as sufficient information about the person as possible. With a wide array of information about an applicant you are in a better position to make a balanced decision about their potential for success.
- Positions should have clear job descriptions that clearly identify not just the skill, education, and experience requirements, but also the traits and characteristics that will lead to success so that these can be matched carefully against applicants.
- Sensitive positions should be identified with clear criteria that will allow applicants to be screened out based on the established criteria and level of risk associated with the duties of the job. People should be carefully matched against the position requirements and not placed in positions that have high risk associated with them.
- A specific training and development plan should be put in place when hiring all applicants, but particularly higher risk ones, to increase the likelihood of their success. In other words, the organization needs to invest in increasing the odds for success.

Conscious changes in work procedures that monitor performance and facilitate success should be considered when possible and if feasible to provide additional safeguards when a person with a criminal history is hired. For example, many organizations that deal with young people and hire volunteers have implemented procedures such that adult staff is never alone with a child. This significantly reduces the risk of improper behavior.

We know that some people will raise the issue regarding this approach being different treatment and that it is discrimination. While we understand this viewpoint, we subscribe to the view that we are taking a higher risk in hiring the person; therefore, we should be allowed to compensate for that risk by taking extra steps to minimize it. We also believe that as time passes by and a person proves himself or herself, the extra precautions will become less necessary. It comes down to that old adage that trust must be earned.

Summary

PreemploymentDirectory.com's 2005 Employers' Background Screening Practice Survey results indicated that 62% of businesses that responded to the survey have a background screening policy in place. Extrapolating from these data, then, suggests that there may be well over a third of businesses that do not have a background screening policy. Juxtaposing this against the estimated 80% to 96% of firms that state they are conducting some form of background or reference check means that there are many firms actively involved in conducting screenings that are operating without a policy in place.

In addition, the survey results indicated that the vast majority of firms that have a background screening policy have had them in place for over 2 years. Because a reasonable standard for updating policies is around 2 years, it may mean that it is time for a good number of these policies to be updated. Background screening has significantly evolved over the last 2 years with changes in the FCRA, the FACTA amendment, and data protection having become a really hot item. These changes need to be reflected in an effective background screening policy.

This chapter has given you detailed insight into the ingredients that should be included in a comprehensive background screening policy. While we fully understand that each organization will have unique circumstances that it must address and their own nuisances, we believe that we have provided a solid core that is applicable to most businesses. We have provided you with sample language to consider along with the intent of each section and the considerations that elaborate on the business rationale for the approach we have taken. This chapter should provide you with the groundwork to be able to create a comprehensive and effective background screening policy.

Glossary of Important Terms

Criminal background check review committee—team that has been chartered by the organization to review situations when a negative criminal record is identified that must be evaluated to determine the applicant's employability. In general, the committee is used to review criminal convictions that fall into a gray area with regard to the applicant's employability, where a determination needs to be made regarding appropriately applying the EEOC rules for handling criminal records, or the hiring manager wants to recommend hiring an applicant despite being notified that the person is ineligible for being hired. These committees are typically made up of representatives from security, HR, and legal.

Nationwide database or national criminal search—search of available databases in the majority of states or across multiple jurisdictions taken from various sources, such as prison records or court indexes available from some courts. Although the report is valuable because it is national in reach, it is not a substitute for a real criminal search of state courts at the courthouse level. The national criminal searches are only intended as an inexpensive and instant "prescreen" tool or as a secondary search to supplement a courthouse search. The point is to be very careful about using national databases as a sole source of information.

Post employment background checks (a.k.a. continuous or infinity screening)—conducted for current employees for a number of reasons including the employee is applying for a new position or is being transferred to another position; government requirement, e.g., DOT drug testing; accident investigation; workplace violence incident investigation; or employee's behavior is bizarre or severe enough to trigger a threat assessment. It may include searching criminal records, motor vehicle records, educational records, previous employment history, Social Security number, previous addresses, and other records as deemed appropriate based on the requirements of the specific position being applied for or the nature of the situation that triggered the background check.

Preemployment background checks—conducted for applicants for employment and may include searching criminal records, motor vehicle records, educational records, previous employment history, Social Security number, previous addresses, and other records as deemed appropriate based on the requirements of the specific position being applied for.

Provisional hires—practice of hiring an employee contingent on the individual providing required information at a date after their employment has commenced.

Reference checks—conducted for applicants for employment and may include verification of previous employment status, position, compensation, dates, performance, verification of information provided on the completed application for employment, the applicant's resume, or on other forms used in the hiring process, etc., and any other legal information that would provide information regarding an individual's employability.

Sensitive jobs—typically the jobs that pose the greatest security risk or the greatest potential to create liability for the organization because of the nature of the work being performed. This includes jobs that deal directly with the public or require employees to go into people homes, have contact with children, elderly or other vulnerable populations or where employees have access to sensitive information, broad access to premises or handling cash, valuable merchandise or financial matters or have a significant responsibility for internal/external safety and/or security such as security personnel, nurses, physicians, etc. Each organization will have unique definitions of sensitive jobs.

Suggested Reading

Andler, Edward C., Dara Herbst: *The Complete Reference Checking Handbook: The Proven (and Legal) Way to Prevent Hiring Mistakes*, 2nd ed. New York, AMACOM, a division of American Management Association, 2003.

Caterinicchia, Dan: *Safeguarding HR Information: Take a Look at Some New Ideas for Preserving Your Employees' Confidential Data*. HR Magazine, SHRM.

Nadell, Barry: *Sleuthing 101, Background Checks and the Law*. Chatsworth, CA, InfoLink Screening Services, 2004.

Nixon, W. Barry: *The Complete Hiring Process to Screen for Violence Prone Individuals*. Lake Forest, CA, National Institute for Prevention of Workplace Violence, 2001.

Post training background investigation courses. California Commission of Peace Officer Standards and Training, 2001 and 2002.

Rosen, Lester S.: *The Safe Hiring Manual*. Tempe, AZ, Facts On Demand Press, 2004.

Make or Buy[1]

The purpose of this chapter is to increase business awareness of the essential elements that should be considered when creating a background screening program. As was discussed in the previous chapter, it is critical that a comprehensive and well-defined policy exists that addresses the full realm of issues associated with background screening. Once the policy is in place, the next decision that must be made is to decide if screenings are going to be conducted by in-house staff or by an outsourcing firm that specializes in background screening. We believe this is an important decision that must be carefully weighed because in the end this process should strengthen the organization's overall selection process and contribute to the firm's capability to hire the right people.

This chapter focuses on identifying the factors that need to be considered in making this "make or buy" choice. We also identify the most important issues that should be considered to evaluate external service providers if the decision is made to utilize one. You should be aware that two leading studies that have been conducted regarding background screening practices have indicated that approximately 80% of businesses use the services of an external firm to conduct their background checks:

□ □ □ ▬▬▬▬▬▬▬▬▬▬▬▬▬▬▬▬▬▬▬▬▬▬▬▬▬▬▬▬▬▬▬▬▬▬

- The Society for Human Resource Management's (SHRM) 2004 Survey on Reference Checking indicated that over 80% of businesses that responded to their survey were conducting some form of background checks
- PreemploymentDirectory.com's 2005 Employers' Background Screening Practices Survey produced a similar result with 82% of respondents indicating they conduct screenings (see http://www.workplaceviolence911. com/docs/03_2006_results.pdf)

▬▬▬▬▬▬▬▬▬▬▬▬▬▬▬▬▬▬▬▬▬▬▬▬▬▬▬▬▬▬▬▬▬▬ □ □ □

In addition, it should be noted that, based on the results of the Preemployment Directory.com's 2005 Employers' Background Screening Practices Survey, the vast majority of companies place the responsibility for oversight of background screening in the human

---

[1] This chapter is based on the publication *The Comprehensive Guide For Selecting a Background Screening Firm* published by PreemploymentDirectory.com, a division of the National Institute for Prevention of Workplace Violence, Inc., January 2007.

resources department (HR), with security being a distant second. However, especially since 9/11, there has been a marked increase in the security department involvement in the screening process.

The "Buy" Decision: Outsourcing the Background Screening Function

Our focus in discussing outsourcing is to help businesses select providers that operate in compliance with all governing laws, that have established business practices that demonstrate excellence in protecting consumer personal data based on "best practices," and that adhere to the spirit of the accreditation standards promulgated by the National Association of Professional Background Screeners (NAPBS).

We firmly believe that businesses need to consider the selection of a background screening firm as seriously as the selection of a CPA firm. Keep in mind that a good background screening firm can keep you out of trouble, while one that does not protect applicant or employee data can get you into a lot of hot water.

These are some of the key factors that firms should consider in selecting an external background screening firm:

- Verification of identity
- State, county and multi-juridictions (national*)
- Criminal and civil background check including current warrants as well as felonies and misdemeanors, when available
- Reference check and previous work history
- Verification of education and professional license records
- Motor Vehicle records
- Sexual offender search
- Terrorist search
- Credit history
- Other searches as deemed necessary
- Review the vendor services that are provided and ensure that they have "full service" capability that will meet your business and hiring needs.

The services that are now available include the following.

Verification of Identity

The traditional approaches to verifying identity are Social Security numbers and date of birth, which in essence ensure that the person's name and birthdate match. While this approach has been very successful over the years, as is the case with any process, it has its problems. With the ready availability of high-tech duplicating technologies, fake documents abound, and people even use the Social Security numbers and dates of birth of those who are deceased. This practice often involves use of dates of birth for relatives or for babies who die. Also, there has been no shortage of issues associated with stolen Social Security numbers and with them being used for identity theft and other fraudulent purposes. This problem has reached such proportions that most organizations significantly restrict the use of Social Security numbers, and this information is treated as highly sensitive data to be maintained confidentially. In addition, it is highly likely that new privacy legislation will be enacted that will substantially eliminate the use of Social Security numbers and dates of birth as identifiers by businesses.

The successor to identity verification will be biometric solutions, which have the capability of virtually eliminating false positive identifications as sophisticated combinations of techniques become readily available and are harder to duplicate. Duplication is difficult because a physical trait like a fingerprint is translated into an electronic code and verification requires the person to actually present his or her finger. Techniques involving fingerprinting, palm prints, iris scans, retina scans, gait maps, etc., will revolutionize the identity verification process (biometrics is covered in more depth in a subsequent chapter).

State, County, and Multijurisdiction (National) Checks

Nationwide database or national criminal searches are searches of available databases from many states' repositories, gleaned from various sources such as prison records or court indexes available from some courts. Although the report is valuable because it is national in reach, it is not a substitute for a real criminal search of state courts at the courthouse level because many state repositories do not contain all the records, may not have been updated at the time of search, and may contain inaccurate information. The national criminal searches are only intended as an inexpensive and instant "prescreen" tool or as a secondary search to supplement a courthouse search. The point here is to be very careful using national databases; do not rely on these as a sole source of information.

Criminal and Civil Background Checks

Criminal and civil background checks should be conducted in all the counties where a person has previously lived, along with a search for current warrants as well as felonies and misdemeanors, when available. Keep in mind that a person convicted of crime may have moved from the county where he or she was convicted, so just checking their current county may not be enough.

Most states prohibit checking arrest records, a practice that is also generally frowned upon by the Equal Employment Opportunity Commission (EEOC); however, there are some states that allow this practice. Even in these states, employers are warned to be careful in how they use arrest records, and it is recommended that you seek the counsel of your labor attorney in how to proceed.

Similarly, while we recommend that businesses inquire about misdemeanors, it must be remembered that the use of misdemeanors in making employment decisions is regulated at the state level, so be sure to check with legal counsel regarding their use in your state.

Reference Checks and Previous Work History

Checking the previous work history of applicants is critical to determining work habits and can offer powerful insights into their capabilities and how the person may "fit" with your firm's culture. While it is important to check references, the unfortunate reality is that most employers have relegated themselves to only giving out the title of the position the person occupied, dates of employment, and verification of salary. Consequently, good references take a lot of effort to get despite the fact that 40 states actually have qualified privilege laws on the books that indemnify employers from being sued for giving out reference information in good faith.

Bob Rosner, author of "Working Wounded: Advice That Adds Insight to Injury," in an article in *Workforce Magazine*, stated with regard to reference checking, "The courts recognize that you and the prospective employer do have a common interest in discussing the attributes of an employee (the legal term is a 'qualified privilege')."[2]

Table 6-1, as an example, provides an overview of California's qualified privilege:

Table 6-1 Qualified Privilege

You should be aware that a supervisor (employer) can legally release employment information if it is done properly. An employer has a right and duty to carefully inquire into a potential employee's work-related background. In responding to such inquiries, it can be legal to provide both positive and negative information about a current or former employee, as reference givers are protected under the legal doctrine of "qualified privilege." That is, an exchange of information between employers (who have a common interest in hiring qualified applicants) regarding previous work history of an employee made as part of a reference check is protected from suits for defamation if the statements regarding an applicant's previous work history are made in good faith to persons having a legitimate need to know.

The protection of QUALIFIED PRIVILEGE exists only when the following conditions are met:

- The information must be given in good faith. Unfounded suspicions about the employee should not be implied or specifically expressed. For example, if you thought that a former employee had stolen state (company) property but you didn't have solid evidence to support that suspicion, it would be inappropriate to mention this during a reference check.

- The truth of the information can be substantiated. However, the truth is not an absolute defense to a charge of defamation if you have abused the privilege by acting with malice. That is, you communicated the information maliciously and with the intent to harm the individual.

- The information should be limited to the inquiry. For example, if you are asked questions about the employee's absenteeism or tardiness, you should not mention that he or she has filed numerous grievances if these issues are unrelated to the question. When certain negative information is volunteered, the motive of this supervisor (employer) could be questioned or a case could possibly be made that personal malice was involved.

- The information must be given during the proper time and proper manner. For example, it would be inappropriate for a supervisor (employer) to discuss the reasons for an employee's termination at an office Christmas party where spouses, etc., were present who did not have a business-related need to know this information.

- The information must be communicated to the proper parties. Excessive publication of information will defeat the privilege. That is, discussing confidential information with those who have no reason to know takes the statement outside the protections of qualified privilege.

- The requested information must be strictly related to the requirements of the job.

Verification of Education and Professional License Records

Never has it been more important to verify educational credentials. We have entered an era where not only are fake degrees readily available along with accompanying official transcripts, but also many entities are offering "buy a degree" programs where students do not need to attend any classes.

As the recruiting area for more and more jobs has continued to expand into the international arena, an additional area that employers will need to pay increasing attention to is validating the equivalency of foreign degrees with U.S. university standards.

---

[2]   State of California.

Motor Vehicle Records

While most employers that hire drivers clearly understand the need to check driving records and verify driving licenses, more employers need to remember if an employee runs an errand on company business and has an accident, your company may be held liable for any damages. Consequently, any individual who at any time may use a vehicle on company business, whether private or company provided, should have their driving license and record checked. It should also be noted that driving licenses are currently an excellent source of verifying date of birth and past addresses.

The Department of Transportation requires that all truck drivers for companies holding federal contracts with them have their licenses and driving record verified. (This is covered in more depth in Chapter 2 on Legal Issues and Requirements.)

Sexual Offender Search

The headline that no company wants to see is that one of their employees has been arrested for sexually molesting a minor, particularly if it relates to the workplace. Beyond the negative imagery of this type of headline, if you have people working with children, the elderly, or vulnerable populations, care must be taken not to hire sexual predators who could cause harm to these individuals and land you in a significant negligent hiring liability situation.

Terrorist Search

We live in a time period where terrorism is very real, which means that employers need to practice due diligence in checking applicants to protect against employing an individual who is associated with a terrorist group. See Appendix E for some of the terrorist searches that are available.

The Patriot Act requires background checks on scientists who work with certain toxins. The law also bans citizens of rogue states, felons, illegal aliens, and certain other individuals from working with the substances. The Department of Agriculture suggests that employers obtain criminal background checks and verify references and addresses and that they check against the FBI terrorist watch list. It is also very important to check residency status of regular, temporary, contract, seasonal, and volunteer workers. (See more in Chapter 2 focused on Legal Issues.)

Credit History

The most important factor in conducting credit checks on applicants is that you can attribute it to a reasonable business consideration and/or the nature of the work that will be performed. Conducting a credit check on a controller who will have signature authority over large sums of money or who can make financial commitments on behalf of the firm is obvious, while checking the credit of an administrative assistant who at most manages your department petty cash for $100 might be a different story. There are also firms that conduct credit checks on all of their new hires, making it a hiring standard and practice created by policy that impacts every new hire equally.

Courthouse Searches

At this time, the most accurate and reliable process for checking criminal backgrounds is a direct courthouse search. Consequently, an important factor for you to consider is whether the screening firm has the capability to perform all the checks you deem necessary. With the background screening industry having rapidly expanded, there is now a network of courthouse record researchers. However, as is the case with most things, not all court searchers are made equal. Because these individuals will be accessing personal identifiable information about an individual, you have to make sure that the background screening company has carefully selected these searchers to avoid issues relating to fraud, identity theft, etc.

Turnaround Times

In today's demanding labor market, "time to hire" is very important to many organizations, and the push is to continually shorten the time frame to get every position filled. Consequently, background screening should not be a bottleneck in the overall hiring process, or you may miss out on a valuable hire. Turnaround times for background checks range from seconds to days depending on the nature and depth of the request. You have to keep in mind that it is important for you to determine these turnaround times across the spectrum of checks you will need. If you need to make an offer tomorrow, it does you little good to choose a firm that has a 4-hour turnaround for a criminal check but takes 3 days to verify educational history and credentials.

Methods to Meeting Your Order and Reporting Needs

This may include Internet-based tools that allow you 24/7 accesses from any computer device at anytime from anywhere, as well as providing fax, email, interactive voice response, and electronic file transfer. Ultimately, the service provider should be able to deliver reports to you via the technology and method that best fits your business requirements. It is equally important that you feel confident of the provider's capability to adjust as your needs evolve.

Educational Verification

Consider the following.

- There are more than 300 unaccredited universities now operating. While a few are genuine start-ups or online ventures, the great majority range from merely dreadful to out-and-out diploma mills—fake schools that will sell people any degree they want.
- It is not uncommon for a large fraudulent school to "award" as many as 500 PhDs every month.

With the closure of the FBI's diploma mill task force, the indifference of most state law enforcement agencies, the minimal interest of the news media, and the growing ease of using the Internet to start and run a fake university, things are rapidly growing worse Bear, John: *Diploma Mills: The $200-Million-a-Year Competitor You Didn't Know You Had,* 2004, http://www.quackwatch.org/04ConsumerEducation/dm1.html).

The scary part is that these data are based on research from April 2004 and it is highly likely that these institutions have significantly increased. The lack of law enforcement resources focused on eradicating these fake degrees virtually ensures they will continue to proliferate.

Whether you want to protect your business against a fictitious degree or you just want to be sure that an applicant has the requisite knowledge and skills to be able to successfully perform the job you are filling, verification of educational and institutional credentials is essential. Also, with international recruiting becoming a reality for more and more jobs, the need to be able to equate foreign degrees to U.S. degrees will continue to increase.

Private Investigator License

If your firm has offices in multiple states, you want to hire a firm that can meet your needs in all the states where your offices are located, or you may need to deal with multiple service providers. Working with multiple providers will likely impact the time and efficiency of your staff, pulling them away from other important tasks.

Limitations of National Databases

National databases, more accurately described as multijurisdictional databases, do not have complete coverage of all state repositories, prison records, federal records, etc. In fact, the idea of a "national" database can be misleading because it infers the data sources consist of some sort of complete library of the nation's criminal records. In fact, each jurisdiction collects its own data in varying degrees of accuracy and completeness and in a variety of formats. Given these limitations, service providers should have a statement explaining the limited nature of the information and reaffirming that when they obtain information from these national databases, it is verified through much more reliable sources. This should be part of their normal operating procedure and training for their staff.

Compliance with Legal Requirements

Require the vendor to certify their compliance with all applicable federal, state, and local privacy, EEOC/discrimination, consumer reporting, data destruction, and other governing laws.

This should include written procedures to ensure that all information sent to clients complies with the law, such as arrest records, sealed or expunged records, etc. This is very important because if the service provider inappropriately sends this type of information to your representatives, they can create potential legal liability for your organization. For example, if a service provider inappropriately sends you information on a criminal conviction that has been sealed or expunged and you use this information to disqualify a candidate, it could raise cause for a legal action against your firm. Another area in which laws have evolved due to considerable privacy concerns deals with the maintenance of records and data destruction. You should thoroughly examine the suppliers' procedures to ensure compliance with Fair and Accurate Credit Transactions Act (FACTA) and other legal requirements.

Errors and Omissions Insurance

Require the vendor to maintain sufficient *errors and omissions insurance* coverage to protect your firm. Have your risk management department or insurance broker identify a sufficient level of insurance that should be in force for a firm your size and have the vendor list you as co-beneficiary. Make sure that the insurance carrier will notify you of any significant changes in the policy (e.g., it has lapsed or a reduction of the amount of insurance below an acceptable level).

Negative Hit Policy and Procedure

Ensure the vendor has a written policy and procedure that clearly articulates the process that will be used when a criminal hit is reported. At minimum, this should include who will report it, how it will be reported, specific information that will be included, process for reverifying information, etc. This is very important because you want to make sure you are making decisions based on accurate information and many databases and sources used for checks may not have the most current or complete information.

"No Contact" Policy and Procedure

Ensure that the vendor has a written policy and procedure in place to avoid contacting a current employer if the applicant has requested that they not do so. Because many current employers will terminate an employee if they know they are actively seeking another position, having a service provider contact a current employer could be "the kiss of death." You could end up on the hook for causing the applicant to lose their job, which is a direct path to a lawsuit. There needs to be a fool-proof process in place to prevent this from occurring.

Certification of Staff Acceptability

Ensure that the vendor certifies that all staff—regular, part-time, and temporary—have been criminally screened at time of hire and that ongoing checks are made to ensure employees continue to have acceptable work backgrounds. This should be a contractual agreement that is part of the service delivery contract. In today's work environment this should be an "ongoing" requirement, which means just conducting a background screening at the time of hire is not sufficient. The service provider should have in place a process that periodically verifies the status of their employees and/or their subcontractors.

Ensure that the vendor discloses all subcontractors that will be involved with the processing of personal identifiable information or will have access to this information and certifies that all of their staff—regular, part-time, and temporary—have been criminally screened at time of hire and ongoing checks are made to ensure employees continue to have acceptable work backgrounds. Ensure that your service provider(s) and their employees are held to the same standards you have established for your employees. Require that new vendors that are hired during the duration of the contract be held to these standards and require the vendor to provide periodic reports verifying this procedure is being followed and to allow their processes to be audited for verification purposes.

Ensure that the vendor certifies that all employees of the vendor and their subcontractors that are involved in processing or who will have access to personal identifiable information sign a confidentiality and nondisclosure agreement that meets your company requirements. The confidentiality and nondisclosure agreements should include language that addresses new hires as well as employees leaving the firm. Your legal counsel needs to create and review these agreements. This is important because if anyone in the "supply chain" that deals with personal identifiable information does not maintain information in a confidential manner or inappropriately uses that information you could end up being blindsided and pulled into a legal action.

Bona Fide Business Verification

Ensure that the vendor has a written policy that details how they investigate and certify that all their subcontractors are bona fide businesses involved in the legitimate processing of personal identifiable information for a permissible purpose as defined by Fair Credit Reporting Act (FCRA). With the unfortunate ChoicePoint situation (identity thieves stole sensitive information about thousands of consumers; see more in-depth coverage in Chapter 7 on Data Protection) that occurred in 2005, one of the key learnings was that firms that provide confidential and personal identifiable information have to be very diligent in making sure that their clients are truly "who they say they are." ChoicePoint agreed to a record settlement of $10 million with the Federal Trade Commission, and this is a mistake that no firm wants to replicate.

There are now a number of services available that provide vendor verifications to ensure that companies are legitimately in the business they claim.

Table 6-2 Permissible Purpose as Defined by the Fair Credit Reporting Act–604 [15 U.S.C. § 1681b]

In general, Subject to subsection (c), any consumer reporting agency may furnish a consumer report under the following circumstances and no other:
In response to the order of a court having jurisdiction to issue such an order, or a subpoena issued in connection with proceedings before a federal grand jury.
In accordance with the written instructions of the consumer to whom it relates.
To a person which it has reason to believe:
(a) intends to use the information in connection with a credit transaction involving the consumer on whom the information is to be furnished and involving the extension of credit to, or review or collection of an account of, the consumer; or
(b) intends to use the information for employment purposes; or
(c) intends to use the information in connection with the underwriting of insurance involving the consumer; or
(d) intends to use the information in connection with a determination of the consumer's eligibility for a license or other benefit granted by a governmental instrumentality required by law to consider an applicant's financial responsibility or status; or
(e) otherwise has a legitimate business need for the information in connection with a business transaction that is initiated by the consumer; or
(f) or to review an account to determine whether the consumer continues to meet the terms of the account.

Release of Information

Ensure that the vendor's policy addresses that personal identifiable information will only be provided to authorized representatives of your firm. Service providers need to have procedures and safeguards in place that ensure that information is only released to appropriate and designated individuals within your firm. This procedure needs to be verified to ensure that information does not get communicated to the wrong persons who should not be privy to the information or could misuse it.

Disclosure of Litigation

Require the vendor to fully disclose previous litigation involving data breaches within the last 5 years and any that occur while the contract is in place. Make sure this language is built into your contractual agreement. You need to have fore knowledge of previous data breaches that have occurred in the recent past so that you cannot be accused of negligent selection or retention of a service provider. Besides this potential legal ramification, this information is important because you want to carefully examine the processes and procedures that the firm has put in place as a result of the breach to ensure that appropriate data protection actions have been implemented.

"No Resell" of Information Clause

Verify that a written policy exists that states that applicant or client personal data information is never resold. Make sure this language is built into your contractual agreement and that violation of the provision is immediate grounds for voiding the contract.

Systems Integration

Ensure that the vendor has the capability to interface and/or integrate their database with your human resources information systems (HRIS) and/or employment information system(s) to allow information to seamlessly flow in and out of your organization's HRIS. Through information dashboards, employers should be able to access all the information that is relevant to making hiring decisions from one place and one source versus the old process of having to go to multiple sources and data feeds. The desired result is to have the ability to go to one place to order and retrieve screening information along with other employment related information in one report that facilitates hiring decision making.

Predetermined Hiring Criteria

Check to see if the vendor has the capability to use smart programming systems, which can be programmed with predetermined hiring criteria so each report on every applicant is graded consistently and fairly. There are two important issues to be concerned with in this part of the evaluation. First, with today's technology, you can preprogram systems to "select or reject" applicants based on predetermined criteria you have established. Using these rules, a system can electronically evaluate all the information to yield individual search decisions as well as an overall recommendation. Putting this type of automated decision assistance tool into place can be much more efficient than manually reviewing and grading reports. In addition, using a "smart" system can ensure that your process applies consistent criteria and that it is equally applied to all applicants. This clearly helps to reduce possible discrimination issues. Despite these very positive attributes, care needs to be taken that these systems are not programmed to simply identify "pass/okay to hire" or "fail/no hire" decisions, which could run afoul with EEOC guidelines to prevent discrimination against hiring individuals who have previously served time in prison. Of course, the quality of the outcomes will be based on the quality of the decision factors that are programmed into the system. To illustrate the potential problem, a decision tree that automatically predetermines that no one with a felony conviction for embezzlement within the last 7 years would be eligible for hire for a CFO position would automatically be programmed into the decision making process which would likely meet the EEOC guidelines. Whereas automatically disqualifying a candidate for an equipment maintenance position who had a felony conviction 15 years ago might run afoul with the EEOC guidelines. The key is to evaluate the job relatedness of the conviction to the nature of the work to be performed and how long ago the incident occurred. While there are no specific criteria for time, the more time that has passed since the incident occurred, (particularly beyond 7 years), the less likely it will be considered as relevant to current qualifications.

Training

Ensure that the vendor has a documented training process in place for all staff whom will be involved in processing or will have access to personal identifiable information. This training should be offered at the time of hire and on an ongoing scheduled basis to ensure competency levels are maintained. At minimum, the training should cover:

- Legal requirements for conducting background screening
- Effective data protection and privacy to ensure security of information
- Essential elements of implementing an effective background screening policy including FCRA required forms
- How to implement an effective background screening program

Require the vendor to provide periodic reports that demonstrate that the training is occurring as scheduled.

Development or Review of Background Screening Policy

Check to see if the vendor will assist you in developing an effective background screening policy, if needed, or, if one already exists, whether they will review your policy and make recommendations for improvements. Given the myriad of legal requirements and the complexity of compliance, it is important that your background screening policy stay current and continue to meet not just your internal requirements but also those of the law. A good background screening firm will be on top of new legal requirements, court interpretations, and emerging issues that need to be addressed at a policy level, and your firm should tap this expertise to keep your internal policy up to date.

Software for creating a comprehensive background screening policy, or to compare your existing one to, is available at www.Workplaceviolence911.com either online or on a CD-ROM.

Demonstrated Financial Stability

Make sure that the vendor has demonstrated financial stability over the last 3 years. Have your controller or CPA review:

- Their debt ratio and outstanding debt to analyze whether they are within acceptable industry standards and do not indicate potential problems in the near term
- That they have sufficient cash, credit, and liquid assets to fund continued investments in technology to maintain a competitive position

System Security and Data Protection

Ensure that the vendor has a system security that provides a high level of data protection. In addition, make sure that the service provider has an information security policy that addresses the following:

- Verification of identity
- State, county, and multijurisdictions (national)
- Criminal and civil background check including current warrants as well as felonies and misdemeanors, when available
- Reference check and previous work history

Have your information technology staff verify that the vendor and any subcontractors that are involved with processing personal identifiable information:

1. Have system security in place that fully meets your data security requirements and meets background industry standards as defined by NAPBS. (See www.NAPBS.com for full listing of standards.)
2. Have procedures in place to mask some or all of the Social Security number from all reports, as well as obscure the year of birth.
3. Closely scrutinize data security processes for communicating and securing data if the firm utilizes independent contractors or home operators for court record verifications or sends data offshore for processing. In addition, if such practices are used by the vendor, you should have your legal counsel define contractual language to be included in the vendor's agreement with their contractors that addresses:

   a. The appropriate type and amount of errors and omissions insurance coverage that needs to be in force with your firm named as co-beneficiary
   b. The contractors and their employees are held to the same requirements and standards as the vendor's employees
   c. Specific procedures exist to ensure your data are protected
   d. All data protection laws are strictly followed
4. Have your security staff verify that the vendor and any subcontractors that process personal identifiable information meet your physical security requirements for securing their systems. They should also meet background industry standards as defined by the NAPBS. (see www.NAPBS.com).

Quality Assurance Policy

Ensure that the vendor has a documented quality assurance policy and ongoing processes in place to ensure the highest report accuracy. Verify that records of quality audits are maintained for all their sources of data and information. While every organization needs to have quality assurance, it is even more critical for background screening firms to have stringent quality requirements and guidelines in place because errors in their process do not just create an internal problem, but could very well prevent someone from getting a job. Several background screening firms have really taken the quality focus to heart and have gotten ISO 9000 certified.

Service Level Agreements

Check to see if the vendor offers service level agreements to back up their claims regarding the quality of their work and service commitments. As an external service provider, it is easy for firms to publicize what they will do. However, as the old adage goes, those that have service-level agreements are willing to "put their money where their mouth is." In other words, they go beyond mere rhetoric about their service and back it up with specific guarantees.

The "Make" Decision: Establishing an In-house Background Screening Operation

Let us now explore some of the essential considerations if you decide to keep the background screening process in-house.

As we discussed above, the FCRA is the primary law that governs background screening and it does not apply to activity by in-house personnel as long as a report from a consumer reporting agency is not used to assist in any part of the investigation. However, it should be noted that many states, California in particular, have statutes that require that individuals who are subject to employment screening are able to obtain a copy of the background check whether or not an adverse action has been taken. Applicants also have the same rights to notice and consent whether the employer hires an outside company to conduct the investigation or does the background check itself. (California Civil Code §1786).

Given the above, we strongly urge that in-house staff follow the guidelines defined by the FCRA for conducting background checks. We consider this to be a "best practice" approach because it will likely protect the company from the perception of unfairness, while adequate training on these guidelines will help to prevent actual wrongdoing. This of course will help to prevent any law suits. The key point here is that if applicants believe that they have been treated fairly, they are less likely to suspect you did something wrong or unfair and therefore less likely to seek legal counsel. In addition, because each state has various requirements for applying FCRA-like laws on employers, it is in your best interest to make sure your staff is educated on the laws in the states in which you operate, and that periodic checks and procedural updates are performed.

The fundamental FCRA guidelines are:

1. An employer must certify to the background screening firm it is working with that it will follow the FCRA (FCRA Section 604). Prior to supplying a background report, an employer must certify to the background screening firm that the employer will follow all the steps set forth in the FCRA. These include:

   a. That the employer will use the information for employment purposes only.

   b. That the employer will not use the information in violation of any federal or state equal opportunity law.

   c. That the employer will obtain all the necessary disclosures and consents as discussed below.

   d. That the employer will give the appropriate notices in the event that an adverse action is taken against an applicant based in whole or in part on the contents of the Consumer Report.

   e. That if a special type of consumer report is requested, called an Investigative Consumer Report, the employer will give the additional information required by law.

2. An employer must obtain a written authorization & release and a separate disclosure from a job applicant before obtaining a background report (FCRA Sections 604 and 606). Before obtaining a background report from a background screening firm, the employer must obtain two separate documents:

   a. There must be a clear and conspicuous language informing the applicant that a background report may be requested. This must be provided in a "separate document" other than just in your employment application; although we suggest that you include language there as well.

   b. The employer must obtain written consent from the applicant.

      i. Release and disclosure can be in the same document, as long as the language does not distract from a clear and conspicuous disclosure or obscure the message that a report is being requested. The fact that a report is being requested must be absolutely clear.

ii. You should be aware that if you request a background screening firm to obtain employment references and it goes beyond merely verifying factual matters, such as the dates of employment or salary, and involves asking for information such as job performance, then that falls into a special category of consumer report called an Investigative Consumer Report.

The following procedures must be followed for this type of report:

(1) You must clearly disclose to the applicant that an Investigative Consumer Report is being requested. This information can be included in the initial disclosure, or the consumer must receive this additional disclosure within three days after the request is made.

(2) The disclosure must tell the applicant that they have a right to request additional information about the nature of the investigation.

(3) If the applicant makes a written request, then the employer has five days to respond with additional information and must provide a copy of a document prepared by the Federal Trade Commission called, "A Summary of Your Rights Under the Fair Credit Reporting Act."

3. If adverse action is intended as a result of a background or consumer report, the applicant is entitled to certain documents (FCRA Section 604). If an employer receives a background or consumer report, and based upon information contained in the report decides to take an adverse action such as not hiring the applicant, the applicant has certain rights. It is important to note that if the decision to not hire the applicant was in whole or part based on the background or consumer report, the applicant has a right to receive that report. Before taking the adverse action, the employer must provide the following information to the applicant:

a. A copy of the background report.

b. The FTC document "A Summary of Your Rights Under the Fair Credit Reporting Act."

c. The purpose is to give an applicant the opportunity to see the information or report that is being used to make a decision not to hire him or her. This provides an opportunity for the applicant to contact the employer and the background screening firm to dispute the information or to explain inaccurate or incomplete information.

d. With regards to how much time should be given to an applicant to clear up alleged mistakes or inaccurate information, the FCRA is silent on this point.

4. Notice must be given to an applicant after an adverse action (FCRA section 615). If after sending out the documents required in Step 3, the employer makes a final decision, the employer must send the applicant a Notice of Adverse Action informing the job applicant that the employer has made a final decision, along with another copy of the FTC form "Summary of Your Rights Under the Fair Credit Reporting Act."

The next step is to designate the department that is responsible for managing this activity. Some of the key points to consider in making this decision involve evaluating the following:

Table 6-3 provides a "point-counterpoint" discussion.

Table 6-3 Point-Counterpoint

Which organization function should be responsible for background screening?	
Security	**Human Resources**
Security departments', specifically corporate security departments, scope of responsibility has changed to overall security posture within an organization. This has been continually demonstrated by the emergence of the corporate security officer (CSO) who is responsible for all security-related activity in a business.	Background screening is part of the hiring process, which in turn is part of normal operations in HR. Thus, HR is best suited to integrate it into the overall employment and hiring process.
Security departments normally have a different perspective regarding risk in a business and usually take a more conservative approach to risk-taking.	• Aspects of the background screening process need to be integrated into the hiring process: Offer letters (offer contingent on satisfactory results from background screening) • Employment application (permission to check background and ground for dismissal for misrepresentation) • Authorization forms handed out with employment application
Security has a working knowledge of criminal statutes and conviction information. The security officials can efficiently determine the severity of the offense and determine overall risk to the business.	
Security departments often are not susceptible to hiring pressure from Operations. They are much more likely to have a narrower interpretation of policy.	HR already maintains confidentiality in many of its dealings with employee information so this will fit right in with that process.
Security personnel are skilled in interviewing and determining deception.	HR maintains employee records and already has processes in place to comply with record retention and data destruction laws.
If the day-to-day hiring motion is "owned" by HR, security could be integrated into the approval process once the background check is completed. Most HRIS networks can accommodate multi-departmental review of candidates.	HR already has expertise in handling employee relation situations, thus if there is an adverse action necessary, HR is trained in how to handle it. Employees are accustomed to using HR for employment-related procedures.
Security personnel are much more familiar with criminal record interpretation, which varies from state to state and in the federal courts. These staff members are more adept at uncovering resume fraud schemes. If HR "owns" hiring, security "owns" security risk. Both have a role in background checking since the security department inherits the results of a bad hire. Proactive reviews of hires by an objective party like security will avoid costly terminations and hiring miscues of risky individuals.	Background screening data is easily integrated into HRIS for one-place access, improved security, and control. HR is already familiar with basic requirements of background screening, thus minimal training is necessary. HR is already equipped with the capability to handle potential questions and legal issues that may arise regarding discrimination, privacy, data destruction, investigations, etc.
At a minimum, security should be consulted in formulating policy and process.	

(Continued)

Table 6-3 Point-Counterpoint—Cont'd

| | HR already involved in getting hiring forecasts, which is built into the staff allocation process. |
| | HR is knowledgeable in creating job descriptions which "sensitive jobs" essential requirements should be integrated into. |

Conclusion

The authors believe that while there are clear and distinct advantages to assigning the responsibility for background screening to the HR department, the best situation is to forge a partnership between security and HR. Both have an expertise that is needed to make the background screening activity as successful as it can be. Security professionals, who generally have a law enforcement background or connection, have access to an information network and resources that are foreign to or not accessible to most HR professionals. Likewise, HR professionals have considerable expertise in skills assessment and the selection process, which is essential to hiring people who will "fit" in the organization. Some companies have set up background screening review committees that are composed of HR and security managers, along with legal counsel. This committee reviews any borderline cases where operations management may want to hire a candidate that has a questionable background. In addition, these committees provide oversight to the identification and revision of "sensitive jobs." Successful background screening operations have learned to maximize both of these areas of expertise to improve the hiring process and provide a secure work environment.

Once the department decision is made, you will then need to determine how much staff is needed. To a great extent, this will depend on the anticipated level of hiring activity, factoring in the average work time involved in conducting a background check, training time, the desired turnaround time, time off, and desired applied time. You will also need to determine if you are going to have a specialist who will focus on conducting background screening or if these duties will be incorporated into an existing job, such as a recruiting assistant or other support staff. A key factor in making this decision will be the anticipated volume and the size of your operation. Even in a small company, which by necessity will have combined positions, we highly recommend that you go the specialist route. This will allow an employee to become fully competent in the legal requirements and nuances associated with conducting background checks. Choose someone who has great attention to detail and make sure they document procedure and keep detailed records on each case.

Please note that with internal staff performing these activities, you will also have to forecast openings, staff development, performance reviews, and other management-related activities.

Next you will have to define the training requirements, frequency of training, and timing to ensure that staff is fully competent. New staff should be fully trained before they start conducting background checks, which means they need to receive training immediately upon starting work. You should also have annual follow-up training that includes updates and new information. Online training is a very good solution for this type follow-up training because it can include interactive exercises and assessments to test and reinforce knowledge acquisition. The training content should match the training defined in the coverage of outsourcing the background screening activity above. Note that staff will have to have a thorough knowledge of your background screening policy because not only will they need to apply it in every aspect of their background screening role but also because they will be called upon for "expert" input.

In the final analysis, we clearly understand that each company must make the decision for itself regarding whether to conduct background screening with internal staff or to outsource this functionality based on its unique business circumstances. Not withstanding this understanding, in general we believe that outsourcing background screening offers many advantages over doing it in-house.

We believe that outsourcing offers these advantages:

- You do not have to be concerned about staffing an operation and the associated responsibilities that go along with this, e.g., managing, hiring, employee relations, performance reviews, etc.
- You can focus your internal staff on more strategic tasks central to the core mission of your business.
- You can focus on measuring performance and quality of services based on a contractual agreement and relationship.
- Your cost will be based on usage, meaning you will not be paying for downtime or slow activity periods.
- You avoid ongoing overhead costs such as salaries, benefits, training, administrative, facilities, etc.
- Your chance of legal liability decreases significantly.

Summary

In this chapter we have presented the essential factors to consider in setting up an internal background screening operation or to select an outside firm specializing in this area. This is a unique decision to each firm, and there are successful models operating both with internal background screening operations and external firms. As we mentioned earlier in the chapter a majority of firms have chosen to outsource their background screening work and likewise most firms assign the responsibility for this function to the HR department. Beyond the in-house or outsource decision, we believe it is paramount that your business understands the serious impact that implementing an effective background screening operation can have on the quality of hires your firm makes. And, as I am sure you are aware, the life blood of any organization is the quality of the people it hires.

The New Focus on Protecting Personal Identifiable Information

The focus of this chapter is on protecting the information that is gathered during the background screening process. Background screening is a critical tool for organizations to deploy in the fight against workplace violence, employee fraud, sabotage, terrorism, as well as information, identity, and property theft that are plaguing them today. Unfortunately, along with background screening comes the burden and responsibility to protect the information that is collected. With this focus in mind, we believe that to have a background screening program that operates at maximum effectiveness it must be part of a larger business strategy that is focused on protecting the organization's resources.

We believe that *resource protection* is the next evolution of *loss prevention*. Loss prevention is a well-developed discipline within the security field that has emerged as a crucial function in the fight to protect organizations' resources and assets. It is our belief that in addition to the spotlight now being focused on the importance of the field of loss prevention, this discipline may be on the verge of a new paradigm forming that focuses on resource protection.

As is true with any new way of viewing something, the beginning stages are the hardest because it is when the most storms occur between those who want to hold onto the current view of the world versus those who are embracing a new calling. We believe that resource protection better embraces the strategic nature and forward thinking that is necessary for the rapidly changing, instant response-demand, technology-based, and dispersed organizations of the future. One significant difference is that resource protection starts at the strategy level, meaning that for an organization to succeed at truly protecting its resources, it must incorporate strategies designed to accomplish this as part of business strategies when they are conceived. We have seen increasingly over the past several years a loss prevention plan attached onto an existing business strategy implemented as a band aid approach that has contributed to data breaches, fraud, and property losses.

The time has come for security management to move beyond simply focusing on creating incremental improvement in loss prevention to implementing a new way to address this problem that will produce quantum improvement in the overall protection of their organizations' resources. The resource protection approach embraces the Enterprise Risk Management concept proposed by the Committee of Sponsoring Organizations (COSO) of the Treadway Commission. Enterprise risk management provides a comprehensive way for organizations to avoid surprises (resource loss) by assuming that every risk can be avoided, accepted, reduced, or shared. It is the responsibility of the leadership of the organization to determine the risk tolerance associated with each major business strategy, which will subsequently define the resource protection strategy. Note that oversight for COSO is made up of the following organizations:

- American Accounting Association
- American Institute of Certified Public Accountants
- Financial Executives International
- Institute of Management Accountants
- The Institute of Internal Auditors

Signs That the Current Approach is Not Working
Identity Theft

Identity theft has been intruding into individuals' lives for a number of years; however, it took a tipping point event such as identity thieves stealing sensitive information about thousands of consumers from ChoicePoint Inc. to catapult the issue into a national business issue. While the ChoicePoint Inc. situation made the issue of data protection a problem for companies across the board, it particularly focused attention on data protection in the background screening process. Although the media made very little distinction in its portrayal of the ChoicePoint Inc. breach situation, the reality is that the data breach actually occurred in the Public Records division of the company, which does not provide background screening information. (In Appendix F, read the National Association of Professional Background Screeners disclosure about this situation.)

In 2005, which has been dubbed the "year of the data breach," the nonprofit Identify Theft Resource Center reported 158 incidents of large data breaches at companies, universities, and government organizations.

Unfortunately, "We are not seeing the change in behaviors (by organizations) as rapidly as we would have thought because the numbers are not going down," said Linda Foley, Executive Director of the San Diego based Identify Theft Resource Center.[1] The number of breaches in 2006 reached over 303, which dramatically illustrates her point. Overall, the Identity Theft Resource Center has reported that in 2006 more than 18.8 million individuals were affected by data breaches.

Some of the more noteworthy events included the following:

- CardSystems Solutions Inc.—disclosed that 40 million records had been breached when hackers infiltrated computers at a credit card processing center.
- DSW Shoe Warehouse—disclosed that 1.4 million records were hacked, exposing a database of customers and credit card numbers.
- Bank of America—disclosed that computer tapes containing personal information for credit cards used by federal employees were lost and they contained 1.2 million records.
- AT&T—hackers gained access to an AT&T computer system and stole credit card information and other personal data from thousands of customers of one of the company's online stores.

---

[1]   Data Theft Growing in Scope and Cost, Experts Say, *The Orange County Register*, January 2, 2007.

- Time Warner—announced that tapes containing personal information on about 600,000 current and former U.S.-based employees had been lost by Iron Mountain Inc, a Boston-based records management and storage firm.
- Marriott International Inc.—discovered that the personal data of 200,000 people was missing after a backup tape went missing from a Florida office. The tapes contained Social Security numbers, bank, and credit card numbers.
- Ameriprise Financial Inc.—had a laptop stolen that contained personal information on 158,000 customers and 68,000 financial advisers.
- Honeywell International—suffered a breach when 19,000 current and former employees' personal information was posted on an Internet Website.

Millions of people are affected by incidents of lost or stolen personal data at federal government agencies. Most of the 800 incidents of data losses that have occurred since 2003 have never been publicly reported. There was a not-so-surprising revelation that the vast majority of these incidents were not accidental misplacements but rather outright thefts of computers or data disks containing sensitive information.

Some of the more noteworthy events included the following:

- A laptop stolen from the home of a Department of Veteran Affairs employee contained the names, birthdates, and Social Security numbers of 26.5 million veterans.
- A hole in the Chicago Board of Elections' Website was discovered that exposes Social Security numbers and dates of birth of more than 1 million voters.
- UCLA disclosed that a database containing the personal information of some 800,000 students had been breached.
- A contractor for the Agriculture Department inadvertently released the Social Security and tax identification numbers of about 350,000 tobacco farmers and landowners in response to a public information request.
- The Defense Department lost a portable data drive that included personnel records of more than 200,000 marines who served from 2001 to 2005.
- Identity thieves used a Hamilton County, Ohio, Website to steal the Social Security numbers and other personal data of hundreds of Ohio residents.
- A hacker gained access to names, Social Security numbers, and other details on 106,000 University of Texas at Austin students, faculty, and alumni.
- A laptop containing personal information of more than 133,000 Floridians with driver's and pilot's licenses was stolen from a government vehicle.
- A hacker gained access to computer databases containing Social Security numbers and other information on 64,000 current and former students and faculty members at the University of Texas at San Antonio.

Educause released results of a survey indicating that about a quarter of 400 colleges said that over the previous 12 months, they had experienced a security incident in which confidential information was compromised.[2] It should also be noted that this is not just a U.S. problem. One of Canada's major credit reporting agencies, Equifax Canada Inc., had a serious breach in its Montreal office where an employee stole 2000 consumer files. In addition, experts say white collar crime and identity theft are on the increase in South

---

[2] http://www.latimes.com/technology/la-me-ucla12dec12,0,5352062.story?page=2&track=rss

Africa, and it is costing the economy in excess of R 40-billion a year. A recent example reported by *Engineering News of New Zealand* is a glaring example: A 29-year-old alleged fraudster claimed at different times to have been a dentist, chartered accountant, chef, doctor, and cell phone company executive. Many experts are starting to state that identify theft may be the fastest growing crime worldwide.

While the above information certainly illustrates the seriousness and pervasiveness of the problem of identity theft for businesses, unfortunately there are more issues beyond this that security professionals must deal with in these tumultuous times.

Employee Fraud

The Association of Certified Fraud Examiners (ACFE) released a study this year of 1134 occupational fraud cases investigated from January 2004 to January 2006. In addition, according to a study conducted by the Ipsos Reid Corporation for Ernst and Young, the average employer spends about $1500 on office supplies due to loss from theft. The same report goes on to state the cost can even triple if upper-level management are the ones responsible for the theft. All in all, those pads of papers, Post-Its, and pens going home with employees cost the average business at least $19,000 per year.

The Ipsos Reid report indicated the following statistics associated with different types of workplace fraud as reported in their survey:

- 37% Theft of office supplies
- 18% Claiming extra hours worked
- 13% Stealing product/money
- 12% Pocketing money from cash sales
- 8% Inflating expense accounts
- 2% "Cooking the books"
- 6% Kickbacks
- 2% Improper use of company vehicle
- 1% Creating phony invoices
- 21% Workers aware of fraud in their workplaces

Some noteworthy examples of employee fraud are listed below:

- A bookkeeper at the Center for Hematology has been accused of misappropriating money from the Center for Hematology in Boca Raton for a total of $6 million.
- A project consultant for a construction and development company pleaded guilty to stealing about $600,000 from her employer.
- Mutual fund shareholder accounts at the Principal Financial Group were drained of some $167,000, and a former employee of the company has been charged with theft.
- A bookkeeper at BHD Corp., a North Palm Beach based home builder, made out more than 100 checks to herself, spending thousands of dollars on dog clothing, doll collections, and jewelry. The company's losses forced it to lay off 20 employees.
- Sharon Kay Smith, 47, formerly of North Palm Beach, was charged in May with writing more than 400 checks totaling $402,817 on the account of Quality

Swimming in Boca Raton to herself and her own company. Smith was a bookkeeper for 8 years at the swim lessons company. Her case is pending.

- An attorney's assistant was busted and charged with transferring money from attorney Cari Podesta's office trust account to her own bank account. The former assistant pleaded guilty to grand theft, admitting that she took $241,000 from her boss.

- A patient coordinator was charged with embezzling $99,245 from a Boca Raton plastic surgeon's office where she worked for 2 years. She told police that she also stole $3,153 from her next employer, a dental clinic.[3]

Property Theft

According to the National Retail Federation, retail crime losses reached a record high of $37.4 billion nationally in 2005, and the biggest crime category is internal theft, which accounts for 47% of the incidents.

Accidental Leaks and Sabotage

Of the respondents to a survey conducted by Ponemon Institute on insider threats, 61% indicated that accidental data leaks occur "frequently" or "very frequently" because employees or contractors lack sufficient knowledge about preventative measures or because employees or contractors are careless. In addition, almost half of respondents, or 48%, claimed that corporate sabotage, such as the deliberate destruction of information technology equipment, occurs "frequently" or "very frequently" because employees or contractors are malicious or disgruntled.

At the far end of the continuum of sabotage is the spectrum of workplace violence or, even worse, terrorism.

While these situations are rare, the reality is that they are occurring and, as our society and business community continue to be more focused on information technology, it is likely that we will see more "malicious" attacks of this nature. On January 16, 2007, Homeland Security Secretary Michael Chertoff focused attention on possible terrorist threats when he asked business leaders to explore the insider threat to critical infrastructure systems to identify "sleepers who could be the source of the threats." The private sector controls about 85% of the nation's water, energy, transportation, and other critical infrastructure.

The following are a few real-life examples of saboteurs from the "Insider Threat Study: Computer System Sabotage in Critical Infrastructure Sectors" that illustrate the serious nature of these threats to the business community:

- A system administrator, angered by his diminished role in a thriving defense manufacturing firm whose computer network he alone had developed and managed, centralized the software that supported the company's manufacturing

---

[3] Embezzling on the Rise ... With Women at Front of Curve? Embezzlement by Women Skyrockets; No Longer Just a Man's Crime, Larry Keller, *Palm Beach Post* Staff Writer, *Palm Beach Post* (Florida), December 4, 2006.

processes on a single server, and then intimidated a coworker into giving him the only backup tapes for that software. Following the system administrator's termination for inappropriate and abusive treatment of his coworkers, a logic bomb previously planted by the insider detonated, deleting the only remaining copy of the critical software from the company's server. The company estimated the cost of damage in excess of $10 million, which led to the layoff of some 80 employees.

- An application developer, who lost his information technology sector job as a result of company downsizing, expressed his displeasure at being laid off just prior to the Christmas holidays by launching a systematic attack on his former employer's computer network. Three weeks following his termination, the insider used the username and password of one of his former coworkers to gain remote access to the network and modify several of the company's Web pages, changing text and inserting pornographic images. He also sent each of the company's customers an email message advising that the Website had been hacked. Each email message also contained that customer's usernames and passwords for the Website. An investigation was initiated, but it failed to identify the insider as the perpetrator. A month and a half later, he again remotely accessed the network, executed a script to reset all network passwords, and changed 4000 pricing records to reflect bogus information. This former employee ultimately was identified as the perpetrator and prosecuted. He was sentenced to serve 5 months in prison and 2 years on supervised probation and ordered to pay $48,600 restitution to his former employer.

- A city government employee who was passed over for promotion to finance director retaliated by deleting files from his and a coworker's computers the day before the new finance director took office. An investigation identified the disgruntled employee as the perpetrator of the incident. City government officials disagreed with the primary police detective on the case as to whether all of the deleted files were recovered. No criminal charges were filed and, under an agreement with city officials, the employee was allowed to resign.

The Impact of These Calamities on Organizations

The ACFE reported that the average business loses the equivalent of 6% of revenue to fraud each year. The fraud examiner's study found that small companies endure disproportionate losses from embezzlements. The median loss at firms with fewer than 100 employees was $190,000 per scheme, compared to $159,000 overall, the study concluded.

In addition, the findings of the Ponemon Data Breach Study indicated that information losses cost U.S. companies an average of $182 per compromised record in 2006, compared to an average loss of $138 per record in 2005, for an increase of about 31%. The report, which is based on interviews held with 56 individual companies known to have experienced a data loss in the last year, maintains that roughly $128 of the 2006 figure is related to indirect fallout from information leaks, such as higher-than-normal customer turnover. Other associated costs spurred by data mishandlings or thefts were an average price tag of $660,000 per company in expenses related to notifying customers, business partners, and regulators about data leaks. Ponemon contends that each company surveyed sacrificed roughly $2.5 million in lost business because of data leaks. Companies in the study paid almost $300,000 on average for other efforts aimed at responding to record losses, such as setting up customer support hotlines or offering credit monitoring services to help protect against related fraud. "The burdens companies must bear as a result of a data breach are significant, making a strong case for more strategic investments in preventative measures," said Dr. Larry Ponemon, Chairman of Ponemon Institute.

In addition to the very tangible financial losses identified above there is another huge risk. In a survey of CEOs conducted by *The Economist* entitled "Reputation: Risk of Risks," The Global Risk Briefing sponsored by Ace, Cisco Systems, Deutsche Bank, IBM and KPMG, December 2005, *reputation* was identified as the most significant risk threat to business, with 84 percent of respondents noting that risks to their company's reputation had increased significantly.

Along with the reputation issue comes the issue of trust that an organization has from its customer, vendors, employees, and community. A study conducted by Unisys indicated that many business leaders do not trust their own companies to secure or manage sensitive information. Mike Gibbons, Vice President and General Manager, Enterprise Security, Unisys[4] stated "... given how devastating a breach of trust is to a company's reputation and bottom line" he was very "concerned with the lack of preparedness among business leaders to monitor and protect the trust their companies had built over the years." This suggests that there is a vacuum in leadership in addressing this important issue.

What Should be Done to Fix the Problem?

First and foremost, we believe a significant contributor to the escalation of data breaches, fraud, and employee theft has to do with the piece meal and patchwork approach that has been taken to prevent loss. Add to this separate silo approaches to informational and physical security and you have a formula for disaster, which is exactly what we have on our hands. It appears that many organizations have accepted that the 5% to 7% estimated loss from fraud is a given and they have built this into their business plans. We believe a more enlightened approach would be for the leadership of organizations to decide to invest at least half of the cost of this 5% to 7% annual net drain on company profits to develop an enterprise approach to resource protection. This would mean once the plan was implemented, the ROI on the program would be realized in a relatively short time period of several years, which would be a pittance to significantly reduce the 5% to 7% loss level down to around 1% or 2%.

We recognize that an enterprise resource protection approach is a major undertaking for an organization. We also believe the time has come for senior management in organizations to move their thinking from the view that data protection is a security strategy to understanding that securing data is a business strategy that is focused on creating competitive advantage. It contributes to the creation of unique value for your customers. As referenced earlier in a Ponemon Lost Customer Information study in 2005, the marketplace has demonstrated the reality that businesses suffer greater breach incident impact from lost customer confidence and business than what the actual breach itself costs. The survey revealed that:

- 20% of people said they immediately closed their accounts or stopped doing business with the company.
- Companies reported the percentages of all customers lost following incidents ranged from 2.5% to 11%.

---

[4]   Unisys Trusted Enterprise Index Reveals Major Gaps in Maintenance of Security and Privacy; IT and Business Leaders Disagree on Top Attributes for Building and Eroding Trust; Most and Least Trusted Industries Identified, Ponemon Institute, September, 2006.

Another study released in December 2005, conducted in Canada by Leger Marketing and sponsored by Sun Microsystems of Canada, showed 58% of consumers said they would immediately stop doing business with a company that experienced a breach that put their personal information in jeopardy.

These data illustrate that firms that experience significant data breaches lose customers. The marketplace is telling us that they want to do business with companies that have a commitment to securing their data and security can play a significant role in helping to develop a strategy that will help avoid data breaches being a reason for losing customers.

One contributing factor may be that no one in a company has really been put in charge of privacy and data protection with the responsibility to address the issue across the enterprise. Interestingly enough, despite a continuous flow of breaches, negative press, and millions of records being lost, 70% of recently surveyed companies indicated that their organizations had no privacy department. In addition, 75% did not have a chief privacy officer in place to manage the tricky and complex issues associated with employee privacy.[5] "Emerging technologies, such as those associated with electronic monitoring of employees and the storage and access of personal information have brought the issue of privacy to the forefront. It's surprising to see that more organizations are not formalizing their policies and procedures. There are not a lot of guidelines in place for organizations, and we need to take these issues out of the shadows and tackle them head on in a way that ensures privacy of the individual and privacy of the corporation at all levels," says Jay Jamrog, Senior Vice President, Research at Institute for Corporate Productivity.[5] Of the 70% of organizations without a privacy department, 53.8% said human resources (HR) oversaw privacy compliance, while 23.9% said it was the legal department's responsibility. Almost 5% said compliance fell under security, and 17.7% indicated "other," which included information technology, corporate auditing, and records management. A significant move in this direction is for an organization to put a senior manager in charge of privacy and resource protection for the enterprise. Some organizations have gone as far as to create a chief privacy officer. The way in which organizations choose to put resource protection on the table at the senior management level will surely vary; however, the key issue is that someone has to be responsible for this endeavor across the enterprise. This issue is very similar to supply chain management, which not too long ago was scattered all over the organization; however, more organizations today have recognized the power of putting a senior manager in charge of harnessing this issue across the enterprise and to keep a high level focus on it. The $10 million ChoicePoint settlement should be a wakeup call that this is a business competitiveness issue and it is time to give it the focus, resources, and effort necessary.

While we believe there is strong upside potential for significant results from an enterprise approach, we also know that this type of undertaking is not a quick fix, which means operational security measures must still be taken in the interim.

Organizational Security

Here are some the measures that can be taken now that will move organizations closer to creating a secure data protection environment.

---

[5]   The Institute for Corporate Productivity (i4cp; formerly HRI), in conjunction with HR.com, conducted the Employee Privacy Practitioner Consensus Survey in January 2007. A total of 145 organizations participated.

Data Protection

In line with the Enterprise Resource Protection approach, "Employers should think of their personal employee data as they do their money, intellectual property, or trade secrets," says Gary Clayton, CEO of the Privacy Council, a division of Jefferson Data Strategies LLC, in Dallas.[6] This mindset will lead to a higher-level strategic focus on planning how to protect the important resources of the organization.

Flowing from this strategic focus should be a complete understanding of the internal and external processes and data flows that involve personal employee information. Employers must understand the business processes from collection through disposal, as well as the company's legal obligations.[7]

In other words, organizations must understand the life cycle of the data at each point and review the risks, exposures, and legal requirements. When considering the life cycle of employee records, there are a number of focus areas that must be paid attention beyond the information that is being stored or disposed of.

Organizations must also pay attention to:

- Appropriate means of classifying the information—Is it sensitive information?
- Tracking the information—Where is it? Is it in storage or in motion?
- Access control—Who has permission to access the information? What are the protocols for accessing the information and an audit trail of who has actually accessed the information?
- Legal requirements.

Actions That Can Be Taken to Protect Data at Each Phase During Its Life Cycle

Although most survey data indicate that there has been a significant increase in the number of organizations that are conducting background checks, it is a sad commentary that one of the key insights from an in-depth analysis of actual insider data breach situations identified a lack of conducting background checks as a key problem. Clearly, there are organizations that have not gotten the message. In the research conducted by Defense Security Research Center entitled *Ten Tales of Betrayal: The Threat to Corporate Infrastructures by Information Technology Insiders Analysis and Observations*, (Shaw, Eric D. Fischer, Lynn F., Sept 2005) no basic background checks were completed on any of the subjects as the they were hired.

—*Nancy Mross*

Table 7-1 discusses personnel screening issues by case.

---

[6]   Safeguarding HR Information, Dan Caterinicchia, *HR Magazine*, 2006.

[7]   Safeguarding HR Information, Dan Caterinicchia, *HR Magazine*, 2006.

Table 7-1 Personnel Screening Issues by Case

Subject and Victimized Organization	Screening/Selection Problem	Prior Known Offenses or Undetected Risk Factors	Tracking Problem
The Crasher	Referred by brother, professor, no background check	No	No
The Data Destroyer	No background check	Multiple prior offenses: forgery, grand larceny, disorderly conduct	Yes
The Hacker	No background check, prior conviction	Published hacker	Yes
The Intruder	No background check	No	No
The Time Bomber	No background check	No	No
The Extortionist	N/A (overseas client)	No	No
The Saboteur	Delayed background check	Prior hacking, extortion	Yes
The Thief	No background check, recommended by brother	Published hacker	No
The Attacker	No background check	Yes (juvenile)	No
The Manipulator	Hired by father, no background check	No	No

Source: Defense Security Research Center, *Ten Tales of Betrayal: The Threat to Corporate Infrastructures by Information Technology Insiders Analysis and Observations.*

Data Input

One of the most important rules to understand about collecting data is that you should only collect data that you need and only at the time when you need it. Keep in mind that the earlier you collect information, the longer the time period is that you are likely going to need to protect it. According to Linda Foley, co-founder of the Identity Theft Resource Center (ITRC), "too much information is being collected at the wrong period of time." According to Linda, "you don't need a Social Security number until you're going to do a background check and potentially offer them the job." Taking a minimalist approach will help reduce the risk and better use the organization's resources.

Accordingly, employers should look very closely at the personal information they ask job applicants and employees to provide and when they ask them to provide it. For example, at what point in your hiring process should an applicant complete your employment application form? From a data protection viewpoint the response would be, only at the point when we need it, which would likely be at the point where we have determined that the person is a serious contender for the position and we are preparing to conduct a background check. While there may be legitimate reasons to have the application completed before this phase, keep in mind that once we collect the information we must protect it. The days of "while we have him/her here, let's get all the information we are going to need" may be over.

Once the data have been collected, it is important to classify it as sensitive or not because the way we protect these two sets of information will be very different.

We also need to give some forethought to the implications of the form in which we receive data. Paper documents require much more space for storage, which translates into facility cost, and physical security measures will be needed to protect them. While electronic data can be stored much more efficiently, it requires information technology security measures to protect it.

The decision regarding form will vary by organization based on numerous factors. The important point is to determine the direction you want to go so that all of your actions support that direction. For example, if you choose to move in the electronic form direction, you should advise job applicants that you will only accept electronic resumes and you should establish an electronic employment application.

Storing Data

One of the key first steps that businesses need to take to protect sensitive information is to establish a strong access control process. This starts with identifying who will have access to sensitive information and to what degree. A classification system that is appropriate for the organization and individual positions must be developed that controls the access to information. The process needs to be based on the responsibilities associated with each position in the organization as well as the "need to know" principle and not simply tied to a department. For example, not every employee in the security department would be granted access to highly sensitive information unless there is a need for that specific position to use the information in conducting their job duties. Temporary employees should be prohibited from gaining access to such information regardless of their position.

The organization needs to undertake a careful examination of the information that is actually needed to carry out the responsibilities of each position. For example, does a supervisor really need personal identifiable information on file about employees who report to him? Beyond knowing the person's name, what bearing does the person's address, marriage status, number of family members, Social Security number, date of birth, drivers license, etc. have on his ability to effectively supervise the person? Keep in mind that the focus needs to move to "need to know" and impact on ability to perform the job. Think about it. Does a supervisor of truck drivers who needs to assign someone to a route that requires a specific level of commercial driving license need to have this information in their own file? Or could he easily retrieve this information from a self-service HR center or an electronic system that has been established to respond to this type inquiry. The risk of having all kind of information lying around because we might need it some day may be a thing of the past and give way to secure retrieval processes.

Increasingly, we are likely to see more information and documents put in electronic formats, which will facilitate the use of electronic access controls. This is the world of information technology solutions such as passwords, firewalls, intrusion detection devices, encryption, etc. It is also highly likely that the advances in identity verification and authentication will aid in this process as well.

Firms should apply many of the advances in physical access control to this process. For example, there are automated access control systems that use biometrics for individuals seeking access to a facility. The system is linked to a background screening system, which will instantly identify if the person has a criminal history. This type of system could easily be applied to current employees seeking to access sensitive information. While this approach may have many merits and the capability to ferret out people with a questionable past, it will not be able to identify the person who is stealing information or committing fraud for the first time or who does not have a criminal record. This means that organizations will have to devise multiple approaches to reduce the risk of unauthorized individuals accessing sensitive information.

To secure electronic data that are being stored, the date should be encrypted as much as possible. Encryption translates the data into a secret code that can be unlocked only by using a key or password. The current industry standard is 128-bit encryption and a commercial tool at that level based on standard cryptographic algorithms—namely, Advanced Encryption Standard, Triple Data Encryption, or Blowfish.[8]

Organizations that have business continuity plans that call for offsite storage should also take measures to ensure backup media is encrypted to prevent unauthorized individuals from accessing information if backup media is lost, stolen, or misplaced. The need for encryption of backup data should be considered by large, medium-sized, and small businesses. In addition, because many entities use contractors and other business associates, proof that backup data are securely protected must be provided by these services.

Beyond the storage of data, an organization must also put processes in place to be able to track data as it moves through its life cycle and to secure it while it is being transmitted.

Tracking is concerned with knowing where the data actually are located and deploying appropriate protection while it is housed in a particular location and/or while it is in motion. This includes data that pass through a Web portal or company network. Charles Kolodgy, Research Director for Security Products at IDC, states that to keep such data secure, employers should require employees to sign onto company networks through a Secure Sockets Layer (SSL) connection. SSL uses a cryptographic system that uses two keys to encrypt data—a public key known to everyone and a private or secret key known only to the recipient of the message.[9]

In addition, Kolodgy says to consider Outbound Content Control (OCC) tools, which include blocking employee access to certain Websites but also can screen transmission of electronic messages for certain sensitive data patterns. For example, if a message has a nine-digit-number set in a message set in 3-2-4 sequence, such as Social Security numbers, an OCC tool can block that traffic without actually reading the message. Content monitoring and filtering technology not only provide employers with the means to control how their employees communicate but also gives them eyes into what sensitive data their employees are accessing and trying to send outside the network.[10]

The point is that just having great protection for data while it is stationary is not enough; you must also be able to protect it while it is in motion.

[8]   Safeguarding HR Information, Dan Caterinicchia, *HR Magazine,* 2006.

[9]   Safeguarding HR Information, Dan Caterinicchia, *HR Magazine,* 2006.

[10]   Misuse and Theft of Sensitive Data by Employees Creates New Security Compliance Market, StevensPublishing.com.

Data Destruction

Under the Fair and Accurate Credit Transaction Act of 2003 (FACTA) amendment to FCRA, organizations that maintain or otherwise possess consumer/applicant information derived from consumer reports are required to "take reasonable measures to protect against unauthorized access to, or use of, the information in connection with its disposal." While this may not be a difficult task to undertake for disposal and destruction of data in paper form, it is a much more challenging task with electronic media. At this point, experts say there is no foolproof system for destroying digital data so that they can no longer be accessed.

According to Rita L. Attebery of the Phoenix Group in the white paper *Proper Handling of Sensitive Consumer Information,* written for the National Association of Professional Background Screeners (NAPBS), the Federal Trade Commission (FTC) requires companies that maintain or otherwise possess consumer/applicant information derived from consumer reports to "take reasonable measures to protect against unauthorized access to, or use of, the information in connection with its disposal."

Section 216 of the FACTA requires the FTC to issue these disposal regulations in order to prevent sensitive financial and personal information from falling into the hands of identity thieves or others who might use the information for harmful purposes. The rule requires measures to be taken that would prevent unauthorized disclosure of consumer/applicant information and reduce the risk of fraud or related crimes by ensuring that records are appropriately redacted or destroyed before being discarded.

The "reasonable measures" standard may include:

- Burn, pulverize, or shred papers containing consumer report information so that the information cannot be read or reconstructed.
- Destroy or erase electronic files or media containing consumer report information so that the information cannot be read or reconstructed.
- Conduct due diligence and hire a document destruction contractor to dispose of material specifically identified by this rule.[11]

California businesses are required by law to destroy records containing personal information by shredding, erasing, or modifying the information to make it unreadable.

The flip side of data destruction is data retention requirements, which must also be given close attention. See Table 7-2 for information on data disposal and also see the section on Data Retention towards the end of this chapter for coverage of this issue.

Employee Fraud

Effective fraud management programs almost always provide significant cost savings. The ACFE estimates that U.S. companies receive a 7:1 return on preventative and detective antifraud programs.

Also, a lot of energy has been put into developing tools and methods for protecting firms' information from external sources and, while this is important given the rapid growth of internal breaches, firms' energies need to invest more in developing innovative approaches to address this growing problem.

---

[11] Larry D. Henry, Esq., Effects of 2003 Amendments to the Fair Credit Reporting Act, as presented to NAPBS National Conference, Scottsdale, AZ, March 29, 2004. 3 16 CFR Part 682 © 2004 Phoenix Group, Inc.

Table 7-2 FTC Disposal Rule for Credit Reports, Effective June 1, 2005

The FTC recently issued regulations governing proper disposal of consumer report information (the "Disposal Rule") under the FACTA. FACTA amends the FCRA. Effective June 1, 2005, the Disposal Rule is aimed at reducing the incidence of identity theft and related fraud by requiring businesses to properly dispose of the type of consumer report information regulated by the FRCA.

The Disposal Rule applies to every business, regardless of size or number of employees, that maintains or acquires "consumer report information" or information "derived from consumer reports." A "consumer report" as defined by the FCRA includes background reports that an employer receives from a credit reporting agency or similar third party vendor related to the character, general reputation, personal characteristics, mode of living, credit worthiness, credit standing, or credit capacity of an applicant or employee.

The Disposal Rule requires businesses to prevent unauthorized access to discarded consumer report information using "reasonable measures" such as burning, shredding or pulverizing of papers, erasing electronic media (*e.g.*, wiping hard drives), destroying electronic media (*e.g.*, smashing computer disks), and establishing "policies and procedures governing disposal, as well as appropriate employee training."

In the event a business contracts with an outside vendor to dispose of such records, it must exercise due diligence in choosing a reputable company and enter into a written contract that identifies papers and/or materials as consumer report information and requires compliance with the Disposal Rule.

Violations of the Disposal Rule could create significant legal exposure. Depending on the type of action brought (*i.e.*, individual or class action) and whether the violation was negligent or willful, the FCRA provides for a range of civil liabilities and penalties, including actual damages, statutory damages up to ,000 per violation, punitive damages, civil penalties up to $2,500 per violation, costs and reasonable attorneys' fees. We hope you find the above helpful. We would be happy to assist you in reviewing your current disposal practices and implementing enhanced disposal policies. Please feel free to contact David Weinstein at (312) 201-2685, Sherrie Travis at (312) 201-2198, or any other partner in our Employment and Labor Practice Group.

Source: *Client Bulletin, Employment and Labor Practice,* June 2005, published by Wildman, Harrold, Allen & Dixon LLP. Used with permission. Copyright 2005. Wildman, Harrold, Allen & Dixon LLP. All rights reserved. This publication should not be construed as legal advice or opinion on specific facts.

Donald Harris, President of HR Privacy Solutions LTD, states "organizations must think of personal employee data like a legally controlled substance."

It is impossible for a business to simply keep its information in a vault for protection because most jobs in the organization require constant use of information and access to it for very acceptable uses: salespeople must have company information with them to do their jobs, financial managers must have access to business performance information, HR must have access to sensitive information to properly evaluate personnel actions, and security must have access to sensitive information to conduct investigations or carry out other duties. So, part of the challenge that an organization is faced with is making the necessary information available to those that legitimately need it and keeping it out of the hands of those who have no need for it or, worse may have a malicious intent. This poses perhaps the biggest challenge for organizations because oftentimes it is the same people who have a legitimate need for the information to perform their jobs who also have malicious intent. And, because these individuals do not walk around with a neon sign saying "I intend to steal the organization's information today, embezzle funds from the organization, or misappropriate resources," the organization is faced with implementing other measures to address the potential threat.

Despite the reality that there is no shortage of information technology, solutions are being introduced to protect the organization's resources and, in fact, vendors are flooding the market with such offerings. However, the fact remains that technology is a tool that is meant to achieve established business objectives and goals and can never be a solution on its own. Business strategy drives technology, not the other way around. Just as is the case with implementing a new software application or security procedure, fully protecting data is still more about the process than technology tools.

The best defense against data loss is what it always has been—establishing clear business objectives, effectively communicating the desired outcomes, providing for two-way communication up and down the management chain, providing training, and developing, as well as implementing, an effective policy with clear procedures.

The first step in introducing a new business process is to be clear about the business objectives and goals that you want to achieve and to be sure that everyone in the organization understands the desired outcomes. Once the outcomes have been effectively communicated throughout the organization, it is necessary to define the roles and responsibilities of all parties. This includes defining "proper and improper use of the organization's resources." An example of this is identifying in an employee conduct policy that taking home a laptop or office supplies without authorization is considered theft. Being explicit and clear helps to avoid confusion and misinterpretation.

Defining what is acceptable use of resources (e.g., data, etc.) should be done very meticulously and individualized for specific organizational functions. Do yourself a favor and avoid the convenience trap of trying to come up with a one-size-fits-all "acceptable use" approach. It will only water down your effort because by definition it would have to be based on the lowest common denominator, which means you have started out compromising your security virtually before you get started. Think about it! In what other important areas of the business do we focus on meeting the minimal requirement?

The most effective approach for a business process as important as this is to form a cross-functional team to determine the right parameters for securing the organization's resources:

- Is it acceptable for the group in question to store customer data on their desktops?
- What if an employee's "desktop" is a laptop that leaves the building each night?
- How much customer data can employees carry out of the building and still comply with an acceptable use policy?
- Can users print lists of customers and/or prospects?
- What is the acceptable use of USB devices? Which customers do users have rights to access data for—should the northwest U.S. regional salesperson be downloading lists of European prospects?

These are the types of things you need to determine. It is not easy, but it is worth the effort in the long run.

Also, let me state emphatically that no "acceptable use" policy will ever cover every possible resource loss scenario. Rather, it is important to define guidelines and mandate that employees are trained to understand what behavior they should be looking out for, and what types of systemic weaknesses they should be bringing to management's attention. Provide clear direction on broad types of user actions that constitute risk and are outside acceptable use, and then give them a place to report this behavior. Help them understand that a user querying for customers that are not in his or her area of interest—like the "top 5 percent of revenue generators"—is a possible threat to the organization, and tell them who needs to know about this activity.

This leads to one of the other critical steps that historically organizations like to skimp on—training. It is important to thoroughly teach your employees what they may and may not do with data, teach them what is acceptable use, define risky behavior, and enforce the rules, when necessary. Employees must be taught loss-reducing strategies and how to watch for aberrant behavior. Once they understand the issues and how they can help, you may be surprised at how willing they are to avoid getting your company in the news for the wrong reasons.

Your official policy should make it clear the true cost to the company of a lost laptop or personal digital assistant. Help employees to understand that the more data there are on the laptop, the greater the risk is to the organization. If a user realizes that the hardware cost is the least of it, he may be less likely to leave his laptop unattended at a coffee shop or in an unlocked car. In today's regulatory environment, as the VA has shown, thefts must be reported as if each was a malicious attempt by identity thieves, even though it is often a teenager hoping to score a new laptop.

System owners do not want to be the source of a data leak; they'll help you resolve issues if you help them understand the level of threat. You're competing for limited resources, but the clearer the message; the more likely they are to respond positively.

One of the steps in implementing a new business process that is frequently overlooked is to make a conscious effort to find out whether the policies you've defined are seen as intrusive to any group's ability to perform its tasks and to fully explore perceived resistance. Oftentimes inside what is perceived as resistance is information that is key to improving the process and its implementation. Creating an environment where people are free to express their concerns and issues will make your process even stronger if you carefully listen to what is being communicated to you. Remember that history has taught us that users will find ways around your perceived intrusive policies that impede people's ability to do their job if they do not understand the rationale for your decisions.

Also keep in mind that you should be designing your policy for the 95% of employees who are willing to follow your policy and not for the 5% who are going to find a reason not to follow it or to work around it no matter how sound it is or how much you explain it. These are performance problems, not process design issues.[12]

Data Retention

According to the white paper by Rita L. Attebery of the Phoenix Group, many of the federal laws applicable to private sector employers have specific record retention requirements for employment records. Although the FTC has not specified a retention requirement for consumer/applicant records, the FCRA statute of limitations imposes a determination for the retention period for these records.[13]

Prior to FACTA, there was a strict 2-year statute of limitations period, beginning from the day of the report or other alleged violation of the FCRA, which barred the consumer/applicant from filing a claim if the suit was not filed within that 2-year period. Now, after FACTA, the applicant/employee has up to 2 years after the applicant/

---

[12]   http://www.networkcomputing.com/showArticle.jhtml?articleID=193003915
[13]   1 15 USC 1681p (618 of FCRA).

employee *discovers* the alleged violation to file a claim, but in no case can they file beyond 5 years. Formerly, the statute of limitations was extended only if the applicant/employee was misled by an entity that was required, under the law, to disclose the information to him/her.

A discovery date for the beginning of the statute of limitations is a soft date, especially if relying upon the applicant's memory. More than ever, it is important for organizations to keep good records of:

- Dates of reports
- Adverse action letters
- All contacts by the applicant
- All mailings to the applicant
- All emails
- Receipt of all disputes (Do not accept email disputes or requests for files.)
- Conclusion of each dispute process
- All reports/inquiry list given to applicant
- Fax logs
- Telephone logs
- Mail logs

Best practice suggests organizations keep consumer/applicant records for at least 6 years. The extra year should be sufficient to cover the processing time for a claim to be served and company lawyers to request information in defense of the suit; however, it may be helpful to keep records even longer. Courts generally will accept a company's records over the unsubstantiated statement of an applicant/employee, which can enhance the possibility of having the lawsuit dismissed in the initial motion in the case.[14] One final point that goes beyond the focus of protecting data for the purpose of maintaining privacy of the records and to prevent inappropriate access that is also important for security professionals to be knowledgeable about is the new.

Federal Rules of Civil Procedure on Electronic Discovery

In the article "Avoiding the Perils of Electronic Data" published in *HR Magazine*, Bill Roberts gives a great overview of this issue.

The unique challenges posed by maintaining and tracking such hidden electronic data require working with information technology staff, legal counsel, and business units to formulate an effective electronic data retention policy.

The need for such policies has never been greater. The proliferation of computers, networks, cell phones, digital voice recorders, digital cameras, personal digital assistants, flash drives, and every other manner of digital storage systems have accelerated its complexities.

What's more, lawyers have never been savvier about using electronic discovery, and computer forensic experts are more skillful at digging out damning details, including data users thought had been deleted or didn't know existed. And there have never been more electronic documents to mine.

---

[14] Larry Henry, Esq., Effects of 2003 Amendments to the Fair Credit Reporting Act, as presented to NAPBS National Conference, Scottsdale, AZ, March 29, 2004. © 2004 Phoenix Group, Inc. and Fair Credit Reporting Act & Background Checks: *Employer Best Practices White Paper, Proper Handling of Sensitive Consumer Information*, Rita L. Attebery, for NAPBS © 2004 Phoenix Group, Inc.

These trends are creating an important role for security in reducing the risks associated with the mismanagement of these digital files. In so doing, security can help reduce the risk of stiff sanctions, costly settlements, and public embarrassment for businesses.

In 2005, Cohasset Associates, the American Records Management Association, and AIIM International conducted a survey of 2054 professionals involved in records management; only 65% said their retention program covered electronic records. (This is in a world where 95% of documents are in electronic form and only 30% are ever committed to paper.)

Email is the biggest problem for most employers. According to the American Records Management Association from the Roberts article, only 34% of firms have email retention policies. "Email is still the No. 1 target in litigation," says Nelson. "Most smoking guns are found in email."

Some of the key issues that need to be addressed follow.

Hard Drives

Hard drives also present dangers that businesses should take very seriously. According to Bill Robert's information technology staff, routinely wipe a drive clean soon after an employee leaves, reformat it, and give it to a new worker, destroying potentially important hidden digital data. That can be a significant issue, as illustrated by the case of *Liggett v Rumsfeld*, 2005 WL 2099782 (E.D. Va. 2005).

> *In an action for employment discrimination on the basis of race and for unlawful retaliation, the plaintiff sought an adverse inference instruction for evidence spoliation. Specifically, the plaintiff claimed the DLA failed to preserve his computer hard drive. The DLA did not image the plaintiff's hard drive although it claimed the plaintiff had used the computer to view pornographic Websites. The court noted the DLA "should have preserved or 'imaged' the hard drive of [the plaintiff's] computer as evidence, however, DLA's failure to do so does not in and of itself suggest fraud or fabrication of evidence."[15]*
>
> *While the court dismissed the case for unrelated reasons, it issued a strongly worded ruling that the defendant should have preserved the hard drive data. The department was lucky; the court could have fined it for not keeping the electronic documents.*

To guard against such problems, experts now encourage companies to keep a mirror image of a hard drive used by any former employee who left under suspicious circumstances, threatened a lawsuit, had access to confidential information, or handled intellectual property or copyrighted material.

The Peril of Purging

The case of *Zubulake v UBS Warburg* established precedent on the following electronic discovery issues.

- The scope of a party's duty to preserve electronic evidence during the course of litigation
- Lawyer's duty to monitor their clients' compliance with electronic data preservation and production
- The imposition of sanctions for the spoliation (or destruction) of electronic evidence

---

[15]   Summary based on *Case Law Update and E-Discovery News*, October 2005, volume 5, issue 10.

During the case, parties discovered that certain backup tapes and emails were missing. The court found that the defendant had a duty to preserve the missing evidence, since it should have known that the emails may be relevant to future litigation and the courts wrote that "almost everyone associated with Zubulake recognized the possibility that she might sue." The court also found that the defendant failed to comply with its own retention policy, which would have preserved the missing evidence.

Further in the case, sanctions were issued against the employer for failing to produce backup tapes containing relevant emails and for failing to produce other relevant documents in a timely manner. The employer recovered some of the deleted relevant emails, however, some of the emails were never produced, including an email that pertained to a relevant conversation about the employee. The court determined that the employer had willfully deleted relevant emails despite contrary court orders. Additionally, the court declared that litigators must guarantee that identified relevant documents are preserved by placing a "litigation hold" on the documents, communicating the need to preserve them, and arranging for safeguarding of relevant archival media.[16] Roberts reiterated a key point that the court stated in the above case, "a litigation hold has long been an important concept in discovery. In blunt terms: once sued, you have to stop shredding documents. A party also has a responsibility to preserve evidence whenever a suit appears likely. The trigger could be the filing of the suit or something that was said or written months earlier suggesting the possibility of a suit. The minute the company faces litigation—or even the possibility of litigation—it should take steps not to purge electronic documents that might be evidence." The bottom line from the Zubulake case is the fact that many emails had been destroyed, the judge took the rare step of ruling "adverse inference"—telling the jury to assume that the defendant had purged the missing evidence because it would have hurt its case. The judge also levied expensive sanctions. UBS Warburg shelled out $29 million in penalties and damages."[17]

See Table 7-3 for some common sense actions that enhance the security of data.

All of the information covered above must be crafted into a comprehensive data security policy that addresses the protection of personal identifiable information, what it is, the importance of it to the organization, and the overall strategy to protect it. The policy should explain your code of ethics and conduct. It should also include specific rules regarding the use of office supplies, company equipment, return policies for terminated employees, and how sensitive data should be handled such as encryption on laptops, etc.

Because this policy will impact every function in the enterprise, it will require the input of a cross-functional team. Participation should include operational management along with the following disciplines or areas of expertise, legal counsel, security, HR, and subject-matter specialists, as needed. The leadership of the organization must set the tone for the creation and implementation of the policy by making it clear that the protection of personal information is important to the organization and that significant resources are being committed to protect it.

See an example of General Electric's Candidate Data Protection Standards Policy in Appendix F.

---

[16] The above summary of the *Zubulake v UBS Warburg* case is based on information presented by Kroll Ontrack, Legal Resource at http://www.krollontrack.co.uk/legalresources/zubulake.aspx

[17] Avoiding the Perils of Electronic Data, Bill Roberts, http://www.shrm.org/hrmagazine/articles/0107/0107roberts.asp

Table 7-3 Some Commonsense Actions That Should Be Taken to Enhance the Security of Data

- Do not collect any personal data you really don't need.
- Keep file drawers locked and set computers to revert to password needed if idle for more than a few minutes.
- Identify workers with employee numbers, not Social Security numbers.
- Lock the HR (and security) office whenever not occupied by authorized personnel.
- Have (trustworthy) person present whenever offices are cleaned or serviced.
- Change locks and passwords immediately if a key person quits or is terminated.
- Never discuss personal information in an email or by cell phone.
- Check your files several times a year to see who has accessed them.
- For sensitive documents, remember that "once you have read it, lock it up or shred it."
- Develop a plan to handle a breach if it happens.
- Document all of the above in company policy.

'Halloween Weeks's Scariest Possibility for Business: Data Breach,' HRDailyAdvisor@mail55.subscribermail.com, hrdailyadvisor@blr.com, 10/30/2006

The following areas should definitely be addressed in your policy:

- Data management, access, tracking, and storage
- Data retention
- Data destruction
- Breach prevention through early identification and problem resolution
- Breach incident management and notification
- Education and training for supervisors, employees, vendors, and customers
- Remote workforce security
- Vendor data security plans

Most of the above points that deal with technical solutions have been touched upon throughout this chapter; however, we want to emphasize that the most important focus areas deal with people—breach prevention through early identification and problem resolution; and training.

Breach prevention through early identification and problem resolution deals with establishing processes and procedures to identify "at-risk employees." These are employees that are highly stressed, disgruntled, upset over personnel action(s), subject to disciplinary action, etc. The organization needs to flag the situations that can contribute to individual employees becoming an "at-risk" employee and develop interventions that will appropriately address the situation. In addition, the organization needs to preidentify the predictable organization-induced stressful events that may lead to employees becoming "at risk." These could include significant changes in job responsibilities, demotions, mergers of departments, disciplinary actions, implementation of policies that are perceived as unfair, layoffs, terminations, etc.

Possible interventions to address these could include referring an employee to the employee assistance program, performance coaching, or job removal. Each organization will need to establish the spectrum of possible actions based on its' policies and work environment. See Tables G-1, G-2, and G-3 in Appendix G for specific items based on lessons learned from the *Ten Tales of Betrayal: The Threat to Corporate Infrastructures by Information Technology Insiders Analysis and Observations.*

In addition, training your people is one of your best defenses against data loss. Employees will be much more likely to follow the processes you have implemented once you make them aware of them and teach them the importance and how to apply the tools and processes. However, don't stop there; make sure there is a plan for training new and promoted employees. Also, do not overlook the critical importance of making sure that your vendors understand your requirements related to data protection and that you require them to have a data protection plan as well.

Table 7-4 provides a "point-counterpoint" discussion.

While we believe all the points identified are true, we believe that the most telling statement above deals with the time-old concept of the "police policing the police." History has taught us that it is generally best to have an independent body that audits the work of another function so that conflicts of interest are minimized, fraud is more difficult to perpetrate, mistakes or sabotage can be discovered, and the process can have an independent assessment, which gives a higher level of integrity to the effectiveness of the process.

Accordingly, we recommend that a cross-functional team that consists of at least HR, security, finance, internal audit, information technology, and operations management be convened to develop a policy and procedure for protecting sensitive information throughout the enterprise. Once the policy is developed and implemented, we believe that the security department should have the responsibility for monitoring adherence to the policy and internal audit have the responsibility to audit functions for compliance. We believe this closely aligns with the responsibility of the security department and that they are best suited to handle this responsibility across the enterprise. This will also contribute to raising the stature of the security function as one that is valuable to the success of the enterprise.

Table 7-4 Point-Counterpoint

Which function should be responsible for data protection?

Security	Human Resources
Securing and protecting are primary responsibilities of the security department and protection of personal identifiable or sensitive information fits right in with this.	Most personal identifiable or sensitive information is collected for hiring or an employment action that HR controls, so this responsibility should also be in human resources.
Security personnel are trained to protect the organization's resources and are the best qualified to protect the organization's information.	HR already maintains the confidentiality of information, so this is simply an extension of current duties.
There is a potential conflict of interest with HR having the responsibility for protecting information that supports their work. There should be an independent layer that serves this function.	HR regularly uses and accesses sensitive information so they should be responsible for protecting it.

Summary

Our focus in this chapter has been on identifying the essential ingredients that should be considered to create a complete program to protect the sensitive information that is gathered during the background screening process. One of the fundamental premises of data protection is to only collect information that you need, because once you decide to collect it, you must protect it. Thus, we need to scrutinize processes and procedures to cleanse them of unnecessary data collection. While this may reduce some information or revise when you collect the information, the stark reality is that you will still need to collect background information. Thus, in the end, you must have a comprehensive plan to protect the data that you will be collecting.

It is our contention that while the background screening process is a critical tool for organizations to deploy in the fight against workplace violence, employee fraud, sabotage, terrorism, as well as information, identity, and property theft, it is still only part of a larger business strategy that should be focused on protecting the organization's resources. We have proposed that organizations consider taking an enterprise resource protection approach that we believe is the next evolution of loss prevention. Essentially, we believe that the time has come for security management to move beyond simply focusing on creating incremental improvement in loss prevention to implementing a new way to address this problem that will produce quantum improvement in the overall protection of the organizations' resources.

A tipping point event that catapulted this issue into a national business spotlight was the ChoicePoint Inc. situation in which identify thieves stole sensitive information about thousands of consumers. Make no mistake about it—ChoicePoint was not alone; according to the Identify Theft Resource Center, there were *158 incidents affecting more than 64.8 million people in 2005 which earned it the title* "year of the data breach." These events served as a wakeup call for corporate America, who started to realize that data breaches not only cost them money to address the loss of the data but, more important, contributed to the "risk of risk,"—namely, company reputation, trust in the brand, lost customers, lower stock prices, etc. Data protection suddenly grew into a business competitiveness issue.

With this recognition, we have started seeing a number of organizations move to put a senior manager in charge of privacy and resource protection for their enterprise. Some organizations have gone as far as to create a chief privacy officer. This is a great step toward creating a data resource protection strategy that will culminate in the organization managing the protection of data throughout its life cycle of existence in the organization and policies that govern how the data must be managed and protected at each point as they travel through the organization.

Interestingly enough, study after study have identified that beyond all the high-technology tools and sophisticated programs, at the heart of a truly effective data resource protection plan is a rock solid background checking policy or, as the study *Ten Tales of Betrayal: The Threat to Corporate Infrastructures by Information Technology Insiders Analysis and Observations* reported as the top lesson learned, the failure to screen candidates before they are hired or admitted to the worksite was the most significant finding related to prevention and vulnerability.

Infinity Screening: Never-Ending Background Screening[1]

With contributions by William Bollinger, Billie Lee, Rick Dyer, and Kenneth Sekella

Despite preemployment screening having reached record levels over the last 6 years, employee misconduct and illegal activity on the job have increased at an unprecedented level. One can only imagine the levels of illicit behavior that may have been reached if organizations were not conducting background screening at heightened levels. Based on the dichotomy of this higher level of screening and higher level of misconduct, it is an inescapable conclusion that conducting preemployment screening is not sufficient to stem the tide of the onslaught of employee fraud and identity, information, and property theft. The focus of this chapter is on the emerging concept of *Infinity Screening,* the process of conducting post-hire screening of employees on a continuous or regular basis, which holds the potential to be another valuable tool to fight these issues that are plaguing today's organizations. (Please note that the terms *Infinity Screening, post-hire screening, continuous screening,* and *post employment screening* are used interchangeably through this chapter.)

Continuous Screening—An Idea Whose Time has Come

First, we need to acknowledge that the concept of ongoing post-hire screening is not a new one. It has been going on for years. Educators, physicians, nurses, commercial truck drivers, etc. have all been subject to having their credentials and licenses periodically checked by their employers. In addition, many employers have had policies for a long time that require employees to update their files regarding educational credentials, licenses, changes in their driving license status, felony convictions, etc.

The new wrinkle is that with advances in information technology, organizations now have the capability to get continuous feeds of information on a daily basis for many

---

[1] The content of this chapter is substantially based on materials from the booklet, *The Advent of Infinity Screening: Continuous Post-Hire Screening that Never Ends,* published by the National Institute for Prevention of Workplace Violence, Inc.

information areas, if they so choose. Consequently, a whole new opportunity to access information is being made available to organizations today that heretofore did not exist.

We view this as truly a golden opportunity for employers to improve the management of risk associated with hiring employees. Currently, preemployment background screening is focused on screening prospective employees to verify information provided during the hiring process and to identify any discrepancies or questionable issues in the person's background. Post-hire screening arms management with the information needed to put themselves in the position of being able to make an informed hiring decision based on a review of the available information.

Too often, managers make faulty assumptions when they hire a new employee. They presume that because the person starts a job with a clean criminal, credit, or driving record, this means the person's record will remain this way. Unfortunately, we are dealing with the hiring of human beings whose thoughts, beliefs, values, and behavior are not etched in stone and change with time. A person continues to evolve in many areas of their life as their employment tenure continues and the situations in which an individual may find himself or herself change as well.

Let's take the employee who was hired as a bookkeeper and had a stellar background check when he or she was hired. The bookkeeper has now been with their firm for 10 years and finds themselves overwhelmed with debt and has a gambling problem, and their child comes down with a serious medical problem that health insurance is going to only minimally cover. The bookkeeper sees a loophole in the company's financial tracking system and exploits this to embezzle funds so they can pay for their child's medical bills. The firm recently decided to implement an Infinity Screening process and created a policy that states all individuals in sensitive jobs (Figure 8-1) that involve the oversight of company funds will be subject to a biannual check of their credit, bankruptcy filings, habit of bouncing checks, etc. When the post-hire screening is conducted on this employee, the file is flagged because of serious credit problems. This triggers the firm to audit the bookkeeper's files and they discover that their books are being "cooked." This is the potential power of Infinity Screening.

Sensitive Jobs

Sensitive Jobs are typically the jobs that have the greatest potential to create liability for the organization because of the nature of the work being performed. This includes jobs that:

- Deal directly with the public

- Require employees to go into people's homes

- Have contact with children or elderly

- Have access to sensitive information

- Have broad access to premises

- Are responsible for managing cash, valuable merchandise, or financial matters

- Are in a position which yields considerable influence on the affairs of the organization or have a significant responsibility for internal/external safety and/or security, such as security personnel, nurses, physicians, etc.

FIGURE 8-1 Characteristics of sensitive jobs.

Many firms have learned this lesson the hard way; that somewhere down the line the same employee who started with a clean record can turn in a different direction.

Regular post-hire background checks are the only way an employer can know of changes in employees' status that may have a negative impact on the company. Some firms have relied on voluntary reporting, but this has not worked for obvious reasons. See Table 8-1 for information on protecting children with improved screening services.

Managing Risk

Infinity Screening helps to manage risk because having current information on employees positions enables you to make proactive decisions versus being caught off guard in a reactionary position after something has already happened. In other words, post employment screening allows employers to stay ahead, quantify their risk, and know where and in whom their risks lie; most important, it helps with the management of risk and avoiding surprises.

Many of the risk factors that organizations face have been identified in other chapters—however, just to remind you of some of the more salient ones, see the following:

- Employees are responsible for approximately 60% of losses due to fraud, information, and property thefts.
- U.S. organizations lose an average of 6% of their revenues to all forms of occupational fraud according to the Association of Certified Fraud Examiners. The cost of fraud from such things as employee espionage or identity theft is estimated around $6 billion annually.
- The number of workplace violence homicides has actually decreased over the last several years. However, horrific incidents continue to happen and cause tremendous suffering and financial burden on employers; 5% of U.S. companies have serious incidents of workplace violence.
- Researchers from the National Institute for Occupational Safety and Health (NIOSH) estimate that the average cost of a workplace homicide is $800,000.
- Negligent hiring lawsuits that result in a jury trial cost, on average, over $3 million to employers that lose, while cases settled prior to trial are running around $500,000.

In addition to the above culprits, immigration is likely to be added to the list of risk factors, if pending federal legislation on immigration ends up in its current form. The Department of Homeland Security (DHS) has already put a serious focus on immigration and has focused a considerable effort on employment of legal aliens. In addition, virtually all of the current immigration bills that are pending at the federal level include a provision for ongoing verification of immigration status and steep penalties for noncompliance. So, it is highly likely this factor will need to be addressed by organizations in the very near future.

There has been a lot written about the pilot immigration system that is intended to provide businesses with a means of verifying immigration status and its challenges. There has also been wide market acceptance of a private immigration system provided by I9 Form Inc., which their customers love. See Table 8-2 for information on continuous screening and immigration.

Table 8-1 Protecting America's Children with Improved Screening Services
Sonya D. Van Norden, Executive Director, Boys & Girls Club of Stamford, CT, Boys & Girls Clubs of America Affiliates Take Background Checks to the Next Level

For Boys & Girls Clubs of America (BGCA), the nation's fastest-growing youth service organization serving more than 4.4 million children, background checks are a critical component in creating a safe haven for its members and providing peace of mind for their parents. Unfortunately, criminal records research is notoriously limited, expensive, and sluggish.

BGCA's affiliates, representing some 3700 club locations, were challenged to find a way to speed up the process and maintain accuracy without breaking the bank. In their search for a more sophisticated background check solution, a handful of affiliates earlier this year stumbled across a technology that would not only enhance their core process but also take their screening program to new heights.

BGCA mandates that all of its affiliates screen employees and volunteers at least once every 2 years. While this provides some assurance, its not always enough. Courts are notorious for being entangled in red tape, so it can take months, sometimes years, for an infraction to be reported. Moreover, people are dynamic. It's dangerous to assume a person with a clean record will keep it that way. Some BGCA affiliates wanted to close these gaps in the flow of valuable information by conducting checks more routinely.

While more frequent screening was needed, as a non-profit organization the chapter budgets were too tight to support manual ongoing monitoring. Regular screening of thousands of volunteers and employees would be financially impossible since numerous, costly hand searches would have to be conducted for each person in each county in which they had resided over the past 7 to 10 years. Turnaround time was critical for BGCA. The volume of new volunteers and employees is high, and there is usually an immediate need to fill open positions. Many of the affiliates have access to the FBI or state police for screening, but these solutions rely on fingerprinting or other tedious processes that can take weeks to provide results. Moreover, the FBI's database has often been deemed limited in scope and accuracy by third-party researchers.

Verified Person's Assure provided a background screening solution that, for the first time, enabled Boys & Girls Clubs affiliates to accurately and cost-effectively conduct both preemployment and frequent ongoing criminal checks of their employees and volunteers.

Instead of relying on outdated manual processes typically used for criminal screening, Verified Person's solution leverages its proprietary, advanced screening technology combined with a criminal record database to automate the process and deliver faster, more reliable search results.

An increasing number of courthouses have embraced the digital revolution. Verified Person has undergone the arduous task of aggregating and standardizing criminal record data directly from state-and county-level courts, covering nearly 76 percent of the U.S. adult population.

In addition to providing BGCA with the ability to perform continuous and streamlined searching, the solution allows affiliates to specify which criminal offenses are most pertinent to company policy and to be alerted to new infractions in real-time. To increase accuracy and eliminate frustrating false positives, Verified Person matches court records against a detailed profile of the individual in question that includes date of birth, aliases, and a complete address history.

Verified Person is applying technology and the pace of business to bureaucratic criminal records collection and management processes, so Boys & Girls Clubs can close gaps in information flow and mitigate a myriad of threats. Now, instead of screening employees and volunteers prehire and once every 2 years, 20 BGCA affiliates are screening each person as often as twice a month, or 24+ times per person per year. Since the solution leverages efficient screening technology, Verified Person is providing this service at an extremely low cost, eliminating concern over budget constraints. As one of the first organizations to deploy ongoing criminal and sex offender screening, these Boys & Girls Clubs affiliates can feel secure that they're doing everything they can to protect the children and communities they serve. With the initial success, word of the new screening solution is spreading throughout the organization to other affiliates.

Printed with permission of HRO Today and Verified Person.

Table 8-2 Continuous Screening and Immigration
Kenneth F. Sekella, VP, Operations, Form I-9 Compliance, LLC

The Immigration Reform and Control Act of 1986 (IRCA) made all U.S. employers responsible to verify the employment eligibility and identity of all employees hired to work in the United States after November 6, 1986. To implement the law, employers are required to complete Employment Eligibility Verification forms (Form I-9) for all employees, including U.S. citizens.

Since the passage of IRCA, employers have had the responsibility to ensure that the Form I-9 be completed by the employee and the company no later than close of business on the employee's third day of employment services. The initial screening that an employer must conduct involves reviewing documentation presented by the employee and recording document information of the form presented. Proper documentation establishes both that the employee is authorized to work in the U.S and that the employee who presents the employment authorization document is the person to whom it was issued. In terms of the screening process (review by the employer of acceptable documents) employees are not required to be document experts. In reviewing the genuineness of the documents presented by employees, employers are held to a reasonableness standard.

The vast majority of U.S. employers do not participate in the employment verification pilots available through the DHS and the Social Security Administration. These agencies provide database checks for determining the employment eligibility by checking among other items, the validity of a "Resident Alien Card" (Form I-551), Social Security number, and an unexpired foreign Passport with attached DHS Form I-94 indicating unexpired work authorization. The use of these databases, called the Basic Pilot Program, takes the guesswork out of the visual inspection process of documents described above. As the quality and quantity of fraudulent documents have increased dramatically in recent years, the use of database verification is viewed as a key measure in preventing the hiring of illegal aliens.

In terms of the retention requirements of the Form I-9, all of an employer's current employees, unless exempted from the guidelines, must have I-9 Forms on file. A retention date can only be determined at the time an employee is terminated. It is determined by calculating and comparing two dates. To calculate date "A", the employer adds 3 years to the hire date. To calculate date "B", the employer adds 1 year to the termination date. Whichever of the two dates is later in time is the date until which the employee's I-9 Form must remain in the employer's employment eligibility verification file.

During the time that an employer is required to keep a Form I-9 on file, it is faced with the responsibility of continuous monitoring under special circumstances. The employer must track the expiration date of documents of non-citizens, the movement from company-to-company of employees working in the United States under H1 B visas, and ensure that the employees with expiring work authorization documents secure appropriate updated documentation. Additionally, if an employee's name changes for any reason, the employer is required to update the I-9 Form with the new information.

Even though the Form I-9 is one of only two federally required employment forms (the W-4 is the other), historically the attention paid to this form has been minimal. The screening (for accuracy and completeness) of the I-9 Form at the time of hire is oftentimes left to lower level human resources (HR) staff who are rarely trained in how to scrutinize this completed document. Thus, most I-9 Forms will have some errors, omissions, or internal discrepancies. The risk for the employer for maintaining defective forms is the potential to be fined by DHS, or other federal government agencies. Screening via visual inspection of documents has not worked since IRCA was passed; thus, there are 13 million illegal aliens in the United States. The federal government attempted in 2006 to deal with the issue of illegal immigration by passing bills in both the House of Representatives and the Senate that included a requirement that all employers must use the Basic Pilot Program. Unfortunately, mid-year elections in 2006 got in the way of any legislation reaching the President's desk. To date, at least two states, Colorado and Georgia, have passed legislation that requires that employers who conduct business with these state governments use the Basic Pilot Program to verify the work eligibility of newly hired employees.

(Continued)

Table 8-2   Continuous Screening and Immigration—Cont'd

The issue of initial and continuous screening of I-9 Forms and supporting documentation can be effectively dealt with through the use of "smart," Web-based electronic I-9 Forms that seamlessly integrate with the Basic Pilot Program. *Form I-9 Compliance, LLC* has developed such an "error-detecting" electronic I-9 Form (with an electronic signature) that ensures that the initial screening and processing cannot be done incompletely. If incorrect data is entered, such as transposing digits in a Social Security number, such errors will be uncovered if the Basic Pilot Program is queried.

In terms of the continuous screening required of the I-9 Form and supporting documentation as outlined above, clearly a form such as the one *Form I-9 Compliance, LLC* has created, provides a "Best Practices" approach (through the issuance of email alerts) to the ongoing tracking and re-verifying of data required by DHS, and provides a level of verification of work authorization that, in all likelihood, will become a federal requirement.

Fiduciary Responsibility

Beyond managing risk, the management of a business has a fiduciary responsibility to appropriately manage and protect the assets of the business. It is through the administration of its fiduciary responsibility that an organization must ultimately determine the company's appetite or tolerance for risks, those risks it will take, and those it will not take in the pursuit of its goals and objectives. The COSO Enterprise Risk Management framework referenced in Chapter 7 can be very beneficial at this stage: a comprehensive way for organizations to avoid surprises (resource loss) by assuming that every risk can be avoided, accepted, reduced, or shared. It is the responsibility of the leadership of the organization to determine the risk tolerance associated with each major business strategy.

Once the level of risk that a firm is willing to accept has been determined, it is their senior management's responsibility to ensure that the company implements an effective and ongoing process to identify risk, define the potential impact, and then take appropriate action to proactively address these risks.

Negligent Retention

Negligent retention is the legal doctrine that has evolved out of numerous court cases. The underlying premise of negligent retention is that if an employer is aware that an employee has been violent or has violent tendencies or should have been aware of the problem and did not take reasonable actions to address the situation, then the employer can potentially be held liable for their employee's actions. This concept has been applied to a wide array of employment situations.

Let's look at a hypothetical situation to see how this might apply.

You have a driver who delivers products to your clients and through an Infinity Screening process you find out he was convicted of driving while intoxicated last month. You can make a decision regarding continuing to allow that person to deliver your product, changing their assignment, terminating the person's employment, or taking other appropriate actions. Without this information being brought to your attention, you could have faced a situation where the driver has an accident while making a delivery and seriously injures someone. You then find out he is driving on a suspended license and has been convicted of a DUI. This is not a pretty picture or a situation that will make you or your attorney happy because it likely to lead to the company getting sued for negligent retention.

In court, several questions are likely to be raised:

- Is it reasonable to expect that the company should have been aware of their employee's driving record?
- Were there reasonable steps that the employer could have taken to have had current information on their employee's driving record?
- If they had been aware of it, what action would they have likely taken?

While we cannot speculate on the decision that a jury might make in this type of situation, you can clearly see where this line of questioning is leading. We believe that firms can avoid this situation altogether by staying informed about their employees' records through Infinity Screening. Preemployment screening reduces the risk of a bad hiring decision; post employment screening reduces the risk to which a company is exposed over the long term. These are the actions that a responsible employer should be aware of in their workforce and may become a new standard for judging if an employer took reasonable steps to provide a safe work environment.

In other words, Infinity Screening has the potential to help organizations overcome the "zone of vulnerability" that exists when firms just conduct preemployment background screenings.

Table 8-3 refers to when a firm conducts preemployment screening only.

Table 8-4 refers to when a firm conducts both preemployment and post-hire screening.

In essence, the Infinity Screening process has the potential to extend risk management over the employment life cycle from the time that a person applies for a job with a firm to when the person becomes an employee to the time when the person exits the organization and is no longer an employee.

Several firms have continuous screening tools to help employers. These firms include Liberty Alliance, National Background Data, and Verified Persons (Table 8-5).

The good news is that these new tools will make higher quality information available to assist managers with internal hiring and employment actions. The bad news is

Table 8-3 Firm Conducts Preemployment Screening Only

	Applicant	Employee
"Bad" hire capability for illegal activity	⟶	Zone of Vulnerability
Prehire capability for security	⟶	Zone of Vulnerability

Table 8-4 Firm Conducts Both Preemployment and Post-Hire Screening

	Applicant	Employee
"Bad" hire capability for illegal activity	⟶	⟶
Prehire and post-hire capability for security	⟶	⟶

Table 8-5 National Background Data/CrimWATCH

Post-Hire Criminal Screening Services

New services are available to address the need for post-hire criminal screening, otherwise known as Infinity Screening. These services monitor active employees to make sure they still meet your employment screening standards. National Background Data (NBD), LLC, the leading provider of criminal history database information to the background screening industry, offers an innovative post-hire criminal monitoring solution—CrimWATCH. CrimWATCH is a recurring criminal records search service that enables organizations to stay abreast of active employees' criminal history. CrimWATCH regularly scans nationwide criminal databases to conduct ongoing background checks on active employees.

CrimWATCH includes features that are essential for ongoing background checks, such as:

- A criminal records search from automated data sources, including:
  - Proprietary Offender Data (POD)
  - Department of Corrections (DOC)
  - Administrative Office of the Courts (AOC)
  - Department of Public Safety (DPS)
  - Traffic Court
  - Terrorist and fugitive watch lists including Office of Foreign Assets Control (OFAC)
  - Sex Offender Registry
- Access via an XML interface or a Web application
- An automatic search requiring minimal effort from your organization

CrimWATCH incorporates all of these features to deliver an Infinity Screening solution that is easy to use. To use CrimWATCH, simply select the type of criminal searches to be conducted, and upload your active employee data (names, Social Security numbers, and dates of birth). Then each month, CrimWATCH automatically conducts nationwide criminal background searches using the employee data provided. If criminal records are found, a notification is sent via email. Once the employer verifies the employee's active employment status, the criminal records may be viewed to determine if the employee still meets the employer's criminal background policies.

Not only can you take preventative measures with CrimWATCH, you can also implement a more comprehensive approach to your workplace crime mitigation strategy. This will help reduce workplace theft and violence while improving your efforts to create a more safe and secure workplace. CrimWATCH is used in conjunction with NBD's background information services. This proprietary service is available through NBD's exclusive Solution Provider Network of over 300 professional background screening companies. If you want to protect your business, minimize risks by implementing Infinity Screening.

Source: National Background Data

that implementing an Infinity Screening program requires a considerable amount of forethought to address the legal requirements, HR, and employee relations issues associated with this type of program. In addition, firms must carefully consider a myriad of other issues to ensure not only consistent employee practices but to also ensure that decisions are made that are congruent with the firm's culture and HR philosophy. To ignore this reality will only lead to future legal and employee relations issues that could have been avoided with forethought and planning.

This is an example of a situation that has turned into a problem:

Thirty-one employees of H & M International Transportation—many of them members of the International Brotherhood of Teamsters labor union—were fired in November from jobs at the Union Pacific Railroad without the hearing required by union bylaws. The men, convicted felons who have served their sentences and reentered society, disclosed this information completely when they were hired. Last March, they did so again when told under threat of firing that they must complete forms characterized as credit checks. After submitting the required information, the workers also completed an Internet test on railroad safety and security. Eight months later, they were notified by telephone or letter that H&M was instituting an "involuntary separation of their employment," apparently as security risks. None of the workers has been involved in criminal cases since employment; nor has misconduct on the job been alleged. On the contrary, some of them have received raises and promotions. All have worked overtime, some 14 days straight, before being fired.[2]

Legal Requirements

Because we have discussed risk, it is important to mention the legal issues associated with Infinity Screening. Most firms are well aware that the primary legal requirement for conducting background screening is defined by the Fair Credit Report Act (FCRA) as amended by the Fair and Accurate Credit Transactions Act (FACTA) amendment, and this is equally true for Infinity Screening. FCRA provides the requirements for using consumer reporting agencies, which includes background screening firms; however, if a business does its own background screening using internal staff and does not use a consumer report in any part of their process, they do not have to follow the FCRA requirements. Although this may be the case, with the numerous state requirements, we strongly encourage organizations to still follow the FCRA requirements to avoid even the appearance of unfairness. Doing this will also put them in a rock solid position should their process get challenged. This is a best practice approach. In addition, firms must be cognizant of abiding by state laws that deal with consumer reporting agencies where they conduct business as well. In addition, there are also legal requirements in several industries regarding background screening:

Medical and health care facilities are required to make sure that medical licenses and certifications are current and meet established standards.

The U.S. Department of Transportation (DOT) requires employers to monitor their employee's driving records on an annual basis. DOT employers who fail to conduct this screening are subject to penalties and fines.

Billie Lee, President, First Advantage–Transportation Services Division, shared with us that there has also been a movement by many state regulatory agencies to put in place employer notification services (ENS) programs that notify employers of changes to a driver's record in a timely manner. Today, 10 states currently offer some form of an ENS program (Arkansas, California, Illinois, Michigan, Nebraska, New York, North Carolina, Oregon, Virginia, and Wisconsin).

She further indicated that in many cases, the state agency actions have been taken to support compliance with regulations such as the Federal Motor Carrier Safety Administration (FMCSA) requirements regarding commercial drivers and driving violation

---

[2] http://www.rainbowpush.org/FMPro?-db=rp5h%2fdata06%2fdetailpress.htm

reporting. These state actions have also resulted in voluntary programs for employers who choose to promote driver and highway safety.

Specifically, these programs often accomplish two goals:

1. Ensure that an employer is notified when a conviction or other change occurs on an employee's driver license.
2. Reduce the time between when a conviction or other status change occurs on a driver's record and when the employer is notified so that the employer can take the appropriate action to reduce risk of an accident or other type of loss.

First Advantage–Transportation Services Division is one of the leading firms that support businesses by providing services to address DOT requirements. (See Appendix H for full Service Description.) They offer a unique mix of core competencies including a long history of leadership and strong relationships with state departments of motor vehicles to obtain driving record reports online, to provide paperless driver monitoring to their customers, and to help mediate the relationship between the state and the employer.

They service over 3700 DOT-regulated private transportation companies that are required to prescreen their potential employee drivers as well as annually review the driving record reports on their current employee drivers. Additionally, they provide driving records from all 50 states, in most states instantly, and offer a national monitoring solution that can be scheduled to provide driving record reports on a monthly, quarterly, semiannual, or annual basis. Monitoring is customized through a user-friendly Web interface that includes such features as exception, expiration and high-risk reporting, standard violation codes on driving records (violations, suspensions, revocations), scored driving records, and more.

In addition, Ms. Lee shared that even companies that are not legally required to monitor their employees but have employees that drive as a part of their job function have started understanding they too need to be alerted to activity that might disqualify the employee from using a company vehicle or from driving as part of their regular job function. Many of these firms have realized that regularly reviewing their employees' driving records on a more frequent basis increases driver safety, reduces the company's exposure to lawsuits, results in an overall reduction of risk, and decreases both hard and soft costs.

Whether or not they may be compulsory for a company, driving monitoring programs are increasingly understood as a critical component to managing risk. With the important ramifications of driving monitoring programs only continuing to expand, companies need to fully understand the capabilities of providers and be confident that the chosen provider can continue to deliver in this quickly evolving area of post-hire screening.

Section 19 of the Federal Deposit Insurance Act prohibits any person who has been convicted of any criminal offense involving dishonesty, breach of trust or money laundering, or has agreed to enter into a pretrial diversion or similar program in connection with a prosecution, from becoming or continuing as an institution-affiliated party; owning or controlling, directly or indirectly, an insured institution; or otherwise participating in the conduct of the affairs of an insured institution without the prior written consent of the FDIC. Banks and brokerage firms have their guidelines as well.

Important Considerations in Implementing an Infinity Screening Program

Development of a Background Screening Policy

One of the important first steps is to develop a comprehensive policy that sets the tone and provides the framework for how post-hiring screening will be handled in your organization. See the background screening policy in Chapter 5, which includes in-depth coverage of what to include in your policy.

The essential ingredients that must be included in a background screening policy are the following:

- Notification and consent—notifying an employee that it is the organization's intent to conduct a background check on him/her and having them sign a written authorization and consent form. Employers must ensure that such checks are done with consent. Ensuring that employees are given proper notice is a very important part of positioning the organization to be able to act at a later date should something go awry with the employee's behavior. It should also be noted that having the traditional statement that "omission of information or giving false statements is grounds for termination" may not be sufficient to address the consent issue. We recommend that organizations include authorization and consent language in their employment application and also have employees sign a separate authorization and consent forms. We actually suggest you have two forms, one for preemployment that is signed by a person who is applying for a position and second for a new hire that is now an employee. The signing of this second form can be incorporated with new hire orientation. Note that we are not aware of any legal issue prohibiting combining these into one form; however, we believe separating them puts the firm in a stronger position should the process come under challenge.

- Define when the background screening will be conducted. Will it be on a regular time schedule such as quarterly, annually, or at random? Will it be situation driven such as when the employee is being considered for a promotion, transfer, or significant increase in job duties that warrant it? Will it be event driven by such things as whenever an accident occurs that leads to lost time due to an injury?

- Define the positions that will have background screens conducted on incumbents. Some firms conduct background screenings on all positions, while most firms target specific jobs that have been designated as sensitive nature to have background screenings conducted on incumbents.

- Sensitive jobs—One of the important areas that the policy should address is to classify jobs on the basis of their sensitivity or the risk factor that is associated with a specific job. In this context, risk refers to the risk of an incumbent being able to commit fraud, embezzlement, steal confidential information or property, or has the potential to inflict harm on people, etc.
  - For example, a chief financial officer who has signature authority for up to $100,000 has a greater risk factor than a receptionist who cannot approve any expenditure. This is important because the greater the risk, the higher is the sensitivity of the job and, therefore, the greater the precautions the employer should take, such as regularly checking the chief financial officer's credit and criminal record.

- Unfortunately, "very few employers tailor the background information they collect to the requirements of the job," says Lewis Maltby, President of the nonprofit National Workright Institute.
- Types of checks to be done
  - Identity validation and address history
  - Criminal record
  - Previous employment history
  - References
  - Social Security verification
  - Education verification
  - Driving record
  - Credit history
  - Credential and license verification
  - Immigration status
  - Terrorist list
  - Drug screening
- Point of hiring training of managers—We recommend providing a short online training or briefing to hiring managers at the point when they have an opening and will be involved in filling it. This way, the "do's and don'ts" will be fresh in their minds.
- FCRA process—Even if internal staff conducts background screening, we strongly encourage employees to follow the FCRA process.
- One of the unique challenges that must be addressed deals with outsourced service providers, e.g., contractors, subcontractors, temporary agencies, professional employment organizations (PEOs), etc. Aside from permanent employees, companies need to be especially aware of outsourced staff, subcontracted companies (e.g., administrative assistants, cleaners, guarding companies, and all personnel who come onto a company's premises). As part of service contracts, companies should insist that their suppliers have a background screening policy that meets their standards and includes ongoing screening. This should be built into the contractual agreement and periodic reviews should be implemented to ensure their policy is being adhered to.
- It cannot be emphasized enough that individuals from suppliers pose as much a risk as any permanent staff member and very often are even more of a potential threat with unrestricted access to all areas, some times with after-hours servicing. For example, consider the unsupervised access that night cleaning crews have to your facilities.
- Creating a discrimination free process—While in most cases organizations today are very knowledgeable in not intentionally establishing discriminatory practices, organizations need to continue to be diligent in avoiding disparate impact from programs they implement that inadvertently have a discriminatory effect. *Disparate impact* is a technical equal employment opportunity term that refers to policies, programs, processes, or actions that an employer takes that on the surface appear to be nondiscriminatory, but the net effect is that a disproportionate number of

protected class members are excluded as result of its use. A classic example is using arrest records as a hiring criterion. A significant amount of research has established that members of minority groups, who are a protected class, are consistently and significantly arrested at higher levels than are members of nonminority groups. Thus, using arrest records as a hiring criterion has the net effect of excluding a disproportionate higher percentage of minority group members from consideration for jobs.

- What happens when a negative hit occurs on an employee?
  - Probably the most important issue that your policy needs to be written to address is "what happens when a negative hit occurs on an employee."
  - We believe that there are several key ingredients that should be included in the organization policy to address this issue.

Notification and Appeal Issues

The employee who has a negative hit should be notified confidentially by security regarding the negative information. The policy and the employees' rights under the policy should be explained and the employee should be given an opportunity to affirm or deny the information.

If the employee disputes the information, he should be advised that the organization will give him the time frame that has been defined in the policy to bring in information that refutes the information that has been identified. Each firm will have to determine what is viewed as a reasonable time frame and whether time off to deal with this issue will be granted with or without pay. In addition, the organization should seek validation of the information from the sources that provided it to ensure its accuracy.

Access to Records

Who needs to know about the information and to be involved in decision-making regarding the situation?

Due to the highly sensitive nature of the information involved and also the potential for even the fact that a negative hit occurred to taint future decisions regarding the employee, it is crucial that a minimum amount of people are involved in this situation. Supervisors and managers should specifically be excluded at this stage because until the information is verified to be accurate, they do not have a need to know.

We recommend that security handle this stage because, despite HR having a neutral role, they are frequently involved in career mobility discussions and their view of the individual could inadvertently be tainted as well. It is cleaner for security to handle this because they are not regularly involved in career mobility discussions and decisions.

Once the negative hit is affirmed as being accurate either by the employee or via verification of background records, HR needs to be bought into the loop. At this point, the following six-point analysis needs to be considered before determining if supervision needs to be informed.

1. The employee's **tenure of employment with the organization.**
2. The employee's **tenure in the current position.**
3. The employee's **record of misconduct,** meaning any violations of policy that matches or is reasonably connected to the nature of the negative hit. It is very important to

understand that this is not a review of the employee's performance that is not relevant to the situation at hand. If an employee is a stellar performer, you have to treat a negative hit the same as you would treat it for a poor performer.

4. **When** did the negative event being reported actually occur? Unless the person is in an executive or high level position, in general, if the negative event occurred more than 7 years ago, it is likely that you should consider it as being irrelevant.

5. The **relevancy** of the negative event to the employee's position. For example, if the employee is in a job that handles money or approves substantial sums of money and the negative hit is an embezzlement conviction within the last 7 years, then it is relevant. If they were convicted of a DUI and the position does not involve driving, it is most likely irrelevant.

6. Ask your labor attorney if, in the future, this employee commits a violation of policy that is connected to the negative hit and the organization is sued, the organization will be able to **defend the decision to keep this person employed** in their current position? In other words, will the rationale and decision making be considered "reasonable" in the courtroom. This should be your litmus test.

The above six-factor analysis must be considered in tandem, which means each situation will need to be judged on the facts that specifically relate to the situation.

Security, HR, and legal should convene to discuss the situation. Some organizations call this a *background screening review committee*. The intent of this committee is to provide an objective body to review the totality of the circumstances surrounding a situation and to apply a consistent framework to how decisions are made.

If the decision from this group is that the employee should be retained in his or her position, then the employee should be informed and advised that this issue has been maintained in the utmost of confidence. He or she should be advised that his or her supervisor has not been informed about the situation.

If the decision is that the issue is of sufficient concern, then the employee's operational management will need to be involved in the situation. Each organization will have to determine which specific level of management to involve in the decision making process to resolve the situation.

Some thoughts to consider are that future retaliation or discrimination charges arising from the negative hit will be easier to defend if the immediate supervisor has no knowledge of the negative hit and situation. On the other hand, the higher the level of position that has knowledge of the negative hit and situation, if this person has a tainted view of the employee, he or she can have a pervasive negative influence on future actions toward the employee.

Determining Appropriate Action to Take

The same factors that were reviewed by security, HR, and legal will need to be reviewed with the input of operational management and any other relevant information.

Conduct a risk assessment—One option available at the point that the above team has been convened is to make a decision to have an in-depth background check conducted of the employee to see if there is any other relevant information to consider. If the situation is related to violence, then an individual threat assessment may also be in order.

Making an Effective Business Decision

The final decision should be based on the merits of the facts involved, consistent with the organization's policies, practices, and culture and in compliance with any relevant legal requirements. The EEOC guidelines regarding the use of criminal records to not automatically disqualify an individual from consideration without a legitimate business reason for doing so should be paid close attention to.

- Make sure that your background screening policy is consistent with the organization's employee monitoring and on/off duty behavior policies and practices.

- A policy needs to be very clear regarding not creating an "expectancy of privacy" and openly communicating to employees about how the firm intends to monitor their records in areas to be covered (e.g., criminal records, licensing, etc.) based on the nature of the responsibilities assigned to specific job function and the qualifications for the job. Make sure that the background screening policy language regarding "no expectancy of privacy" is consistent with the organization's Employee Monitoring Policy, if the organization has one.

See Table 8-6 for tips on staying within the law when monitoring employees.[3]

In addition to ensuring consistency with employee monitoring policies, organizations that have a policy that regulates off-duty conduct need to ensure that the language is consistent with their background screening policy as well. This is necessary because the focus of post-hire background screening is predominantly off-duty behavior, such as arrests, convictions, credit history, driving record, etc.

Regulating off-duty behavior is another one of those emerging legal areas on which some businesses are pushing the envelope. However, "lifestyle discrimination," as this area

Table 8-6 Monitoring Employees: Tips for Staying Within the Law

---

Employers currently have a lot of leeway in monitoring their employees. However, the law in this field is evolving rapidly, as technological changes and increasing concerns about privacy pressure legislators and courts to take action. If you decide to monitor your workers, consider following these tips:

Adopt a policy. Tell your workers that they will be monitored, and under what circumstances. If you indicate that you will respect the privacy of personal phone calls or email messages, make sure that you live up to your promise. The safest course is to ask employees to sign a consent form, as part of their first-day paperwork, acknowledging that they understand and agree to the company's monitoring policies.

Monitor only for legitimate reasons. You will be on safest legal ground—and waste less time and money—if you monitor only for sound, business-related reasons. If you have a reasonable suspicion that a particular employee is engaging in unauthorized use of your equipment, that would certainly qualify as a legitimate cause for monitoring.

Be reasonable. Employees will not perform their best work if they are in constant fear of eavesdropping, being watched, snooped on, or overreaching monitoring.

Source: http://employment.findlaw.com/employment/employment-employee-more-topics/employment-employee-privacy-computer-email.html

Copyright 2006 Nolo.

---

[3] Larry D. Henry, Esq. *Effects of 2003 Amendments to the Fair Credit Reporting Act*, as presented to NAPBS National Conference, Scottsdale, AZ, 3/29/04. 16 CFR Part 682 © 2004 Phoenix Group, Inc.

has come to be known, is one that employers would be wise to tread into slowly because in the privacy conscious world of today, it will likely invite litigation. Nevertheless, private employers have been able to successfully exert themselves in this arena and the laws in many states are fairly open in terms of which policies the law specifically prohibits.

For example, in Texas, except in certain occupations, arrests, and convictions, state laws do not limit employers' rights to choose to employ or not employ individuals with criminal convictions and arrests. Employees whose off-duty behaviors lead to arrests and convictions may face termination. However, this represents another area in which employers must tread carefully. If the employer has sufficient facts to conclude that an employee committed work-related misconduct that led to an arrest, the employer is not required to wait for a conviction before terminating that employee. If an arrest causes the employee to violate the employer's work rules, such as attendance rules, resulting adverse employment action will generally be defensible. Even misconduct that is not specifically work related could impact the employer. For example, repeated arrests for domestic violence could indicate a threat of future workplace violence. Arrests for off-duty conduct involving dishonesty could also justify a work-related concern on the part of the employer. If the employer has a reasonable concern about continuing to employ someone who has been arrested or convicted, termination will usually be safe, but individualized deliberation is always advisable.[4]

The Business Owner's Toolkit (http://www.toolkit.com/small_business_guide/sbg. aspx?nid=P05_5650 Copyright 2007, Business Owner's Toolkit), suggests that "to determine whether there is any action that you can take regarding an employee's lawful off-duty conduct, ask yourself the following questions:

1. Is there a relationship between the off-duty conduct of the employee and the performance of the employee's job?
2. Does the employee's off-duty conduct put your business in an unfavorable light with the public?
3. Does the employee's conduct have a potential for harming the business?"

In addition, some common types of legal off-duty conduct that employers may have the ability to sanction and have a legitimate right to be made aware of include off-duty conduct, either accidental or intentional, that embarrasses the company, jeopardizes the company's ability to do business, or damages its corporate reputation. According to the Business Owners ToolKit, "this includes actual damage to business property and assets, both tangible and intangible (reputation). "Employers may sanction employees for . . . disreputable conduct that hurts the employer's business or reputation despite an employee's privacy or wrongful discharge claim.

Technically speaking, past conduct is off-duty because it occurred during a time when an employee was not working for the corporation. Undisclosed prior convictions and arrests, which have been "paid for" or vindicated, no longer render the employee illegal, but if "your business requires employees to work alone in customer homes, potential harm to the company [may be] enough to sustain a termination even though no actual business loss is demonstrated.[5]"

---

[4]   Texas Lawyer, 07/25/2005, Stephanie G. John, © 2005. American Lawyer Media LP.
[5]   http://www.d.umn.edu/~scastleb/off%20duty%20on%20guard.doc

Policy Implementation

Once the policy has been created, it is necessary to develop an implementation plan.

The first step should be to think through how you want to treat employees who have a blemished record and to define a predetermined set of guidelines which can be communicated to all employees. The important point is to match the criteria with the areas on which you intend to collect data.

You should decide, upfront, how as many situations as possible will be handled. Some items to consider are the following:

- If your organization has not been asking applicants to complete an employment application that asked about felony convictions for at least 7 years, then you may have hired employees that have a record, but it is unknown to you. Be prepared for a few surprises.

- Did the employee misrepresent information that was supplied on their employment application? (This presumes that you had applicants complete an employment application that included a question regarding felony convictions at the time they were hired.) You should anticipate that there will be employees who previously lied about or omitted relevant information regarding their felony convictions. Decide, upfront, how you are going to handle these situations. Whatever approach you decide to take (e.g., forgive them, grandfather them, discipline them, etc.), it is best to have a consistent and standard approach that is applied across the board to avoid discriminatory actions.

- How to handle convictions that fit your criteria that have occurred after the employee was hired.

With the above sorted out, you will then need to decide whether you are going to invite employees to "self-identify" and, if so, whether each situation will be judged on its own merits or you are going to grandfather them and grant immunity for their previous indiscretions.

We know that each organization will have to examine its own culture, philosophy, HR policies, and way of doing business to arrive at a set of criteria and approach that will appropriately fit their organization.

Communications and Training

The communications and training plan should have the goal that every employee will be fully informed about and understand the new policy. To achieve this, you will need not only to announce the policy through the normal channels that your organization uses to communicate to employees but also ensure that every employee understands the policy and how it could impact them individually.

Some ideas on how to communicate the policy:

- General announcement of the policy via email from the CEO. This should advise employees that this is part of an overall enhanced focus on providing a safe work environment and improving profitability by reducing loses due to fraud and theft.

- Briefing of supervisors on the new policy on their responsibilities under the new policy and how it will impact employees.

- Conduct briefing meetings with employees and provide supervisors with a briefing kit on the new policy that can be distributed to employees in the meeting. Ideally, these briefing meetings should be led by an HR representative. Give each employee an acknowledgement form to sign that states that they received a copy of the policy, a briefing on the policy, and to acknowledge that the person fully understands the policy. We suggest that you give them a reasonable amount of time to read, review the policy with their spouses or whomever they choose, and then turn in the signed document. One week should be more than sufficient to accomplish this.

- Schedule a prominent article on the new policy in your organization's newsletter with a Frequently Asked Questions section. This should follow the CEO letter.

- Schedule a second prominent article on the new policy in your organization's newsletter. This should be scheduled after the employee briefing sessions have been completed.

- Post the new policy and Frequently Asked Questions on the organization's Intranet site.

- If the organization has an internal job posting or bidding process and will be conducting background checks on applicants for selected positions, include information about the background screening policy and how to access it.

- Include an overview of the policy during employee orientation.

Employee Relations Issues

The nature of the employee relation issues that may arise in an organization will have a lot to do with the existing culture of the organization and its employee relations philosophy. Even though these factors will match the uniqueness of the organization, there are some issues that are likely to arise in most organizations:

We have already dealt with the number one issue that frequently arises—how to deal with long-term employees whose criminal history suddenly becomes known.

We have also shared some perspective on managing negative hits, which are inevitable.

A highly predicable issue that will arise will be "invasion of privacy." If your organization has already implemented employee monitoring in other forms, you may have already dealt with some segment of your employees on this issue. If so, you should certainly learn from the introduction of that program. The key issues to focus on when addressing this issue are:

- Creating a safer work environment.
- Market competitiveness (maximize profitability by reducing cost of fraud and theft).
- Overwhelmingly, employees are trustworthy and honest.
- Reduce fraud, pilferage, and property, information, and identity theft.
- No right of privacy while working and using company-provided equipment.
- Will take reasonable approach only focused on information "we need to know" and will avoid being overly intrusive.

- In most cases, only security or HR will have knowledge of information. Operational management will only be informed when there is real need to know, which will generally be the exception, not the norm.
- Hot line to "whistleblower ombudsman" for any perceived abuses that will be investigated

We have already addressed the discrimination issue, which is one that is likely to come up as well.

Table 8-7 provides a "point-counterpoint" discussion.

Table 8-7 Point-Counterpoint

Continuous screening of employees will become the next big thing in background screening. Managing risk along the employment life cycle for employees will need to be monitored.

Security	**Human Resources**
Politicians have realized that getting people jobs is an important political issue and are likely to restrict massive efforts to conduct post-hire screening.	Despite preemployment screening having reached record levels over the last 6 years, employee misconduct and illegal activity on the job has increased at an unprecedented level. To help turn the tide and close the window of vulnerability, post-hire screening is a much needed risk management tool.
With close to 90% of companies conducting some form of background screening, are we reaching the saturation point where a backlash is going to occur by job seekers that enough is enough and businesses have no additional "need to know" more about their personal background?	With the ready availability of continuous screening, courts are going to want to know why employers did not take this step as part of their due diligence.
This may be another example of "a whole lot to do about nothing" because the bad guys that have something to hide are starting to figure out sophisticated ways to cover their tracks, which means all the background checking will be on good honest employees who have nothing to hide.	Since a newly hired employee passed the preemployment screening they should not be concerned about a post-hire screening. If there is nothing to hide what is the problem? Post-hire screening is not new, many industries such as financial services, health care, trucking, etc. already check employees licenses, certifications, records, etc. on a continuous basis.
It only stands to reason that the more we continue to do these types of background checks the more likely businesses are going to run into legal problems and have them challenged.	

Contributed by Rick Dyer, Liberty Alliance.

Summary

Post-hire screening deals with the "real" risk created by employees over their employment life cycle with an organization. Consequently, it reduces the long-term risk to which a company may be exposed by positioning the organization to avoid surprises and to be able to make informed decisions about risky situations or behavior. Infinity Screening is a process that focuses on prevention of incidents versus reaction once they have occurred. It has the potential to significantly reduce the zone of vulnerability that an organization is exposed to when it only conducts preemployment background checks.

A fundamental premise of effective management and decision making is that the higher the quality of information that is possessed, the better are the decisions that will be made. Infinity Screening provides management with valuable information on employees' past and current behaviors that positions them to be able to make the best possible decisions about employment actions.

Infinity Screening is an idea whose time has come. It will help to improve the organization's risk management posture and contribute to the reduction of the costly drain on profits from illegal activities such as fraud, information, identity, and property theft. Businesses should embrace this opportunity to be able to further manage their risk by being able to identify potential problems in a proactive manner. In addition, having current information on employees' behavior positions the organization to be able to make decisions not only to reduce risk but also to ultimately create a safer workplace. While it is a well-known premise that "knowledge is power," in this case we know that having the right information at the right time can empower management to better manage all of the organization's resources and assets to improve overall business performance.

9

Screening Strategies for Temporaries, Casual Labor, Consultants, Contractors, and Vendors

It may be hard to believe in this day and age, but it is not that uncommon for an organization to have no idea of the backgrounds of the people who are not employed by their organization but are working on their premises or have wide or even unlimited access to their workspace, proprietary paperwork, and various computer and information technology (IT) systems. Often times, background checking costs and speed at which nonemployee staffing resources are needed quickly overshadow the process of ensuring the temporary personnel, contractor, or vendors are screened.

This is especially true for growing businesses and businesses that are geographically dispersed. Many of the decisions to bring on temporary help in its various forms are left to local managers, decentralized human resources (HR), or operation staff that do not have HR or security on site. Often, the operational need may outweigh the risk of not screening the temporary worker or contractor. In these cases, the risk can often be mitigated by limiting the access or hours the individual has access to the IT systems or facilities. For example, the computer systems the temporary worker has access to may be safeguarded with limited or partitioned access to critical areas of the system.

Realistically speaking, it is probably not practical to do a background screen on every person who enters your premise. But there are ways to "screen" nonemployees by using a combination of identity, background screening, and physical security techniques to reduce the risk to your organization. Before entering into a discussion of how to effectively screen nonemployees, we should first define each of the constituent groups we will be discussing.

Temporary Employees

This term refers to a quasi-employee who is not normally carried on your employment roll. However, there are some companies or organizations that employ temporary workers who are not sent from a third party provider. For example, a company may employ summer hires and call this group "temporary," but, in reality, this is a classification of a type of employees. The term of employment is limited to a specific period. Also, there are employers who emulate the temporary process by putting a 90-day probationary period in their hiring policy. This process can curtail the effect of a bad hire without concern for a long period of HR and management counseling and progressive discipline. However, most real temporaries are provided through a temporary service. These companies specialize in creating pools of candidates for their clients.

The temporary worker or "temp" generally fills a variety of job functions; normally only as a temporary fill in for an absent, permanent employee. The permanent employee may be ill, on some form of leave, or on vacation; however, the day-to-day work still needs to get done. Temporaries typically fill entry-level positions that require little training. However, the job could be a more complex position (i.e., accounting professional) that may apply standard skills to many fields or industries. These individuals will have access to your facilities, other employees, and often the IT systems, on some level.

Many organizations, looking to fill a permanent position, bring on temporary laborers in order to test drive the applicant in the work setting to make sure he or she is a good job fit. This process is referred to as temp to perm. The advantage here is the organization and the temporary worker get to review the cultural cohesiveness, skills needed, work habits, and overall job fit for both parties. A full on-boarding process will accompany this candidate once the trial period is over. In the interim, the temp is still employed by the temp agency and can elect not to return at some point after trialing the job. Conversely, the company may do the same by contacting the third party provider and asking that the candidate not be assigned to the organization. In employer markets, this is very effective in the selection process. The risks being the temporary, who is actually looking for a full-time position, is usually looking elsewhere and may be offered a permanent position during the trial period and the company has to go back to the hiring well to find a candidate. Many well-qualified candidates are lost to other organizations in this scenario.

Casual Labor

Often an organization will need individuals to act as arms and legs for a day or maybe two in order to complete odd jobs or assignments. Another name for this workforce is day labor. There are day labor forces in most cities that can accommodate this need. Although there is often criticism levied here for unscrupulous employers who use undocumented labor for this mission, there are legitimate agencies that screen the workers and can provide a legal workforce. Many of these workers are not expecting or even looking for a long-term assignment as they are often very transient.

Contractors

There can be some confusion around comparing and contrasting contractors and consultants; however, several clear distinctions that can be made between the two. Contractors are usually brought into your organization to complete a job that has a clear scope that has been defined by your internal organization involving a project of some sort. The most obvious of these would be a cleaning, or security officer contract. Another example could be construction or a refurbishing project for a facility. The work is outlined in a contract or an attached scope of work, deadlines are outlined and deliverables clearly mapped. The job is temporary in nature and often involves skills or work that is not core to the business. Installing an HVAC system to your building, constructing work stations, or building a receptionist position, or painting your office space are all examples of contractor-type tasks. Often, there are levels of access necessary depending on the job but often the access is to space. However, there could be contractors that install IT systems or software systems in your computers or servers. Each contract job should be reviewed in detail to understand the access to people and systems before access is granted.

Visitors

Anyone who comes to your facility or business could be classified as a visitor. However, most individuals who visit your facility fall under one of the other categories. For example, sales personnel who come on behalf of a vendor or a potential vendor should be dealt with under the vendor protocol, in most cases. Many times, this type of visitor is coming to your facility on a one off basis. Whether or not they become a vendor is yet to be determined. Family and friends of employees definitely fall into this category as do stockholders or business associates of executives who meet on an infrequent basis. There are several protocols that can and should be adopted for the visitor.

Consultants

Normally, consultants differ slightly from contractors in that their focus is often on the core of what the business or organization is involved in. The consultant, for a period of time, can have the access rights of an employee. They are often seen as a part of the business.

Consultants can be on site representatives of a manufacturer or supplier of key fixtures, furniture, facilities, or technology. They work closely with senior management and often have access to projects and/or information that many of the full time employees may not be privy to. For example, the consultant may be working on a merger or acquisition that is proprietary or even secret. They may be used to perform due diligence on the target organization or even act as an agent. The level of information the consultant has access to might be staggering and the trust that is required is equally weighty.

Vendors

Salesmen, delivery personnel, truck drivers and pizza delivery staff all fall into this category. They often have a daily relationship with the organization that may extend for years. Every morning the bakery truck pulls up with a load of bagels for the office or a meal provider comes in to set up for a luncheon. When the elevator needs repair, a call is made to the building landlord, who sends in a vendor from a local servicing center. The local shredding company comes by each month to clean out the shred bins. All of these, and many more, are consider vendors. The local soft drink vendor or the vending machine delivery truck is a part of your business. After 9/11, heightened question and concern arose as to who was should be given access to the back door of your business. The personnel are employees of another organization, and therefore, are not of your choosing. In the 1972 Munich Olympic Summer Games murder of the Israeli athletes, a portion of the PLO terrorists got into the Olympic Village posing as ambulance drivers. Emergency personnel are "vendors" in the sense that they are sent from the hospital, ICU, etc. and are providing a service. And, most security officers allow them "in" without question.

In the following table, we will outline the various constituent groups and the risks that are associated with each. Some of these groups can use a strategic background screening to mitigate certain types of risks. It will be noted if screening is not the recommended security or HR alternative. But even in the most limited relationships, some screening might be advised.

Table 9-1 describes constituent groups and associated risk.

The follow screening strategy and/or associated security layering is suggested by constituent groups. There can be specific exceptions, but, in general, this strategy should be seen as a baseline.

Temporary screening is normally performed by the temporary agency from which the personnel is sourced. However, your organization should consider the risk before determining the level of screen you specify be performed. Discuss the access requirement of the temporary and then determine the level of check. At a minimum, an identity and some level of criminal background check should be performed. The depth at which the background check is preformed is debatable as the number of temporaries is considerable and the turnover is often high. But consider the risk thoroughly.

Agencies often have negotiated packages of checks with their provider. They normally use a third party provider to complete the check. In return, you benefit from the volume discounts they receive. You are paying for the background check indirectly. The level of transparency of the fees varies. But discussion and disclosure of what the agency pays for these checks should be determined. Ask specifically what they mean by criminal background check, and remember the limitations around national criminal files in the private sector.

You should be given the opportunity to review the results of the screen. The consent and waivers signed by the applicants for those individuals assigned to your organization should allow you to review the results. Do not trust the agency to interpret the results. Ultimately, your organization bears the risk—especially in the area of violence. Contractually transferring the risk is not enough. Make sure you know who and what potential risk you are inviting through your physical and virtual doors.

Casual labor is normally economically and practically difficult to background check. There are agencies that will have pools of workers that have passed a background check. However, depending on your immediate need or staffing time frame, you might fall short of your needs in your search for a screened workforce. Therefore, a good alternative might be to have a supervisory strategy closely overseeing the day labor forces you cannot economically screen. If the work is to be performed in a high-security area, alternative workforces should be sought.

Cleaning, security, maintenance, and various other core services employ the use of contractors as part of the day-to-day business. There should be a clear screening strategy performed by the contract company with apparent audit provisions. Internal thefts are often blamed on these types of contractors, but in reality a good screening strategy will often mitigate this concern. Poor screening policy will result in higher theft, which can, of course, be detrimental to your business. There should be a provision within the

Table 9-1 Table of Nonemployee Constituent Groups and Associated Risks

Constituent Groups	Associated Risk
Temporary Employees—temporary to permanent personnel, normally third party or agency provided.	Depending on the level of complexity of the assignment and level of access granted, the greatest risks a company will take on when using a temp are typically theft and violence. At a minimum, identity verification and criminal background checks need to be performed.
Casual Labor—day labor, manual laborers, transient or migrant workers, packers and movers, skilled labor helpers.	The risk can be minimal if adequate security procedures are in place. Violence or other criminality may be a concern with this sector. Good oversight and management are critical, especially if the labor will be commingled with your regular staff.
Contractors—Construction, installation, skilled labor for a specific task normally not related to the core business of the organization. Cleaning services, security officers, and plant and building maintenance are all examples of contractors.	Access and commingling with permanent employees is likely here. Violence or other criminal behavior that spills into your organization is possible. Since the contractor is responsible for skills and qualifications, skill screening would not normally be necessary. Contract staff can often have extensive access to systems, including many or all areas and layers of the organization. Identifying the personnel and some level of screening is best practice.
Visitors—This could be family and friends of employees to visitors to local church groups. Most visitors who have businesses purposes are classified, for this discussion, as vendors.	Allowing visitors escorted access can be problematic. Most businesses should require a picture form of identification and a business card is often required.
Consultants—Software consultants, security or HR consultants; outside auditors and experts in many fields related to any business or organization.	Of all the nonemployee groups, normally the consultant has the most access to assets including systems and employees, and typically proprietary information and trade or company secrets and strategies as well. These individuals should be screened similarly to your most trusted employees.
Vendors—Suppliers of commodities, deliveries, scheduled services, service-oriented company representative.	The turnover and inconsistency of these relationships make it difficult to have a permanent knowledge of who will be assigned to your company or organization. Vendor representatives often have just as much access to company assets as do contractors or consultants with no real rules or security process in place. For example, truck drivers are often given access to back-of-house areas where inventory is stored.

contract between your cleaning, security, building maintenance, and/or other day-to-day contractors that requires screening be performed on their representatives.

In practice, the level of screen should be in line with the level of screen performed on your employees as they relate to criminality. The risk associated with contractors that have access to your work space normally centers around theft, violence, and sexual misconduct. The cleaning crew, as an example, might have physical access to the server rooms or technical closets. Additionally, the security officers have keys to back doors, alarm panels, and storage areas. Good screening strategies may even exceed the employee requirements. Your organization should have the legal right to review the information if necessary to make sure no one is given an access card that is a potential risk.

Your procurement partner, legal department, and functional management who might have contract administrative responsibilities need to be comfortable with your plan and oversight. In the case of a third party provider, you may be well served to have the contractor use your provider but, as a minimum, you should be comfortable with the level of search conducted. For example, you may require the contractor to go to the local Bureau of Criminal Identification and have a fingerprint check. This is certainly a thorough check focused on criminality. But remember, the cost might be higher than you are currently paying for an identification data point match strategy with your employees. So, be consistent; match your level of check with your employee base. You should use some or most of the suggestions listed for the construction contractor like baggage inspection and contractor badging for added layers of security. For cleaning crews, team cleaning, meaning the cleaning crew cleans areas as a team, is recommended. However, this approach is often seen as inefficient. But this requires less supervision at times and can result in less theft and horseplay.

The contractor might be a part of a construction crew who is covered under contract or part of a set crew of casual labor brought in to help move furniture, tear down walls, or set up for a conference or event. Usually, the ability to screen these individuals is not only costly but logistically difficult. Good security management is needed here. Recommended security strategies include:

1. Baggage or lunch box inspection—both ingress and egress
2. Laptop registration at entry and exit
3. Stringent sign in and sign out procedures
4. Badging strategy that is enforced and communicated to the staff
5. Additional security staff to monitor the contractor staff
6. Restricted entry clearly marked and enforced
7. Separate lounges for drivers and construction personnel
8. Contractual requirements for screening of personnel by the contracting company
9. Audit clauses and negotiated levels of checks for key contractors

Other strategies include limiting the hours of access to high security space and use of card key systems. Movement can be contained if your staff is diligent and watches for individuals who wait for authorized employees to enter and then tailgate behind them. Security awareness and a culture of security mindedness are critical.

Anecdotally, the security author always commented to other security professionals that the losses of laptops, desk change, and other small items increased on the last day a contractor crew was on site. This is not conclusive that the crew was responsible, but it does mean that a higher level of security should be enforced when a large group of "nonemployees" are on site during a particular period of time.

Visitors create a different form of risk. Leaving aside the ongoing vendor visits, these visitors may include customers or sales visits, employee family visits, or tours by various groups from stockholders to the Boys Scouts to a local elementary school class. The number of visitors you have each day may make any sort of screen economically impossible. However, there are more and more databases that can be hit that could assist. But as a minimum, identification check should be completed. Some companies require photo ID badges for all visitors. This acts as a record as well as a deterrent. Scanning technology is currently being used in some schools to check visitors. The scans hit against a sex offender database (www.raptor.com). Additionally, a good visitor badging process should be enforced, and escorts should be used. The host employee should notify reception personnel of any visits prior to their arrival. In most cases, unannounced visitors should not be allowed in. And, of course, no one should be given access to any employee just by demanding entrance. These processes prevent angry customers, family members, or curious passer bys from gaining access.

Consultants can be given extraordinary access to employees, information, and technology and therefore should be screened accordingly. In fact, it is highly recommended that the level of background check should include a level of check that is in-line with the check you would do on an executive of the firm. This should include:

1. Identification of the individual with a data tool. In some cases, a fingerprint check might be appropriate if allowed by law.
2. Full battery of criminal background checks including the federal searches.
3. Full battery of civil searches including federal civil.
4. Credit check.
5. Verification of past consulting assignments.
6. Verification of education and certifications.
7. Reference checks.

The overall cost might be considerably higher than the check performed on your employees, but the risk is often greater. Make sure you really know to whom you are showing the keys to your kingdom.

Vendors can be like the contractors you use every day. They are given extraordinary access to your facilities but often not access to IT systems or the general employee body. Many organizations can, for instance, have delivery truck drivers be directed to driver lounges while their trucks are being loaded or unloaded. Other vendors might only ever need to visit the lobby or your office or factory. While others are escorted to the location they are working in, like a vending machine vendor. Companies often require the vendor to provide the names of the vendor representative who will be coming to your organization. This is sometimes seen as a prudent practice, especially in high security facilities or areas. Sudden changes in assigned personnel can indicate a potential intrusion attempt. Changes of vendors usually can be confirmed with a telephone call or email.

In any event or situation, it is imperative to consider the practicality of doing some sort of screen on nonemployees. Risks vary based upon other security processes you may have in place. The policy you need to adopt should be simple in its core. Do you know who you are allowing access to your business, organization, or information? If you do not, you may pay handsomely.

Table 9-2 provides a "point-counterpoint" discussion.

Table 9-2 Point-Counterpoint

Screening should not end with your employees. Often, the risk associated with individuals who are temporarily or contractually connected to your organization can bring equal or greater levels of risk.

Security	Human Resources
Do the work to find out all the constituent groups that are connected to your organization and research the level of access they have to your employees, assets, information, and systems.	While scrutiny of temporaries and others contractually providing services is important, we need to avoid becoming the "Gestapo" and need be cognizant about the growing privacy laws that must be adhered to.
Whenever possible have a screening strategy for each of the groups that have access to your organization whenever practical.	We must be careful in the groups we "target" and ensure we have consistent criteria to avoid violating discrimination laws.
Make sure you audit the background screens to make sure the service provider is fulfilling your requirements.	We agree that an audit should occur and believe that this should be the responsibility of the Purchasing and Procurement Department.
Failure of individuals to pass the background check based on preset criteria should be reason enough to restrict the movements of the contractor, temp etc. or forbid them access to your premises. Don't take risks on known previous offenders.	While we agree that verifying the backgrounds of these third party individuals is important we have to be careful to not cause our suppliers to violate EEOC guidelines which restrict automatic disqualifications of previously incarcerated persons.
If for some reason a third party supplier can't do a background screen, then you will need to put additional layers of security around the individual. An example would be to have the non-screened personnel escorted or supervised closely.	Having multiple layers of security is fine; however, we can't create a fortress around our facilities or management practices which may impede our ability to retain customers, may not scare customers, or frighten potential new hires. Remember, ultimately we have to support the business succeeding and balance the risk of a given action.

Summary

1. Identify your nonemployee constituent groups of individuals that may be a part of your organization.
2. Analyze what this person(s) have access to, whether it be your other employees, customers, information, space, or systems.
3. Consider and require a screen be completed by the "owner" of the person or persons whenever practical.
4. If a screen is not practical or possible, develop additional layers of security to mitigate risk to your organization.

10
The Special Case of Sexual Offenders

David Allburn

Security professionals are expert observers. When it comes to protecting their business's valuable assets, these guardians know what to look for, how to see it, and what to do about it. Reducing or eliminating security-related threats to a business's reputation is increasingly being recognized as a very important role for the security function. Accordingly, savvy security professionals are recognizing that when their client participates in community-focused programs, which generally involve supporting or working with youth-serving groups, a special category of risk needs to be addressed, the potential for child sexual abuse. As security professionals increasingly focus on contributing to the overall businesses success, they are recognizing that understanding sexual predators' modus operandi is now a necessary knowledge base that they must possess to protect the children of their employees, the community and the company's valuable reputation. With this as a backdrop, the purpose of this chapter is to increase the awareness of security professionals about how sexual predators operate so that they are better prepared to mitigate the very real risk that their businesses could be exposed to.

Can we Just "Spot" These Predators?

Many still think the typical child molester is a creepy looking predator that jumps out of hiding places to kidnap and molest children. They are wrong. Some think the predators disguise themselves as did the wolf in "Little Red Riding Hood." Still wrong. In fairytales the disguise fools the children. In real life it fools the uneducated among us as well. One of the purposes of this chapter is to make it harder for predators to fool you.

Picture this scene: a guy gets out of his car and stops traffic so a mother duck can parade her brood of tiny ducklings across the busy street. A picture like that appears every spring in hometown newspapers. That picture illustrates how we misperceive the sexual predator (child sexual abuse) threat found in community youth sports, after-school programs, mentoring, scouting, kids clubs, even summer camps, the YMCAs, foster parenting, and day care. Think about that picture of "a mother duck parading her brood of ducklings across the street." Can you identify who represents the predator and/or the victims in the picture?

All agree the ducklings represent the victims. Some think the cars represent the predator because they could squash the ducklings. Wrong! Others think the predator might be represented by the guy standing in the road, as if pretending to save the ducks while he selects his next victim (perhaps Peking duck is on his mind.) Better reasoning, but still wrong. The predator is represented by the mother duck, because it's the image least likely to be suspected. Juxtaposing this situation on a human scenario the best disguise is to be an authentic, trusted, admired pillar of the community, church-going family man who sacrifices his time to mentor and help children. Remember the Catholic Church debacle or Congressman Foley. All are individuals who on the surface would be the least suspected as sexual predators.

Another point that is not likely to surprise many is that over 90% of sexual predators are male, although female predators tend to use more physical violence and coercion than do the males. Men tend to be more cunning, patient, and shrewd in their deception technique.

Not the Usual Suspects

The reason everyone is so shocked when one of these predators gets led away in handcuffs is precisely because he was so effective at hiding in plain sight. We say to ourselves, "Surely this minister, congressman, governor, chamber of commerce president, head of the community youth organization, coach was an exception. Nobody could have ever been so suspicious and cynical as to have suspected him!" They are right. Nobody would have dared suspect. But they should have.

The unsuspected should have been inspected. Their backgrounds should have been scrutinized like others who will be working with children or other vulnerable groups. All staff and volunteers who will work with these populations should equally, fairly, and thoroughly be scrutinized. If this scrutiny is done with modern tools and with the skeptical experience of security professionals to advise the process, it is likely any red flag will be recognized. This chapter explains how and why to do such checking, what to watch for in adults and youth who might be molesting right now, and how to deal with the "appearances of potential for complaint" (APC's) that arise from modern background checking methods.

Clinging to the myth that the socially skilled "nice person" just apprehended could not possibly be a predator, we typically say to ourselves, "This exception was so off the charts nobody could have or would have believed a mere child's complaint anyway." This is part right, part wrong. We are more right than we know when speculating a child's complaint would not have been believed. Later in this chapter, the sad reasons for disbelieving victims' disclosures are discussed. But we are wrong about that off-the-charts part. Whose charts? Of course, by this we mean the predator was nice, friendly, and wonderful in every way. His appearance and behavior were the opposite of what we have been conditioned by myth and publicity to expect a predator to look and act like. (Remember the mother duck.) Actually, his entire social structure is the profile of the sophisticated, socially skilled sexual predator described in detail by FBI expert Kenneth Lanning's 2001 study "Child Molesters, a Behavioral Analysis" and by forensic psychologist Carla Van Dam's 2006 book *The Socially Skilled Child Molester*. Consider: Who would have suspected the 30-year Boy Scout veteran chosen to develop scouting's national child protection program? Did anyone have an "uneasy feeling" about the prominent CEO of the Big Brothers Big Sisters affiliate? . . . about the local pediatrician? . . . the kids' volunteer soccer coach? . . . the youth minister? . . . the summer camp counselor? . . . the leaders responsible for hiring them? Should we suspect everyone who is successful and volunteers to help kids?

No. The solution rests precisely in the qualities that distinguish the security professional: doing more and better observing. This is scrutiny, not suspicion. The rest of the solution is a safe and respectful way to act on the "APCs[1]" that informed eyes might notice.

Table 10-1 discusses what to watch for when adults are around children.

This table reprints part of the April 2007 *"Let's Talk"* brochure posted by "Stop It Now," one of the country's best known programs to stop child molesting where it starts. The entire document is posted at this organization's Website (http://www.stopitnow.org/warnings.html). This posting lists the more obvious appearance of potential conflict. Later in this article, it is discussed how to safely and discreetly deal with such observations to the advantage of the group and the client.

Table 10-1 Helpline

What to Watch for When Adults Are Around Children

Have you ever seen someone playing with a child and felt uncomfortable? Maybe you thought, "I'm just overreacting" or "He/she doesn't really mean that." Don't ignore comments or behaviors; learn to talk about them or ask more questions about what you have seen. The checklist below offers some warning signs.

Do you know an adult or older child who:

- Refuses to let a child or teenager set any of his or her own limits (tells a teenager that only a parent can decide when privacy is allowed in the home, even in the bathroom)?

- Insists on hugging, touching, kissing, tickling, wrestling with or holding a child even when the child does not want this affection?

- Is overly interested in the sexuality of a particular child or teen (talks repeatedly about the child's developing body or interferes with normal teen dating)?

- Manages to get time alone or insists on uninterrupted time alone with a child?

- Spends most of his/her spare time with children and has little interest in spending time with people his/her own age?

- Regularly offers to babysit many different children for free or takes children on overnight outings alone?

- Buys children expensive gifts or gives them money for no apparent reason?

- Offers alcohol or drugs to teenagers or children when other adults are not around?

- Frequently walks in on children/teens in the bathroom?

- Allows children or teens to consistently get away with inappropriate behaviors?

Any one of these behaviors does not mean that a child is in danger. But if you answered "yes" to more than one of these questions, begin to ask your own questions and get help. Trust your gut. For information and advice on how to talk to someone, or for resources, please call our toll-free helpline at **1.888.PREVENT (1.888.773.8368).**

---

[1] Appearances of Potential for Complaint™ (APCs) is a trade-marked phrase by Safe Harbor Resources, a research nonprofit based in Ohio and dedicated to finding more effective ways to screen for sexual predators. www.safeharborresources.org.

Client Reputation is an Asset Worth Guarding

The assets most security professionals are hired to protect are tangible ones like property, people, equipment, money, and vehicles. There is opportunity to add value by protecting an important intangible asset as well—the client company's reputation, sometimes called brand equity. (Everyone knows the brand Kleenex. Fewer know the Kimberly Clark Company that makes it.) A firm's reputation is on the line more often than civic-minded companies might think. Such companies often express support for the communities they live in, by sponsoring youth-serving activities like sports leagues, mentoring, homeless shelters, scout troops, after-school programs, county fairs, and holiday concert events. Some do even more, such as encouraging employees to donate time to help manage or staff groups and their events. Often the client's highest officers will serve on the board of directors of such groups, guiding and governing them, but seldom visiting the events themselves where the children gather. These firms get favorable publicity in return, ranging from signs in the Little League outfield, logos printed on flyers and brochures, all the way to applause at big fund-raising and society recognition banquets and congratulations on their various Websites.

When a sexual molestation scandal occurs in a youth-serving group, the public image of the group's benefactors is tarnished along with the reputation of the group itself. Parents and the press speculate about who is to blame. They ask about scrutiny, about precautions, security, and whether someone shirked their duty of care. "Why didn't anybody notice what was going on?" "Where did their volunteers come from?" "Who set up that deficient environment which proved dangerous to children?" Boards of directors start thumbing through their insurance policies while news reporters look for another car window to shove a microphone into. In virtually every case there were warning signs not noticed, hunches not mentioned, vigilance not maintained, scrutiny not done.

Get Assigned if Possible; Volunteer if Necessary

It is ideal if client security personnel participate in the youth-serving group's events or in its governance. Discussions about client security scope and duties should not discourage the community involvement but should include some mention of the reputation risk posed by it. If the assignment cannot be formally extended to include the community activities, ask if the client might "appreciate the effort made" by the security department to volunteer some "in-kind" community service of its own, and within the same group. This has the important effect of placing experienced, skilled eyes on the scene, as well as gaining some client goodwill.

The Emperor's New Clothes

To best understand America's attitude about worker screening for sexual predators, readers should recall the old fable, "The Emperor's New Clothes,"[2] because conventional

---

[2]   The emperor was so powerful and vain (and vindictive) that none dared disagree with him. Some clever tailors convinced him the new clothes they "made" for him were invisible to any who did not appreciate the emperor's wisdom. Since the emperor thought himself wisest of all, he was first to be duped into parading around naked, bragging about the new clothes. The fable demonstrated how it was in the self-interest of all the emperor's courtiers and attendants to go along with the ruse, no matter how ridiculous it actually was.

screening[3] for sexual predators is like a mirage or a shared hallucination: it seems to offer what it does not. Thus it appeals to those who fervently wish such a distasteful "issue" as sexual predators, so full of stigma and disgust, would just go away. But the appeal is not reality as well know the helpless victims[4] who are terrorized into lifetime silence and post-traumatic stress disorder (1) PTSD[5] by the threats of the predators.[6]

Legislatures assumed a person could not be a "sexual predator" unless a judge said he was and enacted laws making the criminal history the "gold standard" of worker screening. While such criminal history records information (CHRI) checks can reduce risk of <u>loss</u> by discouraging lawsuits, they have little effect upon the risk of *harm* faced by victims. That's because so few of the predators ever get caught, ever thereby acquire a criminal history in the first place. Portraying insurance policies taken out against the loss risk as if they also managed the harm risk is a cruel hoax that can attract, not repel, sexual predators. Civil scrutiny methods exist that can expose the APCs defined above, and that meet the Federal Trade Commission (FTC)'s criteria for an "employee misconduct investigation" exempted from most Fair Credit Reporting Act (FCRA)[7] notification and disclosure requirements.

Sexual Predator Inquiries Versus Preemployment Background Checks

Unfortunately, most screening service providers, and especially officials who hire them, think sexual predator inquiries and preemployment background checks are pretty much the same and done for the same purpose. They are not.

Table 10-2 attempts to show how certain features of screening for preemployment and predator prevention will differ. Consider how each difference might suggest alternate approaches to seeking and using the results.

There remains controversy over whether and to what extent the screening industry's federal laws and rules expressed in FCRA/Fair and Accurate Credit Transactions Act (FACTA) and certain FTC interpretations apply to unpaid volunteers. Safe Harbor Resources recommends that organizations take the precaution of choosing to be governed by these rules for all workers, even unpaid interns and volunteers, because today's

---

[3] Conventional screening is based on criminal history records information, which assumes one is not a sexual predator until and unless one has been adjudicated guilty of a crime related to that offense. This screens for existence of a legal label, not for existence of behavioral indications of a likely psychological addiction to sex with children.

[4] Victims are mostly grade-school children, often male, more likely female. One in four little girls, one in six little boys, according to the National Center for Missing and Exploited Children.

[5] PTSD is post-traumatic stress disorder, the preferred diagnosis and treatment modality for terrified war veterans and child sexual abuse survivors.

[6] Predator threats: President Bush declared CSA to be terrorism when establishing the Immigration and Customs Enforcement Department of Homeland Security. According to the American Professional Society on the Abuse of Children, it is the threats, much more than the actual sex itself, that terrorize children into lifetime silence. The threats are so severe as to make PTSD the most often diagnosed aftermath of CSA victimization, and rank CSA in the top five adverse childhood experiences with lifelong consequences that include drug addiction, suicide, obesity, self-mutilation, and uncontrollable anger. Source: Website for the Department of Homeland Security, ICE fact sheet.

[7] FCRA is the Fair Credit Reporting Act, and its update is the Fair and Accurate Credit Transaction Act (FACTA). While obviously aimed at credit reporting, its definitions and controls apply to all "consumer" reporting as well, including background checking.

Table 10-2 Reasons for Differences Between Preemployment and Predator Preventive Screening

	Preemployment Screening	**Sexual Predator Prevention Screening**
Disqualifications sought.	Disqualifying **convictions.**	Disqualifying **behaviors.**
Years into the past scrutinized.	Typically up to 7 years, by statute.	All the way back to the childhood home and teen years. Predators are often exposed to CSA in their childhood homes or got caught while babysitting.
State-legislated "duty of care" met by criminal history checks.	Presumption against negligent hiring if check is single state only.	Predators relocate away from venues where complaints or arrests occurred.
Identifiers used, e.g., name checks vs fingerprints.	Name checks deemed sufficient. Credentials assumed valid.	Predators often use a fake name, even maintain a "library" of fake names with clean backgrounds included.
Who provides the references?	Applicant.	Predators maintain "trophy testimonials" to offer as references. Develop your own.
When is background check done?	**Pre**hire; discrimination issues have high level of sensitivity for applicants.	**Post**-hire. Can check deeper into past, verify names with photos, Can protect sources, terminate worker safely.
Time and cost constraints.	Fastest and cheapest that meets legal minimums.	Must be thorough and repeated periodically after hire.
Periodic rechecking.	Once determined "not a criminal," employers usually don't recheck. Some laws, union contracts, forbid it.	Predators are addicted to CSA, offend repeatedly until either caught (3%) or grow too old. In 2007 Michigan began checking teachers for convictions every 6 months.
Sources available for checking.	Available "public" sources that record formal legal complaints.	Private and nonpublic records that show informal complaints, suspicions, results of others' scrutiny and hesitation to recommend.
Employer's purpose for doing the background check at all.	To avoid downstream liability.	To eliminate the victim's risk exposure to harm; protect organization's brand equity.

philanthropic and selfless volunteer becomes tomorrow's reimbursed or paid worker without notice to the screener.

Another difference arises among the motives of the workers[8] themselves. Volunteers are presumed to donate their time because they want to do good, to help, often

---

[8] *Children workers* is shorthand for all volunteers and paid staff who have any contact with the children in youth-serving groups. In organized gatherings such as at churches and after-school programs, it can and should include contract workers such as janitors and even other adult groups regularly meeting in adjacent rooms. All have facilitated "bonding" of charming pedophiles with the children.

to support their own children in group activities outside the home. Job seekers, in general, are perceived to be driven by the need to earn a living.

Finally, it is important to recognize that the sexual predators who threaten children are not "waiting outside the gate" striving to get in. They are already "in," usually having been screened in by a process adapted from preemployment screening. Getting screened in is prized by molesters because it tends to discredit any complaints made by courageous victims. Adults patronize the confused child victim by reasoning, "It's not possible because we screen everyone here … ." Officials excuse superficial screening policies with "nothing's perfect." It is possible that states and jurisdictions with primitive screening policies could become magnets for sophisticated pedophiles, attracting them with unintended security offered by the superficial screening.

Duty of Care Versus Duty to Warn

The duty of care is a legal requirement to make a reasonable effort to screen the workers and protect the children as a matter of public policy. Most states, with the "help" of privacy, pro convict employment, and civil liberties advocates, have crafted compromise legislation defining what constitutes meeting that duty. The compromise usually attempts to disallow convictions unrelated to the work at hand to be seen or considered by prospective employers. It also limits how far into the past such convictions may be reported by screeners, with bizarre exceptions based on how much the worker is to be paid (apparently afterthoughts about criminal executives.)

Some states tried to preclude lawsuits by codifying a presumption against negligent hiring (lawsuit cannot be based on it) when an employer conducts the one-state-only check. Take, for example, a fact sheet from Florida[9] that states, "The statute specifically provides that if an employer requests and obtains from FDLE (Florida Dept. of Law Enforcement) a state criminal history check, the employer has satisfied the criminal background investigation requirement for the presumption."

This statutory language attempts to save Florida employers money in two ways. First, it tries to preclude successful lawsuits for negligent selection if the offending worker lived in Florida continuously for at least 5 years AND the employer checked Florida's CHRI. Second, it tries to save their employers the cost of checking other states' CHRI. Many states have made similar attempts to save employers the expense of other state checks. Other laws attempt to limit how far into the past inquiries may be made, to conceal offenses that do not pertain to the job being offered, even to expunge "old" offenses. These are foundering as courts realize[10] such laws absurdly ignore three facts: predators have discovered the automobile, predators lie, and the mere passage of time alone does not cure sexual predators of their addiction. As the popular passage of Jessica's Law, the Adam Walsh Act, and others like it set up registered sex offender rules, courts have begun to realize how such laws jeopardize children in clumsy attempts to benefit employers and appease advocates. The duty of care is being defined by a

---

[9] FDLE Fact Sheet September 1, 2005 Criminal History Record Checks. FAQ #1. http://www.fdle.state.fll.us/jla/attach/jla_background_faq.pdf

[10] It is the author's opinion that this and similar statutes are doomed because advocates such as the National Center for the Prosecution of Child Abuse operated by the American Prosecutors Research Institute are educating judges and legislators about the absurdity, even negligence, of allowing such obviously insurance industry–serving statutes to persist.

consensus of court decisions as a duty to acknowledge that predators move, lie, and repeat their crimes. To continue using screening procedures that assume they don't, is "negligent" thinking.

The duty to warn is beginning to gain respect and support in the courts, primarily due to some egregious cases with outcomes clearly against public policy. As a case in point, two families with children enrolled in a church school became aware that one of the teachers was sexually abusing their children. Outraged, they quickly removed their children from the school, but fearing a defamation lawsuit they did not file a formal complaint. When a new family with similar-age children moved in next door and prepared to enroll their children in the school, the previous families chose to warn the newcomer. Word leaked back to the teacher, who promptly sued for defamation, won, and won again on appeal. The hapless families are punished every month as they support a rumored lavish lifestyle of the former teacher. Whispering a warning that somebody is committing a heinous crime can be actionable at law, especially if the one issuing the warning has unwisely failed to make formal complaints and reports first. Stories like that tend to sober policy-makers into a conservative stance when it comes to upgrading their vigilance about sexual predators. They reason:

- What if we find something that looks bad?
- What if we fire the person and he or she sues us?
- What if we're asked to provide a reference on that person applying for a child-caring role?
- What if we keep quiet and he or she harms one of our enrolled children?

This generates a multifaceted liability dilemma. Dare we not scrutinize more, and thereby risk being found negligent? Or dare we scrutinize more, and thereby risk discovering unpleasant facts about trusted workers that force us to face tough choices between duties of care, of warning, and risks of a defamation action? There are even more dimensions to the dilemma. What if parents doubt the veracity of previous declarations of safety? What if the doubt spreads to the overall judgment capacity of leadership? These are not theoretical worries. Such doubt can cause a run on the bank as parents simultaneously disenroll their children en masse if rumors of doubt take root.

Loss Risk or Harm Risk?

Most leadership and policy makers privately focus on the risk of loss, looking for the most cost-effective insurance that covers "jackpot jury awards." For public consumption the emphasis is all on child protection, often citing the existence of insurance coverage as "proof" they have little actual risk of harm to the children. Actually these risks are entirely different, and need to be managed differently. The reasons for this unusual disconnect are found in the research knowledge base. See Table 10-3, where a simple calculation reveals it "takes" thousands of victims for every single lawsuit that arises from their victimization. The largest reasons are victims' reluctance to ever disclose the crime, the tendency for adults to disbelieve their reports, the typical years-long delays before disclosures are made, the overloaded underfunded social service agencies charged with initially investigating, the elapsing of statutes of limitation that preclude the lawsuits, and the high cost and expertise required to investigate and prosecute the crime.

Table 10-3 Attrition in Complaints Reaching Authorities

Consider: Only 1 in 15 victims ever complains, and most "wait" over eight years, often well into adulthood, before doing so. (Perhaps only 1 in 30 disclose while still in their childhood.) FBI studies revealed a "courageous child" had to disclose to an average of six different adults before being taken seriously, implying that perhaps a majority of disclosures fall on deaf ears and die there. Assume that a generous 1/3 of the victims' disclosures survive. Leadership has an incentive to suppress complaints, so fewer than 1 in 4 gets forwarded to Child Protective Service agencies despite "mandatory reporter" laws. CPS accepts only 1/3 of cases to investigate, and only declares 1/4 of those as "founded" for presentation to Law Enforcement. Only 1/3 of such cases result in a conviction, which is necessary before a civil lawsuit can commence. Multiplying those fractions produces: $1/15 \times 1/3 \times 1/4 \times 1/3 \times 1/4 \times 1/3 = 1/6480$. This implies that it "takes" over 6000 victims to be produced for every single lawsuit risk faced by the insurance provider. Even if the imprecision of the estimates makes us revise the statement to say "thousands," is it any wonder that insurance providers consider child protection more of a public relations issue than a claims-loss issue?

Incidence and Prevalence[11]: Dispelling the Myths

This craving and addiction to sex with children afflicts men about 10 times more often than women, and like most addictions it is more or less resisted, not ever cured. Child molestation is a process, often a lengthy one spanning years. It is not an "event" except for rare and sensational kidnappings. In a broad sense this disorder has occurred uniformly over all centuries and peoples. However, in America as in practically all current societies, to act on the impulses is criminal. Research shows some racial differences in victimization rates.[12] Whites in poor, rural, single-parent families and Blacks or Latinos in inner city environments experience higher rates than average.

Most pedophiles begin offending during adolescence, where babysitting is a favorite because the victims are too young to complain. It is variously estimated that such

---

[11] In the child sexual abuse literature, *incidence* refers to the annual rate of new victim reports. Due to heightened awareness and enforcement, the *incidence of new victims* has been declining over the past decade. Prevalence has been applied to the percent of all adults who are estimated to have a diagnosable degree of this mental disorder. Since they are highly stigmatized and their acts are criminal, pedophiles rarely report themselves and counts are impossible. In one study, however, a large number self-reported their groomer-type pedophilia under conditions of anonymity in order to be studied. (Able and Abel, G.G., Becker, J.V, Mittelman, M.S., Cunningham-Rathner, J., Rouleau, J.L. and Murphy, W.D. (1987) Self-reported sex crimes of non-incarcerated paraphiliacs. *Journal of Interpersonal Violence*, 2(6):3-25. These studies estimated an average of 150+ victims per offender, a less-than-3% chance of ever getting caught, and the likelihood that more than 5% of adult males and 0.5% of adult females had this affliction and acted upon its impulses.

[12] Child Abuse and Neglect 1983; 7(1):91-105. In this study of 246 Texas counties … the greater the proportions of single mothers and working mothers in a community, the greater its rate of maltreatment; the greater the proportion of families with annual incomes over $15,000, the lower the county maltreatment rate…Differential patterns of results were observed for Anglo, Black, and Mexican-American segments of county populations. Socioeconomic status of counties was a significant predictor of Anglo rates; greater urbanization was a significant predictor of increased rates of both Black and Mexican-American maltreatment.

irresistible pedophilia[13] occurs in fewer than 1 in 200 men and 1 in 2000 women. These are smaller numbers than described in many studies because they exclude the "soft" offenses such as peeping, flashing, or fondling. But due to these pedophiles' tendency to affiliate simultaneously with multiple youth-serving groups and professions, the chance that one has infiltrated any given youth-serving staff is much higher than the apparent incidence in the general population. An annual study[14] of improper sexual conduct insurance indicates each year that 1% of churches file claims for protection from negligence suits from unwittingly allowing a pedophile to work or volunteer who molested an enrolled child. Other vulnerable program types are youth sports, mentoring, foster care, education, 4-H,[15] Boys-Girls Clubs, YW-YMCA, Scouting, health care, and childhood disability. Any activity that regularly gathers children is a potential, even likely cafeteria of victims for the sophisticated pedophile.

Other mythology involves leadership. The famous "It can't happen here" myth is so obvious that officials now catch themselves before uttering it. The problem is the word "it." The leadership means the sexual abusing itself. Of course "it" never does happen on the premises during gatherings of children. All that happens there is the predator's survey to select victims with the most appeal, and the introductions to begin a relationship designed for exploitation in private, outside and apart from events where potential victims are gathered. Other myths are "We don't hire that kind," and "We've known their families for generations so it's impossible for any of them to be a pervert like that." Predators know that where these myths are cherished, there is opportunity.

Affliction or Addiction?

In the 1980s, *pedophilia* became a medical term; that is, it was assumed to be a disease that could respond to treatment. Legislative-mandated treatment as a condition for release, even early release, hangs on as a logical sounding means to deal with prison overcrowding. Clinical treatment specialists, especially those competing for lucrative state contracts to perform the mandated "treatment" of sex offenders, contend that the treatment reduces offending. It probably does, but only by small hard-to-measure amounts at best.[16] This notion is controversial. Measurement is based on police apprehensions or "recidivism," arguably itself reduced by the sharing of deception technique among

---

[13]   *Pedophilia* is used loosely to refer to the addiction predators have for sex with children. More precisely, pedophilia and the associated paraphilias are defined with respect to the age of the victim in the *Diagnostic Statistical Manual* of the American Psychiatric Association. Pedophilia indicates obsessive-compulsive preference for sex with pre-pubescent children. Ephebophilia is the same affliction directed toward adolescents. Large-scale studies have shown this class of mental disorder to exhibit powerfully addictive characteristics only responsive by degree to treatment (*DSM-IV*).

[14]   James Cobble, executive director of Christian Ministry Resources quoted in Christianity Today, August 2003, Vol 47, Web edition. Although this citation is for 2003, the survey has continued annually, and so has the result: 1% of churches file insurance claims for protection from anticipated or actual lawsuits over child molestation. http://www.christianitytoday.com/ct/2003/augustweb-only/8-18-31.0.html?start=1

[15]   Adult volunteers for 4-H are numerous. In Ohio alone there are 21,000+. Nationally, there are over 1.3 million Scout leaders.

[16]   Stop It Now: "With specialized treatment, a person with a history of having sexually offended who accepts full accountability for his or her crime can learn to control his or her abusive behavior. Without treatment, the sexual recidivism rate for sex offenders is 17 percent. With treatment sexual recidivism among sex offenders drops to 12 percent (Hanson, R. K., et al. First report of the collaborative outcome data project on the effectiveness of psychological treatment for sex offenders. *Sexual Abuse: A Journal of Research and Treatment*, 2002; 142:169–197.)

"students." According to Stop It Now,[17] modern therapy intensely administered under controlled conditions accomplishes some reductions in both appetite and offending. This author believes it is disingenuous to portray low recidivism figures as an indication that serial sex offenders are being "cured" or are not reoffending at all or as much. The groomers "learn from their mistakes" to be sure, but what they learn is how to be more proficient at deception[18] so as to better elude detection and prevent disclosures. Such "learning" includes how to more thoroughly terrorize victims into not disclosing, how to please therapists, as well as how to elude detection.

The Sexual Predator's Decision: to Groom or to Grab

Convenient labels for sexual predators were coined by forensic psychologist and author Carla Van Dam as "groomers" and "grabbers" in her 2006 book, *The Socially Skilled Child Molester.* Grabbers mostly represent the loss risk; groomers mostly represent the harm risk. The styles and characteristics of the two types are summarized below from the book and from numerous private discussions with published researchers.

Youth-serving groups are magnets for "groomer-type" pedophiles who pose as wonderful selfless volunteers, are authentic pillars of the community, and get gratefully and promptly hired. They quickly ingratiate themselves with all, ascend into policy-making roles, and operate an unsuspected assembly line for years, preparing future victims while molesting current ones and dumping no longer wanted ones. Half of all child sexual abuse occurs outside the home, with most of it done slowly and patiently by groomers who are trusted and admired by victim, family, and coworkers alike.

With victims terrorized or shamed into lifetime silence, there are no complaints, no embarrassing investigations, convictions, or downstream lawsuits. No lawsuits means the risk of loss (of assets into jackpot jury awards) has been "managed." Since complaints are already rare (because only 1-in-15 victims ever disclose, and they wait until their adult years to do it) only 3% of all molesters are ever caught. And those are mostly comprised of the crude "grabber-type" pedophiles with few victims each, not the socially skilled and prolific groomers who average 150+ victims.

This is one of the more profound insights to be gained from this chapter. While we proactively conduct preemployment background checks with the intent to weed out "individuals with a problematic background," the stark reality is that 97% of persons who have molested a child have never been arrested for this heinous crime. This does not mean we should stop the preemployment screening, but only that we need to take additional and more relevant steps to identify persons whose past behavior gives "Appearance of Potential for Complaint."

The Grabbers

Grabbers tend to pounce and abduct. Theirs is an obvious crime of impulse, opportunity, and violence. The so-called "premise precautions" like windows, lights, double-teaming, and transportation procedures can thwart this type. Preemployment screening is actually

---

[17] Stop It Now.

[18] See *Predators: Pedophiles, Rapists, and other Sex Offenders*, Dr. Anna Salter, Basic Books, 2004. Her studies of sex offenders using polygraph techniques reveals predators' astonishing determination and pride at acquiring extraordinary deception "skills."

designed to thwart just the grabbers, especially those released from prison who have been designated as registered sex offenders. A fingerprint-based criminal history background check (FBI and all states lived in prior) can meet a duty-of-care defense if the scope of the check was not limited to just one state or length of time lived there. To view typical "grabbers" tune in or replay the televised Internet stings at this URL: http://www.msnbc. msn.com/id/9878187/

Apprehension of these clumsy and mostly unsophisticated grabbers is sensational news and greatly pleases the public as indicated by the ratings and the response of TV talk show hosts. (Only a very few held high-profile jobs or were prominent in the community.) The grabbers have such an uncontrollable urge to molest children that it apparently overcomes all logic and suspicion, even to the absurd occurrence of an offender getting caught on TV and reappearing again in the same sting later.

In November 2006, a Texas prosecutor committed suicide as police were outside his door to serve an arrest warrant for soliciting sex with a minor. Meanwhile, U.S. Congressman Foley was being exposed for importuning congressional interns. In 2005, the head of the Child Protection Division of Boy Scouts of America was jailed for distributing child pornography across the continent, and a Pennsylvania-based private investigator brought a West Virginia prosecutor to justice for covering up a school superintendent's long career of child sexual abuse. If such educated men can succumb to their addictive compulsion to have sex with children, the self-deception required to justify it must be strong indeed. Despite all this, the groomer-types simply do not fall for such obvious tactics as the TV stings.

The Groomers

The groomer-types are much more patient, intelligent, and cunning. They seduce and desensitize the usually prepubescent victims and their caregivers for months before gradually introducing sex. They convince victims the sex is normal, a sign that they are "grown up now" and are "in love" because "that's what people in love do," etc. They explain that parents "conceal the facts from kids" because they want to "hold kids back," etc. Pop culture, fashions, and television abet this.

The profile of the groomer as a "pillar of the community" was published by the Office of Juvenile Justice and Delinquency Prevention, authored by Kenneth Lanning,[19] former FBI profiler and one of the top experts in the CSA field. One of the more bizarre characteristics shared by groomers is their compulsion to save and collect "trophies," that is, child pornography, often of the offender's own victims.

A worldwide clearinghouse for such outlawed activity was discovered in Germany by Homeland Security's Immigration and Customs Enforcement Bureau. Its customer list was dominated by North American child porn collectors, all fantasizing and congratulating each other over their pictorial "conquests." The National Center for Missing and Exploited Children operates a computerized face-recognition program so that victims appearing in child porn depictions can be identified later to support indictments. There has been some success at overcoming legal defense contentions that viewing child

---

[19] Kenneth Lanning: "Child Molesters, a Behavioral Analysis." Downloadable from the Website of the National Center for Missing and Exploited Children, www.missingkids.org. Single printed copies are available. Mr. Lanning operates CAC Consulting.

porn is a victimless crime. Through computer technology, the victims are being found to testify.

The victims, once groomed and effectively brainwashed into cooperating, are usually molested repeatedly for many months, even years, until they age-out of being attractive. When tiring of their current victims, predators dump them, terrorizing them into lifetime silence and shame so intense it often becomes PSTD. The terror is effective. Only 1-in-15 victims ever complain. They "wait" an average of 8 years before disclosing. The terror is recognized. In 2003 President Bush declared child sexual abuse to be "terrorism" and attached the Immigration and Customs Enforcement[20] Bureau to the Department of Homeland Security, tasking them with detecting and deporting aliens who were sexual offenders.

While the PTSD deeply harms and silences victims, it also manifests subtle behavioral symptoms that can be observed and reported while the victim is being molested. This brings the matter into the realm of reporting. All states have mandatory reporting laws requiring medical, education, and religious professionals to report signs of abuse to Child Protective Services officials. The statutes protect their identities to some extent. Will the security or human resource (HR) professional become one of these mandatory reporters who could be prosecuted for not telling? Should they be? But the whole purpose of this chapter is to enable better child protection through observation and safe reporting of behaviors that might contain an APC. How to report is taken up later in the chapter.

Groomers represent the greater threat to children outside the home, but all the attention of press and law enforcement goes to the grabbers. When a local newspaper runs a photograph of a minister being led away in handcuffs for molesting a child, there is such community shame that the story is seldom followed up except to allow the defense to proclaim "This was an isolated incident." It rarely is. The isolated incident was not the sexual abuse; it was getting caught for it. The sad fact is that the minister is likely to have been molesting children for years at the various churches he was assigned. The author visited a local town reporter after such an incident had been reported that week in a distant county. The minister had led a local congregation over 12 years ago. Asked for her reaction to the story, the reporter silently produced a 12-year-old photograph of that minister when he was in charge of the local church, holding two beautiful toddlers on his knees. "Those are my children," she said. No further discussion ensued.

Groomer's Contingency Planning

In the rare cases where a groomer blunders and gets caught or he or she insufficiently terrorizes a dumped victim, all kinds of contingency plans he has prepared in advance get triggered. The plans include encouraging all the predator's associates and peers to cherish the myths, remember all the good things the predators does, and discredit the statements of the victim. The plans include reminding officials that their personal reputations are on the line along with the predator's because they chose him while they were guaranteeing parents no abuse could possibly happen here. All get subtly reminded of a few scandalous cases of overzealous prosecution and community hysteria leading to a foster

---

[20] ICE: http://www.ice.gov/doclib/pi/news/factsheets/accessfactsheetv31.pdf

family's false indictment (and to the making of a movie about it). Predators always have Plan A, Plan B, and more to cope with that possibility. As an example, Mr. Lead Wey,[21] a (now former) senior vice president of Cleveland, Ohio,'s largest bank, was apprehended in Dayton, Ohio, almost a 4-hour commute from his Shaker Heights mansion. He was later learned to have been going through the required "6-months get-to-know-you period" at two other churches in towns located on his route.

Groomer's Method of Operation

Grooming itself has been defined as a criminal act in the United Kingdom's[22] Sexual Offenses Act of 2003 since it is a process of exploiting a trust relationship for the purpose of committing an illegal act. The opportunity to form such relationships is why groomers infiltrate youth-serving groups. The grooming opportunity always requires that the predator engage and beguile the victim, often with the infamous attention–affection–gifting cycle used on needy and needful children. First exploiting their gratitude, next grooming the child's caregivers or parents, the predator ingratiates himself with the whole family, taking care to have the child notice all the approval the predator is winning. As an example, with preferred younger children, the predator will arrange to have horseplay with the child in view of the parents, tickling and laughing while the parents beam with approval. During the session, it is arranged to "accidentally" brush or touch the child's privates, transferring the apparent approval to that act along with all the other benign ones. Later when the sexual touching is being done intentionally, the predator reminds the victim, "Mommy and daddy laughed when we did this before, remember?"

Disrupting the Grooming: The Predator's Achille's Heel

Infiltrated sexual predators are by definition undetectable. Think about it. If they were detectable, they would have been ousted already. Because these groomers are so well "protected" by their facades of respectability, trust, and admiration, they face perhaps less than a single percentage-point likelihood of being arrested. Others may harbor "misgivings or hunches," but most will neither share them nor act upon them due to inability to recognize their validity or due to fear of retribution.[23] All the while the predators satisfy their habit by simultaneously grooming new potential victims, molesting current ones, and reinforcing their warnings to previously dumped ones. Using engineering and militaristic terms, the author recognized this as an assembly line, and that its disruption is the most calamitous event or risk the predator faces. Also realized is that it is relatively easier to disrupt an assembly line than it is to substantiate and bring criminal charges against individuals.

Natural Selection Creates Groomers

One reason groomers tend to elude suspicion and molest many while grabbers get caught and molest few is simple natural selection. It is enormously difficult and costly to lead the double life of the groomer. Only the intelligent socially skilled minority of pedophiles

---

[21]   Article published in the Dayton Daily News, Aug 20, 2002: "Bank Executive Held on Sex Count."

[22]   The United Kingdom's Sexual Offenses Act of 2003, Section 15, criminalizes grooming of a person under 16 by a person over 18, and includes grooming via the Internet.

[23]   See Introduction, in *The Socially Skilled Child Molester,* Carla Van Dam, Haworth Press 2006.

manage to elude detection long enough to perfect their deception skills and become expert at acquiring trust and admiration. The efforts of law enforcement cull the ranks of pedophiles, apprehending mostly clumsy grabbers and probably a rare few groomers who blunder early in their "careers." What is left is a population of pedophiles who are mostly accomplished socially skilled groomers. Arguably due to this natural process, more are entering the groomer ranks than are leaving them due to old age and poor health. It is a known method of operation for groomers to keep the focus of the groups they infiltrate on countermeasures to detect and prevent grabbers. This generates a smug "We're safe!" feeling among parents and leadership that tends to discourage any complaints that might otherwise leak out.

Misperception of Sexual Abuse as an "Event"

Law enforcement and policing are propelled by an "event" mentality. A crime gets "committed." That is why when a person is indicted by the grand jury, there must be cited "counts" of repeating the offense, and separate evidence must be accumulated to support each such "count." However, except for the sensational grabber cases, victimization is not an event. It is a process. Just as it is a crime to engage in organized racketeering, likewise one must be prosecuted for specific instances of infraction, not for the process itself. Thus many social scientists observe that law enforcement is by nature not crime prevention. It requires that a victim be created first. In some jurisdictions this is changing with the creation of crime prevention units; however, this is occurring at too of a slow place.

Official Government Statistics

Many cite "official sources" to illustrate their point of advocacy, whether it is rehabilitation, clinical treatment, better background checking, or sentencing alternatives, revisions to laws, etc. Virtually all statistics on this topic make a statement similar to, "Severe underreporting may affect this data." Indeed, just three facts—the small fraction of victims who complain, the small fraction of perpetrators apprehended, and the need to get caught again in order to be counted as recidivism—explain much. As an example of policy being misguided by official government statistics, consider the studies of incarcerated pedophiles that sought to establish a connection between victimization and perpetration: Did being molested as a child cause people to become molesters? As the studies began, word quickly spread among inmates that the results were going to be considered by parole boards. A wave of "poor me" stories erupted, supporting a cause-and-effect theory called "the abuse cycle."[24] Corrections officials assumed the cause and cure of

---

24   Abuse Cycle, Becker, J. and Murphy, W., *What We Know and Don't Know About Assessing and Treating Sex Offenders*, Psychology, Public Policy and Law 4 (1998): 116-137 "While past sexual victimization can *increase the likelihood* of sexually aggressive behavior, most children who were sexually victimized never perpetrate against others." A spate of studies on juvenile offenders was reported during the 1990s in the journal *Child Abuse and Neglect*. A consensus conclusion was that being a child sexual abuse victim tended to make the victim more susceptible to additional abuse, and in some cases appeared to foster earlier sexual curiosity, which in turn was interpreted by some as being "more sexually aggressive." Author-psychologist Anna Salter demonstrates in seminars how claims of childhood sexual abuse by inmates could not be corroborated and tended to be retracted when the polygraph was introduced. In her article published by *Psychiatry*, Vol 6, Issue 10, pp 433-437, "Adolescent Sexual Offenders," Eileen Vizard states, "However, there is no clear evidence that male victims of sexual abuse in childhood are at higher risk of becoming perpetrators in adult life than are non- victimized young people."

pedophilia had been discovered and got rules written to support early release programs based on group therapy. Later, the abuse cycle was found to mostly explain juvenile offending and victimhood claims of incarcerated adults seeking sympathy from parole boards.

Criminal History is Rare, But it is Essential to Check it Thoroughly

Because the groomers are seldom complained about, they are rarely apprehended. Therefore, they have fewer or no previous convictions or criminal history records information. Those who have been fingerprinted in connection with an arrest frequently seek plea bargains, claim their mandated treatment "worked," and vigorously pursue expungement. And they relocate away from the state or jurisdiction that keeps the record. An FBI fingerprint check is the best first step. When no records are found at the national level, the prints should be checked in the states of residence because not all data flow upward to the FBI. If the FBI records indicate use of other names, all those names should be run against one of the major database services.

Unusual Sentencing for Some Sex Offenders

Two unusual pleas are encountered in sex offender cases, especially older ones. The Alford plea is made when the accused agrees to plead guilty without admitting guilt. It is an administrative plea allowing the accused to receive less or no jail time and perhaps to accept parole, only because there was insufficient investigation resource to prove innocence. Another type of outcome is the Special Sex Offender Sentencing Alternative. This plea arrangement calls for the conviction to be set aside while the offender undergoes treatment and parole. If he violates parole, the conviction is entered; if he completes parole, the conviction is expunged. Both of these arrangements are similar to the consent decree imposed on commercial firms caught violating federal laws. The cheater agrees to accept a penalty or pay a fine "without admitting guilt," in return for which the government agency agrees to not demand a criminal prosecution. Because these require sophisticated negotiation with expensive legal talent, it is generally the groomers who take this position and are able to hire the right level of representatives.

"Risk Management Advice" for Youth-Serving Groups

Most youth-serving groups are nonprofits that depend on donations or philanthropy for funds, and on numerous volunteers for work. They must minimize every expense in order to deliver their badly needed services to the community. A prime candidate for such cost reduction is the background check. As with all precautionary measures, many fervently believe the risk should not apply to THEM because child molestation occurs elsewhere, to others. Cherishing the "It can't happen here" myths, the background check is considered an unfunded mandate ... to be winked at where possible and grudgingly performed to the least allowable degree. The attitude is, "Let others who actually HAVE that problem spend their money to solve it." Please note that we recognize that there are plenty of nonprofit organizations to which this "wink" factor does not apply and that vigorously pursue background screening tactics.

In a well-intended effort, advisors and authors[25] on the topic of managing volunteers have wrestled to bring down this perceived high cost of background checking. They have carefully parsed the duties and job descriptions of the volunteers and paid workers according to how much "continuous child contact opportunity" each role involves. Then they ratchet down the scope and cost of the inquiries according to how much "risk exposure" each job description has. Such "tiered precautions" assume the scrutiny required should match the degree of contact that a role has with children. They further assume that more contact opportunity means more molestation opportunity. Thus they reserve the costly checking for the fewest workers, the ones who have direct and repeated contact with the children such as teachers and bus drivers. Although well intended, such an analysis plays into the hands of the predator because it assumes that grooming is done on site, on premise, and during group events. It is not.

Once the predators has selected likely victims and met with them once or twice, most of the grooming will proceed outside of the group meetings. Coaches will give private lessons; teachers will tutor; mentors will push for overnights; drivers will arrange for unaccompanied transport; and they all will woo the family in order to be seen approved by the child. Then come zoo and museum educational visits, the man-to-man talks, sharing of intimacy, Internet chat room, email, and finally clandestine sex. Bad enough if it would stop there. It does not. Remaining is the most ruinous step of all: dumping. In that step the predator convinces the child that it was her or his fault, not the predator's, and that disclosure will bring all manner of ghastly threats to fruition, including murder, loss of family, and jailing of parents, even loss of eligibility for God's grace, an outcome termed as "soul murder."[26] It is no wonder that the frequent result of such psychological punishment is life-long PTSD.

The "Adverse Childhood Experience" Studies

Drs. Vincent Felitte and Robert Anda conducted the Adverse Childhood Experience Studies for the Centers for Disease Control and Kaiser Permanente HMO. Visit http://www. ACEstudy.org for details. Sexual abuse is a significant adverse childhood experience, responsible for enormous and continued misery in later life, not to mention significant overconsumption of societal services including law enforcement, corrections, welfare, counseling, and other dependencies. In these lengthy and high-sample studies,[27] Dr. Felitte proves the relationship between adult susceptibility to disease processes and self-destructive behaviors, and having experienced child abuse.

---

[25] Linda Graff: *Beyond Police Checks, Better Safe,* and *Risk Management in Volunteer Programs and Community Service.* Books published by Linda Graff & Associates, available from http://www.lindagraff.ca More resources available from the Nonprofit Risk Management Center and Girl Scouts of the USA.

[26] Leonard Shengold: *Soul Murder Revisited, Thoughts About Therapy, Hate, Love, and Memory* (Yale University Press, 1989, New Haven). "The dramatic term *soul murder* probably was coined in the nineteenth century; it was used by the great Scandinavian playwrights Henrik Ibsen and August Strindberg. Ibsen defines it as the destruction of the love of life in another human being. In psychiatry, the term was made familiar by the paranoid psychotic patient Schreber, whose *Memoirs* (1903) were the subject of one of Freud's long case histories (1911)."

[27] "Turning Gold into Lead." Research paper by Dr. Vincent Felliti et al, describing how self-destructive behaviors are actually simple coping mechanisms for the PTSD effects of child abuse. Felliti VJ, "Reverse Alchemy in Childhood: Turning Gold into Lead. The Adverse Childhood Experiences Study." (With commentary by Betsy Groves). *Family Viol. Prev. Fund Health Alert* 8:1-12, 2001 (http://www.endabuse.org/programs/healthcare/files/HA_8_1.pdf)

Appearance of Conflict of Interest

The appearance of conflict of interest is a well-litigated and defined legal concept. Better yet, it is very well understood by the general population. If, for example, your brother runs a paving company, everyone knows you are not eligible to be appointed highway commissioner, never mind that you have not nor ever intend to award a "sweetheart con- tract" to your brother. And there is no point trying to sue for "unfair discrimination." While it may seem, or actually be, unfair to *you*, it is demonstrably and by definition "fair" to the public.

Safe Harbor Resources bases its investigatory inquiries on the fact that precluding such appearances of conflict of interest has been adjudicated as good public policy. The same notion can apply to child workers. It is an obvious conflict of interest to volunteer in child caring roles if one's ulterior motive is to molest the children. Although such a conflict (if it exists) is not publicly apparent, and probably is concealed with all the skill and guile the predator can muster, if indications of it can reasonably, legally, and afford- ably be sought, *they should be*. Furthermore, there is such a conflict if the results of a civil scrutiny background check credibly match typical or average similar background check results from known sexual predators. Seeking concealed indications of such a con- flict is the purpose of sexual predator background screening. Looking for patterns of APC is a reasonable objective for this screening.

There are some interesting reminders that appearances matter. The first is a book written in the 1970s by John T. Malloy titled *Dress for Success*. It caused a furor because it exposed the biases people employed to hastily judge others merely by the clothes they wear.[28] Appearances mattered. The other reminder involves overweight female TV news anchors who sued their TV employers for wrongful termination and discrimination. Courts ruled it was the public who discriminated unfairly and made ratings tumble, not the broad- casters. Appearances mattered again. These precedents, taken with the conflict-of-interest rulings, form a "liability umbrella" whose lesson is that one may form (and act reasonably upon) opinions about how things *look*, so long as those appearances cause damages the employer is helpless to prevent.[29] When news of a molestation event spreads, parents pull their children out. Such "damage" often closes down a group overnight.

What Does the Security Professional do With Adverse Observations?

If a behavior pattern is suspected to match that of pedophiles, the degree of match is an opinion about how something appears. It is not a suspicion that a person is committing crimes against children. It is a suspicion that a pattern is forming with complaint poten- tial that might damage the organization and/or its sponsors. If a security professional

---

[28] *Dress for Success*: John T. Molloy's 1975 classic. The psychological experiments asked participants to view successive slide images of people, and guess which ones were more successful, likable, confident, attractive, etc. Participants thought they were having their own "taste" tested, and were eager to show how socially sophisti- cated they were. Later it was revealed that the real objective of the tests was to expose people's biases in hastily evaluating others based solely on the clothes they wore. Indeed, clothing was the only difference in the slides. They depicted the same people, just dressed differently.

[29] Appearances matter. Perhaps the most urgent instance of this issue is the selling of replica pistols to youth who brandish them to "get respect" and get shot by police for doing so.

notices such a pattern, the observations go up the chain per policy with the suggestion that leadership "consult" with the person observed and get the behavior stopped. It is important to document along the way that these are observations, not accusations, and that they are strictly confidential. Each party to the report should initial a brief pledge promising to not disclose except on a need-to-know basis. No advice should be implied about what personnel action should be taken by anyone. These precautions should protect all involved, including the person himself who might be unknowingly and innocently engaging in the behaviors. (This is not legal advice because it does not pertain to any specific individual case.)

Deflection, Not Detection

In her book *"Predators, Pedophiles, Rapists, & Other Sex Offenders"* (2003, Basic Books), psychologist Dr. Anna Salter coined the term "deflection" in regard to protecting children from sexual predators. It is an extremely useful idea. Confidential opinions formed about vague and unsubstantiated "appearances," while in many states are fully legal reasons to fire workers, may not be totally *safe* reasons to terminate a paid or unpaid worker's employment. By *safe* is meant reasonably unlikely to cause expense to the employer defending a wrongful termination lawsuit.[30] But termination is not always preferred. There is a benign alternative just as effective for those deserving of extra scrutiny: reassign them. Bona fide roles lacking opportunity for contact with the children can be found in group volunteer settings. (Not in 1-to-1 settings like mentors, music teachers, foster care, etc.) This works because the reassignment thwarts the personal physical contact usually needed to start and exploit the trust bond on which groomers depend.

In the era before Internet chat rooms and cellular phone text messaging, such isolation was good interdiction. It spoiled the opportunity to groom by simply deflecting workers away from the children. Today, however, it is not so simple. As the Congressman Foley case illustrated, introductions and the start of an exploitative relationship were apparently "trolled-for" via personal electronic means without any initial physical contact. Grooming in the 21st century can be subtle indeed. As noted above, the United Kingdom has criminalized communications with children for purposes of grooming. And the ABC TV network has distinguished itself with the Dateline stings.

Recalling that groomers are planners, introducing an improved screening method brings with it the opportunity to discourage groomers up front. Furnishing a frank description of the scope, breadth, and depth of the new behavior-background checking is required as part of the disclosure-and-permissions process. If a worker is predatory these disclosures will be chilling indeed. Simply illustrating the diligence of fingerprint-based criminal history checking and noting the procedure and qualifications of a forensic review board (described below) to consider findings that might be prosecuted is likely to dissuade a predatory worker. Psychologists call this the "sentinel effect." Groomers are smart. They cannot bear the risk of having existing or future grooming disrupted. A key concept here is that it is no longer necessary to formally charge or even identify a possible predator in order to nearly eliminate the children's risk exposure. In a manner that does not provoke

---

[30] Lawsuits and "safe": Any party can bring suit against any other party for any reason real or imaginary. By "safe" is meant the likelihood of winning a retaliation lawsuit is so remote as to assure a personal injury lawyer there will be no possibility of a settlement, let alone prevailing in court.

defamation or wrongful termination lawsuits, workers with risky appearing behavior patterns fade away at the start, or their patterns qualify them for alternative ways to serve, or for separation due to having concealed disqualifying information.

Supplemental Inquiry

Because most predators have already infiltrated organizations, limiting the behavior-background checks to just new applicants is of little benefit. Incumbents, workers already on the job, should be screened also. This requires their permission. Because it is likely they will have been already screened with old methods in a previous year, a supplemental inquiry notice is needed. The notice should describe the new inquiry methods, and make provision for additional methods as may become available. It should provide for routine periodic inquiries and include permission to check with out-of-state venues. The notice frankly states that granting permission for the inquiries is voluntary but failure to grant permission may limit job opportunities involving sensitive positions of trust with children and other vulnerable clients. Circulating the notice is opportunity to calm fears and explain that scrutiny is not suspicion. The additional scrutiny is warranted by how the world works today, not by any necessary suspicion that any individual poses a risk.

Scrutiny, Not Suspicion

Supplemental inquiry means increased *scrutiny*, not increased suspicion. Communicating that difference is essential to gaining support for upgrading an organization's vigilance. Once differentiated from suspicion, workers can become accustomed to having periodic inquiries made. Indeed, beginning in 2007 Michigan teachers will undergo routine criminal history checks every 6 months to detect any disqualifying recent offenses. Although such a plan may seem obvious for merely obeying existing laws let alone protecting the students, as of April 2007, no other similar legislation has been introduced anywhere. Teacher unions oppose such proposals on the basis that they imply unwarranted and intrusive *suspicion*. Officially, "suspicion" attaches to a specific person and is triggered by a complaint or other behaviors that have been observed. There has to be a reason for it. In criminal law, it is called "probable cause." Such does not apply to the notion of *scrutiny*, however. Scrutiny is justified simply by increased knowledge of how predators impersonate trustworthy, admired caregivers, how they exploit relationship opportunities with children, and how they exploit superficial background checking. When predators develop more ways to elude detection, more scrutiny is justified in order to thwart them. Unfortunately, this, too, is misunderstood. As mentioned previously, some policy makers try to link how much scrutiny to conduct, to how much "opportunity to molest" is contained in the job description. Mostly informed by the methods of grabbers, not the subtle groomers, such elaborate constructions miss the point. *Scrutiny is justified by how the predators work, not by how the volunteers and employees work.*[31]

---

[31] Justifying scrutiny. A pedophile revealed to his prison psychologist that he took the Sunday noon contract janitor job at the church because he knew two things: (1) he wouldn't have his background checked because he wasn't on the Sunday school staff, and (2) children always forgot things and came running back alone to the empty rooms to retrieve them. After awhile he got certain children to intentionally "forget" things so they could meet him, receive a secret gift, and the grooming began.

The key point is that new circumstances compel us to ration our limited scrutiny resources differently, to prioritize, not demonize, members of groups whose other members proved dangerous once. In the same way it is good public policy to find jobs for persons being released from prison. But not just "any" job. Embezzlers should not be loan officers; pedophiles should not be school teachers. The problem arises when busy employers play "too safe" and automatically eliminate all applicants with any criminal history at all. Such action gives credence to movements that try to conceal offenses from employers, to guarantee they will not unfairly discriminate like that. The author responds to these advocates by asking that they craft their proposed rules so that inquiry will produce sufficient information to protect children and the vulnerable.

Civil Scrutiny

The groomer type can be deflected if criminal background checking is supplemented by civil scrutiny. This means other than criminal history inquiry. Especially in child protection work it is legal to inquire of nonpublic information sources, and indeed of any source in general that the worker gives permission to check. That is why the supplemental inquiry permissions were discussed above. Examples of civil scrutiny include obtaining the list of ever-lived addresses to compare with those disclosed, and using other methods to expose instances of concealment. For all the counties lived in (or fled from) civil scrutiny seeks indications of domestic protection orders, records from Child Protective Services investigations, turndowns of applications for adoption, foster care, and mentoring. It seeks out "developed references" to interview, other than the "trophy testimonials" furnished by the worker, inquiring back to the childhood home and teenage years to contact babysitting clients and get hints about juvenile offending. Civil scrutiny includes analysis and monitoring of national newspapers for arrest reports, and consideration of complaints whether formalized or not. Using the mechanism of "right of personal access" even confidential reports specifically prohibited from viewing "by the public" may be appropriately elicited for confidential appraisal.

Post-Hire Background Checking and the Equal Employment Opportunity Commission

Much data and information resulting from civil scrutiny are nonpublic information that if "leaked" could expose youth-serving leadership to charges of defamation or at least failure to protect sensitive data. Federal laws specifically prohibit using such information to disqualify job seekers. A key component is the determination of positive identification, and the easiest way to establish that is to ask if a developed reference who says they know the worker recognizes his picture. But sharing the picture before the hiring occurs reveals an applicant's race and age, which may invoke problems with the Equal Employment Opportunity Commission (EEOC). So civil scrutiny is applied after conditional offers of employment or volunteering have been accepted. (The condition on the conditional offer, however, can include satisfactory explanation of adverse appearances that crop up later during civil inquiry.) Results of all civil inquiry must be given to the worker unless there was specific reason to suspect "employee misconduct" in previous assignments. In that case only a summary need be given the worker, and sources may remain anonymous. For more information about worker rights regarding employee misconduct investigations, visit the Website www.PrivacyRights.org, home of California's Privacy Rights Clearinghouse, especially their "Background Checks and the Workplace." Laws and rules governing these disclosures and exceptions are discussed next.

Federal Trade Commission and FCRA/FACTA

The FTC, interpreting the FACTA, defined an "employee misconduct investigation" as not governed by provisions of the FCRA. Thus the FACTA fixed a problem that existed for a decade, requiring employers who suspected worker theft to get the suspect's prior permission before investigating it. This is important to child protection and to security professionals because observing people's behavior and making notes about it, is not an investigation per se, although it can become the basis for starting one. Once the scrutiny begins asking whether an investigation should commence, the matter becomes suspicion. Required conditions must be met to support the decision to commence a misconduct investigation, but results from the civil inquiry described above will easily meet them. This means the APCs, the questionable behavior patterns observed, can have quite serious results. Those APC patterns should reach the hands of expert investigators and prosecutors in child sexual abuse cases, leading either to exoneration or indictment.

It is believed rare for persons to have behavior backgrounds that closely match those of serial pedophiles without actually being one, especially if the background includes illegal collecting of child pornography and concealed instances of complaints about molesting children. Even in such cases the background check does not produce actual legal evidence. It produces clues that suggest evidence might be found. Trained investigation professionals and police are required to transform such vague information into evidence if they can. Will they have opportunity to do so? Not if the current situation remains unchanged. Investigations require trained professionals, take a long time, and cost big money. An example of how this situation thwarts justice is the notorious "Pass the trash" procedure by which school districts avoid troublesome and costly investigations by shuffling predatory teachers into each other's districts, bribing the predator to not bring a defamation lawsuit by promising not to mention his offenses.

How can civil inquiry results be safely brought to the attention of law enforcement without requiring formal criminal complaints first? Turning people over to the police like that is a textbook cause for defamation. Suspicion needs to be expertly substantiated, as they say, "gift-wrapped" for prosecution. Who know better how to do that than prosecutors themselves? That is what Safe Harbor Resources reasoned, as it asked an assembly of 188 sexual abuse prosecutors gathered in Clearwater, Florida, in July 2006, to inspect its civil inquiry procedures and adjust them so as not to inadvertently spoil a downstream prosecution. An informal committee was formed to consider the matter. They encouraged formation of a forensic review board, composed of the national body that trains the nation's prosecutors how to investigate and prosecute child sexual abuse cases. The board's duty would be to stand between the security professional or background screener, and law enforcement, receiving the notes from observed possible misbehaviors, and deciding whether they meet the FTC criteria for a misconduct investigation. If they do, this body would initiate the investigation, review the reports, and do the gift wrapping.

Forensic Review Board

Safe Harbor Resources formed a forensic review board in early 2007. It is composed of investigation and prosecution professionals, the very ones who train the nation's attorneys general how to prosecute the child sexual abuse crime. Members include some of the foremost private investigators in the country that specialize in high-profile sexual abuse cases. The forensic review board is organizing to evaluate the behavior backgrounds containing APCs, to see which ones, in their experience and knowledge, both warrant further inquiry AND meet the FTC-specified criteria for an employee misconduct investigation. Then they, not the background screener, conduct the investigation and report its conclusions to the employer (if they exonerate) to the local prosecutor (if they implicate.) At the beginning of the second quarter of 2007 several national foundations are considering funding proposals, and several state trade associations for the private investigator industry have offered nationally coordinated investigations with fees waived. The National Association of Professional Background Screeners is considering the recommendation to include Forensic Review Boards in its recommended best practices and in its position paper for upcoming U.S. congressional testimony. The project is being supported by the National Foundation to Prevent Child Sexual Abuse. It is anticipated that this will become a national resource for the orderly, legal, and ethical processing of scrutiny results so that individuals' privacy and constitutional rights are fully protected and no longer have to be traded off against the rights of defenseless children.

Conclusion

It is critical for security, HR and management in organizations to understand that while preemployment background screening is very important in the battle to thwart sexual predators other tools are needed since only 3% of sexual predators that are pedophiles have a criminal record. Understanding this reality, it is imperative that the new approaches to gathering information be based on post-hire observation and inquiries. The post-hire civil inquiries add data from nonpublic sources that can expose patterns of concealment and distant offending that are similar to those of serial pedophiles. Used in conjunction with pre-employment screening, these can be powerful tools in the war to combat sexual abuse of children. Remember the groomers operate under the radar, infiltrate our organizations, and have been undetectable. New tools described in this chapter can make them visible.

Keep in mind that while prosecution may be the ideal outcome of identifying a sexual predator, in order to eliminate the risk to the children you must make use of the "sentinel effect." This is the disruption of a sexual predators grooming process with the threat of being exposed. Moving the potential predator to a "nonthreatening position" or one that is deemed nonsensitive avoids running afoul of EEOC discrimination guidelines that focus on the relevancy of the criminal behavior to the nature of the work. In the end, the "sentinel effect" creates a win-win solution that solves the problem while also avoiding costly defamation, wrongful termination, and discrimination lawsuits.

Also, the use of a forensic review board as a qualified intermediary to review the results of your scrutiny and decide whether to investigate has proved to be a very promising resource.

With civil scrutiny methods widely deployed by security professionals, we have the potential to make the focus of a recent article entitled "Unto the Third Generation: A Call to End Child Abuse[32] in the United States within 120 Years" by a respected prosecutor, a real possibility or, at a minimum, put a very large dent in it during this current decade.

Finally, security professionals, due to their special skills of observation and scrutiny, can be a valuable resource in protecting their client firm's reputation when it engages in community activities involving youth-serving groups.

---

[32]   "Ending Child Abuse" Victor I. Vieth et al, Haworth Press 2006.

The Other Side of Background Screening

Kenneth Coats and Scott Silverman

Many previously incarcerated persons (PIPs) that have just been released have stopped searching for a job even before they've tried because they already believe they have little chance of obtaining a meaningful job. The *Chicago Reporter* offers an interesting insight regarding the perspective of prison life and its impact on a person, "After years in a crowded and confined environment, a prisoner reacts to the world's ordinary stresses with despair, hypersensitivity to disrespect, and alternating fearfulness and anger. The regimentation of prison life can erode a person's capacity to plan an orderly day, navigate the subways, make it to an appointment on time, or respond flexibly to the smallest of stumbling blocks. Because they lack usable work experience, many are pessimistic about their prospects for finding employment upon release. This pessimism expresses itself in many ways. Some ignore the future and refuse to make plans for employment. Others make plans that are unrealistic or require illegal behavior."[1]

The one's who conjure up some optimism eventually encounter constant rejection because of their criminal history, and sometimes even verbal ejection from employers' premises; these PIPs determination and confidence plunge leaving them little alternative, but to revert to their familiar criminal activities. This, in effect, leaves the PIPs with little alternative and with no rights to live as other citizens do.

Why is it so difficult for previously incarcerated persons to find steady employment, or employment at all? Employers no longer rely on instinct as their reason to hire a candidate. They realize that they are legally being held liable for anyone they hire who commits an illegal act against another coworker, or anyone else in the course of performing their job. This has resulted in thousands and sometimes millions of dollars lost and the company's disintegrating reputation. Any job that requires a person to work with children must ensure that they protect the children at all times.

Candidates and existing employees are increasingly being carefully scrutinized since the tragic attack on the World Trade Center on 09/11, as well as a myriad of other negative events impacting businesses such as employee fraud, workplace violence, and

---

[1] The Real Cost of Prisons Webblog, April 27, 2005.

identity, information, and property theft. Even corporate executives, directors, and the like are under watchful eye concerning not only business affairs, but their personal lives as well. All of these reasons, plus the fact that background checks are more affordable than ever, have a debilitating effect on the everyday life of the PIP.

A background check generally goes back 7 years, although in some cases depending on the position being applied for they can go back substantially beyond this.

Background checks can research a person's

- Employment history
- Personal and character references
- Education
- Court records
- Social Security number
- Credit report; bankruptcies
- Property ownership
- Military records
- State licensing records
- Arrest and criminal records
- Medical records
- Worker's Compensation records
- Drug and sex offenders lists

With the background check results in hand, the employer then determines the applicant's employable status. Many PIP employment applications are rejected subsequent to a background investigation. In many cases, an arrest record, even when a case was dismissed, can tarnish a person's record and negatively impact a job search. The reality is that most businesses are very reluctant to hire PIPs. For example, a published report by the Northeastern Human Resources Association in June of 2005 stated that roughly 80% of companies surveyed say that even minor crimes reported on an employment application bring up severe red flags when employment decisions are made. In addition, the study stated that 40% of companies who receive more than 10 applicants per opening routinely deny applications before reviewing the circumstances surrounding the crime.

Given this cold reality, the question then becomes, why are employers so reluctant to hire previously incarcerated individuals?

In today's tumultuous times the answers are actually quite simple:

- Businesses want to avoid costly lawsuits.
- Businesses want to avoid the negative impact on their reputation that negative incidents could have.
- Political and community pressures driven by emotional fear of the "bad guys."
- Businesses face continued competitive pressures to manage cost.

As we have pointed out elsewhere in the book, negligent hiring and retention lawsuits can cost businesses millions of dollars. Keep in mind that the frenzy for business to insulate themselves from negligent hiring allegations and lawsuits has been a major driver in the unprecedented growth of the background screening industry. In addition, businesses have learned that high profile negative events can impact business performance, customer retention, market perception, and even stock prices. Businesses are also heavily influenced by political and community "hot button" issues with politicians threatening new regulations and the community threatening to withdraw support. An example of this is the current frenzy around sexual predators or offenders. The politicians, community leaders, and parents are in a feeding frenzy to make sure that anyone and everyone who has contact with children has a background check done on them. While on the surface no one could argue with screening all who come in contact with children as a precaution, the stark reality is that only 1 in 10 of sexual predators have a criminal record. Thus, while conducting a criminal background check will certainly identify persons that should be screened out, the vast majority will easily slip through this process because they have never been caught. The question I am raising is, have we moved closer to achieving the real goal of protecting children or have we simply jumped on the band wagon of something that sounds effective, but actually leads people into a false sense of safety? It is also possible that the funds that are being expended on background screening could be wiser spent on other solutions that get closer at addressing the real issue of protecting our children. (See the Chapter 10 for more information on this.)

Businesses oftentimes find themselves caught in the crosswinds of these types of issues, and needless to say their watchful eye never wonders far from being focused on their bottom line and maintaining their margins. The net of this discussion is that businesses have some very real perceived reasons for wanting to avoid hiring PIPs because of the potential risk to persons and the business itself.

A much bigger question is whether or not their reasons are valid and more importantly the actual impact they have on individuals, the community, and society at large.

What is the impact of employers not hiring previously incarcerated individuals? They are people, too.

Individual Impact

Imagine trying to break up a fight between members of your family or friends. The police were called and because you were there, or wrongfully accused, you are arrested. Subsequent to your arrest, the discovery is made that you are not the culprit and you are released. Months have passed, maybe even years, and you apply for a job you really want. You complete the application and confidently answer "no" to the "Have you ever been arrested for a crime?" question. You are more than qualified and the interview goes well. You are offered the job pending a background check. While perusing your offer letter, you receive a telephone call from the company retracting its employment offer. It is because of the arrest made some time ago. You are shocked, followed by frustration and then anger.

- Here's one reader's reply in Reader's Comments to the *Business Week* Online article "Background Checks That Never End."

Review: I am currently unemployed. I have a felony conviction for larceny from when I was 18. I am now in my thirties, and still this haunts me. I am not even able to be employed in the field I went to college for, due to the non-hiring of felons policy. I strongly believe there should be a limit on the amount of time these checks go back. How many people can say they are the same person now as they were in their teens? Or 15 years ago for that matter? I am over qualified for most of the jobs I apply for, yet I remain unemployable. You can't imagine how frustrating it can be. I agree with background checks but do not agree with the no-felons rule that my state (Florida) has.

- Marc La Cloche faced a classic "Catch-22" upon his return from a twelve-year bid in upstate prisons. He had obtained his GED in prison and was trained as a barber by the State of New York in its prison system. Yet, upon his release, he was denied certification as a barber's apprentice from the State of New York's licensing authorities. New York did not permit him to cut hair—the trade he learned inside New York's prison walls.[2]

- "Robert Jamieson Jr. wrote an article raising a valid point of "when should your past remain in the past?" He uses as an example Warren Taylor Yeakey, a construction crane operator, who operated a crane that caused a fatality. Though Yeakey's criminal history revealed multiple convictions for possession of methamphetamine and cocaine, he did not test positive for drugs subsequent to the accident. Nevertheless, questions were raised regarding his criminal past and the company's decision to employ him.

Jamieson pointedly wrote, "The question I've been mulling—and it is a topic that employers everywhere debate—is whether a man with multiple convictions for possession of methamphetamine and cocaine should be operating a big crane in the first place. The problem in this case—like others where private travails become public tribulations—is what a person's past tells us about them, if anything."

Similarly, Jamieson tells of Rev. Tony Harris who voluntarily stepped down as Seattle University's vice president based on a decade old accusation "he repeatedly made homosexual overtures to a 25-year-old seminary student." Though the university considered this piece of the reverend's history 'old news,' there were others who questioned his past and how it relates to his present character.

Jamieson posed the question, "Should that past have disqualified him for this kind of job?" and added, "In the broad view, society seems rabidly intent on having folks carry human failure around like a permanent scarlet letter."[3]

Where is the line drawn? Is it possible for people to make mistakes—be it minor or critical—and eventually get on with their lives, or are they marked with an eternal curse only to walk the road of rejection and alienation forever?

These scenarios are common and affect the lives of millions of PIPs and the wrongfully accused alike. Because neither know, or even understand the laws concerning background checks and their rights under these laws, most simply throw up their hands and become despondent, unproductive, or even harmful to themselves and society at large.

---

[2] The Real Cost of Prisons Weblog (http://realcostofprisons.org/blog/archives/2005/04/tough_on_crime.html) written by Carolina Cordero Dyer.

[3] *The Seattle Post-Intelligencer* Website (http://seattlepi.nwsource.com/jamieson/293143_robert21.html) written by Robert L. Jamieson Jr.

What is the Potential Magnitude of the Impact?

The U.S. Department of Justice cites that the number of inmates in jails and prisons has exceeded two million for the first time in history in 2002. Not only does the United States imprison more people than any other nation, its incarceration rate of 702 inmates per 100,000 residents is the highest in the world (findings based on the Bureau of Justice Statistics). According to the Legal Action Center, more than 630,000 people are released from state and federal prisons each year with hundreds of thousands leaving the local jails.

Although heinous and serious crimes have been on the decline nationwide over the past 20 years, the number, range, and severity of civil penalties have increased for those with criminal convictions, and in some cases, are applicable to individuals who were never found guilty of a crime. To support this claim, The Legal Action Center (LAC) conducted a meticulous, 2-year study of the obstacles individuals with a criminal background face upon reentering society to attempt to live productive lives. The study found the following startling statistics regarding barriers of ex-offenders:

- Most states allow employers to deny jobs to people who were arrested, but never convicted of a crime.
- Most states allow employers to deny jobs to anyone with a criminal record, regardless of how long ago or the individual's work history or personal circumstances.
- Most states ban some or all people with felony drug convictions (including possession due to substance abuse) from being eligible for federally funded public assistance and food stamp programs.
- Many public housing authorities deny eligibility for federally assisted housing based on an arrest that never led to a conviction.
- Twenty-seven states automatically suspend or revoke licenses for some or all drug offenses; 23 states either suspend or revoke licenses for driving-related offenses.

Table 11-1 details some state restrictions on employers' use of criminal records.

State Laws and Their Impact on Use of Criminal Records for Employment Purposes

While the Federal Credit Reporting Act (FCRA) and Equal Employment Opportunity Commission (EEOC) provide a legal framework under which consumer reporting agencies and employers report and use criminal records, there are a number of state laws that limit the use of arrest and conviction records by prospective employers. These range from laws and rules prohibiting the employer from asking the applicant any questions about arrest records, to those restricting the employer's use of conviction data in making an employment decision. In some states, while there is no restriction placed on the employer, there are protections provided to the applicant with regard to what information they are required to report.

Alabama

Arrest: No Alabama statutes have been located that restrict an employer's ability to obtain and/or use information regarding arrests.

Conviction: No Alabama statutes have been located that restrict an employer's ability to obtain and/or use information regarding convictions.

Table 11-1 State Restrictions on Criminal Record Use by Employers

The following text is an excerpt from Chapter 15 of *The Criminal Record Manual* by Derek Hinton and provided by Mr. Hinton and BRB Publications.

States that Prohibit the Use of Misdemeanor Convictions

Several states restrict the use by employers of misdemeanor convictions. If the arrest prohibition is an attempt by some states to address the credibility issue, the misdemeanor prohibition is an attempt to address the "job related" issue. These states have decided that in some cases, misdemeanor infractions should not be considered by employers—that they are never "job related." The states that to some degree limit employers from reviewing misdemeanor records are—

- **California** In those cases in which probation has been successfully completed or otherwise discharged and the case has been judicially dismissed. In addition, employers are prohibited from asking about certain less serious marijuana offenses.
- **Hawaii** Employers cannot consider misdemeanor convictions for which a jail sentence cannot be imposed. (They are restrictive on felony convictions too.)
- **Massachusetts** Employers cannot inquire into or maintain records regarding any misdemeanor conviction where the date of such conviction or completion of incarceration, whichever date is later, occurred five or more years prior to the date of application for employment, unless such person has been convicted of any offense within the five years immediately preceding the date of such application for employment.
- **Minnesota** Employers cannot consider misdemeanor convictions for which a jail sentence cannot be imposed.
- **New York** Employers may not consider misdemeanor convictions older than 5 years unless the person has also been convicted of some other crime within the past 5 years.

States that Prohibit the Use of Expunged or Sealed Records

An expunged or sealed criminal record is one that a court has ordered to be kept a secret. When ordering a criminal record on an individual, some locales will report that that they may not report the criminal record because it has been sealed or expunged. This absurdity is along the lines of "they made me promise not to tell you that your dog got ran over by a car, so I won't." Sealed or expunged criminal records are controversial, but reporting that an individual's criminal record is not available because it has been sealed or expunged seems one tick disingenuous. Especially ludicrous are those records I have seen that report that there is no criminal record by stating "Record Expunged." Crazy, yet it happens. As a result, some states explicitly prohibit the consideration of expunged or sealed records.

These states are:

- **California**
- **Colorado**
- **Connecticut**
- **Florida** (There are several exceptions.)
- **Hawaii**
- **Illinois**
- **Kansas**
- **Ohio**

Employers are prohibited from inquiring about job applicants' juvenile arrest records that have been expunged.

- **Oklahoma**
- **Oregon**

Employers cannot refuse to hire based upon a juvenile record that has been expunged.

- **Rhode Island**
- **Texas**

(Continued)

Table 11-1   State Restrictions on Criminal Record Use by Employers—Cont'd

- **Virginia**

  A few more states, while not explicitly prohibiting employers from reviewing the records, do allow job applicants to "lawfully deny or fail to acknowledge" sealed or expunged records. Frankly, it is probably unwise to put too fine a point on the legalities of using a sealed or expunged record. An employer using a legally sealed or expunged record to deny employment will probably be challenged, if the reason for the denial is known. Incidentally, if you are using a criminal record vendor, the vendor will probably suppress notations regarding sealed or expunged records.

States that Limit the Use of First Offense Records

Two states give first offenders a mulligan.

- **Georgia** Certain first offender crimes in which the offender has been discharged without court adjudication of guilt are not reportable under Georgia law and a notification of discharge and exoneration is to be placed upon the record by the court. The discharge is not considered a conviction of a crime and may not be used to disqualify a person in any application for employment.

- **Massachusetts** Employers may not inquire or maintain records related to a first conviction for any of the following misdemeanors: drunkenness, simple assault, speeding, minor traffic violations, affray, or disturbance of the peace. (In other words, aside from the simple assault misdemeanor, it sounds like most college students catch a break.)

States That Restrict the Use of Records Based on Time Periods

Some states restrict the use of criminal records based on their age. A sampling:

- **California** A consumer report may not contain criminal information older than 7 years.

- **Hawaii** Employers may not examine conviction records older than 10 years.

- **Massachusetts** Certain misdemeanors (as detailed in the misdemeanor section above) older than five years.

- **Maine** In most instances, an employer must only consider the past 3 years.

State Reporting Restrictions

There is a big difference in a state law that restricts the *use* of a criminal record by *employers* and a state law that restricts what a *vendor* can *report*. Several states restrict what a vendor can report, i.e., they have different limitations than the federal FCRA based on time periods. However, there are many exceptions and many of the states are changing their laws to mirror the federal guidelines. States that recently still restricted vendor reporting of criminal conviction information to seven years were California, Colorado, Kansas, Maryland, Massachusetts, Montana, New Hampshire, New Mexico, New York, Texas, and Washington. However, Kansas, Maryland, Massachusetts, New Hampshire, and Washington waive the time limit if the applicant is reasonably expected to make $20,000 or more annually. In New York, the exception is $25,000. In Colorado and Texas, the figure is $75,000. Is it any wonder that many employers and vendors concentrate on complying with the federal FCRA?

Alaska

Arrest: Alaska has a statute indicating an individual may not obtain non-conviction information or correctional treatment information.

Conviction: There are no Alaska statutes restricting an employer's ability to obtain or use information regarding convictions.

Arizona

Arrest: No Arizona statutes have been located that restrict an employer's ability to obtain and/or use arrest records.

Conviction: No Arizona statutes have been located that specifically restrict a private employer's ability to obtain and/or use conviction records.

Arkansas

Arrest: No Arkansas statutes have been located to restrict any private employer's ability to obtain and/or use arrest records.

Conviction: No Arkansas statutes have been located to restrict any private employer's ability to obtain and/or use conviction records.

California

Arrest: Employers cannot ask job applicants to disclose information about arrests or detentions that did not result in a conviction or that resulted in a referral to and participation in a pre- or post-trial diversion program (*e.g.*, a drug treatment program).

Conviction: Employers can inquire about an applicant's prior criminal convictions if the inquiry is accompanied by a statement that such a conviction will not necessarily disqualify the applicant from employment.

Colorado

Arrest: Colorado law prohibits employers from requiring applicants to disclose information contained in sealed arrest records.

Conviction: Colorado law prohibits employers from requiring applicants to disclose information contained in sealed conviction records.

Connecticut

Arrest: Employers are restricted from requesting or using arrest records.

Conviction: No statute or regulation prohibits the collection and use of conviction information.

District of Columbia

Arrest: No District of Columbia statutes have been located that restrict an employer's right to obtain and/or use arrest records.

Conviction: No District of Columbia statutes have been located that restrict an employer's right to obtain and/or use conviction records.

Florida

Arrest: No Florida statutes have been located that restrict an employer's ability to obtain and/or use arrest records.

Conviction: No Florida statutes have been located that restrict an employer's ability to obtain and/or use conviction records.

Georgia

Arrest: Employers may not use arrest records that have been discharged under the <u>First Offender's Law</u> when making an employment decision regarding a prospective employee.

Conviction: Employers may not obtain or use convictions of those individuals who have had their convictions expunged under Georgia's First Offender's Law.

Hawaii

Arrest: Employers may not obtain or make adverse employment decisions based upon arrest or court record information found on employment applications or other inquiries into an individual's "arrest or court records."

Conviction: Once a conditional offer of employment has been made, but not before, an employer may inquire into and consider an applicant's or employee's conviction record, if that record bears a rational relationship to the job.

Idaho

Arrest: Employers may not obtain or use any record of an arrest without disposition after one year from the date of the arrest without written consent from the applicant or employee.

Conviction: No statutes have been located that restrict an employer's ability to obtain and/or use conviction records.

Illinois

Arrest: Employers may not make adverse employment decisions based upon arrest records, sealed/expunged criminal histories, or arrests for which an individual has pled guilty to a crime, received supervision, complied with the supervision requirements, and received a judgment dismissing the charges.

Conviction: Employers may use conviction information to evaluate prospective employees.

Indiana

Arrest: Employers may obtain limited criminal histories (including arrests, indictments, and convictions) of applicants for employment purposes.

Conviction: Employers may obtain limited criminal histories of applicants for employment purposes.

Kansas

Arrest: Employers may require applicants (and prospective independent contractors) to grant them access to criminal history records to determine the applicants' fitness for employment.

Conviction: A job applicant whose arrest record, conviction, or diversion of crime has been expunged may state that he or she has never been arrested, convicted, or diverted of such crime, except when applying for a position in certain state agencies and commissions or in private security.

Kentucky

Arrest: Kentucky has adopted the federal Uniform Guidelines on Employee Selection Procedures, which encompass any "selection procedure used to make employment decisions."

Conviction: Employers can request conviction records for felonies, most misdemeanors committed within five years of the request, and guilty pleas.

Louisiana

Arrest: No Louisiana statutes have been located that restrict an employer's ability to obtain and/or use arrest records.

Conviction: No Louisiana statutes have been located that restrict an employer's ability to obtain and/or use conviction records.

Maine

Arrest: Non-conviction records may be accessed by employers only with the express authorization of a court or statute or to determine the suitability of prospective law enforcement officers.

Conviction: Employers have free access to conviction records.

Maryland

Arrest: No Maryland statutes have been located that restrict an employer's ability to obtain and/or use arrest records.

Conviction: No Maryland statutes have been located that restrict an employer's ability to obtain and/or use conviction records.

Massachusetts

Arrest: Employers are prohibited from requesting, making record or using an application to obtain information about an arrest, detention, or disposition for any violation of the law that did not result in a conviction.

Conviction: Employers may ask individuals if they were convicted of a misdemeanor with some limitations.

Michigan

Arrest: Employers are prohibited from requesting, making or maintaining records regarding a misdemeanor arrest, detention, or disposition that did not result in a conviction.

Conviction: Employers may inquire about convictions or pending felony charges.

Minnesota

Arrest: Arrest records in Minnesota are public records in the originating agency.

Conviction: The Department of Human Rights has indicated that inquiries about prior convictions do not violate Minnesota law.

Mississippi

Arrest: No Mississippi statutes have been located that restrict an employer's ability to obtain and/or use arrest records.

Conviction: No Mississippi statutes have been located that restrict an employer's ability to obtain and/or use conviction records.

Missouri

Arrest: The Missouri Commission on Human Rights Preemployment Inquiry Guidelines state that inquiries about arrests are unacceptable and inquiries about the number and kind of arrests are inadvisable.

Conviction: Missouri law also prohibits employers from disqualifying individuals based on a criminal conviction unless there is a "reasonable relationship" between the conviction and the individual's ability to perform the job.

Montana

Arrest: The Montana guidelines regarding preemployment inquiries warn employers about inquiring into criminal arrest records.

Conviction: The Montana guidelines state that it is lawful for employers to inquire about criminal convictions.

Nebraska

Arrest: No Nebraska statutes have been located that restrict an employer's ability to obtain and/or use arrest records.

Conviction: No Nebraska statutes have been located that restrict an employer's ability to obtain and/or use conviction records.

Nevada

Arrest: Nev. Rev. Stat. Ann. § 179A.100. The Nevada Human Rights Commission prohibits inquiries regarding arrests.

Conviction: No Nevada statutes have been located that restrict an employer's ability to obtain and/or use of conviction records.

New Hampshire

Arrest: No New Hampshire statutes have been located that restrict an employer's ability to obtain and/or use arrest records.

Conviction: No New Hampshire statutes have been located that restrict an employer's ability to obtain and/or use arrest records.

New Jersey

Arrest: No New Jersey statutes have been located that restrict an employer's ability to obtain and/or use arrest records.

Conviction: No New Jersey statutes have been located that restrict an employer's ability to obtain and/or use conviction records.

New Mexico

Arrest: No New Mexico statutes have been located that restrict a private employer's ability to obtain and/or use arrest records.

Conviction: No New Mexico statutes have been located that restrict a private employer's ability to obtain and/or use conviction records.

New York

Arrest: Employers may not request information relating to an arrest without a conviction, unless the charges are still pending.

Conviction: Employers may only consider (1) an applicant's convictions that bear a direct relationship to the job; (2) whether employment would create an unreasonable risk to property or to the safety or welfare of specific individuals or the general public; or (3) whether the position is in relation to the regulation of child-care facilities. N.Y. Corr. Law. §§23-A 752, 753; N.Y. Exec. Law § 296(15).

North Carolina

Arrest: No North Carolina statutes have been located that restrict an employer's ability to obtain and/or use arrest records.

Conviction: No North Carolina statutes have been located that restrict an employer's ability to obtain and/or use conviction records.

North Dakota

Arrest: No North Carolina statutes have been located that restrict an employer's ability to obtain and/or use arrest records.

Conviction: No North Carolina statutes have been located that restrict an employer's ability to obtain and/or use conviction records.

Ohio

Arrest: Employers cannot question an applicant about an expunged juvenile arrest record. Ohio Rev. Code Ann. § 2151.358(I).

Conviction: Employers may not question applicants about sealed convictions unless the question bears a direct and substantial relationship to the position for which the person is being considered.

Oklahoma

Arrest: Employers may request criminal history records, including arrests, for prospective employees. However, certain "non-serious offenses" as enumerated by statute will be excluded.

Conviction: Employers may request criminal history records for prospective employees. Okla. Admin. Code §§ 375:9-1-1, 375:9-1-2.

Oregon

Arrest: No Oregon statutes have been located that restrict an employer's ability to obtain and/or use arrest records.

Conviction: Employers cannot rely on a juvenile record that has been expunged to make employment decisions. Or. Rev. Stat. § 659A.030.

Pennsylvania

Arrest: Under Pennsylvania's Criminal Record Information Act, employers generally may not have access to the following criminal history records to determine eligibility for employment or volunteer services: (1) records of arrests with no convictions or no disposition reported; (2) expunged or pardoned convictions; and (3) convictions relating to summary offenses. 18 Pa. Cons. Stat. § 9125.

Conviction: Employers may consider a prospective employee's convictions only to the extent they relate to the applicant's suitability for the position for which he or she applied. 18 Pa. Cons. Stat. § 9125. The applicant must be notified in writing if he or she was not hired based in whole or in part on his criminal history. 18 Pa. Cons. Stat. § 9125.

Rhode Island

Arrest: Employers may not inquire about an applicant's arrest records, unless the applicant is applying for a law enforcement or agency position. R.I. Gen. Laws § 28-5-7(7).

Conviction: Employers may inquire about conviction records. R.I. Gen. Laws § 28-5-7(7).

South Carolina

Arrest: No South Carolina statutes have been located that specifically restrict an employer's ability to obtain and/or use arrest records.

Conviction: No South Carolina statutes have been located that restrict an employer's ability to obtain and/or use conviction records.

South Dakota

Arrests: No South Dakota statutes have been located that specifically restrict an employer's ability to obtain and/or use arrest records.

Convictions: No South Dakota statutes have been located that specifically restrict an employer's ability to obtain and/or use conviction records.

Texas

Arrest: The release or use of expunged felony or misdemeanor arrest records for any purpose is prohibited and the person whose records are expunged may deny the arrest and the existence of the expunction order. *Texas Code of Criminal Procedure, Art.* 55.03.

Conviction: No Texas statutes have been located that restrict an employer's ability to obtain and/or use conviction records.

Utah

Arrest: Employers may not ask about arrest records and are advised to limit conviction inquiries to those that are job-related.

Conviction: No Utah statutes have been located that restrict an employer's ability to obtain and/or use conviction records.

Vermont

Arrest: No Vermont statutes have been located that specifically restrict an employer's ability to obtain and/or use arrest records.

Conviction: No Vermont statutes have been located that specifically restrict an employer's ability to obtain and/or use arrest or conviction records.

Virginia

Arrest: Employers cannot require applicants (and agencies cannot require licensees) to disclose information about arrests or criminal charges that did not result in conviction or that have been expunged. Va. Code §19.2-392.4

Conviction: Criminal history record information may be disseminated for investigations of applicants for employment if the job will involve personal contact with the public or when past criminal conduct would be incompatible with the nature of employment under consideration. Va. Code Ann. § 19.2-389.

Washington

Arrest: The Washington administrative regulations declare that pre-employment inquiries regarding arrests must include whether charges are still pending, have been dismissed, or led to conviction of a crime involving behavior that would adversely affect job performance, and whether the arrest occurred within the last 10 years.

Conviction: The Washington Preemployment Inquiry Guide provides that inquiries regarding convictions will be considered justified by business necessity if the crimes inquired about reasonably relate to the job duties, and if such convictions (or release from prison) occurred within the last 10 years. Wash. Admin. Code § 162-12-140.

West Virginia

Arrest: According to West-Virginia's Preemployment Inquiry Guide, pre-employment inquiries into general arrest records are prohibited.

Conviction: Employers are prohibited from obtaining arrest or conviction records unless the employer first obtains the applicant's consent.

Wisconsin

Arrest: Under Wisconsin law, requesting an applicant, on an application form or otherwise, to supply information regarding any arrest record is generally considered employment discrimination and is prohibited.

Conviction: Under Wisconsin law, employers generally may not discriminate against an individual (e.g., refuse to hire, license, bar or terminate from employment) based on arrest or conviction records.

Wyoming

Arrest: No Wyoming statutes have been located that specifically restrict an employer's ability to obtain and/or use arrest records.

Conviction: No Wyoming statutes have been located that specifically restrict an employer's ability to obtain and/or use arrest or conviction records.

In preparing this reference document, GIS attempted to provide a concise guide to those state laws that restrict the use of criminal records in some manner. While we have tried to be thorough in our approach to this subject, the states and references to law noted here do not represent an exhaustive compilation of every statute or regulation that may be applicable to your particular business or locale. The information provided as referenced by the NAPBS, CCH, BNA, EEOC and state statutes herein should not be considered legal advice and should not replace legal counsel sought by your company. GIS assumes no liability for any errors or omissions within this document.

Social Impact

While there is no argument that performing background checks leads to improved safety and security of people at work, there still lies the problem of increasing likelihood of unemployability for PIPs, which ultimately contributes to recidivists. Feeling that they have no control over their lives and feeling marked as outcasts, the recidivist robs, deals drugs, and destroys his or her way back into the already overcrowded prison system. ..."

Language has a very powerful impact on how people view things and what we think of them. We need to change the language we use to refer to persons who have been in prison to start reshaping our view of these people.

Following the line of thinking known as enlightened self interest would suggest that society has a role in helping to ensure that PIPs are rehabilitated, not only for the benefit of society at large, but because recidivists commit much of the crime plaguing communities. According to the Alliance for Previously Incarcerated Persons, one of the key ways people can help is to stop viewing PIPs as the sum of their indiscretions. Such thinking spawned the term "previously incarcerated person," which is said to affirm PIPs' humanity more than words such as "ex-convictor, felon." The wording takes the emphasis off the crimes and places it on the fact that the person has served their time, and it reminds people that PIPs are people too."

The stigmas behind other language has been linked with employers' unease in hiring PIPs, another aspect society needs to change. According to the U.S. Department of Justice, employment substantially reduces the likelihood of recidivism. Preventing PIPs from acquiring jobs may then contribute to a cycle of crime. It is important to remember that enrollment in re-entry programs makes employers more amenable to hiring PIPs.

Source: Ensuring Rehabilitative Success in Social Re-entry, By Vincent Sherry WI Contributing Writer, http://www.washingtoninformer.com/ARPrisonReentry2005June27.html

Dennis Drellishak of Corporate Screening Services, raises a valid question regarding the number of growing companies that conduct background screenings. He asks, "Are we moving towards a point where an unwritten norm will arise regarding what types of crimes make you unemployable and even worse are we creating a class of unemployable people that are part of a criminal class?" This conjures up questions on social, political, cultural, and economical fronts that will need to be perused and resolved.

An Editorial from the St. Joseph's University's campus newspaper *The Hawk* had an interesting perspective on this issue:

Editor's Column: Criminal background checks hinder a new start for students
Issue date: *3/28/07,* **Section:** *Opinion*

Saint Joseph's University joins a number of other colleges in the region and across the nation next year in adopting the policy of criminal background checks on its hopeful applicants. In addition to submitting the standard transcripts, SAT scores, essays, and activities resumes, candidates will have to submit to criminal history investigations before being admitted to many universities.

The premise of this decision is that it will supposedly help decreases incidences of campus crime and result in serious disciplinary action, such as drug use and dealing, violence, and rape. The debate against this position so far has questioned whether or not this precaution is effective, as there is little to no evidence to support it, whether it violates privacy, and if it retries and punishes crimes that have already been served. However, there is one major underlying social issue that could potentially be the downfall behind this plan that has not yet been addressed.

It's the very principle behind legislation such as the No Child Left Behind Act, and other educational programs aimed at raising youths out of neighborhoods plagued with crime, violence and frightening statistics. While a number of studies have illustrated that early education often correlates with positive societal behavior and consequently, a better quality of life, it is higher education, such that of a university, that allows many residents of the aforementioned neighborhoods to better their financial and locative situation.

While the University should have the right to consider who is admitted, it is difficult to see this as any more than a screening measure. While the intention may be to deliberate on these situations on a case-by-case basis, the sheer volume of applications will make this feat impossible. For a school like Saint Joseph's that receives nearly 10,000 applications per year, and only has a handful of admissions counselors, it's hard to believe that this won't simply become something of a screening process, since spending more than five to ten minutes on a single application isn't likely. To read through a statement of conduct and then heavily consider an individual's character before making an admissions decision would become extremely time consuming.

Considering that much of the judicial action that a school like St. Joe's has to confront comes from students who do not have an extensive criminal record in the first place, this plan seems like a fruitless ordeal that will serve little purpose beyond issuing sentences that have already been served.

It is understandable that a selective university is seeking to accept only the best of the best; however, there are ethics involved in this situation. The issue that has been troublingly overlooked here is that college is a perfect opportunity for individuals to separate themselves from environments where crime is a way of life. It is a place where students can find themselves and make life-altering changes. Is screening out those individuals with a rap sheet in one environment really an ethically responsible choice for society to make as a whole? Considering the potential for the long run, no, it isn't.[4]

The greater society pays for this folly in many ways. One is the cost of building more and more prisons, which is not just a result of new criminals being incarcerated, but more so, because of the revolving door that keep offenders coming back, again and again. Some wise person once said that the definition of insanity is "continuing to do the same thing, but expecting a different result." When are we going to learn this truism and stop the madness?

Not employing PIPs is not beneficial to the employer, society, and especially the PIPs, and there's every benefit to gain to ensure they are employed.

First, employed PIPs are least likely to commit crimes resulting in repeat offences.

With an eye toward our prison epidemic, the Vera Institute of Justice released a report recently on imprisonment in America titled "Reconsidering Incarceration: New Directions for Reducing Crime."

Here is a summary of its findings:

- Research shows that while the United States experienced a dramatic drop in crime between 1992 and 1997, imprisonment was responsible for just 25% of that reduction.

- The remaining 75% was caused by other factors, including lower unemployment, higher wages, more education, more high school graduates, fewer young persons in the population, increase in the number of police officers (provided that the number of police did not necessarily translate into more arrests), and decreases in crack cocaine markets.

- The more employment, the less crime. Imprisonment reduces employment, and hence can foster more crime. "Incarceration creates problems of low earnings and irregular employment for individuals after release from prison by dissuading employers from hiring them, disqualifying them from certain professions, eroding job skills, limiting acquisition from work experience, creating behaviors inconsistent with work routines outside prison, and undermining social connections to good job opportunities." Moreover, employers may shun neighborhoods with high incarceration rates, and prison can generate connections to illegal rather than legal employment. As two researchers explain, "the magnitudes of the crime-unemployment effects ... suggest that policies aimed at improving the employment prospects of workers facing the greatest obstacles can be effective tools for combating crimes."

- Research showed that a 10% increase in real wages produced significant decreases in both real property and violent crime.

The report concludes that "the impact of incarceration on crime is limited and diminishing. ..." "Public safety cannot be achieved only by responding to crime after it occurs ..." but by addressing factors that increase crime rates, such as "unemployment, poverty, and illiteracy." "By pursuing crime reduction chiefly through incarceration, states are forgoing the opportunity to invest in these other important areas." State policymakers should "look

---

[4] http://media.www.sjuhawknews.com/media/storage/paper763/news/2007/03/28/Opinion/Editors.Column.Criminal.Background.Checks.Hinder.A.New.Start.For.Students-2793960.shtml.

beyond incarceration for alternative policies" to enhance public safety at lower costs to both our wallets and our humanity.

According the same Vera Institute report, employing PIPs saves money. For every 500 people with criminal records employed in lieu of receiving welfare, a minimum of $4 million is saved annually. For every 500 people employed in lieu of returning to prison, $15 million is saved. It increases safety within communities and gives hope to families of PIPs as well as the PIPs.[5]

The following could not have been better stated than by Carolina Cordero Dyer, Associate Executive Director of The Osborne Association:

> *"... there is plenty of money available for this. The funds are available in state prison budgets, but are being spent on ineffective strategies: locking too many people up, for far too long, based on far too arbitrary sentencing guidelines. Mandatory sentencing laws, such as the Rockefeller Drug Laws and Second Felony Offender laws in New York, should be repealed. Reform of the Rockefeller Drug Law, something the State of New York has been unable to do since 1973, could save $610 million annually if we provided alternatives to incarceration to just 19,000 drug offenders. The price of building the prisons to house those drug offenders saves another two billion dollars in capital costs.*
>
> *Politicians must stop pandering to the public's fears. Tough on crime, the war on drugs, three strikes—these are all empty sound bites that have led prosecutors to seek longer and longer sentences, legislatures to lengthen sentences in order to cure every societal ill. This rhetoric to many of the following:*
>
> - *Criminalizing more behavior led to the incarceration of our young people*
> - *The demonization of prisoners and former prisoners*
> - *The devastation of families and communities, and*
> - *Create barriers to employment for those who have served their time*
>
> *The irony of it all is that so much of what we have done to contribute to this mess has been done in the name of public safety. But to ignore the needs of the 600,000 returning to society does not make our streets safer. It is instead extraordinarily costly, increases the likelihood that new crimes will be committed, and puts further strain on fragile communities.*
>
> *We can do better and we must do better. We must shift our thinking about crime and punishment and turn our focus to crime prevention; addressing the root causes of crime such as lack of employment; and devoting our resources to community building, education, and workforce development that provides jobs at a living wage. The future of our communities and our society depends upon it."*

As we search for a medium to make our work environments and communities safe, while restoring the lives of released PIPs from prison, the exploration will not be easy. But, we must start where we are and provide new and pragmatic avenues for a chaotic dilemma.

The notion that a person serving out their sentence is "paying their debt to society" is antiquated today having been buried along with the hopes, despair, and sheer

---

[5] The Real Cost of Prisons Webblog, April 27, 2005.

desperation that PIPs experience. No sooner has the "debt" been paid and an individual is released from prison, when the individual finds his or her indebtedness to society is actually a life sentence. They have no right to vote in some states; no way of taking care of themselves or their families; no way to begin and live a productive lifestyle. Unless these individuals can find a means to create income and somehow live a meaningful life, they are doomed to become recidivists.

What are Some Possible Alternatives for Addressing this Problem?

Expungement

This issue knows no discrimination and cuts across socioeconomic boundaries, affecting not only low-income areas but affluent neighborhoods as well. Many suburban and downstate lawmakers agree there is a need for expungement. The following is an excerpt printed in *The Chicago Reporter* in November 2004.[6]

> *"We're coming to realize that, if what we're trying to do is to reduce recidivism, we need to focus on employment," said state Rep. Patricia Reid Lindner, from west suburban Sugar Grove. Some lawmakers, initially thought expungement was merely a way to let criminals off the hook, but realized [it was much more than this an actually was a way] to help give people a second chance.*
>
> *State Rep. Mark Beaubien of Barrington Hills, an affluent, predominantly white northwest suburb of Chicago, was Howard's first Republican supporter, becoming a co-sponsor of the 2001 bill to help the innocent to expunge their records.*
>
> *Beaubien had personal experience with the issue: He had helped a relative through the expungement process, but he "would never do it again; it took a year," he said. "I piggyback on what [Congresswoman] Connie [Constance Howard] does, because I believe that people who make small mistakes deserve second chances."*
>
> *"Everyone is for law and order until it's their kid," said Sen. Denny Jacobs, a Democrat who has represented his western Illinois district since 1986. He gets two or three calls a year from those looking for help in getting an expungement. "Usually, it's a parent who says my kid screwed up when he was 18; many times it's drugs. If they had everyone on record who tried drugs, it would be 90 percent of the population."*
>
> *Jacobs, who is white, added that most of the people who want his assistance clearing their records are white and affluent. "I have never had a minority ask me for help on an expungement."*

There is hope for PIPs. An effective avenue to consider is the process of having an individual's record expunged. Because the state and federal governments recognized the PIPs woes and the negative effects this over-looked dilemma has on society, expungement laws were created.

---

[6]   "Seeing Daylight," by Brian J. Rogal.

The purpose of this particular law is to conceal criminal records from the public. Depending on the jurisdiction, this process may be referred to as "erasure, destruction, sealing, setting aside, expunction, and purging." Simplified, an expunged record is to treat it as if it never existed.

Four Key Common Elements of Expungement Among State Statutes

Extent to Which an Individual Can Deny Expunged Record

Expungements are based on the premise that those individuals with criminal records will have trouble reintegrating into society and may face barriers from participating in public life unless they have a legitimate means of being able to honestly deny that they have ever been charged with a crime or possessed a criminal record. As a result, most states permit individuals who have had their records expunged to answer in the negative if asked whether they have been arrested or charged of a crime. Therefore, if asked on a job or school application, an applicant with an expunged record may honestly answer "no" to having been charged with a crime. Additionally, for those states that permit expungement even after convictions, the same negative answer may be given for questions concerning conviction.

It is quicker and easier to obtain an expungement when a charge has been dismissed as opposed to when a case has been placed on a "stet docket" (an inactive group of cases which are generally not reopened).

Rehabilitation—Worthiness of Having Records Expunged

Typically, the waiting period before an application can be made is used as an indication of rehabilitation. In addition, a waiting period free of arrests or any trouble with the law is further used to affirm rehabilitation. State codes also contain provisions on the number of times expungement may be granted.

Expunged Records and Access to Criminal Records

The practical effects of expungement remain questionable when considering the number of people who can still access criminal records even after they have been expunged. It has even been advocated that licensing bodies of professions charged with upholding the public trust should have access to the expunged records of their members.[7]

To quantify the need for expungement currently, over 7 million U.S. citizens who have been arrested for minor offenses are finding it difficult to obtain employment, rent an apartment, and apply for professional licenses. Having an arrest record creates community despair and tax burden as we currently pay $30,000 per incarcerated inmate. These barriers are due to having an arrest record in their background. According to the Bureau of Justice Statistics, a staggering 1 of every 32 Americans currently have an arrest record. With the present state of personal information gathering for government regulations (i.e., Patriot Act, Homeland Security) and private companies, there is a definite need

---

[7] The Electronic Privacy Information Center (http://www.epic.org/privacy/expungement/).

to provide people that have committed low level minor offenses the opportunity to re-establish themselves in society.

Expungement laws are typically based on the principle that an individual will be denied his right of employment based on past criminal history. Because of this, most states allow PIPs who are allowed the right to have the records expunged to now answer "no" if asked on an employment application whether they have been arrested or charged of a crime or conviction.

Of course, the severity of the crime plays a significant roll on whether the expungement is even possible. An individual is more likely to be granted expungement on a dismissed charge. Generally, there is a waiting period that must be satisfied to demonstrate evidence of rehabilitation, along with being free of arrests or trouble with the law. Also, most states regulate the number of times an individual can file for expungement. According to the Legal Action Center, 17 states allow some conviction records to be expunged or sealed, such as first-time offenses. Also, 40 states allow people to seal or expunge records of some or all arrests that did not lead to convictions.

Most individuals seek legal representation when pursuing expungement of their criminal history. Although attorneys are experts in this specialty, this route is expensive and can cost well into the thousands, yet the results may not be desirable depending on the PIPs criminal history. However, in recent years a number of companies have emerged that have made it convenient and more affordable to pursue record expungement.

One such company is ArrestFree.com, which is headquartered in Chicago and is the first technology driven expungement service in the world. ArrestFree.com provides a user-friendly, cost-effective solution to assist people in the expungement or sealing of their minor arrest record. With ArrestFree.com's revolutionary approach to filing for expungement, local consumers now have access to a powerful tool that was previously out of their reach. ArrestFree specializes in providing expungement service to citizens with minor arrest records that are removable in accordance to local state laws. Consumers can now choose from a comprehensive selection of state-of-the-art background searches normally employed by leading private and public companies using ArrestFree's Record Discovery. Individuals can also determine their file for expungement conveniently and discreetly either online or though comprehensive phone support.

Government Support for Previously Incarcerated Persons

In his 2004 State of the Union Address, President Bush stated, "America is the land of second chance, and when the gates of the prison open, the path ahead should lead to a better life." On Tuesday November 27 2007, the Faith-Based and Community Initiative (FBCI) hosted the first White House National Summit on Prisoner Re-entry. The two-day conference was designed to highlight the success of the President's re-entry initiatives in changing lives and improving communities, share top innovations in the field, and to expand partnerships of federal, state, and local corrections agencies with faith-based and secular non-profits that help ex-offenders successfully reintegrate into society.

Employability Support for Previously Incarcerated Persons

Several organizations, such as the Safer Foundation, National Hire Network, Second Chance, the Delancy Street Foundation, and Alliance for Previously Incarcerated Persons, are focusing on helping the social and employment re-entry for PIPs. These organizations share the mission of helping PIPs to move beyond the stigma associated with their past and to gain the social and work skills necessary to succeed in a job to make a promising future for themselves.

Scott Silverman, Second Chance's Executive Director, states that recidivism is an enormous problem in our world today. The prison "revolving door" perpetuates a cycle of incarceration, release, reoffend, incarceration. His organization believes that the key to resolving this problem is to concentrate on the critical first 24 hours of release time. Many who have committed crimes and been incarcerated are released from prison and have nowhere to live and no job to go to. They often believe that the only choice (or easiest choice) is to go back to their old lifestyle, it is what they know, many have never learned the life skills to find and keep a job.

Second Chance is a nonprofit agency that helps individuals with overcoming obstacles to employment, affordable housing, and life skills. Many of these individuals have been recently released from prison, and others have been homeless or unemployed for a long period of time. Second Chance teaches a 3-week nationally recognized job-readiness training class called STRIVE (Supportive Training Results in Valuable Employees). This "tough love" class focuses on soft skills and workplace behaviors that aid individuals in becoming and staying employed. STRIVE also teaches work ethics, instilling a positive attitude and a positive self-image, often things that are lacking greatly in individuals with gaps in their work history or who have been incarcerated. This program has had great success in working with clients who may have felonies in their past.

The STRIVE model is very successful for many reasons, possibly the most important being establishment of a positive self-image. The students often start the class thinking of themselves as "felon" or other negative labels and self-images. After the 3 weeks, they are confident in their skills and abilities and they know how to market themselves to an employer. They are also taught a three-step process on how to approach the topic of felonies with a potential employer. (1) Own the past. Without going into graphic detail, explain the offense, the circumstances, and the mindset at the time. This allows for ownership without excusing past behavior, but also gives context. (2) Describe what steps have been taken to make changes. For example, if the felony was substance abuse related, what self-help groups have been sought? How many months clean and sober? This helps to again show the context of the felony, but also illustrates positive changes. (3) Refocus the discussion to "this is what I can do for your company." This is very important. The bottom line is this is what most employers are most concerned about.

Clients are also taught to make their employment search strategic. There may be certain jobs an individual is precluded from because of their felony, but they could work in a related area. For example, a client who has a forgery on their record may not be able to work in a bank, but could work in an area of customer service where they do not have direct access to money. Another major teaching principle is to NEVER lie at an interview about one's own past. This also includes applications and resumes. This is a losing strategy as often employers can and will do checks on work history or searches on the Internet. An individual's background can be explained, lying cannot be explained and is a certain disqualifier as it speaks volumes about the potential behavior that will be exhibited at a job. Additionally, it also shows a pattern of falling back into old behaviors.

At Second Chance, the staff often observes that the clients with the criminal backgrounds often put forth more effort to do a better job because they have had more barriers working against them. When they do get a job, they want to shine, as to not return to their former lifestyle. They are assisted in finding job opportunities that they will not be automatically disqualified from, as to not set them up for failure. Also, if they can no longer work in the field that they have had experience in, they learn how they might transfer those valuable skills into a different field.

The increase of companies using background screening has a significant impact on everyone's community. Often times, background screening fosters a self-fulfilling prophecy for many individuals who already feel they are unemployable and that they can't find a job with a criminal record. Once that starts to become the mindset of someone just released from prison, going back to their old destructive behaviors can become an attractive alternative. Thus taking a person that could be a productive, member of a community, not to mention a tax *payer*, and instead in some cases causing the crime in their community to increase and spending tax dollars to incarcerate them if they are convicted. It is understandable that many employers want to be careful and make sure that certain jobs (i.e., at schools or banks, etc.) do not have people working there with certain convictions in their past. But employers also need to ask themselves, don't people who are trying to change their lives deserve a second chance to do right? It is the hope of agencies and staff who work with clients with felonies on their record that if an employer feels that they must use background screening, that they will use it as a guide and not the deciding factor of an individual's employability.

Success Stories

- Kelvin Evans

  In 1977 at age 19, Kelvin Evans was arrested and sentenced to life in prison with the possibility of parole. While incarcerated, Kelvin took advantage of several classes that were being offered in drafting, printing, and graphic arts. He developed a passion for bodybuilding and won several titles while incarcerated, in addition to receiving his GED.

  In 1984, Kelvin was eligible for parole and began what would be over a 20-year trip of appearances that brought him in front of the parole board 18 times. After his 13th appearance, in 1996, he was found suitable for parole—only to have the decision overturned 5 months later because he did not have a job lined up. In 2005, after 18 failed attempts, Kelvin was once again found suitable for parole. However, this time, with help from his brother, who contacted Second Chance STRIVES's Prisoner Re-entry Employment Program (PREP), and the assistance of staff members Judi Patterson and Lisa Comaduran, Kelvin was able to enroll in the PREP program while still in prison. At age 48, after serving 28 years 7 months of his life sentence, Kelvin went before the governor and back to the parole board. Because he was able to prove that he was seeking assistance for housing and employment, he was released.

  Considering he had spent 60% of his life in prison, Kelvin had a big task ahead of him. He was accepted into a Second Chance sober living home, which is one of the benefits of the PREP program. In February 2006, he graduated from STRIVE, a 3-week job readiness training program that includes two years of graduate services. Being able to reunite with his family has been one of Kelvin's greatest joys. Being able to purchase a cell phone—which was not in existence prior to his incarceration—was another very big accomplishment. Kelvin remarked that "it really didn't hit me until about 3 weeks after I was out, that I was really out of prison. Prison was all I knew for almost 30 years. Now I am employed as a laborer and working towards obtaining my Commercial Drivers License to drive and purchase a big rig truck."

- Michael Rice: Getting a Second Chance

Growing up, Michael Rice maintained a grade point average of 3.5 and won dozens of trophies and medals in karate competitions. He planned to join the army one day. But harsh realities interrupted Rice's plans. His stepfather, who began abusing him at age three, ended up in jail by the time Rice was 14. "When he went to prison, I had to be the man of the house." At that young age, Rice began dealing marijuana to bring in some money for himself, his mother, and his younger sister. Things went downhill from there. During the next decade of his life, Rice earned money dealing crystal meth and running an escort service. He used drugs heavily himself, got into gangs, and was shot and stabbed. He fathered two children, and was in and out of jail more times than he can count. "I had plans to join the military and go to college, but I was stuck in that fast lifestyle," says Rice, looking back. Because of the environment I was in, the plans I wanted for myself could never happen."

At 25, Rice was again sent to jail for the possession and sale of crystal meth and being armed with a handgun. Just before he was released on parole, Rice attended a presentation by an outreach advocate from Second Chance/ STRIVE, a San Diego organization dedicated to helping people recover from homelessness, unemployment, addiction, and gang involvement. The program offers substance-free temporary housing, permanent housing placement, job readiness training, career clothing, job placement, mental health counseling, and two years of comprehensive follow-up care. Rice knew this was an opportunity to break out of his destructive cycle. Even though he had been released from jail, he asked his parole officer if he could go back and finish his time in order to try Second Chance. "When I was in jail I was doing a lot of life evaluating," says Rice. "I was tired of going in and out of jail, tired of not being in my daughters' lives." Through Second Chance, Rice attended job readiness classes and stayed in a sober living house for three and a half months. "Second Chance taught me discipline and patience," says Rice.

"There's more to life than the fast life. It doesn't hurt to be a law-abiding citizen." Within a week after completing the program, Second Chance helped Michael land his first job in concessions at Petco Park. Soon after, he was offered a job as a trainer at Second Chance. The program's Executive Director and Founder, Scott Silverman, says that Rice's life experiences and high level of integrity make him an excellent trainer.

"I love being a trainer," says Rice, who shows up early most days. "I've seen so many walks of life, I can relate to a lot of the people. It's a wonderful gift." Rice believes that Second Chance is effective because it offers a strong

support system. "If I'm having hard times, if I need to talk to anybody, I can just come here." Silverman also attributes the program's success to its strong community environment and comprehensive follow-up care. "We teach people that it's important to develop relationships quickly and in a positive way," he explains. "My team exudes that and practices that with each other and in their own lives with their families. We become that family for people when they first get out of wherever they've been. One of the things you feel when you're there is that we care about you and it's okay for you to care about yourself." Silverman sees an embodiment of that model in Rice. "He's got a really strong feeling about giving back. He has taken significant time and commitment in turning his own life around, and he understands that in order to keep it, he has to give it away."

Rice, now 28, has reconnected with his two daughters, helped his mother go through Second Chance, and had a baby in December with his fiancée, Patecia, whom he met in the program. "We laugh together. We're both steadily working. She's a good woman," says Rice. "I'm happy with my life now. I take care of her, and she takes care of me." Rice hopes to buy a house by the time he is 30, and hopes to find the time to get back into karate. "I love martial arts," he says, "it's a passion, and I was really good at it." Second Chance/STRIVE has helped over 1,000 people find employment after incarceration, homelessness, or substance abuse.

There is also hope at the federal level for programs that will give people like Kelvin Evans and Michael Rice support to help them make the transition in their lives. President Bush proposed the Second Chance Act, which would offer support services for people who are leaving prison. Specifically the Act was proposed for 4 years and is a $300 million prisoner re-entry initiative to expand job training and placement services, to provide transitional housing, and to help newly released prisoners get mentoring, including from faith-based groups. Said the President, "America is the land of second chance, and when the gates of the prison open, the path ahead should lead to a better life."

Restrictions on Background Checks

A different legal approach that is simultaneously occurring is municipalities that are starting to restrict or eliminate criminal background checks.

Boston Mayor Thomas M. Menino "authorized a new policy two years ago eliminating questions about criminal convictions on all city job applications and dispensing with criminal background checks for applicants for jobs that don't involve working with children or the elderly or accessing residents' homes."

Both Menino and newly elected Gov. Deval Patrick intend to press ahead with a previously announced plan to limit private employers' access to job applicants' criminal records, the better to enforce those obligatory second chances.[8]

Also, on July 1, 2006, a new Boston City Council ordinance took effect. According to the ordinance, "the City of Boston and its vendors cannot conduct a criminal

---

[8] Andrea Estes, Patrick Seeks to Limit Background Checks, *Boston Globe*, Feb. 12, (via No Looking Backwards).

background check as part of their hiring process until the job applicant is found to be 'otherwise qualified' for the position."[9]

On November 1, 2006, Philadelphia City Council proposed a bill modeling Boston City Council's ordinance requiring the employer to determine if the application is "otherwise qualified for the relevant position before the Employer may conduct a criminal background." In addition, the proposed bill not only applies to city agencies and private vendors that do business with the city, but to private companies employing more than 10 people.

On December 2006, St. Paul's Mayor Christopher Coleman issued "a memo to the City Council directing the City's Human Resources Department to reform its hiring process. According to the new procedure, the City will remove the criminal history question from its job applications and delay the criminal background check until the final stages of the hiring process." As part of the memo, the mayor wants the private sector to play a major role backing reforms that remove restriction of employment to people with criminal records.

Tips for Reducing Risk to Employers That Hire Previously Incarcerated Persons

One reason employers often give for refusing to hire individuals with a criminal record is the fear that they will incur liability if they hire a person with a conviction record who later commits a new crime. This is known as negligent hiring.

While state standards differ, a 2005 report put out by the Legal Action Center on "Negligent Hiring Concerns" states the key to determining liability is usually whether the employer could have foreseen the crime: specifically, whether the employee had a history or propensity for harmful behavior and, most importantly, whether the employer knew or should have known of the employee's propensities. Ordinarily, an employer's reasonable efforts to check and consider a prospective employee's background will generally satisfy the legal requirements and eliminate the risk of liability on the employer's part.

Federal law discourages employers from having a blanket policy of denying employment to individuals with criminal histories. Guidance from the Equal Employment Opportunity Commission requires employers to make individualized assessments about the appropriateness of hiring a particular applicant.[10] Employers must give full consideration to certain factors including:

- The nature and gravity of the offense(s)
- The time that has passed since the conviction and/or completion of the sentence
- The nature of the job held or sought

There are resources available to employers who hire individuals with criminal records that can be used as a way for employers to protect themselves.

---

[9]   The National Employment Law Project, http://www.nelp.org/nwp/second_chance_labor_project/.

[10]   Equal Employment Opportunity Commission, Notice No. N-915, Policy Statement on Issue of Conviction Records under Title VII of the Civil Rights Act of 1964, [February 4, 1987].

Bonding Program

The Federal Bonding Program is available to employers who have concerns about hiring qualified but "at-risk" job applicants. The U.S. Department of Labor issues Fidelity Bonds, which are business insurance policies that protect employers in case of theft, forgery, larceny or embezzlement of money or property by an employee who is covered by the bond. The bond coverage is usually up to $5,000 with no deductible amount of liability for the employer. Higher amounts of coverage may be allowed if justified. The bond does not cover liability due to poor work performance, job injuries, or work accidents.

Employee Intermediaries

Employers can partner with local community based organizations that serve as a third party intermediary. These agencies offer support services to the employer by providing:

- Cost savings by lowering the employer's recruitment costs by matching qualified applicants to the employer's available positions
- Prescreening and pretraining that suit the employer's needs
- Retention services to the recruited employee

Table 11-2 provides a "point-counterpoint" discussion.

Table 11-2 Point-Counterpoint

Once a crook, always a crook.	
Security	**Human Resources**
The people who founded this country were outcast and PIPs and look what our country has accomplished. Having a second chance is indigenous to America.	You can spout all the rhetoric you want, but when a PIP rapes someone, or injures someone, or worst case, kills someone it is the company that is going to get sued and potentially be on the hook for millions of dollars.
Incarceration is supposed to be focused on rehabilitation and a person paying their debt to society. People should not continue to be punished once their time is served. People who have demonstrated they are free of crime should have the same opportunity as anyone else to get a decent job.	Risk management is about mitigating or eliminating risk and not hiring people with criminal backgrounds achieves this goal.
"Let he who is without sin cast the first stone." Who amongst us did not do some foolish or even illegal things when we were young? This should not be held against a person forever, if they can demonstrate they have learned and changed.	If there is an equally qualified person that does not have criminal history available for a job, it is only common sense that we would hire them over someone that poses a greater risk to the organization.

(Continued)

Table 11-2   Point-Counterpoint—Cont'd

We have an impending labor shortage and a ready made pool of workers. Now is the time to provide the support services to develop this untapped pool of employees. It is a myth that we don't hire people with problem backgrounds. The truth is we simply don't know about much of the dirt in people's background. For example, 1 out of 10 sexual predators have never been caught, so it is highly likely you have some working for you right now. They may be one of your best workers.	A person that has been convicted of a crime has demonstrated that they have bad judgment. Who is to say that under the right or perhaps the wrong set of circumstances that "poor judgment" will not resurface.

Summary

Many people seeking employment that have been incarcerated are finding great difficulty in obtaining gainful employment due to their past criminal record. Although background checks are a necessary safety measure to mitigate a company's risk it also may contribute to the growing problem of recidivism for the PIP by seriously impairing their access to productive and legal means of making a living. It is a dilemma that our society must grapple with and resolve.

One option to assist in overcoming the barriers to employment for PIP is the removal of certain criminal offenses from a person background by way of expungement. Although stipulations vary by state, typically the criteria requires that a person's offenses be first-time and/or victimless offenses. Most of these stipulate certain time conditions including a specified time in which the person has not had any additional arrests. One of the new breed firms that offers expungement services is Arrestfree.com, which provides services online or by telephone to determine eligibility in their local state.

Another option that has emerged comes from community based organizations that focus on developing life and job training skills to assist PIPs in successfully reintegrating into their community with give job readiness skills. Second Chance is one of the committed organizations that is providing this critical work in many communities throughout the United States.

Finally, the government is also taking much-needed steps to attempt to make jobs more readily available to PIPs. Their efforts include offering tax credit incentives to employers willing to hiring PIPs as well as bonding insurance to provide a safety net for employers to insulate employers from negligent hiring risk. In addition, some municipalities have started to take a critical look at restriction or elimination of the need for criminal background checks. On November 1, 2006, a new Boston City Council ordinance took effect. According to the ordinance, "the city of Boston and its vendors cannot conduct a criminal background check as part of their hiring process until the job applicant is found to be 'otherwise qualified' for the position." Philadelphia has passed similar legislation, and St. Paul is moving to revise their hiring process to reflect a similar intent.

As the prison population in the United States continues to grow with much of this driven by recidivism, it is time to recognize we must do something different. As the old adage goes, "insanity is continuing to do the same thing and expecting to get different results." So we must stop the madness and bite the bullet that one of the primary ways of reducing the vicious cycle of recidivism is to provide meaningful opportunities to PIPs to earn a living.

I think that the Honorable Dennis A. Challeen, District Judge, Minnesota, captures the sentiment the best in his following statements:

"We want them to have self worth so we destroy their self worth.

We want them to be responsible so we take away all responsibilities.

We want them to be part of our community so we isolate them from our community.

We want them to be positive and constructive so we degrade them and make them useless.

We want them to be non-violent so we put them where there is violence all around them.

We want them to be kind and loving people so we subject them to hatred and cruelty.

We want them to quit being the tough guy so we put them where the tough guy is respected.

We want them to quit hanging around with losers, so we put all the losers under one roof.

We want them to quit exploiting us so we put them where they exploit each other.

We want them to take control of their own lives, own their own problems and quit being parasites—so we make them totally dependent on us."[11]

---

[11]   From Stimulus: *The New Zealand Journal of Christian Thought & Practice*, Vol 2, # 3, August 1994, p. 10. http://www.stimulus.org.nz/. Used by permission.

12

International Background Checks: The New Frontier in Employment Screening

Nick Fishman, Jason B. Morris, Les Rosen,
and Michael Damm

"The world is flat," opined Thomas Friedman in his like-titled best-selling book. He was referring to the global economy and how business is no longer confined to borders of one's country or large bodies of water. This concept applies to the preemployment screening industry as well, but we didn't *quite* get there over night.

It is believed that the first preemployment background checks in the United States were conducted as early as the late 1800s by Pinkerton Security Company. No doubt the process was both tedious and time consuming. It was probably limited to a very basic criminal check and education and employment verifications—maybe, even reference interviews. The expense must have been exorbitant making the effort cost prohibitive for anyone except top level employees at the largest of companies. And while the concept of preemployment screening continued into the 1900s, it really wasn't until the early 1990s that it began to evolve into what it is today, a widely accepted and highly utilized tool in the hiring process. Many elements led to the "mainstreaming" of this hiring tool highlighted by both technologies, which made finding the information easier coupled with the increase in employer's awareness of their need for this information. The explosion of this industry led to an effort to regulate; to protect the consumer (applicant), the Federal Trade Commission (FTC) amended the Fair Credit Reporting Act (FCRA) that it established to protect those applying for credit in the early 1970s to include job applicants whose employers conducted background checks. In very general terms, the FCRA made mandatory the need to obtain an applicant's written permission to conduct a background check, defined an applicant's rights to receive a copy of the information contained in a background check, and gave them proper recourse when adverse or incorrect information was contained in the report. In the event that an individual is denied employment by virtue of what is found on the background check, the FCRA also made it mandatory for the employer to notify the applicant in writing why they were not being hired and that they must include a copy of the background check.

While the 1990s is looked upon as the renaissance of this industry in the United States, we could define the late 1990s and our current decade as the New Frontier, for types of information available, methods for obtaining them, and the need for information on job applicants that are not from this country. It was inevitable that as the world was shrinking, our clients and, in turn, our industry were expanding. Globalization was taking place on levels that were never anticipated. First, it was manufacturing that was sent overseas and not too long after that call centers began sprouting in Asia. Let's face it, it was cheaper to do and the productivity was supposedly unmatched. U.S. companies had to keep revenue up and costs down. Over time, we found and continue to find that virtually any job can be exported. Overseas business units, divisions, and offices were and continue to be established all over the map. It only stands to reason that these business units, divisions, and offices need to be staffed with employees. Not to be one sided, while this exportation of jobs is taking place, so, too, are the rates at which U.S. employers are importing talent from overseas. Ergo, the evolution of the International Background Check. This chapter will serve to highlight what employers should know (from a screening perspective) prior to extending a job offer to a foreign national.

Quick Tips for What Employers Should Check on Foreign Nationals

- Criminal record search in their current country of residence (or most recent before the United States)
- Employment verifications (all past employers going back 7 years)
- Education verification (for highest degree attained)
- Homeland Security search (these searches can be called different things, but they are databases of various terrorist watch and most wanted lists from around the globe)
- Legal right to work status (if applicant is brought to the United States to work)

employeescreen**IQ**'s first experience with a requested background check on an overseas candidate came from one of our largest customers in the late 90's. We knew that there were wholesalers out there who had researchers in mostly industrialized nations that could get information. We didn't really know how or where they were getting this information and we clearly communicated this to our customers. Since the person wasn't a U.S. citizen, did we need an applicant release? Were they afforded the protection of the FCRA? Who knew? But we executed the process as if they were. The services available were limited to a criminal record check, employment verifications, and education verifications. The searches were expensive, and they remain so today. It could take weeks to get information returned and complete the check. We needed interpreters to conduct the verifications. Each country seemed to require different information in order to conduct the check.

Criminal Record Search

I liken these initial stages of international screening to the Wild West. Everybody was left to fend for themselves and create their own rules. Let's start with criminal records—specifically, where did you need to search? In the United States, we know that criminal records reside at the county courthouse and that these records are public information and, therefore, without sounding too simplistic, are relatively easy to locate. Very few countries are equally situated, and while records are maintained and stored, they were never arranged for the general public to search them. Further, from country to country there are no standards for where the records are kept. In some countries, the best resource is a local police station or local magistrate. Sometimes, there is a centralized system. Other times, there are courthouses that will maintain such records. Once the best method is established, there's still the question about how they were cataloged, so finding them is difficult.

Also, not to be overlooked is the mechanism we use in the United States to identify where we need to search in order to conduct a thorough background check: the address history search or Social Security number trace. By plugging in an applicant's Social Security number, we are able to generate a history of addresses and names where an individual has resided and used. Although not perfect, the results provide us with a roadmap for where a search must be conducted. Rather than taking the applicant's word for this information, we have a fairly reliable tool to provide insight. This type of search tool doesn't exist in other countries, so without some type of investigation that is both timely and costly, you are reliant upon the applicant to provide you with this vital information.

Now that we've established the fact that countries that actually keep and provide records house them in a variety of places, let's also address the information needed to access the information. It, too, varies from country to country and the most important item that can be done in preparation of a search is to know the information that is required by the particular country in order to execute a thorough search. For instance, in China each person is assigned a work number, somewhat analogous to our Social Security number. In order to access any information in China, you must have this number. In India, students are given seat numbers. These elements are not necessarily used for criminal records but may be important to the education or employment verification process. Requirements directly related to criminal searches include making sure that you have your applicant's complete name. For instance, in most Hispanic nations, individuals have a first name followed by their father's last name and then their mother's last name. In many Islamic counties, a person's name is typically followed by the city or town they are from. For instance, Saddam Hussein's formal name was Saddam Hussein al Tikriti (Saddam Hussein of Tikrit). It is important to make sure you conduct the search under the appropriate formal name. Further, many languages do not have the same characters or letters that we use. For instance, in Israel, they use Hebrew letters. In China, Chinese letters, etc. If the person spells their name in the Latin alphabet, it is still important to make sure that it is spelled out in their native characters or letters. Some important elements in countries like China, Japan, areas of the Middle East, and Israel, where special characters are used, it's important to not only communicate the translation of the letters but also the original characters themselves.

Les Rosen, Employment Screening Resources, further illuminates the identification identifiers that are necessary for foreign nationals.

International Identifiers

Identifiers are just as critical for international background checks as they are for domestic checks in the United States. Background checks cannot be accomplished unless there are sufficient identifiers to make sure the researcher has the right person and that the information returned is actually related to the subject of the search. For private employers, information based upon unique biometric identifiers such as fingerprints is typically not available. Information based upon identification by just a name match only can be very unreliable. Therefore, other means of identification must be used in addition to just the person's name

Domestically, U.S. searches can require identifying data such as name, date of birth, Social Security number and sometimes, even a driver's license number. International background checks are no different. Without accurate and complete identifiers, an international background check may return a report that is either a "false positive" or a "false negative."

A "false positive" occurs where an applicant is falsely associated with a record that does not pertain to them. An example of a "false positive" is where a criminal record is reported as belonging to an applicant based upon "name match only." Without looking at additional identifiers, a person can be falsely accused of having a criminal record when in fact the record belongs to a different person but with the same name.

Similarly, it is also possible to have a "false negative," meaning someone really is a criminal, but a criminal record search missed it. This could happen if there is some name variation in databases that causes researchers to miss a match. For example, an applicant may have a hyphenated last name, or the last names are switched. On occasion, a record may exist with the applicant's identifiers; however, within the case docket, it could be revealed his identifying information was used in an identity theft case.

Another type of identifier is some item of information that is uniquely associated with an applicant that a particular information source requires in order to provide information to an international researcher. For example, in some countries the colleges or universities require a "seat number" or an actual copy of the degree in order to verify educational information.

When dealing with applicants internationally, the problem is compounded by the fact every country is different. Because there are 192 members of the United Nations, there are potentially 192 different systems for identifiers that must be dealt with as part of international screening. Some of the issues are as follows:

1. Names and name variations

The issue of name variations internationally can be extremely complicated for three reasons. First, with so many people in the world, there is a high statistical likelihood that a person's name is not unique and that there are others with the

(Continued)

same name. Second, many cultures have naming conventions that are entirely different than the United States. Some cultures may start the name with the family or clan name, where other cultures may utilize the mother's name as an integral part of the naming mechanism. Many cultures do not have the concept of a middle name. The third difficulty has to do with expressing a foreign name in an English format. For the languages that utilize the English alphabet, the expression of names is somewhat easier, such as names in Italian, German, and Spanish. However, keep in mind that Spanish names can have cultural variations.

When it comes to expressing names that utilize a non-English alphabet, there is room for error and confusion. There is no easy way to translate Chinese, Korean, Arabic, or Japanese names into English.

The two techniques used to render names in foreign alphabets into English are transliteration and phonetic transcription.

Transliteration into English is based upon using a representation of the characters in the original language with English characters so that certain characters in one language always translate into English by use of agreed-upon letters. It is analogous to using a codebook. Transliteration means mapping a name from one language into another. An example is in Iraq, where the Q is pronounced as an English CK.

Phonetic transcription, or "transcribing," is based upon taking the sounds of a foreign name, and attempting to associate the same sounds to the sounds of the English alphabet.

With either method there can be any number of variations. For example, "Osama bin Laden" can be represented as both "Laden" with an "e" or "Ladan" with an "a." First name variations can be "Usama" or "Osama."

One possible best practice is to have an applicant provide their name in their native language. In some countries, a school or employer may require that in order to achieve better identification. However, it may be difficult for an employer to authenticate a name that is expressed in a non-English alphabet.

2. Date of birth

Many countries in the world use a different date of birth mechanism than the United States. In the United States, the customary way to express date of birth is to use month/day/year, so that January 10, 1951, would come out 01/10/51.

However, outside the United States, the English system is often used where the day and month are often reversed, so that January 10, 1951, would come out 10/01/1951. In the United States, an employer would assume that is October 1, 1951.

A person with a criminal record outside of the United States may be able to thwart discovery merely by using the U.S. system for date of birth, which can cause them to be misidentified. The best practice is to ask for and to transmit to an international researcher the date of birth in a manner the clearly indicates which is the month and which is the day.

(Continued)

3. International Identity number

In the United States, the Social Security number has become the de facto identity number, although it was not intended for that purpose.

Elsewhere around the world, there are countries with a national identity number or cards. In order to assist with international identification, employers may need to obtain such numbers.

4. Other information

With so many countries, employers need to understand that the system for obtaining information on applicants can be different for each country. It depends upon the systems and customs unique to a country. Many countries have their own rules about obtaining information such as past education, employment, criminal records, credit reports, driving records, or other data that may be required that is to make sure that you have what the information source requires.

For example, in some countries, in order to get a degree verified, the employer may need a signed release. The release may need to have some sort of identifying information about the person. In India, the best practice is a copy of the degree or at least a "seat number."

For criminal records, it is helpful in many countries to have the mother's maiden name. That is especially true in countries with Spanish as the primary language. A release is also often needed. In some counties, much more detailed information may be needed that can include a national ID number, and the period of time in the country. The local or national police or the judicial system determines those requirements.

It is worth noting that the identifiers that are required can change without notice. The best practice is to provide at a minimum the applicant's full name, date of birth making the month and day very clear, the past address when the applicant lived in the country, and a release.

—*Lester S. Rosen*

Having the proper information ahead of time is vital to an efficient and expeditious search because requesting a search without the proper information can stall the process indefinitely. The scenario plays out like this: a request is submitted for an overseas candidate. The researcher receives the request after a couple days and begins to conduct the search only to realize that the search cannot be completed due to lack of information. The researcher may take days to communicate this back to the credit reporting agency (CRA) or employer. The employer must then get back in touch with their applicant and retransmit the data to the researcher. This back and forth can delay a search for days, or even weeks. Each country has its own unique requirements, and it is imperative that the employer or CRA understands these requirements from the onset.

Now that we've established some of the requirements needed for applicants in particular counties, let's focus on the way courts are structured in various countries. A good example is the Judiciary of Thailand. The courts in Thailand are divided into two parts—administration and adjudication. In regard to actual criminal cases, they are divided into several different courts, which are determined by the types of cases that are being heard, much like in the United States. Before one can even consider conducting a search in these courts, they must first understand the actual structure to begin their quest for the information.

An employer's goal is always to hire desirable applicants as soon as possible, so it is not unusual for them to inquire about how long the check will take. Typically, the more industrialized countries have more evolved and efficient processes. So, for instance, conducting a check in the United Kingdom can be very efficient. Second, the more prevalent the practice, the more you can expect a search to be expedited. The most common countries searched today are those in western Europe and the nations in Asia Pacific (India, China, Japan, etc.). With repetition and familiarity comes a more streamlined process.

From a procedural standpoint, the same rules apply when it comes to applicant releases. You must obtain signed consent from your applicant before conducting a background check. This is absolutely mandatory for conducting background checks on an international scale. The release is similar to its U.S. counterpart in that it defines the information to be sought, but very different when it comes to consumer protection and recourse. Again, in the United States, the CRA and the employer are jointly bound by the FCRA. There is no such thing as a global version of this act. Therefore, an applicant's rights become more fluid. The European Union has created Data Protection Laws, which have been mimicked in several forms in various countries. For example, the U.S Department of Commerce created the Safe Harbor Provisions which certifies that CRA's seeking such information on overseas job applicants are committed to protecting the privacy of personal data that are gathered and maintained on behalf of employers requesting consumer data inquiries. Companies must certify that in relation to personal data collected in the European Union that they adhere to the seven "Safe Harbor Principles" of the U.S. Department of Commerce as outlined in the European Commissions Directive on Data Protection.

The Seven Safe Harbor Principles are as follows:

1. Notice—Notice must be given to the consumer that a check will be conducted with their consent and information regarding the nature and scope of the consumer data available.
2. Choice—The company must afford the individual the opportunity to choose whether their personal information will be disclosed to a third party or will be used for a purpose incompatible with the purpose for which it was originally collected or subsequently authorized by the individual. Therefore, consumer data may be disseminated under these circumstances unless the consumer explicitly "opts-out."
3. Onward Transfer—With respect to the transfer of consumer data to third parties, the principles of "Notice" and "Choice" apply. Accordingly, data is only provided to an employer or its agent for purposes described in the "Notice" section, and will not be disseminated to a third party where a consumer has "opted-out" or, in the case of sensitive information, failed to "opt-in."

4. Access—A consumer may request, in writing, access to all data collected and maintained about him or her. Background Information Services, Inc. affords the consumer a reasonable opportunity to correct, amend, or delete information that is inaccurate or incomplete, except where the burden or expense of providing access would be disproportionate to the risks to the individual's privacy, or where the rights of persons other than the individual would be violated.

5. Pursuant to the United States federal Fair Credit Reporting Act, any citizen of the United States may obtain a copy of their consumer report free of charge. We reserve the right, however, to charge an administrative fee not to exceed $15 to cover the cost of reviewing our records and obtaining and forwarding any information for consumers who are not citizens of the United States.

6. Security—This service takes all reasonable procedures to protect personal and identifiable information from loss, misuse and unauthorized access, disclosure, alteration, and destruction.

7. Data Integrity—The company takes reasonable steps to ensure that data collected is accurate, complete, current, and reliable for its intended use. The company must only collect data that is strictly necessary for the purposes listed.

8. Enforcement—The company verifies adherence to the EU Safe Harbor Policy via in-house verification by the management of the company.

Safe Harbor begins to define the confidentiality of such information and the methods used to transmit and protect such data. However, if you are seeking an international standard remember at this time one does not exist, and we doubt that one will in the foreseeable future.

While procedural requirements for each country can be refined and counted upon, the overall quality of a search cannot. Now there's a mouthful! You might be scratching your head now saying, "Did he really just say that?" And your answer is yes, I did just indicate that the quality of each search can vary country to country, province to province, and jurisdiction to jurisdiction. One thing that you cannot escape is the quality of information. The more industrialized the country, the better you can expect the information to be and the quicker it should be, in general, to complete the search. When a U.S. criminal record search is completed correctly, a criminal conviction will be accompanied with full detail of the offense, including the date of the offense, the charges, the disposition, the sentence, and, most important, the identifiers on file so that you can be assured that the record belongs to your applicant. Remember when conducting international criminal record searches that sometimes a researcher will be forced to conduct a search in a small village with manual files that are not organized for public searches as opposed to having access to an automated computer system to which we are accustomed in the United States. This is not to suggest that you cannot count on the people that you hire to conduct the research (this is a topic for another chapter). Bottom line, a thorough search will always be predicated on the quality of information cataloged at the source. Even when records are found, they often come without the necessary depth we have grown accustomed to getting. You are likely thinking, "If you cannot guarantee the quality or completeness of the research, why go through the time and expense." The answer is the same that I would give if you asked that question of an applicant in the United States: there is no such thing as a perfect background check—meaning that even the best background check cannot be guaranteed to uncover every possible record out there. It is incumbent upon the employer to use their best efforts to identify aberrant past behavior to insulate themselves, their employees, and their customers from incidents in the workplace. If you do not conduct a search, you are guaranteed not to uncover adverse information. By conducting a search, you are giving yourself a chance.

Education and Employment Verifications

This next section will deal with employment and education verifications. First and foremost, it is imperative that verifications are conducted in the native language of the person being interviewed. While many people are bilingual, that doesn't mean that they are 100% fluent in their second language. Mispronounced words can be the difference between a positive and negative review. This is a crucial point to remember and a driving factor in using localized resources.

In addition, the tone of a conversation when it isn't conducted in the native language can transmit different meaning, not to mention that people are generally more comfortable and at ease speaking in their native language. Many times this will also increase the likelihood of them speaking more freely with better detail. A second and seemingly obvious point is that those responsible for conducting the interviews must do so during normal business hours in the country where the subject of the interview resides. You would be amazed how many have tried to time a call at the beginning or end of a U.S. workday, hoping that the employer will be available. This doesn't work.

Another important consideration in conducting international verifications is the cultural differences from country to country. In some parts of the world, the practice of providing information about a former employee is a regular and accepted practice. In other places, it can be seem as an intrusion on personal privacy or just plain rude. For instance, we know that when we conduct a verification in Japan, the answers will be short and clipped. We know that the information given will be just bare bones, mostly just confirmation that the applicant did work there. However, if we conduct a verification in France, for instance, the answers are usually more forthcoming. Please note that it is not our intent to place judgment on these practices, but more so to simply divulge the reality based on very real cultural differences. As a result of this reality, your expectations for the information that you can retrieve must be adjusted for each country.

In the United States, it is common to obtain dates of employment, job title and responsibilities, and starting and ending compensation. Much more information can often be obtained as well. The same cannot be said for employment verifications in foreign countries. In some places, you might only be able to establish that the applicant actually worked for the company you are contacting. In other places, you can obtain dates of employment and job responsibilities. It varies country to country and company to company. As imperative as having the proper applicant information was for conducting the criminal check, so, too, is the importance of having such identifying information for the verification work.

Overseas universities and colleges will not release information and often won't even be able to locate the proper information without the aforementioned identifiers. Similar to the criminal search, the verification process can be derailed without proper information. Also be cognizant of the fact that the types of degrees can vary from country to country.

Homeland Security Search or Terrorist Watch List

An expensive, but important, screening tool for foreign nationals is a terrorist watch list search. Many companies offer a variation of this type of search and usually refer to it by different names. We use the term "employeescreen**IQ** Homeland Security Check." At the end of the day, this search should access various databases throughout the world of known terrorists and, or fugitives. Most lists start by accessing the Office of Foreign Asset Control (OFAC) list. Basically, your applicant's name will be cross-referenced against this and other lists to make sure they are not a known terrorist or fugitive. Our Homeland Security check contains the following databases (this list is not provided as a sales tool, but an example of an extensive watch list search).

National

- Office of Foreign Asset Control (OFAC) Specially Designated Nationals (SDN)
- Palestinian Legislative Council (PLC)
- Defense Trade Controls (DTC) Debarred Parties
- U.S. Bureau of Industry and Security Denied Persons List
- U.S. Bureau of Industry and Security Denied Entities List
- U.S. Bureau of Industry and Security Unverified Entities List
- U.S. Marshals Service 15 Most Wanted
- U.S. Secret Service Most Wanted Fugitives
- U.S. Air Force Office of Special Investigations Most Wanted Fugitives
- U.S. Naval Criminal Investigate Service (NCIS) Most Wanted Fugitives
- U.S. Immigration and Customs Enforcement Most Wanted Fugitives
- U.S. Immigration and Customs Enforcement Wanted Fugitive Criminal Aliens
- U.S. Immigration and Customs Enforcement Most Wanted Human Smugglers
- U.S. Bureau of Alcohol, Tobacco and Firearms (ATF) Most Wanted
- U.S. Postal Inspection Service Most Wanted
- FBI Most Wanted Terrorists List
- FBI Top Ten Most Wanted List
- FBI Seeking Information
- FBI Seeking Information on Terrorism
- FBI Parental Kidnappings
- FBI Crime Alerts
- FBI Kidnappings and Missing Persons
- FBI Televised Sexual Predators
- FBI Fugitives—Crimes Against Children
- FBI Fugitives—Cyber Crimes
- FBI Fugitives—Violent Crimes: Murders
- FBI Fugitives—Additional Violent Crimes
- FBI Fugitives—Criminal Enterprise Investigations
- FBI Fugitives—Domestic Terrorism

- FBI Fugitives—White Collar Crimes
- DEA Most Wanted Fugitives
- DEA Major International Fugitives

International

- Politically Exposed Persons List
- Foreign Agent Registrations List
- United Nations Consolidated Sanctions List
- Bank of England Financial Sanctions List
- World Bank List of Ineligible Firms
- Interpol Most Wanted List
- European Union Terrorist List
- OSFI Canada List of Financial Sanctions
- Royal Canadian Mounted Police Most Wanted
- Australia Department of Foreign Affairs and Trade List
- Russian Federal Fugitives
- Scotland Yard's Most Wanted
- World's Most Wanted Fugitives

I always think it is important to tell our clients that utilize this tool that we have never found an applicant whose name was contained on this list; however, for the nominal fee and the peace of mind provided, it is a great tool in risk management.

Electronic Right to Work Eligibility Status

Another tool that is just beginning to take shape is one that can be utilized when a company seeks to hire a foreign national for work in the United States. Bear in mind that this process can only take place after the individual has started work. By law, all U.S. employers must have their employees complete an I-9 form and show valid forms of identification with the first 48 hours of their employment.

This doesn't only apply to U.S. citizens, but also to those visiting our country on work permits or those planning to become citizens. In an effort to take this process a step further, the Social Security Administration (SSA) and the Department of Homeland Security (DHS) recently introduced a basic pilot program which allows employers to submit the information contained on the completed I-9 and receive eligibility to work status with the click of a button. This program is free of charge, but calls for duplicate data entry and can be a bit time intensive. Of course, whatever the government can do, the private sector can do better and more efficient and a select few progressive companies have developed a system that actually allows the I-9 form to be filled out electronically and submitted to SSA and DHS electronically for instant employment eligibility status. Why is this important for hiring foreign nationals? It's important because if the person does not have a valid green card or work permit, they cannot be legally employed. Further work permits and green cards expire after a period of time and these new systems can alert the employer ahead of time for when the information must be updated (either the person must have their permit extended or their employment must be terminated). The bottom line is that this system will give employers the peace of mind that their employees have the legal right to work in this country.

In summation, screening for foreign nationals is an expanding area within the pre-employment screening field. The popularity of this practice will guarantee that the only constant you'll find for the foreseeable future is change. Change in the rules that govern this practice, change in the reliability, change in the efficiency of the information and process, as well as change in the methods each country utilizes to furnish such records. It is important for CRAs to provide direction as to legalities, protocols, and expectations. It is equally important for the end user to understand what they can expect from in international background check in terms of quality and depth.

In addition to the escalation of background screenings on foreign nationals entering the U.S. job market our neighbors to the north are also seeing a resurgence in background investigations. Michael Damm, President of ISB Corporate Services, one of Canada's leading background screening firms, offers some insight into how background screenings are conducted in Canada.

Buyers' Guide for Hiring a CRA to Conduct International Background Checks

- Is the company Safe Harbor certified with the U.S. Department of Commerce?
- Are they in compliance with the European Union Privacy Standards?
- Have criminal records been obtained by a researcher in the country where the search is being conducted?
- Have verifications been conducted in the native language of the person they are speaking to?

The business of preemployment screening is small in Canada, due to our much smaller population compared with Europe or the United States. As well, our society has not been fast to adopt preemployment screening practices beyond the normal reference calls. This is changing, however, as the world changes and forces more awareness of anti-terrorism legislation and a new cultural climate. Business is realizing all too late that proper screening years ago could have levitated many of their problems with employees early on and given them the resources to grow.

Legally, there have not been many challenges to companies doing background checks on potential employees, but there are some restrictions. The intent of this section is to provide guidance regarding the right way to do background searches in Canada.

So what do you have to watch out for in Canada?

- Human right violations
- Federal and provincial privacy legislation
- Sources of improperly acquired background documents or misuse

Conducting preemployment background checks in Canada has many similarities to the United States, but just as many differences. Canada is unique in its culture, labor laws, and human rights codes, as well as its overriding privacy legislation. Canada has one criminal code—the Criminal Code of Canada (CCC).

If a background company outside of Canada is conducting business in Canada without an established Canadian office and servers in Canada, then it runs the risk of violating some aspect of the three areas above.

Questions cannot be asked regarding race, religion, marital status, or sexual orientation. A clear understanding of Canadian laws and requirements is needed as they vary by province. A good alternative is to work with an established Canadian background screening company for all or part of the screening activity.

Useful Websites to Get You Started

Human Rights Canada	http://www.chrc-ccdp.ca
Criminal Code of Canada	http://laws.justice.gc.ca/en/ShowTdm/cs/C-46
Canadian Labor Code	http://laws.justice.gc.ca/en/ShowTdm/cs/L-2
RCMP Criminal Records	http://www.rcmp-grc.gc.ca/crimrec/crimrec_e.htm
PIPEDA Privacy Act	http://www.privcom.gc.ca/legislation/02_06_01_e.asp

Human rights legislation in Canada varies from province to province and prohibits discrimination on hiring in different areas. Be sure to check with local labor lawyers or an existing Canadian preemployment background company for clarification.

A good example is that you cannot discriminate in your hiring against a person with a criminal record in British Columbia, Quebec, PEI, or the Yukon—but you can in Ontario.

Human right codes allow for the employer to ask if the applicant has used different names in their past to clarify what name is used in the varying educational institutions. The purpose for asking this question, however, must be made clear to the applicant.

Criminal Records

One of the biggest differences, at times considered controversial by anyone outside of Canada, is our Central Criminal Records Database, or CPIC. Canada is very lucky in this respect to have a well-managed, central, countrywide database since 1953. This database is managed by the Royal Canadian Mounted Police (RCMP), and accessed by every police force in Canada as well as NCIC in the United States. It contains all criminal activity data on persons in Canada from convictions, arrests, warrants, suspects and physical descriptions.

In this database, all criminal convictions are recorded, along with details of police involvement or criminal or suspect activity and descriptions. For the purpose of this section, we will focus on what information is used in Canadian preemployment screening.

Searching Courthouse Records—In Canada, this is not an acceptable practice for professional Canadian background screening firms. Searching for courthouse records is hit-and-miss process with more misses than hits due to the number of courts from coast to coast. Companies that are not allowed access to the CPIC system and are attempting to operate in Canada in this sector of the marketplace usually do these. What they are doing is putting their clients at risk as well as fellow coworkers and the general public.

Canadian police departments are hesitant to give access to CPIC reports to out-of-country companies. We are required to have police checks done on all employees who order and view criminal requests as well as go through extensive due diligence by the police force supplying the reports. An audit program is in place, as well, enabling the supplying police department to spot check the end user at any time.

There are two ways to get these reports: the first is to set up a relationship with an existing Canadian-based preemployment background screening company, and the second is to have your Canadian corporate branch order them for you.

Note: Ensure that the resource you use has a direct relationship to access CPIC and is accessing for preemployment screening purposes only and not using a third party. Improper use or access will bear severe penalties as well as put your client at risk.

If a person is charged but not convicted, they can be turned down for the job—but be prepared for a human rights fight. We prefer to apply the rule "innocent until proven guilty." Can you imagine not getting a job you applied for because you defended yourself from an attacker, but due to injuries the attacker suffered he charged you with assault? This is why the common practice in Canada is to acquire the criminal conviction report "CPIC" though a police agency.

Provincial or motor vehicle offenses are not maintained in the CPIC database except for criminal code offenses such as impaired driving or careless driving. For motor vehicle infractions, you need to request a driver's abstract from the provincial motor vehicle departments.

Note: Highway traffic act infractions cannot be used to determine employment except in some provinces where it directly relates to the position held. The job description must specify using a car or driving for this information to be considered.

Procedure—Although the police detachments vary in Canada, they all require a specific form to be completed and signed by the applicant and in many cases witnessed by the company human resources person, along with a photo ID of the candidate. Electronic signatures are not acceptable. This will ensure that organized crime, identity theft issues, and privacy concerns are addressed. Once submitted, the turnaround time for the report is usually 24 business hours. If there is a positive hit and a criminal report does exist, a copy of the report will be printed out.

You are able to acquire a criminal record on any potential employee only once a formal offer of employment has been extended to the candidate. During the interview you can ask, "Have you ever been convicted of criminal offense for which you have not received pardon?" If the answer is yes and they disclose the charge, you must determine if human rights laws apply in that province and whether you can use that information in the final decision making process.

Upon conducting a criminal record search where a record exists, you will receive a document listing where the offense took place, the criminal code charges, and the sentencing. If no hits exist, then all you will get is a "clear." If, however, you require a certified copy for security purposes, it should be requested at the time of the initial request and an additional nominal fee must be paid to the police for them to type a letter on police letterhead.

If a record does turn up and the applicant denied he had one—and is still adamant that it is not he or she—then under the Personal Information Protection and Electronics Documents Act (PIPEDA) privacy legislation you will be making a decision that affects a person on the basis of a document and therefore that person has certain rights. They have a right to view that document and to refute it or even, in the case of a credit report, may have the opportunity to correct errors.

The next step is to have the applicant go to the local police station and supply a fingerprint (the only 100% certain method of confirming a criminal record) and bring that original report to you.

Note: No integration is possible with police systems. The report usually cannot be OCR'ed as it is usually printed at the police station and faxed to you. So for those with automated processing systems and programs, manual entry will be required from this point.

There are several other levels of criminal record reports that can be acquired for preemployment background screening.

Vulnerable Sector Criminal Report—This usually pertains to a person applying for a job with children, the infirm, or elderly. It takes the check one step deeper, and through the CPIC system checks for pardons, sex crimes, or involvement in these types of crimes. It will go to a local level of policing through residential address histories in the CPIC database.

Note: You can get a "clear" if no report exists, but if positive hits exist on a person being searched, you will not get the report or a determination either way (which is a clue the police are inquiring further). Police will contact the candidate directly and have them come in for fingerprinting to ensure the correct person is identified as the candidate before improper accusations are made against an innocent person. Be advised that this can take several months and the report will go directly to the potential employer.

Youth Criminal Records—Only the youth, guardian, crown, or appointed legal counsel can request this report. All you are able to do is supply the form to the employer and then they can pass it onto the youth applicant.

In-Depth Criminal Report—There is a another level of report not commonly requested for preemployment screening but does exist for high-risk or secure positions and can take up to 30 days to return. This goes through CPIC and digs deeper for pardons, suspect information and attempted suicide. It also goes through local police via address history, and much more. This requires a special form and the background company will not be sent the report. It will be sent directly to the firm or organization requesting this and costs considerably more.

Note: Caution should be exercised as human right issues may arise if a decision to NOT hire is based on factors other than a conviction report. Records go back to 1953 and in Canada these records are not restricted to any number of years.

Credit Report—In Canada, we have two credit reporting agencies: Equifax and Transunion.

A personal credit report is pretty much standard and can be part of a preemployment background screening process, if the applicant's position is one that warrants a credit check, i.e., access to money, products, venders, and assets. Again there are controls in varying provinces on when you can deny employment based on credit reports.

Apart from the obvious credit information, these reports confirm name and list alias; they confirm the SIN number (Social Insurance Number), which will identify the status of landed immigrants or Canadian citizens. You will see address histories as well as the last three employers, which is very useful in confirming or identifying past employers.

Note: This is a highly confidential record prized by those seeking to commit identity theft. To acquire this report for preemployment screening, you need specific signed consent for a personal credit report by the candidate. Identifiers are name and address; a date of birth may be needed if multiple people with the same name reside at the listed address. Normal turnaround is same day.

Education Verification—This has become even more important due to recent press about CEOs not having the proper credentials. When discovered, their lack of credentials has had a devastating effect on the corporation. Confirmation of education levels reached or degrees is essential in the hiring process. Initially, it should be established that the learning facility does exist and is not an Internet mill spewing forth bogus diplomas. Next, it is important to contact the registrar's office of that facility and confirm that the candidate completed the level as presented.

Turnaround can take 1 to 3 days and written consent from the applicant faxed to the facility is required. The response is verbal and usually at no cost.

Employment Verification—With the legal climate the way it is, employers can be hesitant to reveal much information about prior employees to background screeners, other than positions held and start and termination dates. It takes varied approaches to gather information that will be of value to your client.

We like to suggest to our clients that they give us a supervisor or associate to talk to. Once we have made that call and gathered the information, we will confirm this through the human resources department.

Note: Written consent is again required from the candidate. At times, it may be necessary for this consent to be sent to the employer being questioned. It is a violation of human rights to ask a person their county of origin or race or how long have they been in the country. You need to extend the conditional offer of employment and then ask for proof that person can work in the respective country. This is easily clarified if a person is applying for work in Canada and their SIN number starts with a "9": they should produce a temporary work permit to confirm they are still legally entitled to work.

License Verifications—If the position being filled requires a license, i.e., welder, mechanic or even a chartered accountant or insurance adjuster, a check should be carried out with the governing professional body, association, or training institute to ensure the license is valid and the party is in good standing within the jurisdiction where he/she will be working.

Motor Vehicle License Checks—Each province has its own rules, guidelines and turn around times ranging from a day to several weeks to online to mail. Canada has no one company or Website that offers online access to all provinces for driver information and products such as driver's license abstracts.

Note: Signed consent is needed in all provinces from the candidate. In Alberta, a third party background company will not be allowed to view the abstract or order it; only the candidate or requesting company directly can order it. Prices vary from province to province.

A great general site to find out how and where to order Canadian driver abstracts by province is http://www.ndaa.org/pdf/drive_abstract_canada_chart.pdf.

Legal Requirement to Work

It is illegal to hire an illegal alien. Therefore, upon processing a conditional offer of employment and the applicant accepting, you can then request the necessary forms be completed. You should obtain a date of birth for the criminal record check, SIN number for the credit check, and even the right to identify whether a person is a landed immigrant or not. But remember, you cannot ask what county they are from.

If the SIN number begins with a 9, then the next step it to ask for work visas, and if they do not have them, you must allow a reasonable amount of time for them to produce them.

SIN Validation—New Canadians with no credit history in Canada will have no record with Revenue Canada. An existing Canadian employer is the only one able to access Revenue Canada to confirm a candidate's employment status in Canada, as a business number will be needed. All others can be confirmed through a Credit Bureau Search.

Terrorism Check—As it is illegal to hire a known terrorist, this search should be carried out on each new hire. This can be done online through the United Nations database as well as the Office of the Superintendent of Financial Institutions Canada (OSFI)-Canadian Sanctions List http://www.OSFI-bsif.gc.ca/osfi/index_ e.aspx?DetailID=525

Drug and Alcohol Testing—In Canada, drug and alcohol testing is not as commonplace as it is in the United States. Drug and alcohol testing is mandated by the Department of Transportation (DOT) on transports crossing the border, commercial airline refueler's, train engineers, and person in high-risk occupations to either themselves or others.

The wording "safety sensitive position" is what determines whether a company can do drug and alcohol testing in that area. A good example is if a person drives a forklift with hazardous materials. It would, however, also extend to the manufacturing line of those materials. Be aware, though, that there will be strong opposition in any field where you wish to introduce drug and alcohol testing. It is essential that a professionally developed policy and procedures manual be created for the area, and this should be completed at least one year in advance of a program being established. This allows enough time to bring the manual into compliance, especially if the facility is unionized.

The reason for this resistance is that although there is a very accurate test to reveal the level of impairment from alcohol through a breathalyzer, the leap to an accurate device for testing the level of intoxication or impairment from drugs has not been made.

A very popular Canadian case is the Entrop case (found at http://www.cdp-hrc. uottawa.ca/hrlc/hrlc2002/entrop.html), which is in appeals.

Post Offer Physical Testing—This is an emerging area that really assists the company's hiring process. Although a person may pass the screening with flying colors and fit a psychological assessment to a tee, he or she may not be physically able to carry out the job. This could potentially result in injury to the candidate as well as having to enter the hiring process again. Again, policy and procedure must be in place as well as minimal standards for each function recorded to avoid discrimination.

Reference Checks—Outside of employment, we see little in the way of personal references as companies are giving very little value to these types of inquires and usually do not want to pay for them. However, if done in a detailed and professional manner, they can reveal much more about the social and psychological aspect of the candidate.

Note: Again, it is always best to have consent signed off in this area.

In closing, the biggest factor in doing preemployment screening in Canada is "consent," following human right guidelines, and protecting the privacy of Canadian citizens. As screenings increase, there will be challenges, legislation, and increased restrictions on access.

Privacy Legislation—The PIPEDA is Canada's federal privacy policy; this applies to all federal employees as well as all employers in provinces that do not have their own privacy policy. British Columbia, Alberta, and Quebec have their own overriding policies. We suggest you research those policies carefully to learn how to do business in those provinces without violating privacy laws.

PIPEDA	http://www.privcom.gc.ca/legislation/02_06_01_e.asp
Alberta	http://www.oipc.ab.ca/pipa/act.cfm
Quebec	http://www.nymity.com/pq_ppips/ppips_reference.asp
Manitoba	http://www.ombudsman.mb.ca/principles.htm
British Columbia	http://www.oipcbc.org/
Northwest Territories	http://www.justice.gov.nt.ca/ATIPP/atipp.htm

Summary

As you can see from the brief information presented in this chapter, the area of international background screening is indeed a new frontier that is changing and evolving. U.S. companies are increasing their talent hunts across national borders and therefore increasing the need for conducting background investigations on the individuals that are hired from other countries. This expansion of the talent acquisition process into the international area is fueling the expansion of background screening firms that conduct investigations in other countries and can fulfill the growing need. In addition, firms headquartered in other countries are starting, albeit slowly, to utilize these services too. For security professionals, this is an early alert that you will need to brush up on your geography and make sure that you are educated about background screening practices around the world. This will require gaining an operational understanding of data protection, privacy, and labor laws of other countries to ensure that your firm is following appropriate protocols and legal requirements. We included information about conducting background investigations in Canada, our bordering neighbor, to give you a glimpse into the types of differences that you will likely encounter as you go from country to country.

For security and other professionals involved in background screening, you will have to put aside your expectation of standard and consistent ways of doing things that you have become accustomed to in the United States as your firm recruits talent from and for other nations. The new expectation will have to be to expect differences in data protection and privacy laws, justice systems, court structure, public records, how records are accessed, what records may be accessed, where records can be accessed, process for transmitting records information across national borders, etc. You would do well to start educating yourself on some of these differences now before you are called upon to implement a program or participate in its development. An excellent source of information is the National Association for Professional Background Screeners (NAPBS), which has launched an educational series that will help you on your learning journey. *The Safe Hiring Manual,* by Les Rosen, is also a good book for information, as well as the International Resource Center at http://www.workplaceviolence911.com/docs/internationalresourcecenter.htm.

Some additional Websites to turn to for information include the following:

- www.preemploymentdirectory.com
- http://www.workplaceviolence911.com/docs/internationaresourcecenter.htm

- www.brbpub.com
- http://www.fedee.com/privacy.html (The Federation of European Employers [FedEE])
- http://www.dataprivacy.ie/4c.htm
- www.eapm.org
- http://www.hrpao.org/HRPAO/LegalCentre/WorkplaceLegislation/
- http://www.rcmp-grc.gc.ca/crimrec/crimrec_e.htm
- http://www.privcom.gc.ca/information/guide_e.asp
- http://www.workplaceviolence911.com/docs/map.htm
- www.NAPBS.com
- www.FREEDOMINFO.ORG
- www.ESRcheck.com
- www.employeescreen.com
- www.lexisnexis.com
- www.isbcorporate.com

You are on the cusp of the dawning of a new frontier and you have the opportunity to position yourself to be a valuable resource to assist your organization on its journey into international background screening.

Future Trends in Background Screening

With contributions by Thomas Lawson and Wanda Hackett

As the capstone chapter for the book, we are going to focus on the future and what it may bring. Our projections are based on our collective experiences and information gathered during our research for this book. This is not intended to be an exhaustive portrayal of what the future may hold for background screening, as if we had a magic crystal ball anyway, but more so the trends "we envision that will impact the screening industry. In the very turbulent times when Russia started on its trek toward capitalism under Mikhail Gorbachov, he once quipped, "The future is not what it used to be," and we believe this is an accurate portrayal of the transformation that is occurring in the background screening industry. With the rapid changes in information technology, the Internet, biometrics, and security and human resource (HR) processes, the landscape of background screening is dramatically changing.

However, I believe to appropriately appreciate the future, we must have a clear understanding of the past, so we asked Tom Lawson, one of the industry's true gurus who has been with it from the start, to share his perspective on where the industry has been.

From an industry perspective, first, we were in the "Credit Reporting Industry." Then we evolved into the "Information Industry." Then, the "Information Brokerage Industry." Concurrent to these terms, there was "preemployment Screening Business," and "Employment Screening Business". Somewhere along the line, we were in the "Information Age", and for a short while were called the "Background Check Business", and we are now, for the most part the "Background Screening Industry".

Well, in the beginning, there were three national companies: Equifax, founded in 1898, but much later started "preemployment Screening" for the quality-employee starved insurance industry, Research Associates, Inc. (RAI) of Cleveland, founded by Robert Petersen, a former FBI Agent, and his partners in 1953; and APSCREEN, founded in 1980. In those days "we" all provided "preemployment screening" in a vastly different way than is purveyed today.

(Continued)

To begin with "preemployment screening" was not the stuff of the "Personnel" Department, it was the stock-in-trade of the Corporate Security Department, and was usually undertaken in sensitive environments such as aerospace, military contractors and the like. In the early days, the best group to belong to, in order to have professional fellowship was the American Society for Industrial Security (ASIS), which hosted the membership of most of the director-level security professionals, throughout the world. It was here that a wayward preemployment screener could find comfort after living all day in a non-existent industry where mere business mortals would regularly utter the words: "why would anyone do background checks?"

In the early days, a good "package" consisted of several things, and no self-respecting screener would be caught DEAD selling "pieces" or "units" which, ironically, in today's world, make up 90% of the background screening products sold. It was not uncommon to find the three of us competing in a very friendly way over two or three dollars (maybe) for a multiple-step candidate identification process, three-bureau credit reports, three-level conviction checks (Fed, State and Muni Courts—and we could then only search these by going to the courthouse, and looking through the large books located on the "public counter"), "Bonded-Requester" or "insurance-grade" driving reports, five years of prior employment (the then FAA requirement for certified persons such as pilots, and other flight crew), education verification (by this we meant "all" education, not a cherry-picking of institutions). And we did it all by taking the order over the phone, or via a facsimile machine, which used thermal paper, exclusively, and, after a year, the printing vanished off of the paper!

Excerpt reprinted with permission from Thomas Lawson, CFE, CII, Apscreen

---

With that perspective on where the industry has been, one of the emerging issues that the business community, in general, is faced with in modern times is "The Threat From Within":

- Employee theft is at an all-time high. The Annual Retail Industry report noted employees are stealing from their employers at an all-time high rate.
- Identity theft continues at an alarming level.
- Up to 60% of applicants lie or misrepresent their backgrounds on resumes.
- Fake degrees are prevalent and still easy to acquire.
- One of 10 applicants has a criminal background.
- Employers continue to lose 73% of negligent hiring cases that go to jury trials.

Not surprisingly, the factors that continue to drive background screening numbers up are not new. According to the 2006 Crime Watch Survey, 55%, of businesses surveyed experienced some type of electronic crime committed by an insider during the past year, with individual company losses up 46% to an average of $739,700. Fewer than 28% of the crimes were referred to law enforcement. This means there is no warrant or court record to report for potential future employers. It also is likely that a high percentage of the people were allowed to resign to avoid negative publicity for the company. That increases the likelihood of the fraud not being visible to future employers.

In addition, the most recent Annual Computer Crime and Security Survey, conducted by the Computer Security Institute and FBI, found that the top four security loss categories—which account for almost three-fourths of the total percent of losses—are viruses, unauthorized access, laptop theft, and theft of proprietary information. The same survey found more than one-third of participants believe at least 20% of overall losses are due to insider threats.

There also is the emergence of the "Gigabyte Gangsters"—gangs and organized crime moving their focus from the streets to the lucrative Internet. Friends, relatives, or spouses of the gang members are getting jobs as retail clerks, mortgage loan assistants, or hotel desk clerks, in positions that regularly view credit card information and personal information so they can steal it for illicit purposes.

Because insider threats are escalating, clients are demanding more real-time information and solutions from the background screening industry to better manage risks and assets. This is likely to drive closer connections between background screening, access control, and overall loss prevention.

Data Protection

According to the Ponemon Institute's data breach study, data breaches in 2006 cost U.S. companies an average of $182 for every compromised record, compared to last year's $138, a 31% increase. The study reports that roughly $128 of the 2006 figure is related to indirect fallout from information leaks such as higher-than-normal customer turnover. Other associated costs spurred by data mishandlings or thefts were an average price tag of $660,000 per company in expenses related to notifying customers, business partners, and regulators about data leaks. Total costs for each cited record loss studied in the report ranged from less than $1 million to more than $22 million.

"The burden companies must bear as a result of a data breach are significant, making a strong case for more strategic investments in preventative measures such as encryption and data loss prevention," said Dr. Larry Ponemon, chairman of Elk Rapids, Michigan–based Ponemon Institute. "Tough laws and intense public scrutiny mean the consequences of poor security are steep—and growing steeper for companies entrusted with managing stores of consumer data."

In charting the most common sources of data leaks, researchers found that lost or stolen laptops remain the top culprit, accounting for 45% of all incidents. Records lost by third party business partners or outsourcing companies represented the second-most popular type of event, representing 29% of reported leaks.

"Experience makes it apparent that attempts to prevent data loss will ultimately fail," wrote Drew Robb in the September 19, 2005, issue of *Computerworld* magazine. His view is that the issue is not whether a business will experience a data breach triggering statutory disclosure obligations and subjecting it to public shame. Rather, the issue is how that business will respond when the inevitable happens.

It is expected that federal legislation will define the necessary response by organizations and will require the use of encryption or some other reasonable means to protect personally identifiable information as it is transmitted, stored, used, and disposed of. It remains to be seen if impending legislation will go the next step and identify mandatory requirements that would actually help prevent data breaches.

One of our predictions is that legislators are going to increase standards for being in the business of collecting, handling, and selling personal identifying information. A possible outcome may be to require background screening firms to have a private investigator license as a standard. Many states already have this requirement.

Systems Integration

As firms move toward sophisticated ways of using and accessing data to facilitate better decision making, enterprise integration continues to drive data management. The trend is having a pervasive impact on security and HR as a driving force of background screening in organizations. The business community is now demanding that background screening information become integrated into greater HR and security information systems via a dashboard, where all relevant data regarding an individual can be accessed rather than having to access a separate data feed.

I believe that the focus on integration of disparate systems into a common dashboard is going to move even faster than what we have already seen. Users are becoming more sophisticated and applying concepts from supply chain management, enterprise integration, and customer relationship management to the employment and on-boarding process. This is going to escalate tools like applicant tracking and background screening being integrated into one system. "Developing an integrated hiring management approach means incorporating elements from the entire hiring continuum: recruiting, sourcing, managing the applicant pool, screening, skills, and behavioral assessments, and reviewing qualifications for federal and state tax credits," according to Bart Valdes, President, Employer Services, First Advantage Corporation. Anyone that has been following First Advantage knows that they are marching toward the creation of "an integrated hiring-management solution" for businesses and this may very well be the model of the future.

In addition, according to the article by David Peck "Know Your Hire," in the *Human Resource Executive Forecast 2007,* published by Human Resource Executive, January 2007. "The sheer volume of [background] data per candidate continues to increase, along with its complexity (and potential for errors)," and he actually thinks it is getting tougher to paint an informative picture of a candidate. He also thinks its going to get "exceedingly complicated to extract the most valuable insights from screening and assessment procedures". If this prognosis of the future is correct than we are likely to see the increase application of data management tools to the hiring process to help sort through the information and give management the information it needs.

The Quest for the Perfect Identifier

Beyond traditional information technology issues, several other technologies are likely to intersect with background screening as data collected by the systems are used as a unique identifier. There has been an explosion of identifying technologies since 9/11, and the trend can be expected to intensify for many years to come as the war on terrorism continues to stimulate investment dollars.

From fingerprints to iris or retina scans, all the way to implantable chips and DNA, the race to find the perfect identifier has heated up. An early shot in this battle was fired by the National Institute of Standards and Technology (NIST) in a recent study that confirms fingerprints are still king. The Fingerprint Vendor Technology Evaluation (FpVTE) 2003 is an independently administered technology evaluation of fingerprint matching, identification, and verification systems. Conducted by the NIST on behalf of the Justice Management Division (JMD) of the U.S. Department of Justice. (http://fpvte.nist.gov/)

Fingerprint identification systems have approached 99% accuracy and, perhaps more importantly, a slim 0.01 false-positive rate—or only about 1 in 10,000 scans resulting in a misidentification. An NIST study tested 34 fingerprint ID systems from 18 companies. About 25,000 people supplied about 50,000 sets of fingerprints—all in about 400,000 distinct digital images of fingers. The best systems reached 98.6% accuracy for a single-print match. Predictably, the more prints matched, the higher was the accuracy rate. Two-finger dactyloscopic (comparison of fingerprints for identification) reviews were accurate 99.6% of the time. Four or more fingers matched had a 99.9% accuracy rate.

The study results are not likely to stem the tide of researchers looking for the holy grail of identifiers. Examples of contenders abound with impressive results. For example, "A test several years ago by the United Kingdom's national standards laboratory found the iris-scanning method to be the most accurate. During the study, the iris scan system never accepted a person claiming false identity."[1]

The next wave of biometric products that are already becoming available are ones that combine two or more biometrics for identification purposes. Several on the market include matching a fingerprint identification combined with an iris scan or a facial recognition with a retina scan, etc. These take the accuracy level even higher than just a fingerprint alone and virtually eliminate misidentification.

Table 13-1 addresses identification methodologies.

On February 17, 2007, the U.S. Patent & Trademark Office announced the development of a Personal Authentication System. The invention relates to a "personal authentication system using biometrics information, which identifies or authenticates an individual by verifying to-be-verified biometrics characteristic data against previously registered biometrics characteristic data". With the advances

Table 13-1 Identification Methodologies

• Bertillonage	• Chips
• Tattooing and branding	• Signature verification
• Bar-coding	• Keystroke retina
• DNA registers	• Iris
• Hands (fingerprints, hand geometry, palm prints, thermograms)	• Eigenface
	• Earlobes
• Voice	• Gait

---

[1] *Security Products Magazine*, August 2005.

occurring in biometric technologies, the leap from this Personal Authentication System to one that uses biometric information to match an applicant or employee to their background information stored in some set of databases cannot be too far away. The real hobgoblin of biometrics may prove to be businesses' difficulty in addressing ethical and moral issues associated with the use of these technologies.

Implantable chips offer the promise of instant access to applicant or employee data and make it easy for individuals to show certain levels of security clearance, ensuring they are who they claim to be.

"The age of Intelligent Identifiers has arrived. The significant advances in technologies are already starting to have a profound impact on the landscape of how background screening will be conducted and the ride is just beginning." One that is emerging now is using driver license photos to detect fraud and find criminals. According to the articles (see footnote #2) "Driver's License Photos Become Fraud-Detection Tool" on *The New York Time*'s Website, the following was reported:

> *On the second floor of a state office building three facial-recognition specialists are revolutionizing American law enforcement. They work for the Massachusetts motor vehicles department. Last year they tried an experiment, for sport. Using computerized biometric technology, they ran a mug shot from the Website of "America's Most Wanted," the Fox Network television show, against the state's database of nine million digital driver's license photographs. The computer found a match. A man who looked very much like Robert Howell, the fugitive in the mug shot, had a Massachusetts driver's license under another name. Mr. Howell was wanted in Massachusetts on rape charges. The analysts passed that tip along to the police, who tracked him down to New York City, where he was receiving welfare benefits under the alias on the driver's license. Mr. Howell was arrested in October.*
>
> *At least six other states have or are working on similar enormous databases of driver's license photographs. Coupled with increasingly accurate facial-recognition technology, the databases may become a radical innovation in law enforcement.*
>
> *Other biometric databases are more useful for now. But DNA and fingerprint information, for instance, are not routinely collected from the general public. Most adults, on the other hand, have a driver's license with a picture on it, meaning that the relevant databases for facial-recognition analysis already exist. And while the current technology requires good-quality photographs, the day may not be far off when images from ordinary surveillance cameras will routinely help solve crimes.* [2]

Another perspective might be the following:

Today (2006)

- Company's workers can pass security checkpoints.
- A radio frequency from the reader activates an implanted chip, which then emits a signal transmitting an ID number.

---

[2] http://www.nytimes.com/2007/02/17/us/17face.html?pagewanted=2&_r=2

Table 13-2 Combined DNA Index System

The Combined DNA Index System (CODIS) is an electronic database of DNA profiles administered through the FBI. The system lets federal, state, and local crime labs share and compare DNA profiles. Through CODIS, investigators match DNA from crime scenes with convicted offenders and with other crime scenes using computer software, just as fingerprints are matched through automated fingerprint identification systems.

Tomorrow (20??)

- Job applicants can wave their arm with an implanted chip over an electronic employment application.
- A radiofrequency from the reader activates their implanted chip, which then emits a signal transmitting employment history, education, criminal record, driving record, etc. associated with the person's biometric signature.

DNA may prove to be the ultimate identifier, even though there are voluminous issues associated with employers having access to this type of information. Even with the challenges that using DNA as a personal identifier must face, the groundwork is already being laid (see Table 13-2).

For the foreseeable future, these high-technology identifiers are likely to battle it out for supremacy as the king of identifiers. Only time will tell which technology prevails.

Table 13-2 discusses the combined DNA index system.

In the interim, integrated biometrics tools are likely to become prominent because "the marriage of integrated computer databases, with their super speed, and biometric identifiers with their accuracy will create an identification capability beyond comprehension;" however, to reach its true potential, it will have to overcome privacy, ethical, moral, and public policy issues, which may prove to be more difficult than the technology solution itself.

Reference Checking Makes a Comeback

David Peck believes that "the tide is turning [for reference checking] ... as executives reassess the time, cost, and risk involved in evaluating candidates". He states that HR Executives are, once again, emphasizing old fashioned reference checks, which when done well, are a highly valuable piece of the hiring puzzle."[3]

We think the jury is still out on whether reference checking is ramping up because company policies that govern the refusal to give out any meaningful information still persist as the primary practice in most businesses. Thus, we believe it is time for us to deal with the reality that most businesses are colluding in an ongoing game of "Russian roulette" by not sharing information about previous employees. The time has come to stop this game now and recognize that "We have met the enemy and he is us," to quote Pogo. We need to break the chains that bind us into colluding in this schizophrenic process of "wanting to get as much information as we can" when we are hiring and then to turn

---

[3] Know Your Hire, *Human Resource Executive Forecast 2007*, November 17, 2006.

around and only give out a minimum amount of information to the hiring manager that wants information from us.

The issue needs to be attacked on several fronts:

First, corporate legal counsels need to be helped to understand the very pervasive impact that their stance on "give out minimum information" has on hiring the best candidates which is the life blood of creating competitive advantage for the enterprise. Security and HR professionals need to develop a conscious strategy to educate their corporate legal counsels on this as a business issue and also their senior management team, who can influence the issue as well. They also need to challenge their counsel to identify alternatives to the minimum information approach, which really came about because of managers and supervisors giving out inappropriate information that created legal exposure for the company. There are always alternatives and options, although to discover them, management will need to challenge themselves to get beyond their current paradigms.

Second, as is the case with most business issues, reference checking is interrelated with other facets of the business, but particularly tied to the training and knowledge of managers and supervisors. The reason we ended up with the mess in the first place is because organizations either did not properly train their supervisors or failed to address inappropriate behavior by supervisors as a performance problem.

Third, security managers need to understand the risk associated with making hiring decisions without having valuable information about a candidate from previous employers. Previous performance and relationships could be the most predictive information that can be gathered in the hiring process to project future success. This should be a part of security managers stepping up to the business partnership role and contributing to the management of business risk, not just risk associated with individuals' actions.

Fourth, security and HR professionals need to make this an issue that the major associations that they belong to start to address. I believe at one time the Society of Human Resource Management (SHRM) had a committee that focused on this issue; however, it appears to have fallen by the wayside at this time. We need to get ASIS International, Security Industry Association, Association of Threat Assessment Professionals, HRM, National Human Resource Association, etc. working together and collectively on this issue.

We also have a radical recommendation that we believe associations should consider that would shake this issue up. Create a bylaw or use another vehicle to implement an agreement that members of the association agree to provide reference checks to other members and hold them harmless in the process. The hard part will be creating an agreement that members can agree to; however, if several associations start doing this it could have an avalanche effect on reference checking.

We strongly believe solving this issue of getting quality information from a reference check is a possible, and will have a tremendous payoff for businesses. This is not mission impossible, but more so one that, with focused attention, diligence, stamina, widespread association, and organizational support, can happen.

Continuous Background Checks

As mentioned in the discussion on Infinity Screening in a previous chapter, with the availability of more and more sophisticated information technology tools and the ability to cross-reference databases and accumulate massive amounts of data, we believe we are going to see continuous post-hire screening drastically increase and become the new norm for businesses.

> *Bill Bollinger, Executive Vice President of National Background Data, said their criminal monitoring service, CrimWatch, will offer firms the capability to proactively monitor background screening information on current employees. This extends a firm's due diligence from the initial contact with employment candidates through the complete employment lifecycle of employees, providing real-time information for the business to make informed risk management decisions. The post-hire services help firms with early identification of potentially problematic situations, to assess risk and be able to take preventative steps before something bad happens. This will be a great tool to help avoid potential negligent retention lawsuits.*[4]

The Background Screening Business Model

With talent acquisition becoming a major organizational issue, the focus of background screening will continue to move toward being an important process to help hire the right person for the business versus the focus being to keep out the bad guys.

We will also see the "need for speed" continue to escalate as clients put continuing pressure on background screeners to provide faster feedback on candidates. This requirement will be on top of the demand for accuracy, meaning providing the right information and ensuring that the information provided is accurate. There are also a number of background screening firms that have become ISO certified, which will enhance their capabilities to provide accurate information. Some of these trend-setting firms include Verified Person and Accurate Background. The movement toward quality information is being driven by both customers and the National Association for Professional Background Screeners (NAPBS), which represents the industry and is driving for industry accreditation standards.

We also believe that we will see a push for background screening services to provide more pinpointed information that fits the unique requirements of clients. This customization will in many ways parallel the push that occurred in manufacturing for mass customization.

Just as we will see the continued push for information systems integration, we are likely to see the continued integration of the processes that make up the hiring continuum. The clear distinctions that we see today between background screening, drug

---

[4]   Robert Capwell, Beyond Pre-Hire Background Checks: Post-Hire Screens Become the Norm, *SHRM Online*, February 2000.

testing, interviewing profiles, psychological and personality assessments, etc. will dissipate and blur as new innovative models and systems are created. Juxtaposed on top of this will be the integration with disparate systems outside of the hiring process, which draw upon similar information even though they tie to security information systems such as

- Access control
- Reported workplace crime
- Safety and threat incidents
- Logs of employee hotline calls
- Geographic crime vulnerability data
- Threat proximity identifying terrorist and crime targets
- Homeland Security information

An example of integration with access control has already emerged with products offered by firms like LobbyGuard and HireRight

> *When someone wants to pay a visit to Davison Elementary, that person swipes his driver's license on the lobby kiosk. It snaps a picture and prepares a one-use visitor badge—while simultaneously checking sex offender registries and the school's internal "do not allow" list. If the visitor is a match for one those lists, the badge isn't printed and the office is alerted.... In the principal's office, workers monitor the kiosk through a Web-based interface. Whenever a red flag is raised about a visitor, an alert pops up on the administrator's screen; it contains the name and photo of the visitor, along with a full background log explaining why they failed the check. If the visitor has a criminal record, its details are shown on screen, as well.*[5]

Part of the new models will also likely involve preemployment and post employment screening moving from strictly being business products to also encompassing consumer products, as well as the lines between products, tools, and services blurring. An example of a consumer product emerging from what has heretofore been a business product is MyBackgroundCheck.com in which the background check is being given to all candidates in a patent pending certificate format that will allow them to reuse the report in other aspects of their lives. Some uses include applying for other jobs, dating services, signing on to social networks, renting an apartment, etc.

Another example that illustrates how lines between products, tools, and services could blur is when tools such as those used for continuous post-hire screening evolve to the point that they are also incorporated into the firm's background screening policies so that they will automatically govern when, how, and when checks are performed.

In addition integration is also likely to occur across the various types of searches that are conducted, e.g., criminal, educational, previous employment, driving, etc. Today, these are all separate databases or sources that must be checked. Tomorrow, we are likely to see the emergence of databases that either house multiple types of information or are linked so that information access is simplified.

---

[5]   http://www.Kioskmarketplace.com/articl.php?id=170908&na=1

Infinity Screening (continuous post-hire screening) is going to expand and is one of the services that will offer security professionals an ongoing opportunity to participate in risk management decision making, which will only raise their stature and perceived value to the organization.

One aspect of the background screening process that is going to continue to evolve is the way court records are kept and accessed. Increasingly, as municipalities can afford it, they are moving to putting court records online. The next frontier will be to standardize the format and processes across city, county, state, and federal levels. Don't hold your breath for this one, but eventually it will happen.

We also expect that background screening is going to continue to expand as more and more jobs require screening. In the near future, we expect requirements to be added for most positions that involve processing consumer credit cards, e.g., hotel clerks, mortgage loan processors, retail store clerks, etc., as well as caregivers in elder services, home service providers, carpet cleaners, home repair, plumbers, electricians, etc., and other workers like vendors who drive an ice cream cart or truck through neighborhoods with that so-familiar melody.

Outsourcing

Another challenge in today's employment marketplace deals with the accelerating trend toward outsourcing work. Outsourcing work to other firms or to freelancers is occurring on a large scale. With the amount of talent existing in the freelancing pool and the acceptability of employing free agents, employers are motivated to use the specialized firms or free agents. This impacts the background screening industry because this is often the Achilles heel of many firm's background screening program—checking the backgrounds of independent contractors or employees of their contractors.

The simple solution is to require every contractor to conduct background checks on employees as a part of all contract agreements. However, if you do not "inspect, what you expect," you are likely to find that many contractors are not complying with the contractual agreement. Businesses have not worried too much about the situation because companies have been able to go into court and use the defense that it was the contractor's employees that caused the problem, therefore the companies have no liability. However, recent cases signal that this view may no longer be acceptable in the courts.

As this new view takes hold, security professional professionals can help businesses close this gaping hole in their background screening program. A starting step should be to require contractors to provide a regular report summarizing background check results while periodically reviewing the contractors' documentation. Security should take an active role in ensuring that this happens.

We also believe that as the recruitment process outsourcing (RPO) trend continues, end user businesses are going to focus on outsourcing the full initial onboarding process that includes full responsibility for conducting background checks on applicants and/or candidates based on a defined contractual agreed-upon process. This will, in effect, transfer the full responsibility, accountability, and liability to the RPO firm. This is going to stimulate more interest by these firms in fully understanding the background screening process so they can effectively manage it.

Marketing

David Sawyer, President of Safer Places Inc. in Middleboro, Massachusetts, offers an interesting perspective on the situation. He believes contractors are going to start to recognize the time has come to diligently perform background checks. Progressive firms will not only start conducting checks but use the information in marketing and advertising efforts to create a competitive advantage. An example of this is "the Smell Good Plumbers" whom are featured in the book *Listening to the Voice of the Customer*. They have a radio advertisement campaign in which they proudly declare that "their plumbers have passed a background check."

International Talent Search

Beyond the outsourcing and freelancing trends we must also recognize that the globalization of the workforce is a two way street. With America having an impending labor shortage in the future, the cold hard truth is we need immigration to meet our economic needs. Thus, we are seeing an unprecedented amount of recruiting across national borders to acquire the talent needed to fill our jobs. According to the Bureau of Labor Statistics, by 2010, the overall labor shortage, measured in unfilled jobs, will be 21.3%. This means that "the competition to acquire new employees and retain existing personnel will reach dimensions that are unthinkable in today's environment," according to the Bureau of Labor Statistics.

And as Jason Morris, CEO of EmployeeScreenIQ, Inc., pointed out in the International chapter, conducting background checks on foreign nationals is rapidly growing. "The international market is growing significantly with more firms having locations outside of the country and more individuals being imported or exported. The labor market is no longer just in the United States," said Morris. As firms address the impending shortage by expanding talent searches beyond the U.S. borders, the searches have moved beyond technical fields, such as engineers, scientists, or nurses, to many other management and professional-level positions. And, white collar, college-educated workers will not be the primary category where the shortages occur. Even larger shortages will appear in lower-level service and production jobs. This is one of the real issues fueling the debate about immigration legislation, as legislators struggle with how to balance national security concerns with the employment needs of the economy.

This impacts background screening because the focus of background checks has been on U.S. employees applying for jobs within the country. A recent survey conducted by PreemploymentDirectory.com found only 47% of businesses conduct background checks on applicants from outside of the country and 70% do not conduct checks on candidates hired in other countries.

This practice is going to change, and international background checks are emerging as one of the next frontiers where background investigations will take hold.

Legal Challenges

Credit Checks

In the article "Stop Using Credit Reports as a Criterion in Hiring," Ben Arnoldly, staff writer at *The Christian Science Monitor*, says that "credit checks are a growing factor in hiring, with 35% of employers checking applicants' credit in 2003, up from 19% in 1996, according to the SHRM. Typically credit reports are done if a person is going to deal with money, says John Dooney, a manager of strategic research at SHRM."

In the same article, Les Rosen, president of Employment Screening Resources, a national background screening firm in California, says employers should look at credit only for jobs where the information is relevant.

He cites a few examples:

- For jobs that involve handling money, people may have the motive to steal if their debts surpass their salary.
- For jobs requiring travel, bad credit could bar applicants from renting cars or buying tickets.
- For jobs managing money, the report can offer some clues on how applicants manage their own.

Particularly in that last scenario, Les Rosen cautions employers to be circumspect because blemishes might be errors or beyond the person's control, such as sudden medical expenses. Legally, employers must receive written permission from applicants to do a credit check and must give those denied because of credit a chance to respond.

While there are many who are dismissing this issue has similar drapings, in my opinion, and needs to be paid closer attention to my businesses, given that the credit reports that are provided to businesses do not show ratings or FICO scores, we believe this issue is likely to grow "legs" and may have a very real impact on the current practices for using credit checks. I recall in the not too distant past when all businesses used educational requirements such as a high school diploma or college degree as their absolute standard. However, when scrutinized under the lens of being a legitimate job requirement and the negative impact on protected class groups, it gave way to the current practice of considering the educational requirement and/or "equivalent experience." This credit checking issue has similar drapings in my opinion and needs to be paid closer attention to by businesses so they do not become the victim of a costly landmark ruling that sets the new direction.

Previously Incarcerated Individuals

Another impending legal battle is likely to emerge over the effect of background checking on previously incarcerated individuals. The following U.S. judicial decision in Hawaii illustrates this point very well:

> *Hawaii's high court ruled that a Home Depot wrongfully fired an employee based solely on his prior criminal record. Under state law, a company must show that the conviction bears a rational relationship to the employee's job before it can take action. The employee applied for a promotion to department supervisor and Home Depot conducted a criminal background check and uncovered a drug conviction. Note that during his tenure with the firm, he had passed three drug tests.*[6]

---

[6] *Wright v. Home Depot,* Hawaii Supreme Court, No. 27190, 2006; Security Management, Legal Report, March 2007.

This is another issue that could pick up steam, although it has a great potential for polarization that could foretell its doom. One could easily see the Democrats lining up on the side of workers, promoting jobs and second chances, while the Republicans line up on the law and order side, with an intent to keep the criminals out of our workplaces. Who knows which way the political winds will blow and take this issue, but one thing is for sure—we are going to see an increase in lawsuits happening in this area.

Ethics and Honesty

Will the increase in background checking stimulate a renaissance on honesty and full disclosure, or will it motivate more creative ways to hide the truth? While this question crosses sociological, psychological, and behavior boundaries, it is our humble opinion that "the cops and robbers" scenario will continue to be alive and well. As background screening gets smarter, faster, and better systems to discover and report problematic behavior, the bad guys will figure out more ways to disguise, hide, or otherwise try to elude detection.

Demand for Return on Investment

The frenzy for background screening is likely to continue for some time to come; however, in the not too distant future, we are likely to see businesses starting to seriously evaluate the return on investment on background screening similar to what happened with medical examinations and drug screening. At some point, background screening firms are going to have to be able to definitively answer, "What is the return on conducting background screenings? And is it worth the investment?"

Cultural Change

Background screening is part of an overall risk mitigation strategy that supports a security conscious culture. To continue to increase their influence and stature in their organizations, security professionals will need to understand the power of an organization's culture in driving people's behavior. Accordingly, security professionals will need learn how to effectively forge alliances and close working relationship with HR, organizational development, and training professionals to inculcate key security processes, like background screening, into well-crafted "organizational change" strategies that institutionalize a security consciousness and actions as the way a company does business. See "How to Create a Security Conscious Culture" in Appendix I.

In closing, as you can see we believe that there is a lot happening with background screening and innovation will continue to escalate. There is widespread belief that background screening will continue to expand and security professionals should view this as another opportunity to further demonstrate the value-added nature of their counsel.

Tom Lawson's View of the Future of Background Screening

- **Global Screening.** Like most of the thorough guys, we're doing a lot more stuff around the world.

- **"Never-Stop" Screening.** Companies, through more available access to information and better written Consent Forms and policies, will be able to constantly update their employees' backgrounds with "Pull Notice" programs through several DMV's, Direct-Purchase Credit monitoring tools, and random drug testing, etc., all of which doesn't sound that new, it just is terrific speech fodder for those who would address industry trade associations—the key is the consent language, and the policy modifications, the information has always been there, and most companies re-screen when they promote anyway, but "24/7-Global" sounds great.

- **More and better automation** and cheaper for the user, since there are more Web-based screening management programs out there, and there is no end in sight. This will also naturally promote laziness, and the inherent desire to put more distance from "them" and the NPRRA and the PRRN.

- **Self-Screening.** A growing number of companies have actually read the FACTA and the FCRA and realize that if they do it themselves, they can save some bucks on the consistencies within the employment class as advised by us responsible members of the industry, not to mention they can buy crappy information and have a feel good party (not to be confused with the Pity Party they are going to have after I've testified against them when their improperly screened employee murdered his supervisor, after being discovered to have molested several children in the company's day-care center) and the Notice requirements are more relaxed, leaving more room for the "closet" screener to forge his own program, independent of industry-advised standards. This is problematic, but get ready, folks, it's here and it's growing. Contrary to this is the increase in potential clients flooding into the industry, because Counsel has realized that Employment Screening is a risky proposition, best left to professional screeners, and better yet, they get the liability at an arm's length, "outsourced" provider.

- **Increasing demand** for the ultimate in incompetent screening tools, Worker's Comp records.

Some companies will improve their screening procedures because their counsel will advise them to, if they are lucky enough to have counsel that reads the cases being filed for "negligent hiring, retention, and supervision."

Appendix A
Sample Forms

50-State Compliant Background Check Disclosure and Authorization Forms

Disclosure Form

In the interest of maintaining the safety and security of our customers and employees, _____ ("the Company") will procure a consumer report and/or investigative consumer report ("background check report") on you in connection with your employment application, and if you are hired, may procure additional background check reports on you for employment purposes. LexisNexis® Authentication & Screening, or another consumer reporting agency, will prepare the report. LexisNexis® Authentication & Screening is located at 700 East Technology Avenue, Building E., Suite 2200, Orem, Utah 94097 and can be reached at 800 631-8777.

The background check report will contain information bearing on your character, general reputation, personal characteristics, mode of living and credit standing. The types of information that may be obtained include but are not limited to: Social Security number verification; criminal, public, educational and, as appropriate, driving records checks; verification of prior employment; references checks; credit reports; licensing and certification checks; and drug testing results. The information will be obtained from private and public record sources, including, as appropriate, personal interviews with your associates, friends, and neighbors.

You may request more information about the nature and scope of any background check reports by contacting: _____ [*Company contact information*]. A summary of your rights under the Fair Credit Reporting Act is also being provided to you with this form.

State Law Notices: If you live, or are seeking work, in California, Maine, N.Y. or Washington State, please note the following information:

CALIFORNIA: You may view the file maintained on you by LexisNexis® Authentication & Screening, and obtain a copy of the file, upon submitting proper identification and paying duplication costs, by appearing at their offices, during normal business hours and on reasonable notice, or by mail. You may also receive a file-summary by telephone. LexisNexis® Authentication & Screening has trained personnel available to explain your file to you, including any coded information. If you appear in person, you may be accompanied by one other person, provided that person furnishes proper identification.

MAINE: You have the right, upon request, to know whether the Company requested a background check report on you. You may request and receive from the Company, within five (5) business days of our receipt of your request, the name, address, and telephone number of the nearest unit designated to handle inquiries for the consumer reporting agency issuing a background check report concerning you. You also have the right to request and promptly receive from all such agencies copies of any such reports.

NEW YORK: You have the right, upon written request, to know whether the Company requested a background check on you from a consumer reporting agency. If a report is requested, you may inspect and receive a copy of the report by contacting the agency.

WASHINGTON STATE: You have the right, upon written request made within a reasonable period of time after your receipt of this disclosure, to receive from the Company a complete and accurate disclosure of the nature and scope of the investigation we requested. You also have the right to request from the consumer reporting agency a written summary of your rights and remedies under the Washington Fair Credit Reporting Act.

Authorization Form

After carefully reading this Background Check Disclosure and Authorization form, I authorize the Company to procure a background check report on me that is prepared by a consumer reporting agency. I understand that, if I am hired, the Company may rely on this authorization to procure additional background check reports during and throughout my employment without asking for my authorization again.

I also authorize the following entities to disclose to the consumer reporting agency and its agents all information about or concerning me, including, but not limited to: my past or present employers; learning institutions, including colleges and universities; law enforcement and all other federal, state, and local agencies; federal, state, and local courts; the military; credit bureaus; testing facilities; motor vehicle records agencies; all other private and public sector repositories of information; and, any other person, organization, or agency with any information about or concerning me. The information that can be disclosed to the consumer reporting agency and its agents includes, but is not limited to, information concerning my employment history, earnings history, education, credit history, motor vehicle history, criminal history, drug test results, military service, professional credentials, and all other information requested by the consumer reporting agency or its agents.

For residents of, or for jobs located in, California, Minnesota and Oklahoma: You may request a free copy of any background check reports on you by checking the box below.

☐ I request a free copy of the report.

I promise the information I provided on this form is true and correct. I understand that dishonesty will disqualify me from consideration for employment with the Company, or if I am hired, that I may be fired.

I agree that a facsimile or photocopy of this form may be used in lieu of the original.

Last Name _____ First _____ Middle _____

Present Address _____

City/State/Zip

_____

Social Security Number _____

Driver's License Number _____

FOR IDENTIFICATION PURPOSES ONLY: Month and **Day** of Birth _____ [*Optional*]

_____   _____

Signature   Date

Pre-Adverse Action Letter for Applicants

[LETTERHEAD]

[Date]

PERSONAL & CONFIDENTIAL

[Individual's Name]
[Individual's Address]

Dear _____ :

Enclosed please find a copy of the pre-employment screening report that we procured from LexisNexis® Authentication & Screening, with your authorization, in connection with your application for employment. Also enclosed is a summary of your rights under applicable law.

[*Option 1*: Please carefully review the report. If you believe that any of the information is inaccurate or incomplete, or if you have any other concerns about the information, please contact _____[*insert name of designated contact person*] no later than _____, 2006 [*insert date that is at least five (5) days after the date of this letter*].

[*Option 2*: Please carefully review the report. If you believe that any of the information is inaccurate or incomplete, or if you have any other concerns about the information, you may contact _____ [*insert contact information*] at LexisNexis® Authentication & Screening.

Sincerely,

_____

[*Company representative*]

Enclosure: FTC Summary of Rights Form

Adverse Action Letter for Applicants

[COMPANY LETTERHEAD]

[Date]

PERSONAL & CONFIDENTIAL

[Applicant's Name]
[Applicant's Address]

Dear _____ :

We regret to inform you that we are unable to offer you a position with the Company. LexisNexis® Authentication & Screening, a consumer reporting agency, provided the Company with a pre-employment screening report in connection with your application for employment. The Company's decision not to offer you employment was based in whole or in part on information contained in this report. LexisNexis® Authentication & Screening is located lat 700 East Technology Avenue, Building E., Suite 2200, Orem, Utah 94097 and can be reached at 800 631-8777.

LexisNexis® Authentication & Screening did not make the decision to take this action and cannot provide you with information about the Company's decision. You, nevertheless, have a right to contact LexisNexis® Authentication & Screening to dispute any information in the pre-employment screening report that you believe to be inaccurate or incomplete. You should already have received copies of any relevant reports, but have a right to obtain additional free copies from LexisNexis® Authentication & Screening. You have sixty (60) days from the date you receive this notice to request additional free copies of any such reports from LexisNexis® Authentication & Screening.

Sincerely,

_____

[*Company representative*]

A Summary of Your Rights Under the Fair Credit Reporting Act

Para informacion en español, visite *www.ftc.gov/credit* o escribe a la FTC Consumer Response Center, Room 130-A, 600 Pennsylvania Ave., N.W., Washington, DC 20580.

The federal Fair Credit Reporting Act (FCRA) promotes the accuracy, fairness, and privacy of information in the files of consumer reporting agencies. There are many types of consumer reporting agencies, including credit bureaus and specialty agencies (such as agencies that sell information about check writing histories, medical records, and rental history records). Here is a summary of your major rights under the FCRA. **For more information, including information about additional rights, go to www.ftcgov/credit or write to: Consumer Response Center, Room 130-A, Federal Trade Commission, 600 Pennsylvania Ave. N.W., Washington, DC 20580.**

- ❑ **You must be told if information in your file has been used against you.** Anyone who uses a credit report or another type of consumer report to deny your application for credit, insurance, or employment – or to take another adverse action against you – must tell you, and must give you the name, address, and phone number of the agency that provided the information.

- ❑ **You have the right to know what is in your file.** You may request and obtain all the information about you in the files of a consumer reporting agency (your "file disclosure"). You will be required to provide proper identification, which may include your Social Security number. In many cases, the disclosure will be free. You are entitled to a free file disclosure if:

  - ❑ a person has taken adverse action against you because of information in your credit report;
  - ❑ you are the victim of identity theft and place a fraud alert in your file;
  - ❑ your file contains inaccurate information as a result of fraud;
  - ❑ you are on public assistance;
  - ❑ you are unemployed but expect to apply for employment within 60 days.

  In addition, by September 2005 all consumers will be entitled to one free disclosure every 12 months upon request from each nationwide credit bureau and from nationwide specialty consumer reporting agencies. See www.ftc.gov/credit for additional information.

- ❑ **You have the right to ask for a credit score.** Credit scores are numerical summaries of your credit-worthiness based on information from credit bureaus. You may request a credit score from consumer reporting agencies that create scores or distribute scores used in residential real property loans, but you will have to pay for it. In some mortgage transactions, you will receive credit score information for free from the mortgage lender.

- ❑ **You have the right to dispute incomplete or inaccurate information.** If you identify information in your file that is incomplete or inaccurate, and report it to the consumer reporting agency, the agency must investigate unless your dispute is frivolous. See www.ftc.gov/credit for an explanation of dispute procedures.

❑ **Consumer reporting agencies must correct or delete inaccurate, incomplete, or unverifiable information.** Inaccurate, incomplete or unverifiable information must be removed or corrected, usually within 30 days. However, a consumer agency may continue to report information it has verified as accurate.

❑ **Consumer reporting agencies may not report outdated negative information.** In most cases, a consumer reporting agency may not report negative information that is more than seven years old, or bankruptcies that are more than 10 years old.

❑ **Access to your file is limited.** A consumer reporting agency may provide information about you only to people with a valid need – usually to consider an application with a creditor, insurer, employer, landlord, or other business. The FCRA specifies those with a valid need for access.

❑ **You must give your consent for reports to be provided to employers.** A consumer reporting agency may not give out information about you to your employer, or a potential employer, without your written consent given to the employer. Written consent generally is not required in the trucking industry. For more information, go to www.ftc.gov/credit.

❑ **You may limit "prescreened" offers of credit and insurance you get based on information in your credit report.** Unsolicited "prescreened" offers for credit and insurance must include a toll-free phone number you can call if you choose to remove your name and address from the lists these offers are based on. You may opt-out with the nationwide credit bureaus at 1-888-567-8688.

❑ **You may seek damages from violators.** If a consumer reporting agency, or, in some cases, a user of consumer reports or a furnisher of information to a consumer reporting agency violates the FCRA, you may be able to sue in state or federal court.

❑ **Identity theft victims and active duty military personnel have additional rights.** For more information, visit www.ftc.gov/credit.

States may enforce the FCRA, and many states have their own consumer reporting laws. In some cases, you may have more rights under state law. For more information, contact your state or local consumer protection agency or your state Attorney General. Federal enforcers are:

Type of Business	Please Contact
Consumer reporting agencies, creditors and others not listed below	Federal Trade Commission: Consumer Response Center – FCRA Washington, DC 20580 1-877-382-4357
National banks, federal branches/agencies of foreign banks (word "National" or initials "N.A." appear in or after bank's name)	Office of the Controller of the Currency Compliance Management, Mail Stop 6-6 Washington, DC 20219 800-613-6743
Federal Reserve System member banks (except national banks, and federal branches/agencies of foreign banks)	Federal Reserve Board Division of Consumer & Community Affairs Washington, DC 20551 202-452-3693

Savings associations and federally chartered savings banks (word "Federal" or initials "F.S.B." appear in federal institution's name)	Office of Thrift Supervision Consumer Complaints Washington, DC 20552 800-842-6929
Federal credit unions (words "Federal Credit Union" appear in institution's name)	National Credit Union Administration 1775 Duke Street Alexandria, VA 22314 703-519-4600
State-chartered banks that are not members of the Federal Reserve System	Federal Deposit Insurance Corporation Consumer Response Center 2345 Grand Avenue, Suite 100 Kansas City, MO 64108-2638 1-877-275-3342
Air, surface, or rail common carriers regulated by former Civil Aeronautics Board or Interstate Commerce Commission	Department of Transportation, Office of Financial Management Washington, DC 20590 202-366-1306
Activities subject to the Packers and Stockyards Act, 1921	Department of Agriculture Office of Deputy Administrator- GIPSA Washington, DC 20250 202-720-7051

Notice to Users of Consumer Reports: Obligations of Users Under the FCRA

All users subject to the Federal Trade Commission's jurisdiction must comply with all applicable regulations, including regulations promulgated after this notice was prescribed in 2004. Information about applicable regulations currently in effect can be found at the Commission's Website, www.ftc.gov/credit. Persons not subject to the Commission's jurisdiction should consult with their regulators to find any relevant regulations.

The Fair Credit Reporting Act (FCRA),15 U.S.C. 1681-1681y, requires that this notice be provided to inform users of consumer reports of their legal obligations. State law may impose additional requirements. The text of the FCRA is set forth in full at the Federal Trade Commission's Website at www.ftc.gov/credit. At the end of this document is a list of United States Code citations for the FCRA. Other information about user duties is also available at the Commission's Website. **Users must consult the relevant provisions of the FCRA for details about their obligations under the FCRA.**

The first section of this summary sets forth the responsibilities imposed by the FCRA on all users of consumer reports. The subsequent sections discuss the duties of users of reports that contain specific types of information, or that are used for certain purposes, and the legal consequences of violations. If you are a furnisher of information to a consumer reporting agency (CRA), you have additional obligations and will receive a separate notice from the CRA describing your duties as a furnisher.

I. Obligations of All Users of Consumer Reports

A. Users Must Have a Permissible Purpose

Congress has limited the use of consumer reports to protect consumers' privacy. All users must have a permissible purpose under the FCRA to obtain a consumer report. Section 604 contains a list of the permissible purposes under the law. These are:

- As ordered by a court or a federal grand jury subpoena. Section 604(a)(1)
- As instructed by the consumer in writing. Section 604(a)(2)
- For the extension of credit as a result of an application from a consumer, or the review or collection of a consumer's account. Section 604(a)(3)(A)
- For employment purposes, including hiring and promotion decisions, where the consumer has given written permission. Sections 604(a)(3)(B) and 604(b)
- For the underwriting of insurance as a result of an application from a consumer. Section 604(a)(3)(C)
- When there is a legitimate business need, in connection with a business transaction that is initiated by the consumer. Section 604(a)(3)(F)(i)
- To review a consumer's account to determine whether the consumer continues to meet the terms of the account. Section 604(a)(3)(F)(ii)
- To determine a consumer's eligibility for a license or other benefit granted by a governmental instrumentality required by law to consider an applicant's financial responsibility or status. Section 604(a)(3)(D)
- For use by a potential investor or servicer, or current insurer, in a valuation or assessment of the credit or prepayment risks associated with an existing credit obligation. Section 604(a)(3)(E)
- For use by state and local officials in connection with the determination of child support payments, or modifications and enforcement thereof. Sections 604(a)(4) and 604(a)(5)

In addition, creditors and insurers may obtain certain consumer report information for the purpose of making "prescreened" unsolicited offers of credit or insurance. Section 604(c). The particular obligations of users of "prescreened" information are described in Section VII below.

B. Users Must Provide Certifications

Section 604(f) prohibits any person from obtaining a consumer report from a consumer reporting agency (CRA) unless the person has certified to the CRA the permissible purpose(s) for which the report is being obtained and certifies that the report will not be used for any other purpose.

C. Users Must Notify Consumers When Adverse Actions are Taken

The term "adverse action" is defined very broadly by Section 603. "Adverse actions" include all business, credit, and employment actions affecting consumers that can be considered to have a negative impact as defined by Section 603(k) of the FCRA – such as denying or canceling credit or insurance, or denying employment or promotion. No adverse action occurs in a credit transaction where the creditor makes a counteroffer that is accepted by the consumer.

1. Adverse Actions Based on Information Obtained From a CRA

If a user takes any type of adverse action as defined by the FCRA that is based at least in part on information contained in a consumer report, Section 615(a) requires the user to notify the consumer. The notification may be done in writing, orally, or by electronic means. It must include the following:

- The name, address, and telephone number of the CRA (including a toll-free telephone number, if it is a nationwide CRA) that provided the report.
- A statement that the CRA did not make the adverse decision and is not able to explain why the decision was made.
- A statement setting forth the consumer's right to obtain a free disclosure of the consumer's file from the CRA if the consumer makes a request within 60 days.
- A statement setting forth the consumer's right to dispute directly with the CRA the accuracy or completeness of any information provided by the CRA.

2. Adverse Actions Based on Information Obtained From Third Parties Who are Not Consumer Reporting Agencies

If a person denies (or increases the charge for) credit for personal, family, or household purposes based either wholly or partly upon information from a person other than a CRA, and the information is the type of consumer information covered by the FCRA, Section 615(b)(1) requires that the user clearly and accurately disclose to the consumer his or her right to be told the nature of the information that was relied upon if the consumer makes a written request within 60 days of notification. The user must provide the disclosure within a reasonable period of time following the consumer's written request.

3. Adverse Actions Based on Information Obtained From Affiliates

If a person takes an adverse action involving insurance, employment, or a credit transaction initiated by the consumer, based on information of the type covered by the FCRA, and this information was obtained from an entity affiliated with the user of the information by common ownership or control, Section 615(b)(2) requires the user to notify the consumer of the adverse action. The notice must inform the consumer that he or she may obtain a disclosure of the nature of the information relied upon by making a written request within 60 days of receiving the adverse action notice. If the consumer makes such a request, the user must disclose the nature of the information not later than 30 days after receiving the request. If consumer report information is shared among affiliates and then used for an adverse action, the user must make an adverse action disclosure as set forth in I.C.1 above.

D. Users Have Obligations When Fraud and Active Duty Military Alerts are in Files

When a consumer has placed a fraud alert, including one relating to identity theft, or an active duty military alert with a nationwide consumer reporting agency as defined in Section 603(p) and resellers, Section 605A(h) imposes limitations on users of reports obtained from the consumer reporting agency in certain circumstances, including the establishment of a new credit plan and the issuance of additional credit cards. For initial fraud alerts and active duty alerts, the user must have reasonable policies and procedures in place to form a belief that the user knows the identity of the applicant or contact the consumer at a telephone number specified by the consumer; in the case of extended fraud alerts, the user must contact the consumer in accordance with the contact information provided in the consumer's alert.

E. Users Have Obligations When Notified of an Address Discrepancy

Section 605(h) requires nationwide CRAs, as defined in Section 603(p), to notify users that request reports when the address for a consumer provided by the user in requesting the report is substantially different from the addresses in the consumer's file. When this occurs, users must comply with regulations specifying the procedures to be followed, which will be issued by the Federal Trade Commission and the banking and credit union regulators. The Federal Trade Commission's regulations will be available at www.ftc.gov/credit.

F. Users Have Obligations When Disposing of Records

Section 628 requires that all users of consumer report information have in place procedures to properly dispose of records containing this information. The Federal Trade Commission, the Securities and Exchange Commission, and the banking and credit union regulators have issued regulations covering disposal. The Federal Trade Commission's regulations may be found at www.ftc.gov/credit.

II. Creditors Must Make Additional Disclosures

If a person uses a consumer report in connection with an application for, or a grant, extension, or provision of, credit to a consumer on material terms that are materially less favorable than the most favorable terms available to a substantial proportion of consumers from or through that person, based in whole or in part on a consumer report, the person must provide a risk-based pricing notice to the consumer in accordance with regulations to be jointly prescribed by the Federal Trade Commission and the Federal Reserve Board.

Section 609(g) requires a disclosure by all persons that make or arrange loans secured by residential real property (one to four units) and that use credit scores. These persons must provide credit scores and other information about credit scores to applicants, including the disclosure set forth in Section 609(g)(1)(D) ("Notice to the Home Loan Applicant").

III. Obligations of Users When Consumer Reports are Obtained for Employment Purposes

A. Employment Other Than in the Trucking Industry

If information from a CRA is used for employment purposes, the user has specific duties, which are set forth in Section 604(b) of the FCRA. The user must:

- Make a clear and conspicuous written disclosure to the consumer before the report is obtained, in a document that consists solely of the disclosure, that a consumer report may be obtained.

- Obtain from the consumer prior written authorization. Authorization to access reports during the term of employment may be obtained at the time of employment.

- Certify to the CRA that the above steps have been followed, that the information being obtained will not be used in violation of any federal or state equal opportunity law or regulation, and that, if any adverse action is to be taken based on the consumer report, a copy of the report and a summary of the consumer's rights will be provided to the consumer.

- **Before** taking an adverse action, the user must provide a copy of the report to the consumer as well as the summary of consumer's rights. (The user should receive this summary from the CRA.) A Section 615(a) adverse action notice should be sent after the adverse action is taken.

An adverse action notice also is required in employment situations if credit information (other than transactions and experience data) obtained from an affiliate is used to deny employment. Section 615(b)(2)

The procedures for investigative consumer reports and employee misconduct investigations are set forth below.

B. Employment in the Trucking Industry

Special rules apply for truck drivers where the only interaction between the consumer and the potential employer is by mail, telephone, or computer. In this case, the consumer may provide consent orally or electronically, and an adverse action may be made orally, in writing, or electronically. The consumer may obtain a copy of any report relied upon by the trucking company by contacting the company.

IV. Obligations When Investigative Consumer Reports are Used

Investigative consumer reports are a special type of consumer report in which information about a consumer's character, general reputation, personal characteristics, and mode of living is obtained through personal interviews by an entity or person that is a consumer reporting agency. Consumers who are the subjects of such reports are given special rights under the FCRA. If a user intends to obtain an investigative consumer report, Section 606 requires the following:

- The user must disclose to the consumer that an investigative consumer report may be obtained. This must be done in a written disclosure that is mailed, or otherwise delivered, to the consumer at some time before or not later than three days after the date on which the report was first requested. The disclosure must include a statement informing the consumer of his or her right to request additional disclosures of the nature and scope of the investigation as described below, and the summary of consumer rights required by Section 609 of the FCRA. (The summary of consumer rights will be provided by the CRA that conducts the investigation.)

- The user must certify to the CRA that the disclosures set forth above have been made and that the user will make the disclosure described below.

- Upon the written request of a consumer made within a reasonable period of time after the disclosures required above, the user must make a complete disclosure of the nature and scope of the investigation. This must be made in a written statement that is mailed, or otherwise delivered, to the consumer no later than five days after the date on which the request was received from the consumer or the report was first requested, whichever is later in time.

V. Special Procedures for Employee Investigations

Section 603(x) provides special procedures for investigations of suspected misconduct by an employee or for compliance with federal, state, or local laws and regulations or the rules of a self-regulatory organization, and compliance with written policies of the employer. These investigations are not treated as consumer reports so long as the employer or its agent complies with the procedures set forth in Section 603(x), and a summary describing the nature and scope of the inquiry is made to the employee if an adverse action is taken based on the investigation.

VI. Obligations of Users of Medical Information

Section 604(g) limits the use of medical information obtained from consumer reporting agencies (other than payment information that appears in a coded form that does not identify the medical provider). If the information is to be used for an insurance transaction, the consumer must give consent to the user of the report or the information must be coded. If the report is to be used for employment purposes – or in connection with a credit transaction (except as provided in regulations issued by the banking and credit union regulators) – the consumer must provide specific written consent and the medical information must be relevant. Any user who receives medical information shall not disclose the information to any other person (except where necessary to carry out the purpose for which the information was disclosed, or as permitted by statute, regulation, or order).

VII. Obligations of Users of "Prescreened" Lists

The FCRA permits creditors and insurers to obtain limited consumer report information for use in connection with unsolicited offers of credit or insurance under certain circumstances. Sections 603(l), 604(c), 604(e), and 615(d). This practice is known as "prescreening" and typically involves obtaining from a CRA a list of consumers who meet certain preestablished criteria. If any person intends to use prescreened lists, that person must (1) before the offer is made, establish the criteria that will be relied upon to make the offer and to grant credit or insurance, and (2) maintain such criteria on file for a three-year period beginning on the date on which the offer is made to each consumer. In addition, any user must provide with each written solicitation a clear and conspicuous statement that:

- Information contained in a consumer's CRA file was used in connection with the transaction.

- The consumer received the offer because he or she satisfied the criteria for credit worthiness or insurability used to screen for the offer.
- Credit or insurance may not be extended if, after the consumer responds, it is determined that the consumer does not meet the criteria used for screening or any applicable criteria bearing on credit worthiness or insurability, or the consumer does not furnish required collateral.
- The consumer may prohibit the use of information in his or her file in connection with future prescreened offers of credit or insurance by contacting the notification system established by the CRA that provided the report. The statement must include the address and toll-free telephone number of the appropriate notification system.

In addition, once the Federal Trade Commission by rule has established the format, type size, and manner of the disclosure required by Section 615(d), users must be in compliance with the rule. The FTC's regulations will be at www.ftc.gov/credit.

VIII. Obligations of Resellers

A. Disclosure and Certification Requirements

Section 607(e) requires any person who obtains a consumer report for resale to take the following steps:

- Disclose the identity of the end-user to the source CRA.
- Identify to the source CRA each permissible purpose for which the report will be furnished to the end-user.
- Establish and follow reasonable procedures to ensure that reports are resold only for permissible purposes, including procedures to obtain:
  (1) The identity of all end-users;
  (2) Certifications from all users of each purpose for which reports will be used; and
  (3) Certifications that reports will not be used for any purpose other than the purpose(s) specified to the reseller. Resellers must make reasonable efforts to verify this information before selling the report.

B. Reinvestigations by Resellers

Under Section 611(f), if a consumer disputes the accuracy or completeness of information in a report prepared by a reseller, the reseller must determine whether this is a result of an action or omission on its part and, if so, correct or delete the information. If not, the reseller must send the dispute to the source CRA for reinvestigation. When any CRA notifies the reseller of the results of an investigation, the reseller must immediately convey the information to the consumer.

C. Fraud Alerts and Resellers

Section 605A(f) requires resellers who receive fraud alerts or active duty alerts from another consumer reporting agency to include these in their reports.

IX. Liability for Violations of the FCRA

Failure to comply with the FCRA can result in state government or federal government enforcement actions, as well as private lawsuits. Sections 616, 617, and 621. In addition, any person who knowingly and willfully obtains a consumer report under false pretenses may face criminal prosecution. Section 619.

The FTC's Website, www.ftc.gov/credit, has more information about the FCRA, including publications for businesses and the full text of the FCRA.

Citations for FCRA sections in the U.S. Code, 15 U.S.C. § 1681 et seq.:

Section 602 15 U.S.C. 1681
Section 603 15 U.S.C. 1681a
Section 604 15 U.S.C. 1681b
Section 605 15 U.S.C. 1681c
Section 605A 15 U.S.C. 1681cA
Section 605B 15 U.S.C. 1681cB
Section 606 15 U.S.C. 1681d
Section 607 15 U.S.C. 1681e
Section 608 15 U.S.C. 1681f
Section 609 15 U.S.C. 1681g
Section 610 15 U.S.C. 1681h
Section 611 15 U.S.C. 1681i
Section 612 15 U.S.C. 1681j
Section 613 15 U.S.C. 1681k
Section 614 15 U.S.C. 1681l
Section 615 15 U.S.C. 1681m
Section 616 15 U.S.C. 1681n
Section 617 15 U.S.C. 1681o
Section 618 15 U.S.C. 1681p
Section 619 15 U.S.C. 1681q
Section 620 15 U.S.C. 1681r
Section 621 15 U.S.C. 1681s
Section 622 15 U.S.C. 1681s-1
Section 623 15 U.S.C. 1681s-2
Section 624 15 U.S.C. 1681t
Section 625 15 U.S.C. 1681u
Section 626 15 U.S.C. 1681v
Section 627 15 U.S.C. 1681w
Section 628 15 U.S.C. 1681x
Section 629 15 U.S.C. 1681y

Appendix B
Survey Results
2005 Background Checking Survey Report Results

PreemploymentDirectory.com

Background Screening Research—March 2006

Publisher Information

About This Report

In June of 2005, PreemploymentDirectory.com conducted a survey on the current practices that businesses were using to conduct background screenings. The survey explored in depth the full realm of checking applicants' backgrounds ranging from the types of checks conducted, to the content contained in background screening policies, to key selection factors in choosing an outsourced background screening firm.

The following is a preliminary look at the results. A detailed in-depth analysis is in progress and, when completed, the results will be released.

About PreemploymentDirectory.com

Preemployment Screening Directory is the largest and most comprehensive Web-based directory of background screening firms designed to make it easy for employers to quickly find a company to meet their screening needs. The Directory consists of four sections to guide employers quickly to the company that will serve them best:

1. U.S. Domestic Section (firms are listed by their location, state by state)
2. International Section (firms that conduct background screening internationally)
3. Vendor Showcase (firms that provide services to the background screening industry)
4. Alphabetical listing

The Directory has over 800 firms listed and is continuously growing. Visit us at www. PreemploymentDirectory.com.

Introduction

In today's turbulent work environments. employers are challenged by identify theft, fraud, workplace violence, theft, sabotage, negligent hiring, terrorism, etc., to name a few of the issues. This may be the "interesting times" that Charles Dickens' famous quote "Shall you live in interesting times" was meant for. Due to concerns about the above issues, background checking has skyrocketed to record levels and is continuing to grow annually. The number of firms that provide outsourced background screening services has leaped to well over 2,000 and is growing daily.

In parallel with the unprecedented growth of the background screening industry, we have seen more concerns about privacy and security of the data obtained. ChoicePoint recently settled an issue surrounding a breach of their data for $10 million. This case, along with numerous others, will inevitability lead to new data protection laws.

Many are predicting the days of using birthdate and Social Security numbers as identifiers are numbered and will give way to biometric solutions, some of which border on science fiction. Consequently, the landscape of background screening will continue to evolve and employers will need to keep up. A very promising trend that has emerged in background screening is that we are increasingly seeing stand-alone screening feeds being integrated into firms' human resource information systems.

A pressing issue that is confronting background screeners is the proliferation of the fake diploma and degree mills. Simply verifying educational background is no longer sufficient. Screeners must now verify that the source of the education is legitimate and, for foreign degrees, their equivalency.

There are also clear signs that background screening is increasingly going global as the economies in India, China, Europe, etc. continue to prosper and recruiters span national borders to find people. The international marketplace is likely to be the brave new world that background screening must master.

Methodology

The survey questions were developed by an advisory committee specifically formed for the purpose of creating the survey. The advisory committee was composed of a variety of human resource (HR), employment, background screening, security and assessment professionals (ATAP), as well as members of several online HR communities. An invitation to participate in the survey was also posted on the home page of The National Institute for the Prevention of Workplace Violence, Website www.Workplaceviolence911. com. Seven thousand emails were delivered and each recipient was sent an email invitation containing a link that directed the participant to the online survey. Three email reminders were sent out to sample members in an effort to increase the response rate.

Key Findings

It was interesting to see that while 80% of employers conduct background checks on applicants, only 58% conducted them on current employees. At one level, this is understandable because it is easier to implement a program focused on job candidates versus having to tangle with the complexity of screening employees. From our experience we believe the trend is toward doing more internal screening; however, we will have to see results from future surveys.

It was also interesting to note that less than 50% of responding firms conduct background checks on applicants from other countries. Given the increasing focus on globalization juxtaposed onto concerns about terrorism and the viewpoint that many of these individuals are from countries outside of the United States, it would appear that our background screening processes are out of sync with this perspective. Or perhaps this reflects the challenges and complexity of conducting international background investigations or vetting with the myriad of legal, privacy, political, cultural, and language issues. Either way, this may be an issue that senior management will want to take a closer look at to ensure that their background screening practices are consistent with their risk management profile.

The most prevalent types of background checks were criminal records, previous work history, and references, and 85% of companies conduct background screenings for all open positions.

Preliminary Survey Results

1) Does your company conduct background checks in the United States on applicants?
   Response Ratio
   Yes = 79.45%
   No = 20.55%

2) Does your company conduct background checks in the United States on employees?
   Response Ratio
   Yes = 58.33%
   No = 41.67%

3) Does your company conduct background checks on applicants from other countries outside of the United States?
   Response Ratio
   Yes = 47.14%
   No = 52.86%

4) Does your company conduct background checks on employees that work in other countries outside of the United States?
   Response Ratio
   Yes = 30.43%
   No = 69.57%

5) What kind of background checks does your company conduct?
Response Ratio
Yes = 30.43%
No = 69.57%

Criminal background check	88.57%
Previous work history	84.29%
Reference check	75.71%
Social Security number verification	64.29%
Motor vehicle records	60%
Education verification	60%

Appendix C
Background Screening Certification Program

Core Curriculum

1. Background Screening and the Fair Credit Reporting Act
2. Legal Aspects of Background Screening II—Includes EEOC guidelines for hiring previous incarcerated persons, use of credit records, Expungement, Patriots Act, Immigration issues, and other federal legislation, etc.
3. Implementing an Effective Background Screening Program, including
   - Overview of National/Multijurisdictional Databases
   - Essential Ingredients for Creating an Effective Background Screening Policy
   - Infinity Screening (ongoing screening of employees)

Electives (choose 3)

1. Lie Detector Tests in the Workplace
2. Drug Testing
3. Workplace Violence Prevention
4. Reference Checking
5. Legal Aspects of Background Screening III—Specialty Industries
   - Healthcare
   - Transportation
   - Financial
   - Nuclear Energy Facilities, etc.
6. An Overview of International Background Screening
7. Characteristics of a Wow! Customer Service Organization

   How an organization creates customer service as a core competency that creates competitive advantage

8. Benefits of Wow! Customer Service
   - How organizations and individuals benefit from adapting Wow! Customer Service
   - Customer service as a stealth sales advantage
   - Heavy focus on WIFM (What's in for me) to stimulate the willingness for significant learning
9. Building Your Wow! Customer Service Toolkit and Transforming Yourself into a Wow! Customer Service Pro
   - The core competencies of delivering exceptional Wow! customer service
   - Creating a personal action plan to master the competencies to become a Pro

Appendix D
Sensitive Jobs Identification Worksheet

The _____ Corporation requires that a criminal background check should be conducted whenever an individual is hired, transferred, promoted, reclassified, or reassigned duties for any position designated and/or is assigned new duties that are deemed as sensitive. A sensitive position is one where any of the criteria listed below is a significant part of the job duties.

Please check all boxes that apply, sign and date the form, and retain it with relevant Human Resource files.

Date:
Employee Name:
Badge #:

Position Title Code/Title:
Action: ❑ hire ❑ transfer ❑ promotion ❑ reclassification ❑ reassigned duties

❑ Senior management (designated levels).

❑ Care, safety, and security of people or property (includes safety, occupational health, security, human resources, child care workers, camp counselors, teachers, etc.).

❑ Direct access to, or control over, cash, checks, credit card account information (includes cash handling or credit card acceptance positions).

❑ Authority to commit financial resources of the organization greater than $_____.

❑ Control over organization-wide or departmental business processes, either through functional roles or systems security access (includes network administrators, system programmers, HRMS, and payroll functional leads).

❑ Access to detailed personally identifiable information about employees, customers, or the public that might enable identity theft.

❑ Possession of building master or sub-master key access to facilities (includes custodial services, security, etc).

❑ Regular operation of company vehicles as part of assigned job duties (includes delivery staff, commercial drivers, sales, field technicians, meter readers, etc).

From the *2005 Employers Practices in Background Screening Survey.*
Copyright held exclusively by the National Institute for the Prevention of Workplace Violence, Inc.

Appendix E
Terrorist Search

Preemploymentdirectory.com

International Resource Center

Terrorist Searches

- **Specially Designated Nationals (SDN) and Blocked Persons**

  16 June 2004, revised 2 May 2005. The U.S. Treasury Department, Office of Foreign Assets Control (OFAC) publishes this list of individuals and companies controlled by targeted countries. The list includes "individuals, groups, and entities, such as terrorists and narcotics traffickers designated under programs that are not country-specific. Collectively, such individuals and companies are called "Specially Designated Nationals" or "SDNs." Their assets are blocked and U.S. persons are generally prohibited from dealing with them."

- The **Excluded Parties List System** provides integrated search access to several debarment lists. (et)

- **List of Parties Debarred for Arms Export Control Act Convictions**

  21 June 2004. The Directorate of Defense Trade Controls of the U.S. Department of State provides two lists—one statutory and one administrative—of companies and individuals convicted of violations involving the Arms Export Control Act (AECA) or the International Traffic in Arms Regulations (ITAR). Both lists are alphabetical and include a Federal Register citation, although not a link to the relevant issue. (et)

- **Entity List**

  16 June 2004, revised 2 May 2005. The U.S. Bureau of Industry and Security (BIS) maintains this list of foreign individuals and companies, which "have been determined to present an unacceptable risk of diversion to developing weapons of mass destruction or the missiles used to deliver those weapons." Changes to the list appear officially in the Federal Register.

Source: PreemploymentDirectory.com's International Resource Center, http://www.workplaceviolence911.com/docs/internationaresourcecenter.htm

- Foreign Terrorist Organizations
- Terrorist Exclusion
- Consolidated list of persons, groups and entities subject to EU financial sanctions
- US Department of State Resources:
- Office of Foreign Asset Control (OFAC) of the U.S. Department of the Treasury

Appendix F
GE Candidate Data Protection Standards

I. Objective

The aim of these Candidate Data Protection Standards ("Standards") is to provide adequate and consistent safeguards for the handling of candidate data by GE entities.

The identifiable information about yourself that you provide to a GE entity as a job seeker for a position with a GE entity (the "Candidate Data" or "Data") will be used for recruitment purposes, and the Candidate Data will be protected in accordance with GE's Standards outlined below and all applicable laws.

By submitting your Candidate Data, you confirm and agree that:

- You have reviewed GE's Standards;
- GE may process the Candidate Data according to the recruitment purposes set out in the Standards; and
- The Candidate Data may be transferred worldwide consistent with GE's Standards.

Your consent is required in order to complete the submittal process. If you do not agree, click on the "x" button in the upper right-hand corner and the submittal process will discontinue.

These Standards, unless noted otherwise, do not form part of any contract of employment, where applicable, offered to successful hires.

II. Scope

These Standards apply to all GE entities that process Candidate Data.

Processing refers to any action that is performed on Candidate Data, whether in whole or in part by automated means, such as collecting, recording, organizing, storing, modifying, using, disclosing, or deleting such data.

Candidate Data are defined as any identifiable information about you that you or someone else provides (on your or GE's behalf) in the context of applying for a position with a GE entity.

These Standards do not cover data rendered anonymous or where pseudonyms are used. Data are rendered anonymous if individual persons are no longer identifiable or are identifiable only with a disproportionately large expense in time, cost, or labor. The use of pseudonyms involves the replacement of names or other identifiers with substitutes, so that identification of individual persons is either impossible or at least rendered considerably more difficult. If Data rendered anonymous become no longer anonymous (i.e., individual persons are again identifiable), or if pseudonyms are used and the pseudonyms allow identification of individual persons, then these Standards will again apply.

III. Application of Local Laws

These Standards are designed to provide a uniform minimum compliant standard for every GE entity with respect to its protection of Candidate Data worldwide. GE recognizes that certain laws may require stricter standards than those described in these Standards. GE entities will handle Candidate Data in accordance with local law applicable at the place where the Candidate Data are processed. Where applicable local law provides a lower level of protection of Candidate Data than that established by these Standards, then the requirements of the Standards shall apply.

IV. Principles for Processing Candidate Data

GE respects the privacy rights and interests of each individual. GE entities will observe the following principles when processing Candidate Data:

Data will be processed fairly and lawfully.

Data will be collected for specified, legitimate purposes and not processed further in ways incompatible with those purposes.

Data will be relevant to and not excessive for the purposes for which they are collected and used. For example, Data may be rendered anonymous when feasible and appropriate, depending on the nature of the Data and the risks associated with the intended uses.

Data will be accurate and, where necessary, kept up-to-date. Reasonable steps will be taken to rectify or delete Candidate Data that is inaccurate or incomplete.

Data will be kept only as long as it is necessary for the purposes for which it was collected and processed.

Data will be processed in accordance with the individual's legal rights (as described in these Standards or as provided by law).

Appropriate technical, physical, and organizational measures will be taken to prevent unauthorized access, unlawful processing, and unauthorized or accidental loss, destruction, or damage to Data.

V. Data Collection

You may use various methods to submit your Candidate Data to GE. These methods may include: (a) e-mail or paper submission to GE personnel; (b) online submittal of Candidate Data processed by a third-party service provider into an electronic database based in the U.S. accessible by GE authorized personnel; or (c) via a GE employment application.

GE may periodically collect further information with your consent or in accordance with applicable laws. For example, GE may collect your feedback and opinions (e.g., surveys) for business purposes, such as improving processes. You may respond to these surveys voluntarily or may elect not to respond and will not suffer reprisals for your decision. These Standards will be applicable to any further information collected including any responses to such surveys.

VI. Purposes and Access for Candidate Data Processing

GE and GE entities process Candidate Data for legitimate human resources purposes. Such processing will be conducted within such purpose limitations and in accordance with applicable law.

Human resources purposes include: identifying and/or evaluating candidates for GE positions; making a decision about whether the individual should be hired; maintaining appropriate record-keeping related to hiring practices; analyzing the hiring process and outcomes; and conducting background investigations, where permitted by law (the "Purposes").

If a GE entity processes your Candidate Data for purposes that go beyond the Purposes described above, the GE entity responsible for the new purpose will ensure that you are informed of the new purposes for which your Candidate Data are to be used, and the categories of recipients of your Candidate Data.

Your Data will be accessed and processed by individuals who are involved in the hiring process for GE and who have a legitimate need to access and process your Data for the Purposes.

VII. Types of Candidate Data

Candidate Data that is processed includes:

- Candidate status
- Work history/job data
- Education
- Compensation
- Employer feedback
- Online questionnaire results
- Candidate contact information
- Previous addresses or names of the Candidate
- Additional information provided by the Candidate (e.g., a cover letter)
- Driver's license number, as needed for certain positions
- References
- Criminal history, where permitted by law

VIII. Special Categories of Data

To the limited extent a GE entity needs to collect any Special Data (such as data containing personal information about racial or ethnic origin, political opinions, religious or political beliefs, trade-union membership, health or medical records, or criminal records), the GE entity will ensure that the individual is informed of such collection and processing. Where required by law, the person's explicit consent to the processing and particularly to the transfer of such data to non-GE entities will be obtained. Appropriate security and protection measures (e.g., physical security devices, encryption, and access restrictions) will be provided depending on the nature of these categories of data and the risks associated with the intended uses.

IX. Security and Confidentiality

GE entities are committed to taking appropriate technical, physical, and organizational measures to protect Candidate Data against unauthorized access, unlawful processing, accidental loss or damage, and unauthorized destruction.

Equipment and Information Security

To safeguard against unauthorized access to Candidate Data by third parties outside GE, all electronic Candidate Data held by GE entities are maintained on systems that are protected by secure network architectures that contain firewalls and intrusion detection devices. The servers holding Candidate Data are "backed up" (i.e., the data are recorded on separate media) on a regular basis to avoid the consequences of any inadvertent erasure or destruction of data. The servers are stored in facilities with comprehensive security and fire detection and response systems.

Access Security

GE entities limit access to internal systems that hold Candidate Data to a select group of authorized users who are given access to such systems through the use of a unique identifier and password. Access to Candidate Data is limited to and provided to individuals for the purpose of performing their job duties (e.g., a human resources manager may need access to a Candidate's contact information for the purposes of setting up an interview). Compliance with these provisions will be required of third-party administrators who may access certain Candidate Data, as described in SECTION XI. TRANSFERRING DATA.

Training

GE will conduct training regarding the lawful and intended purposes of processing Candidate Data, the need to protect and keep information accurate and up-to-date, and the need to maintain the confidentiality of the Data to which employees have access. Authorized users will comply with these Standards, and GE entities will take appropriate disciplinary actions, in accordance with applicable law, if Candidate Data are accessed, processed, or used in any way that is inconsistent with the requirements of these Standards.

X. Rights of Data Subjects

Any person may inquire as to the nature of the Candidate Data stored or processed about him or her by any GE entity. You will be provided access to Candidate Data as is required by law in your home country, regardless of the location of the data processing and storage. A GE entity processing such data will cooperate in providing such access either directly or through another GE entity. All such requests for access may be made by sending a request in writing to:

Human Resources Data Protection Administrator
3135 Easton Turnpike
Mail Drop W2G
Fairfield, CT 06828

Candidate Data will be available for access for a reasonable period of time, and GE will allow you to view your Candidate Data upon reasonable notice and at reasonable times.

You may also contact the Human Resources Data Protection Administrator to ask questions regarding these Standards or your Candidate Data or withdraw your consent. Any letters sent to the Administrator for any other purpose other than the above will not be responded to and will be discarded.

If access or rectification is denied, the reason for the denial will be communicated and a written record will be made of the request and reason for denial.

If you demonstrate that the purpose for which the data is being processed is no longer legal or appropriate, the data will be deleted, unless the law requires otherwise.

If any Candidate Data is inaccurate or incomplete, you may request that the data be amended by submitting a new resume/CV with the updated information (e.g., new home address or change of name).

In addition, you may send an email to CHR.webmaster@corporate.ge.com to withdraw your consent.

XI. Transferring Data

Transfers to Other GE Entities

GE strives to ensure a consistent and adequate level of protection for Candidate Data that are processed and/or transferred between GE entities. A transfer of Candidate Data to another GE entity is considered a transfer between two different entities, which means that even in such "intra-group" cases, a data transfer shall be carried out only if applicable legal requirements are met and if:

- The transfer is based on a clear business need;
- The receiving entity provides appropriate security for the data; and
- The receiving entity ensures compliance with these Standards for the transfer and any subsequent processing.

Transfers to Non-GE Entities

- **Selected Third Parties:** At times, GE entities may be required to transfer Candidate Data to selected external third parties that they have hired to perform certain employment-related services on their behalf. These third parties may process the data in accordance with the GE entity's instructions or make decisions regarding the data as part of the delivery of their services. In either instance, GE entities will select reliable suppliers who undertake, by contract or other legally binding and permissible means, to put in place appropriate security measures to ensure an adequate level of protection. GE entities will require external third-party suppliers to comply with these Standards or to guarantee the same levels of protection as GE when handling Candidate Data. Such selected third parties will have access to Candidate Data solely for the purposes of performing the services specified in the applicable service contract. If a GE entity concludes that a supplier is not complying with these obligations, it will promptly take appropriate actions.

- **Other Third Parties:** GE entities may be required to disclose certain Candidate Data to other third parties (1) as a matter of law (e.g., to tax and Social Security authorities); (2) to protect GE's legal rights (e.g., to defend a litigation suit); or (3) in an emergency where the health or security of a Candidate is endangered (e.g., a fire).

XII. Direct Marketing

GE entities will not disclose Candidate Data outside GE to offer any products or services to a Candidate for personal or familial consumption ("direct marketing") without his or her prior consent.

The restrictions in this section apply only to contact data obtained in the context of applying for a position with GE. They do not apply to contact data obtained in the context of a consumer or customer relationship.

XIII. Automated Decisions

Some countries regulate the making of Automated Decisions, which are decisions about individuals that are based solely on the automated processing of data and that produce legal effects that significantly affect the individuals involved.

In some circumstances, job seekers will be asked to complete a questionnaire where automated decisions will be made based on the Candidate's responses.

Except in limited circumstances (e.g., the screening via computer or telephone for some open positions in GE), GE entities do not make Automated Decisions to evaluate individuals or for other purposes. If Automated Decisions are made, affected persons will be given an opportunity to express their views on the Automated Decision in question by contacting the Human Resources Data Protection Administrator.

XIV. Enforcement Rights and Mechanisms

All GE entities will ensure that these Standards are observed. All persons who have access to Candidate Data must comply with these Standards. In some countries, violations of data protection regulations may lead to penalties and/or claims for damages.

If at any time, a person believes that Candidate Data relating to him or her has been processed in violation of these Standards, he or she may report the concern to the Human Resources Data Protection Administrator.

If the concern relates to an alleged violation of these Standards by a GE entity located in a country other than that of the person or the exporting GE entity, he or she may request the assistance of the exporting entity. That GE entity will assist him or her in investigating the circumstances of the alleged violation. If the violation is confirmed, the exporting and importing entities will work together with any other relevant parties to resolve the matter in a satisfactory manner, consistent with the provisions of these Standards.

If the Human Resources Data Protection Administrator or the local GE entity does not resolve the concern, it may be escalated to GE's Employment Data Privacy Committee. The Employment Data Privacy Committee, chaired by GE's Chief Privacy Leader, is composed of senior compliance specialists who are independent of the business lines of management and who have oversight responsibility for all aspects of compliance with these Standards and for the resolution of all concerns and issues that arise with respect to GE's handling of Candidate Data under these Standards. The Employment Data Privacy Committee may be contacted by email at EmpDataPvcy@corporate.ge.com or by fax at +1-203-373-2181. The Employment Data Privacy Committee will communicate its decision and any associated remedy to the relevant persons.

The processes described in these Standards supplement any other remedies and dispute resolution processes provided by GE and/or available under applicable law.

XV. Audit Procedures

To further ensure enforcement of these Standards, GE's Chief Privacy Leader, along with GE's Global Privacy Council, which is composed of senior privacy officials from each of GE's major businesses, will identify Candidate and employment Data procedures that should be audited. For this purpose, GE will engage its Corporate Audit Staff, who are independent of the business lines of management. Members of the Audit Staff report to GE's Vice President, Corporate Audit Staff, who has an independent line of communication to the Audit Committee of GE's Board of Directors. Reports of the Audit Staff's findings will be submitted to GE's Policy Compliance Review Board and/or GE's Global Privacy Council for review and response. The Board or Council will require an action plan to ensure compliance with these Standards. To the extent such matters cannot be adequately handled with GE's own resources, GE agrees to appoint an independent third party to conduct an investigation/audit of any procedures or issues involving Candidate or employment Data under the Standards.

XVI. Communication About the Standards

In addition to the training on these Standards, GE will communicate these Standards to current and new employees by posting them on selected internal GE websites and by providing a link to the Standards on information technology applications where Candidate Data are collected or processed.

XVII. Modifications to the Standards

GE reserves the right to modify these Standards as needed, for example, to comply with changes in laws, regulations, GE practices and procedures, or requirements imposed by data protection authorities. GE's Chief Privacy Leader, or his/her designee, must approve all changes to the Standards for them to become effective. If GE makes changes to the

Standards, GE will submit the Standards for renewed approval where required by law. GE will inform GE employees and other persons (e.g., persons accessing GE websites to enter Candidate Data such as job application information) of any material changes in the Standards. GE will post all changes to the Standards on relevant internal and external websites.

Effective with the implementation of these Standards, all existing intra-group agreements and applicable company privacy guidelines relating to the processing of Candidate Data will be superseded by the terms of these Standards. All parties to any such agreements will be notified of the effective date of implementation of the Standards.

XVIII. Obligations Toward Data Protection Authorities

GE will respond diligently and appropriately to requests from data protection authorities about these Standards or compliance with applicable data protection and privacy laws and regulations. GE employees who receive such requests should contact their local Human Resources Manager or business legal counsel. GE will, upon request, provide data protection authorities with names and contact details of relevant contact persons. With regard to transfers of Candidate Data between GE entities, the importing and exporting GE entities will (i) cooperate with inquiries from the data protection authority responsible for the entity exporting the data, and (ii) respect its decisions, consistent with applicable law and due process rights.

Addendum

Rights and Obligations With Respect to Candidate Data Collected Within the EU/EEA and Processed Elsewhere

In addition to any rights and obligations that are set forth in GE's Candidate Data Protection Standards ("Standards") or that otherwise exist, the following principles established in light of Directive 95/46/EC ("European Data Protection Directive") will apply to Candidate Data collected by GE entities in the European Union/European Economic Area and processed elsewhere. In jurisdictions where this Addendum applies, the enforcement rights and mechanisms mentioned in the Standards also apply to the provisions of this Addendum. The following are not intended to grant employees further rights or establish further obligations beyond those already provided under the European Data Protection Directive:

> Job seekers may object to the processing of Candidate Data about them on compelling legitimate grounds relating to their particular situation. This might occur, for instance, if the job seeker's life or health is at risk due to the processing of the data. This provision shall not apply if the processing is (i) required by law, (ii) based on the job seeker's individual consent, or (iii) necessary to fulfill a contractual obligation between the job seeker and GE.

> After exhausting appropriate internal dispute resolution processes, job seekers may seek compensatory damages from a GE entity for loss or damage to them caused by a violation of the Standards (including the provisions of this

Addendum) by the GE entity. The GE entity shall not be liable for damages if it has observed the standard of care appropriate in the circumstances.

If any of the terms or definitions used in the Standards are ambiguous, the definitions established under applicable local law within the relevant EU/EEA member state shall apply or where there are no such definitions under applicable local law, the definitions of the European Data Protection Directive shall apply.

http://www.gecareers.com/GECAREERS/html/us/searchJobs/candidate_privacy.html

Appendix G
Betrayal

Table G-1 Key Findings and Implications Relevant to Prevention

Risk Factors Contributing to Heightened System Vulnerability	Implications Related to Prevention of Attacks
Diverse location of subjects within the IT organization	Need for broadly based prevention and detection programs
Presence of very serious subject: employment problems	Need for improved and more aggressive management of at-risk employees undergoing personnel problems with greater emphasis on security risks
Organizational stress as risk indicator	Advisability of increasing alert and monitoring levels during periods of stressful organizational change, improving and increasing stress interventions for employees
Intimidation of manager by offending IT professionals through their control of the system and influence in the firm	Improved management training, enforcement of basic security precautions against overdependence on subjects (two-man rule, etc.)
Problems with probation and termination processes	Need for revised probation and termination procedures to decrease vulnerability to attacks, reduce likelihood of attacks during these periods and to monitor attack risk more effectively

Table G-2 Key Findings and Implications Related to Detection

Indicators of Impending Attack on the System	Implication Related to Detection or Intervention During Periods of Elevated Risk
Use of OPSEC by the subject	Need for regular outside audits and increased use of personnel versus electronic indicators of risk, increased sensitivity to the expression of interpersonal disgruntlement in online formats
Occurrence of personnel problems prior to electronic attacks	Need for improved detection and management of personnel problems, improved communications between personnel and computer security staff, improved policies and procedures, awareness training, integrating management with personnel problems and computer security, advisability of integrating detection of disgruntlement into computer monitoring systems
High frequency of post-termination attacks	Need for improvement in management and security of the termination process and post-termination monitoring of at-risk employees
Personal stress as risk indicator	Advisability of increasing alert and monitoring levels during periods of personal stress in at-risk subjects, more aggressive personnel interventions
Social and cultural conflicts as risk indicators	Advisability of increasing alert and monitoring levels during social and cultural conflicts, intervening aggressively to reduce employee stress
Window of opportunity to intervene prior to attacks	Improved manager, personnel, and security training regarding the risk of personnel problems, need for aggressive detection and intervention and effective interventions to reduce risk
Subjects' use of remote access for post-termination attacks	Need to revise remote access policies and practices, especially after detection of subject risk and during probation and termination periods

Table G-3 Key Findings and Implications Related to Personnel Management

Key Findings: Risk Factors Related to Personnel Management and Policy That Predict to Greater Vulnerability	Implications Related to Personnel Management and Policy
Gaps in personnel and security policies and practices	Need for increased education and proliferation of personnel and security policies and practices, audits of policies and practices
High rates of personnel and security policy implementation and enforcement failures	Need for increased education and proliferation of personnel and security policy implementation and enforcement methods, management training in enforcement practices, case management training, more reliable consequences for violations
Lack of technical and human resources staff and education for policy enforcement	Improved education and awareness training regarding policy enforcement, improved enforcement auditing, increased corporate self-regulation of policy enforcement to avoid liability, government regulation and legislation
Offender ability to avoid detection of policy and practice violations	Improved education and training of personnel and security personnel responsible for policy implementation and enforcement, and improved technical and human resources staff to assist these personnel
Failure of basic screening procedures	Need to increase screening requirements
Failure of traditional screening methods to detect at-risk online activities	Need to broaden and improve screening to improve detection of hacking and other at-risk, online activities and affiliations, use of security audits early in employment in absence of reliable screening methods
Tracking failures	Need to improve availability of information regarding past prosecuted and nonprosecuted violations for preemployment screening

Appendix H
Continuous Screening
Get Support in Implementing a Continuous Post Hire Screening Program

Executive Summary

Today, many employers are recognizing the benefits of driver monitoring and are looking for vendors that can offer such service by state, as well as on a national basis.

Background

Over the last several years, there has been a movement by many state regulatory agencies to put in place Employer Notification Services (ENS) programs that notify employers of changes to a driver's record in a timely manner. Today, ten states currently offer some form of an ENS program (Arkansas, California, Illinois, Michigan, Nebraska, New York, North Carolina, Oregon, Virginia, and Wisconsin).

In many cases, the state agency actions have been taken to support compliance with regulations such as the Federal Motor Carrier Safety Administration (FMCSA) requirements regarding commercial drivers and driving violation reporting. These state actions have also resulted in voluntary programs for employers who choose to promote driver and highway safety.

Specifically, these programs often accomplish two goals:

1. Ensure that an employer is notified when a conviction or other change occurs on an employee's driver's license.
2. Reduce the time between when a conviction or other status change occurs on a driver's record and when the employer is notified so that the employer can take the appropriate action to reduce risk of an accident or other type of loss.

In general most of the programs are similar. However, there are differences among them including whether the program is paper based or electronic, whether it is mandatory or voluntary, whether a full record is returned or only a notification, and in the determination of the enrollment process and costs.

Where to Turn

A company such as First Advantage offers a unique mix of core competencies including a long history of leadership and strong relationships with state departments of motor vehicles to obtain driving record reports on-line, to provide paperless driver monitoring to their customers, and to help mediate the relationship between the state and the employer. First Advantage is also a well-known leader in the employer screening services industry.

First Advantage currently provides risk mitigation, screening, and driving record services to over 2,000 employers. Additionally, First Advantage services over 3,700 DOT-regulated private transportation companies that are required to pre-screen their potential employee drivers as well as annually review the driving record reports on their current employee drivers.

Since First Advantage is uniquely positioned to enable its clients with the ability to request driving records from every state (in most states instantly), it can offer a national monitoring solution by scheduling driving record reports from all states on a monthly, semi-annual or annual basis. Smaller providers are limited in their ability to provide competitively priced driving records to employers, thus restricting their ability to provide a complete and cost effective monitoring solution. Additionally, First Advantage can simplify and enhance this monitoring system through a user-friendly web interface that includes such features as exception, expiration and high risk reporting, standard violation codes on driving records, scored driving records, and more.

Value

Many categories of employers are required by law to screen prospective employees that may drive a vehicle for work. Many employers are also required to annually review those driving records on a post-hire basis. The employers also may require the driver employee to self-report violations and convictions. This usually results in a process that involves manual calendaring and paper-shuffling—an arduous management process for both large and small employers alike.

Even companies that are not legally required to monitor their employees have realized that regularly reviewing their employee's driving records on a more frequent basis increases driver safety, reduces the company's exposure to lawsuits, results in an overall reduction of risk, and decreases both hard and soft costs.

Driver monitoring programs have value to multiple user groups including:

1. Employers that must monitor employee drivers under such programs as California's Employer Pull Notice Program (CA-EPN). (First Advantage offers a full service management of such programs).
2. Employers of CDL drivers that need to be alerted to and verify changes of the driving record that may restrict or otherwise delay on-time delivery of loads.

3. Employers of non-CDL drivers with motor vehicles to be used as a part of their job function that need to be alerted to activity that might disqualify the employee from using a company vehicle or from driving as part of their regular job function.

Driving monitoring programs provide advantages that:

- Ease the workload of managing releases and driver compliance, and in obtaining driver histories.
- Support the company decision process in identifying, and disposition high-risk drivers.
- Provide the company with the information and tools necessary to reduce the risk of Negligent Entrustment while meeting state and federal requirements.

Service Description

First Advantage's driver monitoring service enables companies to monitor the driving records of individuals in all 50 states. This product allows employers with the proper authorization to track the driving records of employees by:

- Scheduling the periodic (monthly, quarterly, annual) ordering of a current driving record on a roster of employees.
- Receiving notification of changes to the employees driving record (violations, suspensions, revocations) as they occur on a roster of employees (i.e. California Employer Pull Notification [CA-EPN] Program).

Along with the core functionality, First Advantage's product also provides clients with the ability to:

- Outsource the release/waiver management responsibility associated with ordering driving records to First Advantage
- Upload batch driver information into the system
- Schedule driving records
- Order ad-hoc driving records
- Participate in a paperless CA-EPN program
- Assess fleet status through a user-friendly "Dashboard"
- Manage/modify driver rosters
- Manage account/role settings
- Receive standard violation codes for ease of interpreting the various state supplied data
- Receive scored driving records for simplification of evaluation
- Set driving record score cut-offs that generate special reporting and notifications
- Receive notifications through preferred means: electronic, fax, and mail based
- Accommodate electronic/digital signatures
- Access multiple products, i.e., Electronic Vehicle Registration
- Manage accounts easily

Scoring Driving Record Reports Support Monitoring Programs for Additional Value

First Advantage has applied its knowledge and understanding of driving records to develop nationwide scoring—based on standard industry points, rules, and indicators that can help better assess a driving record.

With First Advantage scoring, a company can tell at a glance whether more time might be necessary to evaluate a current or prospective employee driver. As companies review many driving records, any visual cue will save time to allow the better management of exceptions.

First Advantage developed a standard set of points, rules and scores that will fit the needs of most businesses, but it can also customize this valuable service to address specific business situations.

Summary

Whether or not they may be compulsory for a company, driving monitoring programs are increasingly understood as a critical component to managing risk. With the important ramifications of driving monitoring programs only continuing to expand, companies need to fully understand the capabilities of providers and be confident that the chosen provider can continue to deliver in this quickly evolving area of post-hire screening.

Questions, please contact:

Christine Hughes
Director of Marketing
First Advantage
Transportation Services Division
E-mail: chughes@fadv.com
Tel: 918-712-9660

Appendix I
How to Create a Culture of Security Consciousness

By Wanda Hackett, Ph.D.

The Importance of Security Consciousness

What's at risk?

- Statistical data
- Examples of employee behaviors that put companies at risk

Scenario

The following describes the transformation of an organization fraught with potential security nightmares into one that is well on its way to becoming more security conscious and much safer.

□ □ □ ▬▬▬▬▬▬▬▬▬▬▬▬▬▬▬▬▬▬▬▬▬

Company A
Security Unconscious—An Organization at Risk

- Inaccurate background data;
- Cursory research to identify sound background check data services;
- Use of a less comprehensive/inexpensive Web-based data base service;
- Database fraught with data entry errors;
- Employees unaware of the relationship between their safety and the importance of an effective background check process; and
- Limited or no employee training in how to implement security policies and procedures effectively.

▬▬▬▬▬▬▬▬▬▬▬▬▬▬▬▬▬▬▬ □ □ □

□ □ □ ▬▬▬▬▬▬▬▬▬▬▬▬▬▬▬▬▬▬▬▬▬▬▬▬▬▬

Company A
Security Conscious—A Transformed Organization

- Focus on achieving the highest possible accurate background data;
- Comprehensive research conducted to identify the most accurate database services available;
- Aware of the strengths, limitations, and costs of database services;
- Security policies developed and implemented with an understanding of how people think and what motivates behavioral change;
- Employees receive effective security consciousness training; and
- Employees make the connection between their personal safety and the organization's security policy

▬▬▬▬▬▬▬▬▬▬▬▬▬▬▬▬▬▬▬▬▬▬▬▬▬ □ □ □

Company A, a midsize information technology company with 500 employees, has been in business for five years. While the company's customer base and market share are growing, infrastructure costs, which include security processes, are carefully controlled. Last year the company had a number of employee security breeches spotlighting the ineffectiveness of its background check process. Unknowingly, they had employed several individuals with histories of endangering the safety of employees, clients, and/or customers; or who posed a security risk with regard to how they had handled proprietary information in the past; or who had histories of misappropriating company resources. Company A hired a security consulting firm to conduct a careful audit of their background check process. After a careful investigation, the consulting firm reported the following findings.

First, the background data Company A received was not always accurate. Once hiring managers realized there were discrepancies in the data they were receiving, they began to disregard the background reports and to make hiring decisions based on their first impressions of applicants.

Secondly, Company A's budget allocation for background check services was inadequate to ensure accurate, nation-wide data. So, while the company was receiving data, it was not the most comprehensive data available, a fact which undermined, in some cases, the effectiveness if the entire process.

Third, while Company A conducted employee background screening training, the training only emphasized the importance of employees following the policy. The training omitted two equally important elements—how to gain employee understanding of the policy at a personal level; and how to get employees to buy in to the policy, and commit to implement the policy consistently. In other words, Company A's training "*told* managers what the rules were." It did not prepare them to develop a plan to engage employees involved in the hiring process to successfully implement the new background screening process.

The security consulting company conducted its security audit and reported a number of findings to Company A management—the bottom line, Company A's background screening practices, including inconsistent implementation of company policy, use of inaccurate data, ineffective training practices, etc., put the company at risk!

Following the security audit, Company A implemented three major actions. First, they engaged in a comprehensive study of background screening companies, to understand what was available in the marketplace, including companies' strengths, limitations, and costs. Second, keeping in mind their specific needs, they selected the most affordable background screening service. Third, the company began comprehensive background screening training to assist employees involved in making hiring decisions to understand what the safety and risk factors were, as well as the relationship between an effectively implemented company background screening policy and *their personal* safety and the company's safety.

Within six months, Company A had significantly reduced the risk of error in its employee background screening process and was achieving the following outcomes:

- Receiving current and correct background screening information to inform both hiring and ongoing employment decisions;
- Consistent implementation, throughout the company, of the background screening policy; and
- Widespread employee understanding of the importance of following security policies and, in this case, employee background screening in order to create a security conscious organization culture.

What Do We Mean by Organization Culture?

One definition of organization culture simply stated is *"the way we do things around here."* The above scenario gives us a snapshot of aspects of Company A's organization culture:

First four years:

- A growing and successful company;
- A fast paced, go with your instincts environment;
- Cost conscious to the point of cutting corners;
- Not always quality conscious;
- Often "telling" employees rather than engaging, including, and asking employees;
- Willingness to examine its performance; and
- Aware of its mistakes.

Year five:

- A growing and successful company;
- Willing to examine its performance;
- Aware of its mistakes.
- Willing to acknowledge the ineffectiveness of its security processes;
- Willing to seek and take expert advice;

- Willing to learn from mistakes;
- Willing to invest in quality processes and training;
- Willing to engage and partner with employees; and
- Willing to learn and change.

The above characteristics of Company A describe a pattern or tendency that informs employee/company action—*the way we do things around here.* This inclination (which we are calling <u>organization culture</u>) describes the organization's beliefs about what is important, what is valued, what contributes to success for individuals and the company, what informs investment decisions, and what is rewarded and punished.

The organizational characteristics that describe Company A's first four years in business are illustrative of a company focused on its business and growth in the marketplace. Those characteristics that describe its fifth year behavior depict a change in some areas of its organizational culture including the addition of a focus on company learning, partnering with employees, quality improvement, and organizational change.

Organizational culture is a very powerful determinant of organizational behavior. Organizational culture can either support changes in policy, procedure, or practice or undermine them. The good news is that you can make changes in your organizational culture as warranted by the internal and external context surrounding your business. The key pre-requisites to making such a change are to understand how organizational culture operates and to recognize when it needs to change to support company vision, mission, and operational strategies.

The next section outlines a number of important factors associated with organizational culture and how it can be utilized to support changes in company policy, procedure, and practice in general, as well as with regard to employee background screening.

Five Important Steps to Creating a Security Conscious Organizational Culture

Step 1: Create a Positive Attitude Toward Change

Organization consultants who study organizational change have discovered that 12% of what contributes to a successful change in policy, practice, or procedure is associated with people's skills and abilities—having the information and tools to make the change. The more important ingredient of successful change, the other 88% is associated with people's attitudes—employees who believe the change will benefit them personally are more likely to successfully implement the change. Therefore, creating a general atmosphere that recognizes *we live in changing times* and approaches change positively (with a carrot) versus authoritatively (with a stick) is key to successful organization change.

Step 2: Support Employees Developing Openness to New Ways of Doing Things

Continuous change is a reality of the 21st Century workplace and much of it is driven by new technology, the need to reduce costs in order to achieve higher profits, the need to ensure a safe work environment, etc. Stop for a moment and count the number of changes you have asked your employees to make in the last year, quarter, and/or month.

If your organization is like many organizations, there have probably been a lot of such requests.

As a consequence, it is important to recognize that when people are asked to change, whether in one's personal life or at work, it often produces an emotional reaction. Some employees will respond with confusion and disbelief, *"Why am I being asked to do this new thing, I don't get it?"* Or *"I can't believe management is asking me to do this."* Others may become angry, *"I don't have time to waste my time with this."* Still others may just shut down, and engage in the following self talk *"I'm going to just hold my breath and do nothing until this stupid request goes away, it's happened a thousand times before."*

Some employees may experience all of the above emotions: confusion, disbelief, anger, and avoidance. These are normal human emotions everyone has experienced at some point in their live. (Reflect for a moment on your own experiences. We bet, if you are honest, you can recall feeling one or more of these emotions when asked to implement a new policy, learn a new skill, or use a new tool. We know we have.) While these emotions are normal, they can also result in people getting stuck, and failing to implement important organizational change, which can then result in the loss of time and money, and too often an unsafe work environment—it becomes a vicious cycle. Therefore, helping employees move through this emotional quagmire as quickly as possible is the goal of management, and the objective of steps 3 through 5, which follow.

Step 3: Ensure the Organizational Leadership Believes the Change is the Right Thing to Do

The next step to ensuring that employees throughout an organization believe the change in policy and procedure is the right thing to do, is to make certain that the leadership (both the formal hierarchy of management, as well as informal leaders within teams and departments) throughout the organization understands the reasons for the change in policy, practice, procedure, etc. and is committed to, and buys in to, supporting the change process. Support includes talking about the change in all employee meetings, attending the training roll out, and even conducting sections of the training (i.e., delivering the introductory section, describing the impact on the company of not making the change, etc.).

Step 4: Assist Employees in Believing the Change is the Right Thing to Do

Telling people to do things is an efficient way to roll out organizational change, but too often it is *not an effective* way. We have learned from the literature on adult education that to optimize the investment made in training and adult learning and support successful organizational change, adults need four things.

- First, people need to understand the problem or the reasons behind what's driving the need for the policy or procedural change.
- Second, people need to understand the risks to them personally, as well as to the company of not consistently implementing the change.

- Third, people need evidence of the effectiveness of the proposed changes (the policy, associated procedures, etc.). In other words, people need to believe the proposed solutions will fix the problem and benefit them personally (e.g., ensure their personal safety as well as the company's).

- Fourth, the communications and training processes describing the policy change and the associated procedural changes MUST include steps 1 and 2 above, be presented in a way that creates a positive attitude about the change, and recognizes that many people may have emotional reactions they will need help in working their way through.

Step 5: Engage in Careful Planning and Monitoring of Outcomes That Recognize Both the Human and Business Side of Organizational Change

The last recommended step is to take what we know about the human side of organizational change outlined above, and integrate it into your organizational thinking and planning to create an effective strategy to guide the implementation of your new background screening policy and associated procedures.

By engaging in a structured planning process that includes having a clear purpose for your change effort, being specific about the results you want to achieve, creating a plan that lists the specific steps you will need to take, identifying the resources (human, fiscal, material, and informational) you will need, and being intentional about how you will monitor and learn from your results, you are much more likely to accomplish your change goals. We recommend the following components be included in your planning.

1. Have a clear *purpose of what needs to change* that includes both the business and the human elements that surround the need for your change in policy and procedure.

2. Describe the specific *desired results* you want to accomplish from the planned change in policy and procedure from the business side, as well as the human side—what problems will you fix (e.g., the threat to the company of hiring or retaining employees whose behavior presents a risk to the company is minimized; company employees understand the potential risk to themselves and to the company of not consistently implementing the background screening policy and commit to implement it fully, etc.).

3. Create a list of specific *steps required* to achieve the desired outcomes some of which might include:

   - What you will do to create a positive attitude toward change in general within your organization (Steps 1 and 2 above);
   - What research you will conduct to understand what change is required given the issues facing your organization, including best practices with regard to policy, procedure, and practice (similar to the knowledge, tools, and resources you are gaining from a review of this book);
   - What steps you will take to ensure the organizational leadership believes the change is the right thing to do (Step 3 above);
   - What steps you will take to assist employees in believing the change is the right thing to do (Step 4 above);

4. Identify the *resources you will need* to fully envision, plan, and implement the change process within your organization (e.g., new information, new ways of thinking—shift in organizational culture, staff, budget, expert consulting, information technology, etc.)

5. *Monitor and evaluate the effectiveness* of your change in policy and procedure including understanding:

   - How the new policy and procedures were received by employees—did they understand the need, see the self-interest, believe the solution would fix the problem, and commit to implement the change consistently?

   - Whether you got the results you expected? Did you meet your goals? Exceed your goals? Fail to meet your expected goals?

   - Do you know why you got the results achieved? What about the change process supported success or failure?

   - What did you learn from the implementation of the change effort and from reviewing your results?

   - How will you use what you have learned to support BOTH the human and business side of the change process? What will you do to keep employees engaged in the process and committed to reaching both their goals and the company's goals for a security conscious environment? What will you have to change in the future in order to develop a more security conscious organizational culture?

Summary

The literature on organizational change informs us that 80% of the major change initiatives implemented in the last 20 years (e.g., quality improvement initiatives, security and safety efforts, team based organization redesign, diversity initiatives, etc.) have failed, not because they were not the right things to do, but we submit, because they were not implemented through a process that recognized BOTH:

- The human side of change (the need to engage with employees, to create understanding, to uncover mutual self-interests and develop a deep commitment to the change effort), and

- The business side of change (e.g., cost-benefit analysis, risk analysis, policy development, and implementation planning and roll out).

Organizational change requires not only changes in policy and procedure, but also changes in organizational culture—you know, in our perceptions of *the way we do things around here*. Some changes in policy and procedure strike at the heart of what employees believe and when it does, a change in organizational culture (the way we think about and do things within the organization) is required.

The MIT organization guru Peter Senge says, "When change and culture meet, culture wins." In other words, the traditional ways we do things within organizations are very powerful and can cut two ways. Our organizational culture can work to undermine the change needed for the company's future success OR by paying attention to what needs to change about a company's organizational culture and implementing that change, success can indeed be snatched from the jaws of defeat. The choice is up to you.

Index